D1268297

GRAMMAR
AND BEYOND 3

Second Edition

with Academic Writing

Randi Reppen
Laurie Blass
Susan Iannuzzi
Alice Savage

CAMBRIDGE
UNIVERSITY PRESS

CAMBRIDGE
UNIVERSITY PRESS

University Printing House, Cambridge CB2 8BS, United Kingdom

One Liberty Plaza, 20th Floor, New York, NY 10006, USA

477 Williamstown Road, Port Melbourne, VIC 3207, Australia

314–321, 3rd Floor, Plot 3, Splendor Forum, Jasola District Centre, New Delhi – 110025, India

79 Anson Road, #06–04/06, Singapore 079906

Cambridge University Press is part of the University of Cambridge.

It furthers the University's mission by disseminating knowledge in the pursuit of education, learning and research at the highest international levels of excellence.

cambridge.org
Information on this title: cambridge.org/9781108779883

© Cambridge University Press 2021

This publication is in copyright. Subject to statutory exception and to the provisions of relevant collective licensing agreements, no reproduction of any part may take place without the written permission of Cambridge University Press.

First published 2013
Second edition 2021

20 19 18 17 16 15 14 13 12 11 10 9 8 7 6 5 4 3 2 1

Printed in Mexico by Editorial Impresora Apolo, S.A. de C.V.

A catalogue record for this publication is available from the British Library

ISBN Student's Book 3 with Online Practice 978-1-108-77988-3

Additional resources for this publication at www.cambridge.org/grammarandbeyond

Cambridge University Press has no responsibility for the persistence or accuracy of URLs for external or third-party internet websites referred to in this publication, and does not guarantee that any content on such websites is, or will remain, accurate or appropriate. Information regarding prices, travel timetables, and other factual information given in this work is correct at the time of first printing but Cambridge University Press does not guarantee the accuracy of such information thereafter.

About the Author

Randi Reppen is Professor of Applied Linguistics and TESL at Northern Arizona University (NAU) in Flagstaff, Arizona. She has over 20 years' experience teaching ESL students and training ESL teachers, including 11 years as the Director of NAU's Program in Intensive English. Randi's research interests focus on the use of corpora for language teaching and materials development. In addition to numerous academic articles and books, she is the author of *Using Corpora in the Language Classroom* and a co-author of *Basic Vocabulary* in Use, 2nd edition, both published by Cambridge University Press.

Laurie Blass has more than 25 years' experience teaching and creating materials for ESL students in the United States and abroad. She is currently a full-time materials developer with a special interest in ESL for academic success and educational technology. Laurie is co-author of *Writers at Work: From Sentence to Paragraph,* published by Cambridge University Press, among many other titles.

Susan Iannuzzi has been teaching ESL for more than 20 years. She has trained English teachers on five continents and consulted on the national English curricula for countries in Africa, Asia, and the Middle East. She has authored or co-authored more than 10 English courses in use today. *Grammar and Beyond* is her first publication with Cambridge University Press.

Alice Savage is an English Language Teacher and Materials Writer. She attended the School for International Training in Vermont and is an author on the Read This! series, published by Cambridge University Press. She lives in Houston, Texas with her two children.

Advisory Panel

The ESL advisory panel has helped to guide the development of this series and provided invaluable information about the needs of ESL students and teachers in high schools, colleges, universities, and private language schools throughout North America.

Neta Simpkins Cahill, Skagit Valley College, Mount Vernon, WA
Shelly Hedstrom, Palm Beach State College, Lake Worth, FL
Richard Morasci, Foothill College, Los Altos Hills, CA
Stacey Russo, East Hampton High School, East Hampton, NY
Alice Savage, Lone Star College-North Harris, Houston, TX

Scope and Sequence

Avoid Common Mistakes	Academic Writing
Remembering the simple present with stative verbs; avoiding the base form of the verb when using the present progressive	**Plagiarism and Academic Honesty** • Avoid plagiarism
Remembering the base form of the verb after *would* and *used to*; remembering the simple past for specific events in the past; remembering the past progressive for background information	**Expository Writing** Writing prompt: *How has globalization changed your country?* • Topic sentences • Support statement with details • Use tables to organize information
Remembering correct subject–verb agreement with present perfect; remembering been for the present perfect progressive	• Essay structure • Write effective thesis statements • Write the introductory paragraph
Remembering when to use the past perfect or past perfect progressive	• Write the first draft • Revise and edit
Remembering *be* with *be going to*; remembering when to use the future progressive, the simple present, or the present progressive	**Comparison and Contrast** Writing prompt: *Compare learning a language with studying math. How do you think the study of these subjects will change over time with new technology?* • Use Venn diagrams • Brainstorm topics and ideas
Avoiding the future form in the time clause; remembering *will* with the future perfect	• Use transitions to show comparison and contrast • Structure a comparison-and-contrast essay

Avoid Common Mistakes	Academic Writing
Remembering *have* + the past participle after a modal; remembering *be* in *be allowed to* and *be supposed to*	• Use modals in academic writing • Write the first draft
Avoiding *must* with future probabilities; remembering *be* + verb + *-ing* with the progressive with modals	• Revise and edit
Avoiding plural noncount nouns; remembering plural forms for count nouns	**Opinion Writing** Writing prompt: *Is disease prevention the responsibility of individuals and their families or of the government?* • Use T-charts to brainstorm and organize ideas • Use precise nouns and adjectives
Avoiding *much* with plural nouns; remembering articles before singular occupations	• Use transitions to show opposing ideas • Add sentence variety • Structure an opinion essay • Use quantifiers and pronouns to hedge
Remembering to form reflexive pronouns with object pronouns; remembering to use singular verb forms with indefinite pronouns	• Plan the essay • Write the first draft • Revise and edit
Remembering to use a gerund after a preposition; remembering to use a singular verb with a gerund subject	**Summary-Response** Writing prompt: *Summarize the article "Creating a Successful Logo." Then choose a logo and analyze it in terms of the criteria in the article.* • Use an outline • Summarize • Write the summary paragraph
Avoiding verb + *that* clauses after *want*; remembering correct word order with a negative form of an infinitive	• Determine and apply criteria • Respond to an article • Write the response • Revise and edit

Avoid Common Mistakes	Academic Writing
Remembering the auxiliary verb + *not* in negative questions; remembering an auxiliary verb + a pronoun in tag questions	**Argumentative Writing** Writing prompt: *Which is more important when choosing a home: location or size?* • Negative and tag questions in academic writing • Identify arguments and reasons • Brainstorm and organize in a T-chart
Avoiding a comma before a *that* clause; remembering a complete verb in *that* clauses; remembering a subject in *that* clauses	• Connect information • Support arguments
Remembering to use statement word order for a noun clause with a *wh-* word; avoiding using *either* instead of *whether*	• Register in academic writing • Argumentative essay structure • Write the first draft • Revise and edit
Remembering to change the form of the verb in indirect speech; remembering quotation marks with direct speech	**Argumentative Writing Using Graphs and Tables for Support** Writing prompt: *Using what you know about the job market, what is a good choice for a career path with a secure future? Include information from graphs or tables to support your choice.* • Understand and use graphs and tables • Brainstorm topics and ideas • Use reporting verbs to introduce evidence
Remembering to use infinitives in indirect imperatives; remembering to use an object pronoun or noun after *tell*	• Analyze information in graphs and other visuals • Make and evaluate claims • Add indirect advice from experts • Write body paragraphs
Remembering a form of *be* in passive sentences; remembering to put *be* before the subject in questions	• Make a logical appeal in the introductory paragraph • Use active and passive voice to discuss visuals • Write the first draft
Avoiding the base form of the verb after *be* in passive sentences	• Use passive voice in academic writing • Revise and edit

Avoid Common Mistakes	Academic Writing
Using *which*, *that*, and *who* correctly; avoiding a second subject in the relative clause	**Expository Writing** Writing prompt: *Explain the advantages and disadvantages of three types of renewable energy and decide which would work best in your country or region.* ● Organize ideas in a table ● Use relative clauses to add information and avoid repetition
Avoiding commas for an identifying object relative clause; avoiding *what* in relative clauses	● Introduce advantages and disadvantages ● Build coherence ● Order ideas in an essay ● Write the first draft
Avoiding a preposition before *when*; remembering a subject in *where* clauses	● Write the concluding paragraph ● Revise and edit
Remembering the simple present in *if* clauses in future real conditionals; avoiding *when* to describe possible future conditions	**Argumentative Writing** Writing prompt: *Research an aging but culturally or historically important building in your city or country. What do you think should be done with it and why?* ● Build support for an argument ● Maintain paragraph unity ● Brainstorm and organize ideas
Remembering a subject in *if* clauses	● Integrate information from multiple sources ● Use impersonal statements ● Use conditionals to support ideas ● Write the first draft ● Revise and edit

Unit	Theme	Grammar	Topics
PART 12 Connecting Ideas			
UNIT 26 page 378	Globalization of Food	Conjunctions	Connecting Words and Phrases with Conjunctions (p. 380) Connecting Sentences with Coordinating Conjunctions (p. 384) Reducing Sentences with Similar Clauses (p. 388)
UNIT 27 page 396	Consumerism	Adverb Clauses and Phrases	Subordinators and Adverb Clauses (p. 398) Reducing Adverb Clauses (p. 401) Subordinators to Express Purpose (p. 403)
UNIT 28 page 408	Technology in Entertainment	Connecting Information with Prepositions and Transitions	Connecting Information with Prepositions and Prepositional Phrases (p. 410) Connecting Information with Transition Words (p. 413)

Avoid Common Mistakes	Academic Writing
Avoiding *either* when joining ideas with *and*; avoiding *too* after a negative verb	**Comparison and Contrast** Writing prompt: *Not all products and services fit the same business model. Some might have a more successful introduction in a mobile setting. For others, a mobile setting would not be appropriate. Compare and contrast two products or services regarding their potential as mobile businesses.* • Use signal words and phrases to compare and contrast • Use Venn diagrams
Remembering to spell *even though* as two words; avoiding *even* in adverb clauses	• Organize comparisons and contrasts • Write concisely • Write body paragraphs
Avoiding *in the other hand*	• Connect the conclusion to the introduction • Write the first draft • Revise and edit

Introduction to *Grammar and Beyond*, 2nd edition

Grammar and Beyond is a research-based and content-rich grammar and academic writing series for beginning to advanced-level students. The series focuses on the most commonly used English grammar structures and practices all four skills in a variety of authentic and communicative contexts.

Grammar and Beyond is Research-Based

The grammar presented in this series is informed by years of research on the grammar of written and spoken English as it is used in college lectures, textbooks, academic essays, high school classrooms, and conversations between instructors and students. This research, and the analysis of over one billion words of authentic written and spoken language data known as the *Cambridge International Corpus*, has enabled the authors to:

- Present grammar rules that accurately represent how English is actually spoken and written

- Identify and teach differences between the grammar of written and spoken English

- Focus more attention on the structures that are commonly used, and less on those that are rarely used, in writing and speaking

- Help students avoid the most common mistakes that English language learners make

- Choose reading topics that will naturally elicit examples of the target grammar structure

- Introduce important vocabulary from the Academic Word List

Special Features of *Grammar and Beyond*

Realistic Grammar Presentations

Grammar is presented in clear and simple charts. The grammar points presented in these charts have been tested against real-world data from the *Cambridge International Corpus* to ensure that they are authentic representations of actual use of English.

Data from the Real World

Many of the grammar presentations and application sections include a feature called Data from the Real World. Concrete and useful points discovered through analysis of corpus data are presented and practiced in exercises that follow.

Avoid Common Mistakes

Every unit features an Avoid Common Mistakes section that develops students' awareness of the most common mistakes made by English language learners and gives them an opportunity to practice detecting and correcting these errors. This section helps students avoid these mistakes in their own work. The mistakes highlighted in this section are drawn from a body of authentic data on learner English known as the *Cambridge Learner Corpus*, a database of over 35 million words from student essays written by non-native speakers of English and information from experienced classroom teachers.

Academic Vocabulary

Every unit in *Grammar and Beyond* includes words from the Academic Word List (AWL), a research-based list of words and word families that appear with high frequency in English-language academic texts. These words are introduced in the opening text of the unit, recycled in the charts and exercises, and used to support the theme throughout the unit. By the time students finish each level, they will have been exposed several times to a carefully selected set of level-appropriate AWL words, as well as content words from a variety of academic disciplines.

Academic Writing

Every unit ends with an Academic Writing section. In Levels 1 through 3, this edition of *Grammar and Beyond* teaches students to write academically using writing cycles that span several units. Each writing cycle is organized around a writing prompt and focuses on a specific type of academic writing, such as argumentative, expository, and summary-response. Students move through the steps of the writing process - Brainstorm, Organize, Write, Edit - while learning and practicing new writing skills and ways to incorporate the unit grammar into their writing. In Level 4, the entire scope and sequence is organized around the types of essays students write in college, and focuses on the grammar rules, conventions, and structures needed to master them.

Series Levels

The following table provides a general idea of the difficulty of the material at each level of *Grammar and Beyond*. These are not meant to be interpreted as precise correlations.

	Description	TOEFL IBT	CEFR Levels
Level 1	Beginning	20 – 34	A1 – A2
Level 2	Low Intermediate to Intermediate	35 – 54	A2 – B1
Level 3	High Intermediate	55 – 74	B1 – B2
Level 4	Advanced	75 – 95	B2 – C1

Student Components

Student's Book with Online Practice

Each unit, based on a high-interest topic, teaches grammar points appropriate for each level in short, manageable cycles of presentation and practice. Academic Writing focuses on the structure of the academic essay in addition to the grammar rules, conventions, and structures that students need to master in order to be successful college writers. Students can access both the Digital Workbook and Writing Skills Interactive using their smartphones, tablets, or computers with a single log-in. See pages xx–xxv for a Tour of a Unit.

Digital Workbook

The Digital Workbook provides additional online exercises to help master each grammar point. Automatically-graded exercises give immediate feedback for activities such as correcting errors highlighted in the Avoid Common Mistakes section in the Student's Book. Self-Assessment sections at the end of each unit allow students to test their mastery of what they learned. Look for 📓 in the Student's Book to see when to use the Digital Workbook.

Writing Skills Interactive

Writing Skills Interactive is a self-grading course to practice discrete writing skills, reinforce vocabulary, and give students an opportunity with additional writing practice. Each unit has:

- Vocabulary review
- Short text to check understanding of the context
- Animated presentation of target unit writing skill
- Practice activities
- Unit Quiz to assess progress

Teacher Resources

A variety of downloadable resources are available on Cambridge One (cambridgeone.org) to assist instructors, including the following:

Teacher's Manual

- Suggestions for applying the target grammar to all four major skill areas, helping instructors facilitate dynamic and comprehensive grammar classes
- An answer key and audio script for the Student's Book
- Teaching tips, to help instructors plan their lessons
- Communicative activity worksheets to add more in-class speaking practice

Assessment

- Placement Test
- Ready-made, easy-to-score Unit Tests, Midterms, and Final in .pdf and .doc formats
- Answer Key

Presentation Plus

Presentation Plus allows teachers to digitally project the contents of the Student's Books in front of the class for a livelier, interactive classroom. It is a complete solution for teachers because it includes easy-to-access answer keys and audio at point of use.

Acknowledgments

The publisher and authors would like to thank these reviewers and consultants for their insights and participation:

Marty Attiyeh, The College of DuPage, Glen Ellyn, IL

Shannon Bailey, Austin Community College, Austin, TX

Jamila Barton, North Seattle Community College, Seattle, WA

Kim Bayer, Hunter College IELI, New York, NY

Linda Berendsen, Oakton Community College, Skokie, IL

Anita Biber, Tarrant County College Northwest, Fort Worth, TX

Jane Breaux, Community College of Aurora, Aurora, CO

Anna Budzinski, San Antonio College, San Antonio, TX

Britta Burton, Mission College, Santa Clara, CA

Jean Carroll, Fresno City College, Fresno, CA

Chris Cashman, Oak Park High School and Elmwood Park High School, Chicago, IL

Annette M. Charron, Bakersfield College, Bakersfield, CA

Patrick Colabucci, ALI at San Diego State University, San Diego, CA

Lin Cui, Harper College, Palatine, IL

Jennifer Duclos, Boston University CELOP, Boston, MA

Joy Durighello, San Francisco City College, San Francisco, CA

Kathleen Flynn, Glendale Community College, Glendale, CA

Raquel Fundora, Miami Dade College, Miami, FL

Patricia Gillie, New Trier Township High School District, Winnetka, IL

Laurie Gluck, LaGuardia Community College, Long Island City, NY

Kathleen Golata, Galileo Academy of Science & Technology, San Francisco, CA

Ellen Goldman, Mission College, Santa Clara, CA

Ekaterina Goussakova, Seminole Community College, Sanford, FL

Marianne Grayston, Prince George's Community College, Largo, MD

Mary Greiss Shipley, Georgia Gwinnett College, Lawrenceville, GA

Sudeepa Gulati, Long Beach City College, Long Beach, CA

Nicole Hammond Carrasquel, University of Central Florida, Orlando, FL

Vicki Hendricks, Broward College, Fort Lauderdale, FL

Kelly Hernandez, Miami Dade College, Miami, FL

Ann Johnston, Tidewater Community College, Virginia Beach, VA

Julia Karet, Chaffey College, Claremont, CA

Jeanne Lachowski, English Language Institute, University of Utah, Salt Lake City, UT

Noga Laor, Rennert, New York, NY

Min Lu, Central Florida Community College, Ocala, FL

Michael Luchuk, Kaplan International Centers, New York, NY

Craig Machado, Norwalk Community College, Norwalk, CT

Denise Maduli-Williams, City College of San Francisco, San Francisco, CA

Diane Mahin, University of Miami, Coral Gables, FL

Melanie Majeski, Naugatuck Valley Community College, Waterbury, CT

Jeanne Malcolm, University of North Carolina at Charlotte, Charlotte, NC

Lourdes Marx, Palm Beach State College, Boca Raton, FL

Susan G. McFalls, Maryville College, Maryville, TN

Nancy McKay, Cuyahoga Community College, Cleveland, OH

Dominika McPartland, Long Island Business Institute, Flushing, NY

Amy Metcalf, UNR/Intensive English Language Center, University of Nevada, Reno, NV

Robert Miller, EF International Language School San Francisco – Mills, San Francisco, CA

Marcie Pachino, Jordan High School, Durham, NC

Myshie Pagel, El Paso Community College, El Paso, TX

Bernadette Pedagno, University of San Francisco, San Francisco, CA

Tam Q Pham, Dallas Theological Seminary, Fort Smith, AR

Mary Beth Pickett, Global-LT, Rochester, MI
Maria Reamore, Baltimore City Public Schools, Baltimore, MD
Alison M. Rice, Hunter College IELI, New York, NY
Sydney Rice, Imperial Valley College, Imperial, CA
Kathleen Romstedt, Ohio State University, Columbus, OH
Alexandra Rowe, University of South Carolina, Columbia, SC
Irma Sanders, Baldwin Park Adult and Community Education, Baldwin Park, CA
Caren Shoup, Lone Star College – CyFair, Cypress, TX
Karen Sid, Mission College, Foothill College, De Anza College, Santa Clara, CA
Michelle Thomas, Miami Dade College, Miami, FL
Sharon Van Houte, Lorain County Community College, Elyria, OH

Margi Wald, UC Berkeley, Berkeley, CA
Walli Weitz, Riverside County Office of Ed., Indio, CA
Bart Weyand, University of Southern Maine, Portland, ME
Donna Weyrich, Columbus State Community College, Columbus, OH
Marilyn Whitehorse, Santa Barbara City College, Ojai, CA
Jessica Wilson, Rutgers University – Newark, Newark, NJ
Sue Wilson, San Jose City College, San Jose, CA
Margaret Wilster, Mid-Florida Tech, Orlando, FL
Anne York-Herjeczki, Santa Monica College, Santa Monica, CA
Hoda Zaki, Camden County College, Camden, NJ

We would also like to thank these teachers and programs for allowing us to visit:

Richard Appelbaum, Broward College, Fort Lauderdale, FL
Carmela Arnoldt, Glendale Community College, Glendale, AZ
JaNae Barrow, Desert Vista High School, Phoenix, AZ
Ted Christensen, Mesa Community College, Mesa, AZ
Richard Ciriello, Lower East Side Preparatory High School, New York, NY
Virginia Edwards, Chandler-Gilbert Community College, Chandler, AZ
Nusia Frankel, Miami Dade College, Miami, FL
Raquel Fundora, Miami Dade College, Miami, FL
Vicki Hendricks, Broward College, Fort Lauderdale, FL
Kelly Hernandez, Miami Dade College, Miami, FL
Stephen Johnson, Miami Dade College, Miami, FL
Barbara Jordan, Mesa Community College, Mesa, AZ
Nancy Kersten, GateWay Community College, Phoenix, AZ
Lewis Levine, Hostos Community College, Bronx, NY
John Liffiton, Scottsdale Community College, Scottsdale, AZ
Cheryl Lira-Layne, Gilbert Public School District, Gilbert, AZ
Mary Livingston, Arizona State University, Tempe, AZ

Elizabeth Macdonald, Thunderbird School of Global Management, Glendale, AZ
Terri Martinez, Mesa Community College, Mesa, AZ
Lourdes Marx, Palm Beach State College, Boca Raton, FL
Paul Kei Matsuda, Arizona State University, Tempe, AZ
David Miller, Glendale Community College, Glendale, AZ
Martha Polin, Lower East Side Preparatory High School, New York, NY
Patricia Pullenza, Mesa Community College, Mesa, AZ
Victoria Rasinskaya, Lower East Side Preparatory High School, New York, NY
Vanda Salls, Tempe Union High School District, Tempe, AZ
Kim Sanabria, Hostos Community College, Bronx, NY
Cynthia Schuemann, Miami Dade College, Miami, FL
Michelle Thomas, Miami Dade College, Miami, FL
Dongmei Zeng, Borough of Manhattan Community College, New York, NY

Tour of a Unit

ACADEMIC

WRITING FOCUS

appears at the
beginning of the unit.

GRAMMAR IN THE

REAL WORLD

presents the unit's grammar in a
realistic context using relatable texts.

Direct Speech and Indirect Speech

UNIT
17 Direct Speech and Indirect Speech

Human Motivation

1 Grammar in the Real World

ACADEMIC WRITING

Argumentative
writing using
graphs and tables
for support

A What makes people work hard at their jobs? Read the article about employee motivation. What type of reward is particularly effective in motivating workers?

B Comprehension Check Complete the chart. Check (✓) whether each reward is external or internal.

	External Reward	Internal Reward
1 Pay raise		
2 Feeling successful		
3 Freedom to work independently		
4 Good salary		
5 Good grades		

C Notice Find similar sentences in the article and complete the sentences below.

1 Lionel Messi _____ , "Money is not a motivating factor… My motivation comes from playing the game I love."

2 Daniel Pink, the author of a book on motivation, _____ an audience once that Google was a great example of a company that supported autonomy.

3 Pink _____ the audience that Google News and Gmail had been created during this free time.

Each sentence tells what someone says. Which sentence gives the actual words of the speaker? How do you know?

WORKPLACE MOTIVATION

Motivation is the desire to do something. Soccer star Lionel Messi **said**, "Money is not a motivating factor… My motivation comes from playing the game I love." Messi meant that he enjoys playing soccer more than making millions of dollars. Can that be true? What other factors are important in motivating people?

Many psychologists believe that there are two types of rewards that affect motivation: external rewards and internal rewards. External rewards are rewards that someone gives you. A pay raise is a common external reward. A good grade at school is also an example of an external reward. Internal rewards are connected to the feelings people have about the work they do. The satisfaction you get when you do something well is an internal reward. Researcher Frederick Herzberg (1923–2000) studied motivation in the workplace for many years. Herzberg **said that** employers must think about factors that affect employees' feelings of satisfaction. Herzberg **explained that** working conditions and relationships among co-workers affect workers' motivation. Therefore, employers need to create an environment that makes employees feel safe, valued, and accepted.

Some studies on workplace motivation have focused on autonomy, which is the freedom to work independently. This is an important internal reward. Daniel Pink, the author of a book on motivation, **told** an audience once **that** Google was a good example of a company that supported autonomy. One day each week, Google engineers focus on their own ideas. Pink **informed** the audience **that** Google News and Gmail had been created during this free time.

Research also shows that appreciation is a powerful reward. In his book *The 1001 Rewards and Recognition[1] Fieldbook*, Bob Nelson described a study on the effects of appreciation on motivation. The study **asked**, "What motivates you?" Workers ranked the importance of 65 motivating factors. Nelson **indicated that** appreciation for their work ranked first for the workers.

The subject of worker motivation is complex. People expect fair pay for their work. However, research **shows that** people find internal rewards more meaningful than a high salary.

[1]recognition: special positive attention

NOTICE ACTIVITIES

draw students' attention to the
structure, guiding their own analysis of
form, meaning, and use.

GRAMMAR PRESENTATION

begins with an overview that describes the grammar in an easy-to-understand summary.

CHARTS

provide clear guidance on the form, meaning, and use of the target grammar, for ease of instruction and reference.

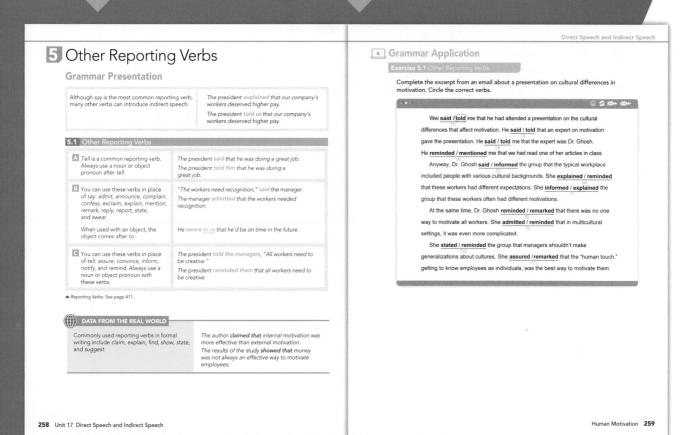

Direct Speech and Indirect Speech

5 Other Reporting Verbs

Grammar Presentation

| Although *say* is the most common reporting verb, many other verbs can introduce indirect speech. | The president *explained* that our company's workers deserved higher pay. |
| | The president *told us* that our company's workers deserved higher pay. |

5.1 Other Reporting Verbs

A *Tell* is a common reporting verb. Always use a noun or object pronoun after *tell*.	The president *said* that he was doing a great job. The president *told him* that he was doing a great job.
B You can use these verbs in place of *say*: *admit, announce, complain, confess, exclaim, explain, mention, remark, reply, report, state,* and *swear*.	*"The workers need recognition,"* said the manager. The manager *admitted* that the workers needed recognition.
When used with an object, the object comes after *to*.	He swore *to us* that he'd be on time in the future.
C You can use these verbs in place of *tell*: *assure, convince, inform, notify,* and *remind*. Always use a noun or object pronoun with these verbs.	The president *told the managers, "All workers need to be creative."* The president *reminded them* that all workers need to be creative.

▶ Reporting Verbs: See page A11.

DATA FROM THE REAL WORLD

| Commonly used reporting verbs in formal writing include *claim, explain, find, show, state,* and *suggest*. | The author **claimed that** internal motivation was more effective than external motivation.
The results of the study **showed that** money was not always an effective way to motivate employees. |

▶ Grammar Application

Exercise 5.1 Other Reporting Verbs

Complete the excerpt from an email about a presentation on cultural differences in motivation. Circle the correct verbs.

Wei **said** / **told** me that he had attended a presentation on the cultural differences that affect motivation. He **said** / **told** that an expert on motivation gave the presentation. He **said** / **told** me that the expert was Dr. Ghosh. He **reminded** / **mentioned** me that we had read one of her articles in class.

Anyway, Dr. Ghosh **said** / **informed** the group that the typical workplace included people with various cultural backgrounds. She **explained** / **reminded** that these workers had different expectations. She **informed** / **explained** the group that these workers often had different motivations.

At the same time, Dr. Ghosh **reminded** / **remarked** that there was no one way to motivate all workers. She **admitted** / **reminded** that in multicultural settings, it was even more complicated.

She **stated** / **reminded** the group that managers shouldn't make generalizations about cultures. She **assured** / **remarked** that the "human touch," getting to know employees as individuals, was the best way to motivate them.

DATA FROM THE REAL WORLD

takes students beyond traditional information and teaches them how the unit's grammar is used in authentic situations, including differences between spoken and written use.

GRAMMAR APPLICATION

Keeps students engaged with a wide variety of exercises that introduce new and stimulating content.

QR CODES

give easy access to audio at point of use in class or for review.

CONTEXTUALIZED PRACTICE

moves from controlled to open ended, teaching meaningful language for real communicative purposes.

THEME-RELATED EXERCISES

boost fluency by providing grammar practice in a variety of different contexts.

Exercise 5.2 More Reporting Verbs

A Listen to the conversation about a presentation on cultural differences in classrooms. Complete the sentences with the words you hear.

David What happened in class today?

Mira We had a guest speaker. He _told us_ about the importance of motivation in the language classroom. He _____ there are two kinds of motivation: intrinsic and extrinsic.

David Right. Last week, the professor _____ there were two different types, and she gave examples.

Mira Yes. So anyway, the speaker _____ he had done a study of students in Japan and students in the United States. He _____ both groups had native-speaking English teachers. He _____ the purpose of the study was to see whether the teachers' remarks had a negative effect on the motivation of the Japanese students.

David What did he find out?

Mira He _____ the study found four ways in which the teachers' behavior had a negative effect on Japanese students' motivation.

David Did he give any examples?

Mira He _____ classroom discussion is one area where there are key differences. He _____ in the Japanese classroom, students generally listen more and talk less.

David And as we know from our reading, Porter and Samovar _____ in the U.S. classroom, some students speak up spontaneously, and that a lot of teachers encourage discussion.

Mira Right. So, he _____ when a teacher criticizes a Japanese group for not participating, it has a bad effect on motivation.

B Listen again and check your answers.

260 Unit 17 Direct Speech and Indirect Speech

HOW TO USE A QR CODE

1. Open the camera on your smartphone.
2. Point it at the QR code.
3. The camera will automatically scan the code. If not, press the button to take a picture.

* Not all cameras automatically scan QR codes. You may need to download a QR code reader. Search "QR free" and download an app.

AVOID COMMON MISTAKES

is based on a database of over 135,000 essays, students learn the most common mistakes English language learners make.

EDITING TASK

gives learners an opportunity to identify and correct the commonly made errors, helping develop self-editing skills needed in their university studies.

ACADEMIC WRITING

concentrates on specific stages of the writing process: Brainstorm, Organize, Write, Edit

---

(Thumbnail page 261 — Direct Speech and Indirect Speech)

C Over to You Compare the behavior of American and Japanese students to students from another culture that you are familiar with. Use sentences with indirect speech.

The speaker said that in the Japanese classroom, students listen more and talk less. That is true in my culture, too. Students show respect that way.

6 Avoid Common Mistakes ⚠

1. For verbs such as **admit, announce, complain, explain,** and **mention,** the object pronoun comes after the preposition **to.**
   He explained ~~us~~ *to us* the objective.

2. Change the form of the verb in indirect speech in most cases.
   He claimed that they ~~had~~ followed the directions.

3. Use beginning and ending quotation marks with direct speech.
   The director said, "All designers may work from home on Fridays."

Editing Task

Find and correct the mistakes in the paragraphs about a memorable event.

One of the highlights of my life happened through an experience at work. It started when my manager announced *to us* us some interesting news. He said, I am starting a company band. Then he asked, "Who wants to join?" I mentioned him that I had played guitar for many years. He said, You should definitely try out.

On the day of tryouts, I was a little nervous because everyone played extremely well. After I auditioned, the manager thanked me and explained me that he will let me know soon.

I forgot about it, so I was very surprised when I got a phone call from my manager a few days later. He said, You can play lead guitar. I said, Wow! That's great! After that, the band practiced a few times a week. A few months later, we played at the company party. We were nervous, but we played well. The president of the company spoke to me later and said I have a lot of talent. I was embarrassed by his compliment, but I said I am proud to play for the company. I will never forget that experience.

Human Motivation **261**

(Thumbnail page 262 — Unit 17 Direct Speech and Indirect Speech)

7 Academic Writing

Argumentative Writing Using Graphs and Tables for Support

Brainstorm | Organize | Write | Edit

In this writing cycle (Units 17–20), you will write an argumentative essay that uses graphs or tables to answer the prompt below. In this unit (17), you will analyze an essay with graphs and then brainstorm ideas about the topic.

Using what you know about the job market, what is a good choice for a career path with a secure future? Include information from graphs or tables to support your choice.

Exercise 7.1 Preparing to Write

Work with a partner. Discuss the questions.

1. Is it important to have a college degree? Why or why not?
2. College tuition in the United States is very expensive. Do you think the benefits of a degree outweigh the costs? Why or why not?
3. A founder of Netscape, an early Internet search company, has said that people who earn a degree in a non-technical field like literature will probably be working in a shoe store upon graduation. Do you agree or disagree? Why or why not?

Exercise 7.2 Focusing on Vocabulary

Read the sentences. Then match the words in bold to the definitions.

1. Steve Jobs, one of the **founders** of Apple Inc., said that quality was more important than quantity.
2. Business leaders **disputed** the government's claim that the number of jobs had grown.
3. The successful campaign against buying the corporation's products **illustrates** the power of the consumer.
4. There is some **ambiguity** in the law, so it is difficult to know if the company did anything wrong.
5. This new technology has the **potential** to change how students learn about science.
6. According to economists, the more you consume something, the more your enjoyment of it will **diminish**. In other words, you will never enjoy it as much as you do when you first buy it.
7. The consequences of the economic crash **extend** beyond the city to the whole country.

a. _____ (v) to disagree with
b. _____ (n) the state of being unclear or having more than one possible meaning
c. _____ (n) people who establish an organization
d. _____ (v) to decrease in size or importance
e. _____ (v) to go further
f. _____ (n) the possibility to develop and succeed
g. _____ (n) an example that explains something

262 Unit 17 Direct Speech and Indirect Speech

(Thumbnail page 263 — Human Motivation)

What Is the Value of a College Education?

(essay text and Figures 1 and 2 — graph and table)

chronic (adj) lasting for a long time, especially something bad

Human Motivation **263**

LEARNER OUTCOMES

are mapped out at the beginning of each writing cycle and section.

REAL WORLD MODEL

incorporates the unit grammar into common types of writing for students to understand and analyze.

SKILL BOXES

provide clear explanations of carefully selected writing skills.

WRITING TASK

helps students develop their academic writing at various stages of the writing process.

Exercise 7.3 Comprehension Check

Read the text on page 263. Work with a partner. Discuss the questions.

1 Summarize the main argument of the text.
2 What benefits of a college degree are mentioned in the text?
3 According to Figure 1, what three countries had the highest percentage of citizens with a college education?

Exercise 7.4 Noticing the Grammar and Writing

Work with a partner. Complete the tasks.

1 Underline the first sentence. Why does the writer use a quote to introduce the topic?
2 Find another quote in the text. How does the writer introduce the quote?
3 Look at Figure 1. What is the writer's purpose in using this graph?
4 Look at Figure 2. What is the writer's purpose in using this graph?
5 What is the source of the information in the graphs?

Understanding and Using Graphs and Tables

Information in academic texts is often presented through graphs and tables. Writers include these to support their ideas or argument. It is important to understand and interpret the information in your graphs and tables, and to draw inferences and conclusions for your reader.

Exercise 7.5 Applying the Skill

Work with a partner. Ask and answer the questions about the information in Table 1.

Table 1. The 100 Best Jobs in the U.S., with Median Salary

Rank	Job Title	Median Salary
1	Software Developer	$101,790
4	Dentist	$165,120
14	Surgeon	$208,000
28	IT Manager	$139,220
42	Lawyer	$119,250
62	Hairdresser	$24,850
66	Medical Assistant	$32,480
76	High School Teacher	$59,170
88	Massage Therapist	$39,990

Source: U.S. News and World Report 2018

1 What information does the table present?
2 What can you infer from the table?
3 In addition to salary, what other factors do you think make a job a "best job"?

My Writing

Argumentative Essays with Graphs or Tables as Support

In argumentative essays, writers present their position, reasons, and supporting evidence. Evidence used in graphs and tables should come from credible sources, such as educational or research institutions, government websites, and respected news organizations.

Exercise 7.6 Brainstorming Topics and Ideas

1 Work with a partner. Make a copy of the chart and complete it.
* Column 1: Write the names of three careers.
* Column 2: Write relevant information from the reading, Table 1, and other credible sources you find. Include the name of the source in parentheses.
* Column 3: Make notes about the career and the information you found.

Career	Information (Name of Source)	Notes

2 In your opinion, which of the careers is the best choice for a financially secure future? Why?

Using Reporting Verbs to Introduce Evidence

Writers use reporting verbs to introduce evidence. Reporting verbs also show readers how the writer feels about the evidence. **Neutral reporting verbs** show a more neutral feeling towards the evidence.

The report **said** that the number one skill employers are looking for is flexibility.

Strong reporting verbs show a strong feeling towards the evidence.

The report **asserted** that the number one skill employers are looking for is flexibility.

Neutral reporting verbs: *advise, accept, acknowledge, recognize, encourage, interpret, analyze, examine, investigate, consider, evaluate*
Strong reporting verbs: *argue, assert, convince, emphasize, indicate, persuade, refute, show, state, stress, support, warn*

Exercise 7.7 Applying the Skill

Use the information from Exercise 7.6 to write a paragraph that asserts which career would best lead to a secure future. Include a topic sentence, at least two reasons for your argument with supporting details and evidence, and a concluding sentence. Use at least one reporting verb to introduce evidence.

APPLICATION EXERCISES

give students scaffolded practice of the writing skills.

Kahoot!

for Grammar and Beyond
cambridge.org/kahoot/grammarandbeyond

What is Kahoot!?
Kahoot! is a game-based learning platform that makes it easy to create, share and play fun learning games and trivia quizzes in minutes. Students can play Kahoot! on any mobile device or laptop with an internet connection.

What can you use kahoots for?
Kahoots can be used for review, formative assessment or homework.

When should you play Kahoot?
You can use a kahoot before starting the unit as a diagnostic, during the unit as formative assessment, or at the end of a unit to test student knowledge.

To launch a live game in the classroom, simply click on "play" when launching kahoot.

Quiz Your English app

Quiz Your English is a fun new way to practice, improve, and test your English by competing against learners from all around the world. Learn English grammar with friends, discover new English words, and test yourself in a truly global environment.

- Learn to avoid common mistakes with a special section just for *Grammar and Beyond* users
- Challenge your friends and players wherever they are
- Watch where you are on the leaderboards

1 Simple Present and Present Progressive

First Impressions

1 Grammar in the Real World

ACADEMIC WRITING

Plagiarism and academic honesty

A When you meet someone for the first time, what do you notice about the person? Read the article about first impressions. What influences your first impressions?

B Comprehension Check Answer the questions.

1 How long does it take to form a first impression?
2 What is the collection of tests known as the IAT helping to reveal?
3 What is one stereotype that young and old people share?

C Notice Find the sentences in the article and complete them. Circle the correct verbs. Then check (✓) the box that best describes the function of each verb.

1 The average person **forms / is forming** a first impression of someone in less than 30 seconds.

☐ general fact or habit ☐ temporary action

2 Handshakes, facial expressions, and general appearance **help / are helping** to create first impressions.

☐ general fact or habit ☐ temporary action

3 Some psychologists today **research / are researching** the factors that influence how people react to others.

☐ general fact or habit ☐ temporary action

4 Specifically, Nosek **investigates / is investigating** our use of stereotypes and attitudes about others in forming first impressions.

☐ general fact or habit ☐ temporary action

What do the verbs in the simple present describe? What do the verbs in the present progressive describe?

FIRST IMPRESSIONS

Here is an interesting fact: The average person **forms** a first impression of someone in less than 30 seconds. *First impressions* **are** the opinions someone **has** about you when you **meet** for the
5 first time. What **is** your smile **telling** the other person? What **is** the way you dress **saying** about you? These factors can make a difference in the way the person **thinks** about you.

Handshakes, facial expressions, and general
10 appearance **help** to create first impressions. People are constantly **forming** these impressions of others. We do not make these impressions consciously.[1] They **are** largely subconscious.[2] However, they **tend**[3] to be extremely difficult to change.

15 Some psychologists today **are researching** the factors that influence how people react to others. For example, psychologist Brian Nosek **is** currently **using** a collection of tests known as the IAT, or

Implicit Association Test, for his research. These
20 tests **are helping** to reveal our thinking processes, both conscious and subconscious, as we form our impressions of others. **Specifically**, Nosek is **investigating** our use of stereotypes and attitudes about others in forming first impressions.

25 Each test **measures** what happens while people **are making** judgments. The results **demonstrate** that people have stereotypes, and that these stereotypes **influence** their first impressions. For example, both young and old people **tend**
30 to associate the word *good* with pictures of young people.

Since first impressions **influence** what a person **thinks** about you to a great degree, it **is** important to always do your best to make a good
35 first impression.

---

[1]**consciously:** aware of what is happening

[2]**subconscious:** existing in the mind but not in one's awareness

[3]**tend:** be likely

2 Simple Present vs. Present Progressive

Grammar Presentation

The simple present and the present progressive both describe present time. The simple present describes things that are more permanent, such as general facts or habits.	*The average person forms a first impression in less than 30 seconds.*
The present progressive describes things that are temporary, such as things in progress now or around now.	*Psychologists are researching the factors that influence how people react.*

2.1 Simple Present

A Use the simple present for general facts and permanent situations.	*People form a first impression within 30 seconds.* *First impressions influence what a person thinks about you.* *I dress conservatively at work.*
B Use the simple present to describe routines and habits.	*The manager asks a lot of questions.* *We work for eight hours every day.*
You can use time expressions such as *always, usually, often, sometimes, never, on Mondays, once a week, two days a week,* and *twice a month.*	*The hiring manager always writes a report after an interview.* *We usually follow her recommendations.* *She doesn't interview candidates on Mondays.* *We discuss the manager's reports once a week.*
C Use the simple present for routines, scheduled events, and timetables.	*The office opens at 9:00 a.m.* *The train to Boston departs from platform 11 at 2:00 p.m.* *"Does the meeting always begin at noon?"* *"Yes, it does."*

▶◄ Irregular Verbs : See page A1.

 DATA FROM THE REAL WORLD

Research shows that we use some adverbs with the simple present more often in academic writing than in speaking.

More common in writing: *typically, frequently, traditionally*	*The email interview typically takes three hours.*
Common in both speaking and writing: *generally, usually, normally*	*The team generally meets on Tuesdays.* *How do you normally handle complaints?*

2.2 Present Progressive

A Use the present progressive to describe what is in progress now or around the present time.

Mr. Rask is interviewing a candidate at the moment. (The interview is happening now.)

We are interviewing candidates all month. (Interviews may not be in progress now, but they are in progress during this month.)

B Use the present progressive to describe temporary events or changing situations.

I am studying stereotypes in the workplace. (My studies will end in the future.)

DATA FROM THE REAL WORLD

Research shows that we often use the present progressive for habits that are noteworthy or unusual. This is sometimes, but not always, because these habits are not desirable. You can use *always* or *constantly* for emphasis. *Constantly* is more formal than *always*.

She is always disturbing me when I am trying to study.

My boss is constantly asking me to stay late at work.

The present progressive form is also common with verbs that describe changing or temporary situations.

The workers at that store are constantly changing. Every week there is someone new.

We are always looking for new ideas and people with special talents.

Grammar Application

Exercise 2.1 Simple Present

Complete the sentences with the simple present of the verbs in the box.

give	have	have	help	~~make~~	meet	show	start	teach	videotape

1 According to many studies, most people _____*make*_____ judgments about others in only a few seconds.

2 Communication trainer Mary Hernandez _____ job seekers make a good first impression.

3 Ms. Hernandez _____ a course called *Making a Good First Impression* at the community college.

4 The class _____ on Mondays and Wednesdays.

5 At the first class meeting, Ms. Hernandez typically _____ students a self-assessment test.

6 The self-assessment test _____ how the students judge themselves.

7 Students almost always _____ a positive impression of themselves.

8 After the self-assessment, Ms. Hernandez usually _____ the students in mock interviews.

9 On the last day of class, students _____ real interviews with a representative from a local company.

10 Ms. Hernandez's class _____ at 6:30 p.m. and ends at 9:00 p.m.

Exercise 2.2 Simple Present or Present Progressive?

Complete the questions about Josh and Rachel with the simple present or present progressive form of the words in parentheses. Then write answers using the information in the picture.

1 Where _are Josh and Rachel working_ (Josh and Rachel / work) this summer?
 Josh and Rachel are working at the Bursar's Office this summer.

2 How often _____ (Josh and Rachel / work)?

_____

3 When _____ (Josh / start his job) in the mornings?

_____

4 _____ (Rachel / talk) to a student right now?

_____

5 How many _____ (students / wait) in Josh's line?

_____

6 _____ (who / make) a better first impression on the students who need help?

_____

7 When _____ (Rachel / finish) work in the afternoons?

_____

8 _____ (who / not help) students at the moment?

_____

Exercise 2.3 More Simple Present or Present Progressive?

A Complete the sentences from a brochure that participants received at a job fair. Use the simple present or present progressive form of the verbs in parentheses.

Welcome to the State Employment Agency

JOBFAIR!

Representatives from over 30 big regional corporations *are participating* (participate) in
(1)
today's state job fair. The job fair _____ (take) place every year. Every year, interviews
(2)
_____ (begin) at 9:00 a.m. and _____ and (continue)
(3)   (4)
throughout the day until 6:00 p.m. The long list of participating companies is on the back of this
brochure. This year, companies A–G _____ (interview) candidates in room 245 on the
(5)
second floor. Companies H–Z _____ (meet) candidates in room 252.
(6)

Tips for Job Seekers

Interviews generally _____ (take) about 30 minutes. An interviewer
(7)
usually _____ (spend) a few minutes reading your résumé. He or
(8)
she sometimes _____ (ask) you to fill out an application. An interview
(9)
typically _____ (end) with a question-and-answer period. The average
(10)
employer _____ (expect) you to know a lot about the company – this is an
(11)
opportunity to demonstrate your knowledge. Also, employers _____ always
(12)
_____ (look) for new ideas, and these ideas may come from you!
(12)

B Pair Work Compare your answers with a partner. Discuss the reason for each of your answers.

A *I used the present progressive in number 1 because the phrase* today's job fair *tells me that the sentence is about something that is happening now.*

B *I agree with you. For number 2, I used . . .*

3 Stative Verbs

Grammar Presentation

Stative verbs describe states and conditions. Generally, they do not describe actions.	*That sounds like a great project.* *We don't have two chances to make a first impression.*

3.1 Non-action or Stative Verbs

Use the simple present with stative verbs. Here are some common stative verb categories:	
Description: *appear, be, exist, look, seem, sound*	*She seems like a hard worker.*
Measurement: *cost, weigh*	*It doesn't cost anything to send your application.*
Knowledge: *believe, forget, know, remember, think*	*He doesn't believe that first impressions are true.* *I know stereotypes aren't true.*
Emotions: *feel, hate, like, love, prefer*	*Employers prefer motivated workers.*
Possession / Relationship: *belong, contain, have, need, own, want*	*I don't have a good impression of him.* *I need a challenging career.*
Senses: *hear, see, smell, taste*	*Can you see the water from your office?*
Perception: *notice, see, understand*	*When you explain the problem in that way, I see your point. I understand your viewpoint.*

▶▶ Stative (Non-Action) Verbs: See page A2.

3.2 Verbs with Stative and Action Meanings

Some verbs have both stative and action meanings. You can use the present progressive with the action meanings of these verbs. Examples of verbs with stative and action meanings include *be, have, see, taste, think,* and *weigh.*

SIMPLE PRESENT (STATIVE MEANING)	PRESENT PROGRESSIVE (ACTION MEANING)
I think first impressions are important. (*think* = believe)	*I am thinking about how to make a good first impression.* (*think* = use the mind)
Do you have an interesting career? (*have* = own)	*Are you having trouble at work?* (*have* = experience)
She is the new manager. (*be* = description)	*She is being difficult.* (*be* = act)
He noticed that he doesn't see very well anymore. (*see* = view with the eyes)	*He is seeing the eye doctor for an exam next week.* (*see* = meet with)

Grammar Application

A Complete the article from a college newspaper. Circle the correct form of the verbs.

A STUDY ON STEREOTYPES

Lisa James is majoring in psychology here at Carlson College. This semester, she **thinks /(is thinking)** about participating in a study (1) on stereotypes in Professor Green's Psychology 101 class. According to Dr. Green, many people **have / are having** fixed ideas about members of (2) their own and other cultures. This is true even when they **know / are knowing** that the stereotypes they (3) **have / are having** are false. (4)

Dr. Green **believes / is believing** that when (5) most people make generalizations about other cultures, they **don't seem / are not seeming** to (6) make these judgments on observation. Instead, they **appear / are appearing** to base their judgments on (7) ideas that they grew up with in their own cultures.

This semester, Dr. Green **has / is having** an (8) interesting time giving his students two tests: a self-assessment test and a personality test. In the self-assessment test, students describe the traits they **think / are thinking** members of their own culture (9) have. The personality test gives basic information about what a person is really like. Dr. Green **believes / is believing** the results of the personality (10) test will conflict with the results of the cultural self-assessment test. Here's an example: People from one culture in the study **believe / are believing** that (11) they are hostile and argumentative. However, when these people take the personality test, they usually **get / are getting** very high scores for kindness (12) and helpfulness.

The results of studies such as Dr. Green's **appear / are appearing** to show that cultural (13) stereotypes are almost always mistaken. Lisa is looking forward to discovering what the tests say about her. Although she believes that she does not have stereotypes about people, she knows that Dr. Green **believes / is believing** that almost (14) everyone has stereotypes of some people.

B Pair Work Compare your answers with a partner. Discuss the reason for each of your answers.

I used the present progressive with the verb think *in number 1 because the action is happening now.*

Complete the conversation about stereotypes at work. Use the simple present or present progressive form of the verbs in parentheses. Use contractions when possible.

Alan Claudia, how are your interview follow-up reports going? Are you still working on them?

Claudia I _____*think*_____ (think) they're going well. I'm almost finished.
(1)

Alan That's wonderful news. How many reports _____ you
(2)
_____ (have)?
(2)

Claudia Eight. I have three more to do.

Alan Oh, I see. So you're just a little more than half finished. Our meeting

_____ (be) always at 4:30 on Wednesdays. Why are you still
(3)
working on them?

Claudia I don't usually take this long, but this time I'm spending a lot of time on the

reports because I _____ (be) very careful. I interviewed a lot of
(4)
people from many different cultures, both young and old, and from cities as well

as from the countryside.

Alan So?

Claudia Some of the reports _____ (be) finished, but I don't want to base
(5)
my judgments on only partial information. I _____ (not think) that
(6)
the information would be useful if it's not complete.

Alan I _____ (know) what you mean.
(7)

Claudia This time, I _____ (have) a hard time separating things like culture
(8)
and appearance from people's actual abilities.

Alan Well, it's good that you _____ (be) aware of it. Let's discuss
(9)
it later.

Exercise 3.3 More Stative or Action Meaning?

A Listen to the interview about first impressions. Write the missing words.

Reporter When you ___*meet*___ someone for the first time, how does
(1)
the person's appearance affect your judgment? Today, we

_____ people to describe how they make
(2)
judgments about others.

Marta I know I _____ unfair stereotypes when I meet
(3)
someone new. To me, older people always _____
(4)
like they need help. When I meet an older person,

I _____ about my grandparents.
(5)
I speak slowly and clearly, in case the person can't hear.

I _____ it's wrong to think all older people
(6)
are like that, but I can't help it.

Marc I feel that I _____ always very fair when I meet a
(7)
new person. I _____ people's appearances don't
(8)
always say who they really are. For example, if I meet a person who

_____ sloppy,[1]
(9)
I _____ that he or she is a lazy person.
(10)

Bin For me, it depends on the situation. When I am interviewing people
at work, I take their appearance very seriously. For example, I always
notice how a person dresses for an interview. If a person's appearance

_____ sloppy or careless in an interview, I
(11)
_____ he or she will be a sloppy and careless worker.
(12)

[1]**sloppy:** messy, not tidy

B Pair Work Discuss these questions with a partner: Which person in A are you most like?
How much do stereotypes affect the judgments you make about people when you first meet
them? Give an example.

*I think I'm like Marc. I don't like to judge someone right away. For example, my
landlord seems somewhat reserved when you meet him, but he's actually a really
nice guy.*

4 Special Meanings and Uses of Simple Present

Grammar Presentation

The simple present is frequently used for summarizing and reviewing as well as for explaining procedures or giving instructions.	*Malcolm Gladwell's book* Blink *persuades the reader to believe in first impressions.* *Participants follow strict procedures for the Implicit Association Test.*

4.1 Special Meanings and Uses of Simple Present

A Use the simple present to summarize scientific writing or review artistic works such as books, plays, and movies.	*The Implicit Association Test measures people's responses.* *Malcolm Gladwell's book* Blink *discusses the importance of first impressions. He argues that first impressions are often accurate, even if the mind doesn't realize it.*
B Use the simple present to explain procedures or instructions.	*To administer the test, we always follow the same procedures. First, we seat participants in every other chair. We don't usually put them next to each other.*
Commonly used expressions that show sequencing include *first, then, next, after that,* and *finally.*	*When you arrive at the job fair,* <u>first</u> *you go to the desk and sign in.* <u>Then</u> *you take a look at the list of companies and plan which companies you want to see.*

Grammar Application

Read the sentences. Then label each sentence *R* (book reviews), *P* (procedures and instructions), or *O* (other uses – facts, routines, schedules) according to where the text comes from.

1 First, students write their names at the top of the paper.   *P*

2 The authors end with a set of tips for always creating good first impressions.   ____

3 The class meets on Tuesdays and Thursdays from 11:30 a.m. to 1:00 p.m.   ____

4 This book helps readers understand the difference between how they see themselves and how other people see them.   ____

5 The required reading for this course is *Making a Good Impression* by Dr. Al Stone.   ____

6 *Making a Good Impression* includes summaries of many of the latest studies on how people make first impressions.   ____

7 To complete the online test, students select their answers and click "Submit."   ____

Use the words to write sentences that describe the main points from an article on the problems with personality tests.

1 personality tests / always / not be / accurate

   Personality tests are not always accurate.

2 job candidates / sometimes / not tell / the truth

   _____

3 a job candidate's score / always / not reflect / the candidate's personality

   _____

4 candidates who take some personality tests twice / sometimes / get / different scores

   _____

5 these tests / not match / people to jobs well

   _____

Pair Work **Choose a situation with a partner in which it is important to make a good first impression, such as a job interview or a first meeting with an important person. Describe the scene and how the person makes a good first impression. Remember to use sequencing words such as *First, . . .*; *Then . . .*; *After that, . . .*; and *Finally, . . .***

On the first day of work: First, the new employee shakes hands and makes eye contact with the people he or she meets.

5 Avoid Common Mistakes ⚠

1 **Use the simple present with stative verbs.**

                 matter
First impressions ~~are mattering~~ when you want to establish a relationship.

2 **Use the simple present to express facts, routines, or habits unlikely to change.**

            require
Sessions ~~are requiring~~ 10 to 15 minutes to complete.

3 **Use the present progressive to show that something is in progress or temporary.**

       isn't interviewing   *is still studying*
He ~~doesn't interview~~ for jobs this year because he ~~still studies~~.

4 **Use the -*ing* form, not the base form of the verb, when using the present progressive.**

       working
He is ~~work~~ as a store clerk.

Editing Task

Find and correct eight more mistakes in the paragraphs about first impressions.

Without a doubt, first impressions are important. Current research ~~is showing~~ *shows* that a first impression can last a long time. These days it seems that everyone talks about the significance of the first 30 seconds of a job interview or a meeting with a client. However, I am believing there is another side to this story.

5   Some people are having the ability to make a good first impression, but the impression may be false. I believe that time and experience are telling the truth about a person's character. Whenever I talk with someone who smiles at me and seems completely charming, I am getting suspicious. I think that the person is not sincere, and that he or she wants something from me. On the other hand, I often find that

10   quieter, more reserved people are more willing to help me when I ask. My colleague Jim is a good example. This fall he is work on a special project, so he is very busy, and sometimes he appears unfriendly. However, he usually stops and helps me when I ask. My friendlier colleagues usually smile, but when I ask them for help, they are making excuses.

15   In short, I am not believing that everyone who makes a good first impression deserves my trust. Maybe I am too suspicious with friendly people, but I will always give awkward or shy people a second chance. After all, I think that I may be one of them.

6 Academic Writing

Plagiarism and Academic Honesty

In this unit (1), you will learn about plagiarism and how to maintain academic honesty at a North American university.

Exercise 6.1 Preparing to Write

Work with a partner. Discuss the questions.

1 What is plagiarism? What is academic honesty?
2 Is plagiarism the same or different in your culture than in North America? Give an example to explain your answer.
3 Why might plagiarism be considered academically dishonest?
4 What are three reasons that students plagiarize?

Read the interviews with three academic professionals: a professor, a librarian, and a writing center tutor.

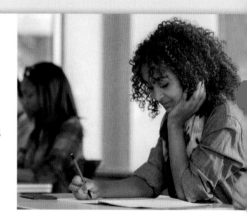

Dr. Moore, *Professor*
Academic honesty is important. If a student pretends that someone else's words are theirs, that's dishonest. If students let someone else write their paper, that's dishonest. If a student submits a paper that was used in another class, that's also dishonest. These are all examples of plagiarism. The rules are simple: Do your own work, use your own words, and don't re-use your work for other classes. If students are having trouble, they should see their professor. At our college, if a student plagiarizes, I have to report it to the Dean[1] of Students.

Dee Mackey, *Librarian*
Students are often confused about plagiarism. If students write something that is not their own idea or their own work, they should cite the source. That means they should say where they found something. When students cite a source, they always need to mention the author and date of publication. They should also cite sources for photos and graphs. Students can use the ideas of another person, but they should use their own words and cite the source. If they are unsure about anything, they should ask for help. Professors and librarians are happy to help.

Jaye Evans, *Writing Center Tutor*
Students plagiarize because sometimes they wait until the last minute, so they don't have time to write their paper. Then they go to the Internet and cut and paste things into their paper, or copy from books or articles. That's never OK. Their professors know that they have copied. Writing center tutors can help, but students have to start working on their papers early. We can't really help them at the last minute.

---

[1]**dean** (n) a head of a department or group at a college or university

Exercise 6.2 Understanding Plagiarism

Answer the questions for each speaker. Then compare your answers with a partner's.

1 What is plagiarism and academic honesty?

Dr. Moore: _____

Dee Mackey: _____

Jaye Evans: _____

2 Why do students plagiarize?

Dr. Moore: _____

Dee Mackey: _____

Jaye Evans: _____

Exercise 6.3 Evaluating Plagiarism

Read the statements. Write *T* (true) or *F* (false) next to the statement. Then write the name of the speaker who helped you decide your answer.

_____ 1 When students cut and paste from the Internet, it's not right, but no one will know. _____

_____ 2 A student writer doesn't have to say where they got a photograph for their essay. _____

_____ 3 The writing center wants students to come to them early. _____

_____ 4 Students should cite their sources when they paraphrase. _____

_____ 5 Having a friend write your paper is plagiarism. _____

_____ 6 Professors don't want to help students with questions about plagiarism. _____

Avoiding Plagiarism

In academic writing, **plagiarism** is defined as taking other people's words and ideas and using them as your own. It is a very serious issue in North America, and it should always be avoided. If you use other people's words or ideas in your writing, you must always give them credit.

Exercise 6.4 Applying the Skill

1 Work with a partner. Make a list of three things you should do and three things you should not do to avoid plagiarism and maintain academic honesty. Use your own words.

2 Share your list with the class. As a class, create an official list of plagiarism "Dos" and "Don'ts."

2 Simple Past and Past Progressive; *Used To, Would*

Global Marketing

1 Grammar in the Real World

ACADEMIC WRITING

Expository writing

A What is a *global market*? Read the article about global marketing. What makes global marketing campaigns successful?

B Comprehension Check **Answer the questions.**

1 What are some reasons customers in China did not buy the dolls at first?
2 Why was the campaign in Malaysia successful?
3 How are advertising campaigns different today from in the past?

C Notice **Read the sentences from the article. Check (✓) the sentence that describes an action that continued for a period of time in the past. Does the verb end in *-ing* or *-ed*?**

_____ 1 Around the same time, another American company **was showing** a series of advertisements in the United States for a shampoo product.

_____ 2 As a result, the company **adapted** its advertising to fit the local culture.

GLOBAL Marketing

In 2017, an American toy company **opened** a huge store on the main shopping street in a major city in China. The store **featured** the company's famous doll. At that

5 time, the sales of the doll **were falling** slightly in the United States, so the company **was working** on developing new markets in other countries. At the store, there **were not** many sales. Customers **would come** in and look,

10 but few **were buying** the dolls. The company **did** some research and **found out** why. The doll's image **did not appeal**[1] to young Chinese women. They **had** a preference for dolls that looked cute and **adorable**.[2] They

15 also **wanted** more affordable prices. The toy company eventually **closed** the store.

Around the same time, another American company **was showing** a series of advertisements in the United States for a

20 shampoo product. In one ad, "real women" **showed** their hair and **talked** about how much they liked the shampoo. These women **looked** like your friends and neighbors, not like models. The advertisements **were** a great

25 success. The company **decided** to create similar advertisements in Malaysia. While it **was working on** these advertisements, it **was** also **doing** research on Malaysian culture. The company **discovered** that

30 some Malaysian women **thought** that it was inappropriate[3] to show their hair in public, so it **realized** that its approach[4] **would not be** successful. As a result, the company **adapted** its advertising to fit the local culture. In the

35 new Malaysian advertisements, the women **did not show** their hair. They only **talked** about it. The ads **were** a tremendous success.

In the past, companies **would create** one advertisement and one product for all

40 markets. Today's markets include places all over the world, and the success of global marketing campaigns depends on two simple rules: understand the local culture and adapt the marketing and product to that culture.

---

[1]**appeal:** interest or attract someone

[2]**adorable:** attractive and easy to love

[3]**inappropriate:** unsuitable, especially for the particular time, place, or situation

[4]**approach:** a method or way of doing something

2 Simple Past vs. Past Progressive

Grammar Presentation

The simple past and the past progressive describe actions in the past.	American consumers *wanted* affordable prices. *While the company was working on these advertisements, it was also doing research on Malaysian culture.*

2.1 Simple Past

Use the simple past to describe actions, situations, or events that are completed. Use the simple past for actions that happened once or repeatedly in the past.	*Company executives decided to market the dolls in China in 2017.* *The dolls weren't popular in China a few years ago.* *What did the company market in Malaysia?* *The company executives visited Malaysia a few times.*
Past time markers, such as *yesterday, last week, two months ago,* and *in 2018* can be used with the simple past.	*A company studied Malaysian culture last year.* *Did it get good local advice last time?* *Who gave the company advice last week?*

▸▸ Irregular Verbs: See page A1.

2.2 Past Progressive

Use the past progressive to describe an activity or event in progress over a period of time in the past.	*The company wasn't selling dolls in China at that time.* *Why weren't many people buying them?* *What was happening during that period?*

2.3 Simple Past and Past Progressive Contrasted

A Use the past progressive to describe background activities. These activities were in progress at the same time as the main event in the sentence. Use the simple past for the main event.	BACKGROUND ACTIVITY *They were planning a new advertising campaign* MAIN EVENT *in the country, so they did some research on the culture.*
B Use the simple past, not the past progressive, with stative verbs.	*The company understood the culture.* NOT *The company was understanding the culture.*

Grammar Application

Exercise 2.1 Simple Past and Past Progressive

A Underline the past forms of the verbs in this paragraph about early American advertising.

Benjamin Franklin is one of the fathers of American advertising. He <u>was</u> an early American politician and inventor. In the early 1700s, Franklin was working in Philadelphia, Pennsylvania, as a publisher and inventor. He published a variety of books, and he was also the publisher of the newspaper *The Pennsylvania Gazette*. He used *The Pennsylvania Gazette* to advertise his inventions. Franklin filled the newspaper with ads. He also advertised books, both his own and other people's. Because of the ads in his newspaper, Franklin was making a lot of money and was selling a lot of books. These were among the first advertisements in America.

B Pair Work Compare your answers with a partner. Discuss which verbs are simple past and which are past progressive.

Exercise 2.2 Simple Past or Past Progressive?

A Read the paragraphs about a successful advertising campaign.[1] Circle the simple past or past progressive form of the verbs. Sometimes more than one answer is possible.

In the years after World War II, the U.S. government **promoted/(was promoting)** milk as
(1)
a health product. In the 1960s, however, soft-drink[2] companies began to market their products
very aggressively. As a result, people **soon drank/were soon drinking** more soft drinks and
(2)
less milk. The California Milk Advisory Board (CMAB) realized that the old health-focused
advertising **didn't work/wasn't working**.
(3)
Beginning in the mid-1970s, milk sales **went/were going** down in the United
(4)
States, and the CMAB **decided/was deciding** to do something to increase sales.
(5)
The CMAB members **learned/were learning** that the majority of people believed
(6)
that milk was good for them, but they weren't drinking it.

In 1993, a new board was formed, the California Milk Processor Board
(MilkPEP). This new board **hired/were hiring** an advertising agency to design a
(7)

new advertisement for milk. The agency **designed / were designing** a very original
ad. The ad showed a person eating something sweet or sticky (like cake or peanut
butter). The ad was funny because the person really needed milk to drink, but he or
she didn't have it. This **became / was becoming** the very successful "Got milk?"³
campaign. In 1994, milk sales **increased / were increasing** by over 10 million gallons a
year. This was a clear indication that the new campaign was a success.

¹**campaign:** series of advertisements
²**soft drink:** a carbonated, nonalcoholic drink, also known as "pop," "soda," or "cola"
³**Got milk?:** an informal way of saying "Do you have milk?"

B Pair Work **Compare your answers with a partner. Then ask and answer questions about
the information in A. Use the simple past and the past progressive.**

A *What was happening in the United States beginning in the mid-1970s?*

B *Milk sales were going down.*

3 Time Clauses with Simple Past and Past Progressive

Grammar Presentation

The simple past and past progressive are used with time clauses to show the order of two past events.	*We changed our minds about the product after we saw the ads for it.* *While he was presenting the product, the audience listened attentively.*

3.1 Using Time Clauses with Simple Past

A Use time clauses beginning with the time words and phrases *after, as soon as, before, once, until,* and *when* to show the order in which two events happened. When the time clause comes first in the sentence, use a comma.	*We found out that the ad wasn't appropriate for consumers when we were doing research on the market.* *When we were doing research on the market, we found out that the ad wasn't appropriate for consumers.*
B Use *after* to introduce the first event.	FIRST EVENT SECOND EVENT *After the store opened, people didn't buy the dolls.*

3.1 Using Time Clauses with Simple Past *(continued)*

C Use *before* to introduce the *second* event.	FIRST EVENT *The company worked with an advertising team* SECOND EVENT *before it marketed the shampoo.*
D Use *as soon as* or *once* to introduce the first event when the second event happens immediately after.	FIRST EVENT *As soon as the company made prices* SECOND EVENT *affordable, sales improved.* SECOND EVENT FIRST EVENT *Women bought the shampoo once the ad fit the local culture.*
E *Until* means "up to that time." Use *until* to indicate the second event.	FIRST EVENT SECOND EVENT *There were not many sales until the company changed its advertising.*
F Use *when* to introduce the first event. *When* means "at almost the same time."	FIRST EVENT SECOND EVENT *When we thought about the low sales, we got a little worried.*

3.2 Using Time Clauses with Simple Past and Past Progressive

A Use the past progressive to describe an ongoing action. Use *while* or *when* to introduce the ongoing action.	ONGOING EVENT *While we were developing an advertising campaign,* INTERRUPTION *I got sick.*
Use the simple past to describe an action that interrupts the ongoing action. Use *when* to introduce the interruption.	ONGOING EVENT *We were discussing the new ad campaign* INTERRUPTION *when we heard about the low sales.*
B Use the past progressive in both clauses to talk about two actions in progress at the same time.	*While they were studying Malaysian culture, they were developing an advertising campaign.*

DATA FROM THE REAL WORLD

In formal writing, *when* is more common than *while*.

when
while

Exercise 3.1 Time Clauses with *After*, *Before*, *Once*, and *When*

Read the sentences about marketing milk. Circle the time words. Underline the time clauses. Label the earlier event with *1* and the later event with *2*.

              1   2

1 (After) World War II ended, the milk companies in the United States wanted people to drink milk. They marketed milk as a health drink.

2 People drank more milk than soft drinks before soft-drink companies started marketing their drinks as "fun."

3 When soft-drink companies began marketing their drinks as "fun," the California Milk Advisory Board (CMAB) realized it needed to market milk differently.

4 The CMAB learned that people thought milk was boring after the board completed its market research.

5 When the CMAB discovered that 70 percent of Californians already drank milk, it decided to create a campaign to persuade them to drink more milk.

6 Before it started a new ad campaign, the new California Milk Processor Board, MilkPEP, learned that most people drink milk at home with foods like cookies and cake.

7 When the new milk ads appeared, they immediately became famous.

8 MilkPEP created a successful Spanish-language milk ad once it had success with the "Got milk?" campaign.

Exercise 3.2 Time Clauses with *As Soon As*, *Before*, *Until*, and *While*

Read the facts about the history of advertising. Combine the sentences with the time words in parentheses. Sometimes more than one answer is possible.

1 First event: Advertising already existed in Europe.
  Second event: Europeans came to the Americas in the 1400s.

  (before) *Before Europeans came to the Americas in the 1400s, advertising already existed in Europe./Advertising already existed in Europe before Europeans came to the Americas in the 1400s.*

2 First event: Europeans were exploring the world from the fifteenth to the seventeenth centuries.
  Second event: They found new and interesting kinds of food and spices.

  (while) _____

  _____

3 First event: European explorers came home.
  Second event: They introduced the items to the people from their countries.

  (as soon as) _____

  _____

4 First event: Europeans didn't know anything about coffee.
 Second event: They read the ads that explained what it was.

 (before) _____

 _____

5 First event: Early advertisements had no words because most people couldn't read.
 Second event: Literacy became widespread in the eighteenth century.

 (until) _____

 _____

6 First event: Newspapers were the most common form of advertising.
 Second event: Radio was invented in the 1920s.

 (before) _____

 _____

Exercise 3.3 Using Time Clauses with *When* and *While*

Complete the sentences from a report on a global marketing lecture. Use the simple past and past progressive forms of the verbs in parentheses.

1 The head of marketing of a restaurant chain __*was speaking*__ (speak) when
 I __*arrived*__ (arrive).

2 When his company _____ (consider) opening new restaurants, they
 _____ (realize) that they needed some vegetarian food items.

3 The market researchers _____ (do) research on the vegetarian consumer
 when the managers _____ (decide) they needed a new, healthy menu.

4 The managers _____ (learn) that they had to eliminate many ingredients
 with eggs and dairy products when the market researchers _____
 (interview) vegan[1] customers.

5 While they _____ (listen) to customers explain how busy they were, the
 market researchers _____ (get) the idea that the company should offer
 delivery service.

6 The head of marketing _____ (think) about opening up restaurants in
 Chicago when he _____ (learn) that more people ordered take-out food
 in New York City than in Chicago.

7 While the managers _____ (contemplate) the idea of
 opening up a place in New York City, a restaurant in a busy location
 _____ (become) available, and the company bought the
 place immediately.

[1]**vegan:** a vegetarian who eats no animal or dairy products

A Over to You **Think about important decisions you have made in your life. Write an answer to one of these questions. Use *when* and *while*.**

- What were you doing when you decided to study here?
- What were you doing when you made an important decision about your life?

  I was working in two different jobs when I decided to take classes here.

B Pair Work **Discuss your sentences with a partner.**

4 *Used To* and *Would*

Grammar Presentation

Used to and *would* describe past routines or repeated actions. *Used to* expresses states or habits that existed in the past, but do not exist now. *Would* can only express repeated actions.	*Our company used to sell shampoo around the world. We would study the local customs. Then we would create local marketing campaigns.*

4.1 *Used To*

A *Used to* is followed by the base form of the verb. It can be used for actions or states.	*Some companies used to ignore local customs.* (But they don't do that now.) *This building used to be a TV studio.* *I used to know the manager's name, but I've forgotten it.*
Use *use to* not *used to* in questions with *did*.	*Where did you use to go to school when you were young?*
The negative is *didn't use to* + the base form.	*Our company didn't use to ask for advice from the local markets.* (But our company does now.)
B Use the simple past, not *used to*, to talk about completed actions in the past.	*The company made its sales goals last year.* NOT *The company used to make its sales goals last year.* *The company made its sales goals for a decade.* NOT *The company used to make its sales goals for a decade.* *The company made its sales goals three times.* NOT *The company used to make its sales goals three times.*

4.2 *Would*

A *Would* is followed by the base form of the verb.	*In the past, companies* would create *one advertisement for all markets.*
A time expression, such as *in the past*, shows the context for the action.	*In the past, we* would meet *for an hour every Friday to talk about marketing techniques.* (But we don't do that now.)
B *Would* is only used for actions, not states.	*Twenty years ago, many smaller companies* wouldn't do *a lot of marketing in other countries.* *Usually, the president of our company* would not attend *our weekly meetings.* *In the past, companies* were not *sensitive to local customs.* NOT *In the past, companies* wouldn't be *sensitive to local customs.*
C Use the simple past, not *would*, to talk about completed actions in the past.	*The sales team* attended *a conference last week.* NOT *The sales team* would attend *a conference last week.*

Grammar Application

Exercise 4.1 *Would*

Complete part of a lecture on the history of radio and TV advertising. Use *would* and the correct verbs in the boxes.

appear	not use	~~produce~~	read

TV commercials developed from radio commercials. In the early days of radio, radio stations sold advertising time to support themselves. Many companies **would produce** (1) entire radio programs in order to advertise their products. Famous Hollywood stars of the day _____ (2) on these programs. In the early days of radio, radio stations _____ (3) ads that were on tape.[1] Instead, people performed the ads live. That is, an announcer _____ (4) an advertisement on the air.[2] Today, some radio ads are still live, but many ads are also prerecorded.

[1]**on tape:** prerecorded
[2]**on the air:** while broadcasting

advertise	buy	create	match

When television appeared, advertisers _____ time
                                                    (5)
during a TV program for their commercials. They _____
                                                                (6)
short, 10-second advertisements to show during these programs. They

_____ a program with viewers who were likely to buy
            (7)
their product. For example, they _____ laundry soap to
                                                (8)
housewives who stayed home and watched serial dramas ("soap operas") during
the day.

Exercise 4.2 *Used To, Would,* or Simple Past?

A Listen to an interview about how TV advertising has changed. Write the correct form of the verbs that you hear.

⌂   💬 ↻ ☰ ✉

Zach How has TV advertising changed over the years?

Dave In the past, we __*used to create*__ commercials with very direct messages.
            (1)
Commercials _____ the consumer exactly what to do. We never
                        (2)
_____ vague[1] about the message at all. In addition,
            (3)
commercials _____ to entertain the viewer.
                            (4)

Zach So, how _____ you _____ an advertising message in the old days?
                    (5)   (5)

Dave A commercial for our product _____: "Drink Fruity Juice."
                                                (6)
We _____ the product several times in a commercial.
            (7)
We _____ the product.
                (8)

Zach What changed?

Dave We _____ some research a few years ago. It _____
                (9)   (10)
that people no longer pay attention to commercials like those. As a result, we

_____ to change our style. Now we are producing "mystery ads."
        (11)
Mystery ads don't show the product until the very end of the commercial. They

entertain the viewer because the viewer has to figure out what the product is.

[1]**vague:** unclear

B Listen again and check your answers.

5 Avoid Common Mistakes ⚠

1 **Use the base form of the verb after *would* and *used to*.**

       live

He used to ~~living~~ in Bangladesh, where he studied economics.

2 **Use *was* or *were* with the verb + *-ing* to describe actions in progress in the past, including in sentences with two clauses.**

                                         was

The new dolls were selling well, and the company ∧ making a lot of money.

3 **Use the simple past when describing specific events in the past.**

                had

She knew that she ~~has~~ a problem in one of her markets.

4 **Use the past progressive to provide background information for an event.**

was studying

I ~~studied~~ business administration in Malaysia when I got my first job.

Editing Task

Find and correct eight more mistakes in the transcript from a meeting.

    Hello, everyone! Welcome to the meeting.

                               was

    As many of you know, this past ∧ year disappointing for many

companies. However, we ended up doing quite well here at ABC Tech.

At the beginning of the year, things looking bad. In fact, our sales fell

5 when I started here. However, our excellent marketing team did their

research, and they create new and extremely successful advertisements

after they discover two shifts in consumer spending.

    The first shift they saw was a shift to green marketing. Last year we

noticed that consumers would paid more for environmentally friendly

10 products. Therefore, our first advertisement of last year showed how

good our smartphone batteries are for the environment.

    The second shift was in who advertised our products. While we wrote our most

recent advertisement, research arrived that showed that celebrities sell products

better. In October we began showing famous actors and actresses using our phones,

15 and last month alone, our sales rise by 25 percent.

    In short, while some businesses were struggling, we increasing our profits.

6 Academic Writing

Expository Writing

Brainstorm 〉 Organize 〉 Write 〉 Edit

In this writing cycle (Units 2-4), you will write an expository essay that answers the prompt below. In this unit (2), you will analyze an essay about globalization. You will then brainstorm and start organizing your ideas in a table.

> How has globalization changed your country?

Exercise 6.1 Preparing to Write

Work with a partner. Discuss the questions.

1 What is globalization?
2 How has globalization affected your country?
3 What types of food used to be popular in your country? What types of food are popular now?

Exercise 6.2 Focusing on Vocabulary

Read the definitions. Then complete the sentences with the correct form of the words in bold.

consumption (n) the using of goods and services
convenience (n) something that causes no difficulty for your schedule or plans and is suitable to your purposes
ensure (v) to make certain that something is done or happens
experiment (v) to test or to try a new way of doing something
increase (v) to become larger or greater
influence (n) the power to have an effect on people or things
relatively (adv) quite good, bad, etc. in comparison with other similar things or with what you would expect

1 In the past, people always had to leave their home to buy food. Now, many shoppers are ordering groceries online because of its _____.

2 Many people prefer to see food before they buy it to _____ that it is fresh.

3 People sometimes reduce their _____ of certain foods when those foods become more expensive.

4 The bad weather in Florida affected the supply of oranges, so the price of oranges _____ a lot.

5 People who live in big cities tend to be _____ more familiar with international food compared to people who live in rural areas.

6 Recently, the popularity of cooking programs on television has had a big _____ on the ingredients that people use. People want to cook with foods they see on TV.

7 Some travelers like to eat familiar food, but others prefer to _____ with unfamiliar dishes.

The Globalization of Italian Cooking

1 Globalization is causing a lot of change in international culture, from the TV shows we watch to the clothes we wear. One major area is food culture. In one survey taken in Japan, Brazil, and Canada, 72% of people said that globalization improved their
5 eating habits. It seems clear that globalization has significantly affected food **consumption** in most parts of the world, but one country whose food has a long history of being "globalized" is Italy. If you walk down any main street in any major world city, you will find at least one Italian restaurant. At the same time, Italy is
10 experiencing changes in its own eating habits due to **influence** from other countries. This influence, which is a result of the broader trend of globalization, has both advantages and disadvantages.

2 Italian families traditionally take a lot of pride in preparing food, but changing trends began affecting the preparation of food
15 more than 40 years ago. People always used to make pasta—a basic Italian food—locally. Families also made the sauces to eat with the pasta at home. However, by the 1990s, people no longer were spending as much time preparing their meals. In fact, these days frozen or take-out Italian meals are very popular in Italy. In
20 addition, dried pasta is now mass-produced and is sold **relatively** cheaply in supermarkets. Ready-made pasta sauces are also popular. For example, one pasta sauce manufacturer saw its sales double in just five years. This trend made meal preparation more convenient, but it diminished an old cultural tradition too.

3 Italians' food tastes are also changing because of
25 globalization. People are traveling more, being exposed to more cultures, and seeing more foreign ingredients and recipes on the Internet and social media. Immigrants to Italy bring their food traditions with them. People's opportunities to **experiment**
30 with foreign food used to be very limited, since only pizza and pasta were available in the local town square. In the past, Italians would rarely have the chance to eat more exotic food, like sushi or curry. Now they can eat at restaurants with foreign cuisine and buy foreign food in supermarkets. Indian, Chinese, and Japanese
35 food have all become especially popular. While this trend is more common in urban areas such as Rome, Milan, and Venice, smaller

towns are experiencing similar changes. Many Italians see this as positive, but others worry that they are losing their sense of nationality as foreign food becomes more common.

40 **4** A third major change in Italy's food culture due to globalization is the rise of large restaurant chains. These chains are often foreign, and their numbers have **increased** enormously in recent years. Many people like the **convenience** of fast food. However, when this trend started, some Italians felt that it was destroying
45 local and national specialties. For example, in 1986, a famous fast-food chain opened a restaurant in a historic Rome neighborhood. Many unhappy people responded by joining the "Slow Food" movement, which encourages people to eat healthy, locally sourced food.

50 **5** In summary, globalization has had a significant effect on the way that Italians eat. Its influence can be seen as both positive and negative. Convenient foods were replacing traditional home-cooked meals at the end of the last century, and the availability of foreign foods and international chains has greatly increased
55 since then. Italians no longer have to rely on food that is produced locally. While some people welcome this extra choice, others fear its damage to Italian traditions, culture, and local businesses. On the other hand, the great popularity of Italian food worldwide will **ensure** that this delicious cuisine never disappears.

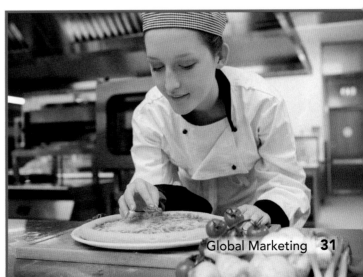

Read the text on page 31. Work with a partner. Discuss the questions.

1 What is the main idea of the essay?
   a Italian food used to be the most popular cuisine in the world.
   b The effects of globalization on Italian food are both positive and negative.
   c The introduction of global fast food in the 1980s changed Italian eating habits.
2 What other types of food or restaurants are mentioned in the essay. Why?

Exercise 6.4 Noticing the Grammar

Complete the tasks. Then compare your answers with a partner's.

1 Underline the use of *used to* in paragraphs 2 and 3. Why does the writer use it?
2 Highlight the use of *would* in paragraph 3. Why does the writer use it?
3 Circle the use of the simple past in paragraphs 2 and 4. Why does the writer use it?
4 Put a box around the use the past progressive in paragraphs 2, 4, and 5? Why does the writer use it?

Topic Sentences

The **topic sentence** tells the reader the subject of the paragraph and the writer's main idea about that subject. It answers the questions: What is the paragraph about? What does the writer want to say about the topic? Writers often start paragraphs in academic writing with topic sentences.

Exercise 6.5 Applying the Skill

Complete the tasks. Then compare your answers with a partner's.

1 Underline the topic sentence of paragraph 2. What is its main idea? _____

2 Underline the topic sentence of paragraph 3. What is its main idea? _____

3 Underline the topic sentence of paragraph 4. What is its main idea? _____

Supporting Statements with Details

In academic writing, writers give **details** - facts, examples, or reasons - that support their statements or opinions and show that they are true.

Exercise 6.6 Applying the Skill

Work with a partner. Use the text on page 31 to complete the tasks.

1 Identify two supporting details for the topic sentence in paragraph 2.

2 Identify two supporting details for the topic sentence in paragraph 3.

3 Identify two supporting details for the topic sentence in paragraph 4.

My Writing

Expository Essays

In an **expository essay** a writer explains and presents important information and viewpoints on a topic.

Exercise 6.7 Brainstorming Topics and Ideas

Work with a partner. Discuss the questions.

1 Besides food, what is one area in which globalization has changed your country?
2 What are two ways it has changed your country?
3 Write a possible topic sentence for a paragraph for each way.
4 Write two possible supporting details for each topic sentence.

Using Tables to Organize Information

Using **tables** can often help you organize information that you can use to support your ideas in an essay.

Exercise 6.8 Applying the Skill

Complete the table below for one of your topic sentences in Exercise 6.7. Add another supporting detail and a concluding sentence.

Topic sentence	
Supporting detail	
Supporting detail	
Supporting detail	
Concluding sentence	

Exercise 6.9 Writing a Paragraph

Write a paragraph about how food has changed in your country. How did it use to be? How is it now? Why did it change? If possible, give a personal example to show the change. Make sure you avoid the common mistakes in the chart on page 29.

1 Grammar in the Real World

**ACADEMIC
WRITING**

Expository
writing

A What are the characteristics of a successful person? Read the article about Mahatma Gandhi and Bill Gates. What qualities do they have in common?

B Comprehension Check Answer the questions.

1 What principle did Mahatma Gandhi support?
2 What does the Bill and Melinda Gates Foundation do?
3 What is the secret of successful people?

C Notice Find the sentences in the article and complete them. Circle the correct verb forms.

1 Although he died in 1948, his life and principles _____ people all over the world since then.
   a inspired   b have inspired   c have been inspiring

2 His example _____ movements for civil rights and freedom around the world ever since.
   a guided   b has guided   c has been guiding

3 Gates _____ the Microsoft Corporation in 1975.
   a founded   b has founded   c has been founding

Which verbs describe actions that are still happening now?

The MAKING of SUCCESS

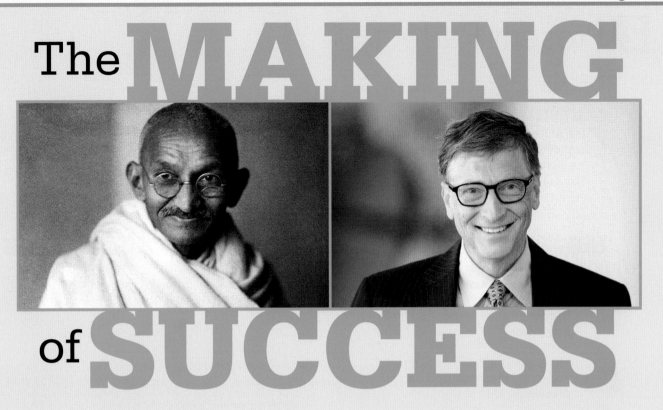

Some people **have said** that a successful person is like a sore thumb: The person sticks out[1] wherever he or she goes. People always seem to notice something special about the person. **Have** you ever
5 **wondered** why? What makes someone successful? For some time, researchers **have been trying** to answer this question. They have **been looking** closely at people who **have achieved** success in their lives, and they **have discovered** some very
10 interesting traits.[2]

Mahatma Gandhi is one person the researchers **have studied**. Gandhi was born in India in 1869. Although he **died** in 1948, his life and principles **have been inspiring**[3] people all over the world since then.

15 Gandhi **believed** in nonviolence, and he used this principle to help India gain independence from the British. His example **has been guiding** movements for civil rights[4] and freedom around the world ever since. In spite of great personal
20 risk, he never **gave up** on his goals to help the poor and the underprivileged, such as ethnic minorities. Additionally, he always **aimed** to live a simple life. At the time of Gandhi's death, the prime minister of India **announced** on the radio: "The light
25 **has gone out**[5] of our lives, and there is darkness everywhere."

Many people consider Bill Gates one of the most successful people in the world, and certainly one of the richest. Gates **founded** the Microsoft Corporation
30 in 1975. In 1994, he **formed** the Bill and Melinda Gates Foundation. Through this foundation, he **has contributed** billions of dollars to organizations and programs working in global health, including public-health organizations, and he continues to work for
35 world health and education.

The secret of the success of Gandhi, Gates, and other successful people is strikingly similar. They **have found** a purpose in life and are not afraid to take action, to take risks, or to work hard. Sometimes
40 they **have failed**, but they **have** always **gone on** to reach their goal.

---

[1]**stick out:** be easily noticed

[2]**trait:** a characteristic, especially of a personality

[3]**inspire:** fill someone with confidence and the desire to do something

[4]**civil rights:** the rights of every person in a society, including equality under law

[5]**light goes out:** an idiom meaning joy and hope disappear

2 Present Perfect

Grammar Presentation

The present perfect is used to describe an event that happened at an unspecified time in the past. This event may be completed, or it may not be completed and may continue into the future.

Winners of the Gandhi Peace Prize **have contributed** to world peace.

Sociologists **have studied** the definition of success for a long time.

2.1 Using Present Perfect

A Use the present perfect to describe an action or event that happened at an unspecified time in the past.	Researchers **have discovered** similar traits in successful people.
The adverbs *already, ever, never,* and *(not) yet* can be used with the present perfect. *Ever* means "at any time in the past."	"**Has** she **received** an award yet?" "Yes, she **has** already **received** two awards." "No, she **hasn't received** one yet." "**Have** you ever **thought** about the meaning of success?" "**I've** never **thought** about it."
B Use the present perfect for actions or events that started in the past and continue into the present.	How long **has** she **been** a successful businessperson?
For, since, so far, and *still* help link between the past and the present. Other common expressions are *all day, all my life,* and *all year.*	She's **owned** a successful business for 15 years. They've **worked** here since May. So far, he **hasn't changed** jobs. I still **haven't learned** to relax on weekends. They've **been** in the lab all day. He **has lived** here all his life.
C Use the present perfect to describe a recent action.	Breaking news: The judges **have awarded** the Nobel Peace Prize.
The adverbs *just* and *recently* emphasize the recent past time.	I **have** just **discovered** the answer. He **has** recently **given** money to the foundation.

2.2 Present Perfect with *For* and *Since*

A Use *for* to show the duration of time of an event that continues into the present moment.	She *hasn't worked* here <u>*for*</u> several years.
B In negative sentences, the preposition *in* may replace *for*.	She *hasn't seen* her <u>*in*</u> several years.
C Use *since* with specific dates or times to show the start of an event that continues into the present moment.	He *has lived* here <u>*since*</u> last year. She *hasn't worked* here <u>*since*</u> 2016.

Grammar Application

Exercise 2.1 Uses of Present Perfect

Read about Blake Mycoskie, a businessperson and a humanitarian. Label the bold and underlined verbs *U* (unspecified time in the past), *C* (time that continues to the present), or *R* (recent action) according to the use of the present perfect.

Blake Mycoskie is an American businessperson. He started a shoe company called TOMS in 2006. He sells a special type of shoe, the alpargata. He discovered the shoe in Argentina. Argentinean

5   farmers **have worn** ^{*C*} alpargatas for over 100 years.

      Recently, experts **have discovered** a link between children going barefoot and getting certain diseases. Mycoskie **has** always **wanted** to help children stay healthy. Therefore, every time someone buys a pair of TOMS shoes, his company gives a free pair of

10   new shoes to a child who needs shoes. Since he started TOMS, Mycoskie **has given** over a 60 million pairs of alpargatas to children in South Africa, Ethiopia, Rwanda, Argentina, Guatemala, Haiti, and the United States.

      More recently, Mycoskie **started** a coffee company. It **has donated** a week of water to people in coffee-producing countries for every bag of coffee that they've

15   sold. Mycoskie's favorite quote comes from Gandhi: "Be the change you wish to see in the world."

A Complete the interview about success. Use the present perfect form of the verbs in parentheses. Use contractions when possible.

| Reporter | Today, we are asking a few people about success. Are you successful? Do you know anyone who is successful? What makes someone successful? |

| Carlos | My friend Marta is successful. She **'s wanted** (want) to own a restaurant for years, and now she _____ (achieve)
(2)
her goal. Three years ago, she bought a restaurant. She
_____ (have) a successful business ever since.
(3) |

| Reporter | How long _____ you _____ (know) Marta?
(4)   (4) |

| Carlos | I _____ (know) her for 10 years.
(5) |

| Reporter | _____ she always _____ (be) interested in food?
(6)   (6) |

| Carlos | So far, that _____ (be) her only interest!
(7) |

| Annie | Well, I think my parents are very successful people. They
_____ (not/have) any problems in years.
(8)
They _____ (raise) five happy, successful children.
(9)
In fact, my youngest brother _____ just _____
(10)   (10)
(graduate) from college, and my older sister _____ recently
(11)
_____ (get) married.
(11) |

| Ian | You know, I _____ never _____ (think) about it.
(12)   (12)
I guess I _____ (not/achieve) anything
(13)
yet. I'm very happy, though! That's my idea of success! |

B Group Work Read the definitions of success. Choose one definition and give examples of it using your experiences or those of someone you know. Use the present perfect and *already*, *never*, *yet*, *for*, *since*, *so far*, *still*, *just*, and *recently*.

Definitions

Success is having a goal and then achieving it.
Success is doing work that you love.
Success is having a lot of money.
Success is having good relationships with family and friends.

I think that success is having a goal and achieving it. My brother has always wanted to climb Mount Everest. He hasn't done it yet, but he has climbed several other mountains.

Exercise 2.3 *For or Since?*

Complete the sentences about successful people. Circle *for* or *since*.

1 Blake Mycoskie has started several businesses **since**/**for** he graduated from college.

2 Bill Gates has worked part-time for Microsoft and part-time for the Bill and Melinda Gates Foundation **since**/**for** the past several years.

3 Bill Gates has given over $32 billion to charity **since**/**for** 2007.

4 Oprah Winfrey has helped poor people **since**/**for** many years.

5 **Since**/**For** several years, actors and pop stars have spent a great deal of their time and money on charity events.

Exercise 2.4 *More For or Since?*

Use the words to write sentences about successful people. Use the present perfect and *for* or *since*.

1 Joe and Ling have a successful marriage. They / be married / more than 30 years
   They have been married for more than 30 years.

2 They / have / only / one fight / they first met

3 They / not spend / a night apart / 1988

4 Mark and Amy have a successful friendship. They / be friends / high school

5 They / speak / on the phone every day / the past 10 years

6 Verónica / be / a successful single parent / many years

7 She / raise / her three children by herself / her divorce

3 Present Perfect vs. Simple Past

Grammar Presentation

The present perfect can refer to events that began in the past, continue until now, and may continue in the future. The simple past expresses completed events.	*"Have you read any books about successful people?"* *"Yes. I read one about Ricky Sánchez last week."*

3.1 Present Perfect and Simple Past Contrasted

A Use the present perfect to refer to events or repeated actions that continue into the present moment.	*Gandhi has inspired people all over the world.* (Gandhi inspired people for many years, and his ideas still inspire people now.)
Use the simple past to refer to completed actions.	*Gandhi promoted nonviolence against British rule.* (Gandhi did this while he was alive.)
B Use the present perfect to refer to an action completed at an unspecified time in the past that has an effect in the present.	*The Gates Foundation has supported health care in poor countries.* (Poor countries are benefiting from this care now.)
Use the simple past to refer to a completed action in the past that doesn't have an effect in the present.	*Bill Gates founded the Microsoft Corporation in 1975.* (This is a fact about Bill Gates's past.)

 DATA FROM THE REAL WORLD

In informal speaking, people sometimes use the simple past with *already* and *yet* instead of the present perfect.	*We haven't finished yet.* *We didn't finish yet.* (informal speaking)
In academic writing, always use the present perfect with *already* and *yet*.	*The foundation has already given millions of dollars to charities this year.*

Grammar Application

Exercise 3.1 Present Perfect or Simple Past?

A Complete the online interview about the actress Marlee Matlin. Circle the correct form of the verbs.

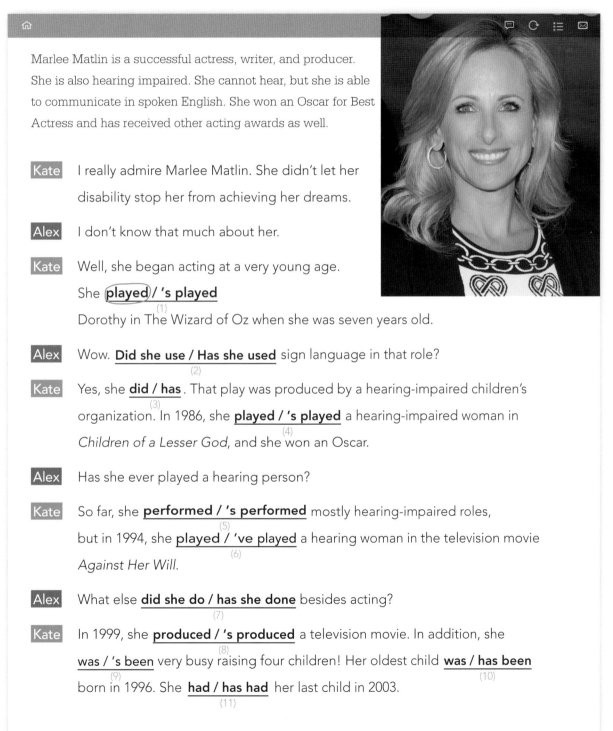

Marlee Matlin is a successful actress, writer, and producer. She is also hearing impaired. She cannot hear, but she is able to communicate in spoken English. She won an Oscar for Best Actress and has received other acting awards as well.

Kate I really admire Marlee Matlin. She didn't let her disability stop her from achieving her dreams.

Alex I don't know that much about her.

Kate Well, she began acting at a very young age. She **played** / **'s played**
(1)
Dorothy in The Wizard of Oz when she was seven years old.

Alex Wow. **Did she use / Has she used** sign language in that role?
(2)

Kate Yes, she **did / has** . That play was produced by a hearing-impaired children's
(3)
organization. In 1986, she **played / 's played** a hearing-impaired woman in
(4)
Children of a Lesser God, and she won an Oscar.

Alex Has she ever played a hearing person?

Kate So far, she **performed / 's performed** mostly hearing-impaired roles,
(5)
but in 1994, she **played / 've played** a hearing woman in the television movie
(6)
Against Her Will.

Alex What else **did she do / has she done** besides acting?
(7)

Kate In 1999, she **produced / 's produced** a television movie. In addition, she
(8)
was / 's been very busy raising four children! Her oldest child **was / has been**
(9)   (10)
born in 1996. She **had / has had** her last child in 2003.
(11)

B Pair Work Compare your answers with a partner. Discuss the reason for each of your answers.

I chose the past for number 1 because the action happened at a specific time in the past – when she was seven years old.

Exercise 3.2 More Present Perfect or Simple Past?

A Read the time line about Diane, a successful clothing designer. Complete the sentences with the present perfect or simple past.

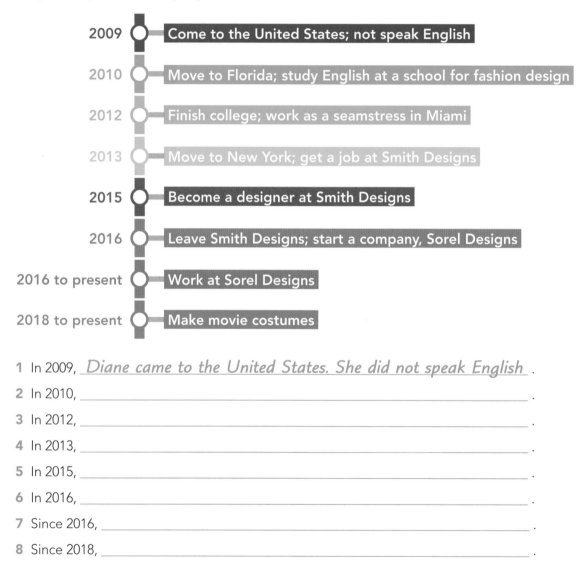

2009	Come to the United States; not speak English
2010	Move to Florida; study English at a school for fashion design
2012	Finish college; work as a seamstress in Miami
2013	Move to New York; get a job at Smith Designs
2015	Become a designer at Smith Designs
2016	Leave Smith Designs; start a company, Sorel Designs
2016 to present	Work at Sorel Designs
2018 to present	Make movie costumes

1 In 2009, *Diane came to the United States. She did not speak English* .

2 In 2010, _____ .

3 In 2012, _____ .

4 In 2013, _____ .

5 In 2015, _____ .

6 In 2016, _____ .

7 Since 2016, _____ .

8 Since 2018, _____ .

B Over to You Think about a successful person you know: a friend, a relative, or a famous person. On a separate piece of paper, write five facts about that person's life and accomplishments. Use the simple past and present perfect. Then share your sentences with a partner.

4 Present Perfect vs. Present Perfect Progressive

Grammar Presentation

The present perfect and present perfect progressive can sometimes have similar meanings. However, the present perfect progressive focuses on the ongoing nature of the activity. The present perfect often suggests that the action is finished.	*I've worn / I've been wearing glasses all my life.* *I've been writing an article about the meaning of success.* (I haven't finished it yet.) *I've written an article about the meaning of success.* (I've already finished it.)

4.1 Similar Meaning: Habitual and Ongoing Actions

A Use either the present perfect or present perfect progressive for habitual actions that began in the past and continue up to the present. Some verbs that show habitual action are *live*, *study*, *teach*, *wear*, and *work*.	*Bill Gates has worked hard all his life.* *Bill Gates has been working hard all his life.*
B Use *how long* to ask about the duration of habitual actions.	*"How long have you lived / have you been living here?"* *"I've lived / I've been living here for four years."*

4.2 Different Meanings: Completed vs. Ongoing Actions

A Use the present perfect for an event that was completed at an unspecified time in the past.	*She has read a biography of Gandhi.* (She finished it. She is no longer reading it.)
Use the present perfect progressive for an event that began in the past and is still ongoing. It emphasizes the duration of the activity.	*She has been reading a biography of Gandhi.* (She is still reading it.)
Stative verbs are usually in the present perfect (not the present perfect progressive). Stative verbs include *be*, *have*, *like*, and *see*.	*They've been good friends for ages.* *He's had a lot of experience in this business.* *I've always liked learning about successful people.*
B Use the present perfect to express *how much / how many*.	*A friend of mine has painted at least 100 paintings.* (*at least 100 paintings* = how many)
Use the present perfect progressive to express *how long*.	*She has been painting for more than 10 years.* (*more than 10 years* = how long)

Grammar Application

Read the sentences. Check (✓) whether the action is completed or ongoing.

		Completed	Ongoing
1	Lara has learned Spanish very well.	✓	☐
2	Michelle has also been studying French and Japanese this semester.	☐	☐
3	Enrico has been learning a lot of languages.	☐	☐
4	Tony has been working as a chef for the past eight years.	☐	☐
5	Alex has been running his own business since he was 19.	☐	☐
6	Joe has lived in Madrid.	☐	☐
7	Ron has been living in California since 2016.	☐	☐
8	We've already eaten dinner.	☐	☐
9	Sasha and Janet have been working there since 2017.	☐	☐
10	Raymond has won three prizes for his poetry.	☐	☐
11	I've been traveling for four weeks.	☐	☐
12	Bryn has been dancing since she was a child.	☐	☐
13	My mother has been cooking since she was 12.	☐	☐
14	Luisa has written four letters to her senator.	☐	☐

A Complete the following podcast transcript with the correct forms of the verbs in parentheses. Sometimes more than one answer is possible.

Zaha Hadid was an architect. She ___*designed*___ (1) (design) many famous buildings around the world, including the Rosenthal Center for Contemporary Art in Cincinnati. Hadid _____ (2) (study) architecture in London in the late 1970s and formed her own architecture company in 1979. Since her death in 2016, her company _____ (3) (continue) to build original and imaginative buildings and structures and _____ (4) (win) many international awards.

Richard Branson is one of the world's most successful businesspeople. He was born in England. He _____ (5) (have) a hard time in school because he had a learning disability.[1] Reading was difficult for him. As a result, he _____ (6) (leave) school at age 16. After that, he _____ (7) (start) his first business. Later, he _____ (8) (open) a record shop called Virgin Records. Since then, he _____ (9) (start) new businesses in many different industries, including transportation, entertainment, and communications.

[1]**learning disability:** a condition that affects a person's ability to learn

B Pair Work Compare your answers with a partner. Discuss the reason for each of your answers.

In number 1, I wrote designed *because the action is complete and it is in the past. So, I didn't choose* has designed.

C Listen to the podcast and check your answers.

D Over to You Think about your life story. Write answers to these questions on a separate piece of paper. Use the simple past, the present perfect, and the present perfect progressive. Share your answers with a partner.

- Have you accomplished something important (for example, learned a language, graduated from high school, saved money for an important purchase)? How did you do it?

- What are some things that you have done recently that make you feel happy? How long have you been doing them?

- What have you been doing recently that makes you feel successful?

5 Avoid Common Mistakes ⚠

1 **Use correct subject-verb agreement when forming the present perfect.**

have
Young people ~~has~~ always gone to college with high expectations.

2 **Use the present perfect (not the present perfect progressive) for a time period that starts in the past and is completed.**

finished
He has ~~been finishing~~ two books since last week.

3 **Remember to include *been* for the present perfect progressive.**

been
The definition of success has ‸ changing over the years.

4 **Use the present perfect progressive (not the present progressive) for actions that began in the past and are still continuing.**

has been
He ~~is~~ studying for six hours, and he refuses to stop.

Editing Task

Find and correct eight more mistakes in the paragraphs about a student's success in his job.

  I am a college student by day and a sous-chef[1] by night. My studies are important,
but my restaurant job ~~have~~ *has* taught me what I really need to know about success. I am
working in the kitchen of Da Lat, a French-Vietnamese bistro, for three years, and the
job has been a wonderful experience for me because I have learned many new skills.

5   First, I have been becoming a much better planner since I started working at
Da Lat. Planning and preparation are very important in a kitchen. If the chef have not
prepared the ingredients well beforehand, it will take too long to make each dish,
and customers will complain. We start our preparation early each day, and by the
time the first customer comes, we have working for 6 hours.

10   Second, I have developing better interpersonal skills. For example, I have
been receiving two promotions in the last two years. Last year, I became a line cook
because I had learned to pay attention to what others might need before they ask.
I think that for the past few months, I am paying better attention in other areas of my
life as well.

15   My college education is important, but I will always be grateful for my job at
Da Lat. This job have given me mental and social skills for my future.

[1]**sous-chef:** the head chef's assistant

6 Academic Writing

Expository Writing

Brainstorm > Organize > Write > Edit

In Unit 2, you studied topic sentences and supporting details, and started planning an expository essay to answer the prompt below. In this unit (3), you are going to learn how to structure essays and write effective thesis statements.

> *How has globalization changed your country?*

Essay Structure

Although there are different types of academic essays, the overall structure and principles are similar. Academic essays start with an **introductory paragraph**, followed by **body paragraphs**, and end with a **concluding paragraph**.

Introductory paragraph - The first paragraph gets the reader's attention by beginning with a **hook**–an interesting fact of statement, a surprising statistic, a quotation, or a question. Then the writer provides some **background information** on the main topic of the essay. The paragraph usually ends with a **thesis statement**, which is the main idea of the essay and often shows the writer's point of view.

Body paragraphs - The next paragraphs develop the main ideas outlined in the introduction and include relevant evidence and supporting information.

Concluding paragraph - The last paragraph presents a restatement of the thesis of the essay, along with the writer's conclusions, recommendations, or predictions.

Exercise 6.1 Analyzing a Text

Work with a partner. Look at "The Making of Success" on page 35. Discuss the questions. Explain your reasons.

1 What is the main idea of the reading?
   a Researchers have been trying to find out what makes someone successful.
   b Gandhi was successful because he never gave up.
   c Successful people share certain traits.

2 What is the hook? What is the thesis statement?

3 How many body paragraphs are there?
   a 2   b 3   c 4   d 5

4 Does the concluding paragraph end in a conclusion, recommendation, or prediction?

Exercise 6.2 Identifying Parts of an Essay

The following sentences are from an essay on the benefits of globalization. Write the paragraph (introductory, body, concluding) in which you would probably find them. Explain your answers to a partner.

1 We are fortunate to be living in the era of globalization. _____

2 While globalization has had a huge influence on every country, the changes have mostly been beneficial. _____

3 Globalization allows countries to exchange ideas, research, and technology more easily. _____

4 For example, consumers all over the world buy products and services from international companies like Microsoft and Apple. _____

5 In summary, globalization exposes all of us to the richness of new cultures. _____

Writing Effective Thesis Statements

A **thesis statement** in an academic essay is usually found at the end of the introductory paragraph. It explains what the essay will be about, and it expresses the writer's point of view. A good thesis statement allows the reader to predict what the rest of the essay will look like. It should *not* sound like a fact, a question, a description of what the essay will contain, or a general idea that everyone agrees on. For example:

Topic	Possible Thesis Statement
The effects of globalization	Globalization has had both positive and negative effects, but the benefits have been far greater than the drawbacks.
The global influence of the United States	It is a mistake to confuse globalization with Americanization.
Foreign direct investment by companies	The rise of foreign direct investment has led to pollution, exploitation of workers, and job losses in less developed countries.

Exercise 6.3 Applying the Skill

Read the statements and evaluate them as possible thesis statements. Check **F** for **fact**, **Q** for **question**, **D** for **description**, or **G** for **general**. Check **T** if the statement could make a good essay thesis.

	F	Q	D	G	T
1 In 1975 Bill Gates founded the Microsoft Corporation.					
2 Should governments lower taxes on international companies to increase jobs?					
3 While successful people may come from different places and background, they all share two important characteristics.					
4 The following essay will explain the drawbacks of globalization.					
5 Successful people and companies are important.					
6 I think Gandhi was an amazing person.					
7 Although globalization is considered beneficial by many, it has actually done great harm to cultures around the world.					

Exercise 6.4 Connecting Topic Sentences to Thesis Statements

In a well-organized academic essay, the topic sentences of the body paragraphs should clearly refer to the thesis statement. Match the topic sentence (1-3) of a body paragraph from three different essays about globalization to its thesis statement (a-c).

1 Because of globalization, farmers in poorer countries have to compete with farms in developed countries that have more resources. _____

2 The rising popularity of foreign restaurants has led to more competition for local businesses. _____

3 As people's eating habits around the world become more similar, national dishes will become less common. _____

   a Globalization has changed many aspects of local culture.
   b Globalization has created some disadvantages in worldwide food production.
   c Globalization has influenced local food service industries.

My Writing

Exercise 6.5 Writing Thesis Statements

1 Look at your work from My Writing in Unit 2. Write three possible thesis statements for the writing prompt.

2 Work with a partner. Discuss and revise your thesis statements.

3 Choose a thesis statement for your essay. Revise the topic sentences and supporting details you wrote in Unit 2, Exercise 6.7, page 33, to match it.

Exercise 6.6 Writing an Introductory Paragraph

Write an introductory paragraph for your thesis statement. Start with a hook. Then describe a specific event or situation as background information. End the paragraph with your thesis statement.

Exercise 6.7 Editing Your Writing

Use the questions to edit your introductory paragraph.

- Did you use the present perfect to write about events that happened at an unspecified time in the past?
- Did you use the present perfect or present perfect progressive to describe situations that started in the past but are still ongoing in the present?
- Did you use the simple past to write about actions that happened at specific times in the past?
- Did you use the simple present or present progressive to write about any current activities?

Past Perfect and Past Perfect Progressive

Nature vs. Nurture

1 Grammar in the Real World

ACADEMIC WRITING

Expository writing

A Have you ever reconnected with someone from your past? Read the article about twins who lived apart for many years. What surprised the twins when they reconnected?

B Comprehension Check Answer the questions.

1 What was surprising about the twins' adoption?
2 What characteristics and interests did Elyse and Paula have in common?
3 What is the nature versus nurture debate?

C Notice Underline the verbs in each sentence.

1 Both girls knew that their parents had adopted them as infants.
2 She had been doing research on her birth mother when she made a surprising discovery.
3 Even more surprising, she learned that she had been part of a secret scientific study.

Which event happened first in each sentence? What event followed? Write the verbs. What do you notice about the form of the verbs?

1 First: _____ Then: _____

2 First: _____ Then: _____

3 First: _____ Then: _____

The SCIENCE of TWINS

[1]**identical:** exactly the same

[2]**DNA:** the abbreviation for deoxyribonucleic acid, a chemical that controls the structure and purpose of every cell

[3]**controversial:** causing or likely to cause disagreement

[4]**dominant:** more important, strong, or noticeable

Twins, especially identical[1] twins, have always fascinated scientists. Identical twins develop from one egg, have identical DNA,[2] and are usually very similar in appearance and behavior. There have been many studies of identical twins raised in the same family. There have also been
5 a number of studies of identical twins separated at birth and raised in separate families. These studies have provided interesting information about the impact of *nature* (genetics) and *nurture* (the environment) on the development of the individual. However, some of the studies have been controversial.[3]

10 Take the case of Elyse Schein and Paula Bernstein. Elyse and Paula were identical twins separated at birth. Both girls knew that their parents **had adopted** them as infants, but neither girl knew about her twin. When Elyse grew up, she longed to meet her biological mother, so she contacted the agency that **had arranged** the adoption. She **had**
15 **been doing** research on her birth mother when she made a surprising discovery. She had an identical twin. Even more surprising, she learned that she **had been** part of a secret scientific study. At the time of the adoption, the agency **had allowed** different families to adopt each twin. The agency **had told** the families that their child was part of a scientific
20 study. However, it **had** never **told** the families the goal of the study: for scientists to investigate nature versus nurture.

When Elyse and Paula finally met as adults, they were amazed. They had many similarities. They looked almost identical. They **had** both **studied** film. They both loved to write. Together, the twins discovered
25 that the researchers **had stopped** the study before the end because the public strongly disapproved of this type of research.

Although that study ended early, many scientists today make a strong case for the dominant[4] role of nature. Schein and Bernstein agree that genetics explains many of their similarities. However, recent research
30 suggests that nurture is equally important. It is clear that the nature versus nurture debate will occupy scientists for years to come.

2 Past Perfect

Grammar Presentation

The past perfect is used to describe a completed event that happened before another event in the past.	Elyse finally met her sister, Paula. Paula *had been married* for several years. (First, Paula got married; Elyse met Paula at a later time.)

2.1 Forming Past Perfect

Form the past perfect with *had* + the past participle of the main verb. Form the negative by adding *not* after *had*. The form is the same for all subjects.	Elyse and Paula did not grow up together. They *had lived* with different families. They were available for adoption because their birth mother *had given* them up. "*Had* she *talked* about the study to anyone at the time?" "No, she *hadn't*." "What *had* you *heard* about this study before that time?" "*I'd heard* very little about it."

▸▸ Irregular Verbs: See page A1.

2.2 Using Past Perfect with Simple Past

A Use the past perfect to describe an event in a time period that leads up to another past event or time period. Use the simple past to describe the later event or time period.	LATER TIME EARLIER TIME She *learned* that she *had been* part of a secret study. LATER TIME EARLIER TIME The twins *discovered* that they *had* both *studied* psychology.
B The prepositions *before*, *by*, or *until* can introduce the later time period.	EARLIER TIME LATER TIME Their mother *had known* about the study <u>before</u> her death. EARLIER TIME LATER TIME Sue *hadn't met* her sister <u>until</u> last year. EARLIER TIME LATER TIME Studies on twins *had become* common <u>by</u> the 1960s.
C The past perfect is often used to give reasons or background information for later past events.	REASON She <u>was</u> late. She *had forgotten* to set her alarm clock. BACKGROUND INFORMATION LATER PAST EVENT He *had* never *taken* a subway before he <u>moved</u> to New York.

DATA FROM THE REAL WORLD

In writing, these verbs are commonly used in the past perfect: *come, have, leave, make,* and *take.*

Had been is the most common past perfect form in speaking and writing.

The twins *had not gone* to the same school as children.

The family thought that they *had made* the right decision.

Psychologists praised the study because the researchers *had been* very careful in their work.

The researchers *had not been* aware of each other's work on twins until they met.

Grammar Application

Exercise 2.1 Past Perfect

Complete the sentences about twins who met as adults. Use the past perfect form of the verbs in parentheses.

1 Two separate Illinois families ___*had adopted*___ (adopt) Anne Green and Annie Smith before the twins were three days old.

2 When the girls met, they were fascinated by their similarities. For example, they _____ (live) near each other before the Greens moved away.

3 As children, both Anne and Annie _____ (go) to the same summer camp.

4 Anne _____ (not / go) to college, and Annie _____ (not / attend) college, either.

5 Both _____ (marry) for the first time by the age of 22.

6 Anne _____ (get) divorced and _____ (remarry). Annie _____ (not / get) divorced and was still married.

7 Both Anne and Annie were allergic to cats and dogs and _____ never _____ (own) pets.

8 Both _____ (give) the same name – Heather – to their daughters.

9 Both _____ previously _____ (work) in the hospitality industry.

10 Anne _____ (work) as a hotel manager. However, Annie _____ (not / work) in hotels; she _____ (be) a restaurant manager.

A Read the article about a famous twin study. Underline the simple past forms. Double underline the past perfect forms.

The University of Minnesota is the birthplace of one of the most important twin studies in the world. It <u>started</u> in 1979. Thomas J. Bouchard <u><u>had</u></u> already <u><u>been</u></u> on the faculty[1] of the university for some time when he began his study of identical twins. Bouchard read an article about a set of twins who had been separated at birth. The twins had recently met and had found many similarities. They found out that they had lived near each other for years. Bouchard was amazed by the twins' story and decided to start the Minnesota Twins Reared Apart Study. Bouchard began to study sets of twins that had been separated at birth. Over the years, the Minnesota Twins Reared Apart Study has studied around 10,000 sets of twins. The study continues today.

[1]**faculty:** the people who teach in a department in a school

B Pair Work Compare your answers with a partner. Discuss the reason for each of your answers.

In line 3, had been *refers to the first event. Dr. Bouchard joined the faculty before the twin study. The twin study began later. The study is the second event, so* started *is in the simple past.*

A Listen to an interview with twins who are actors. Complete the sentences with the verbs you hear.

Claudia Today, I'm interviewing Alex and Andrew Underhill. They appear in the *Spy Twins* movie series based on the books of the same name. How did you get the part in the first *Spy Twins* movie?

Alex A friend ___*had seen*___ the advertisement in the newspaper and later
(1)
_____ us about it. We _____
(2)   (3)
any acting before then, but we _____ to try out anyway.
(4)

Claudia How many twins were at the audition?

Andrew When we got there, we _____ (5) that about five other sets
of twins _____ (6) for the audition.

Alex We also noticed that all the twins were wearing matching outfits. Until that
audition, we _____ (7) never _____ (7) the
same clothes in our whole lives. We decided to run out to the nearest shopping
mall to buy some matching clothes. The audition _____ (8) just
_____ (8) when we _____ (9) .

Claudia _____ (10) you _____ (10) the *Spy Twins* novels
before your audition?

Andrew Yes. The third book _____ (11) when we
_____ (12) to the first audition.

Claudia What's it like being twins? Are you two close? Do you do the same things?

Alex Yes, in lots of ways.

Andrew We definitely think the same way.

Alex Right! Once, we took the same test
in school. Of course, we were in the
same grade, but we had different
teachers. We had exactly the same
answers correct, even though we

_____ (13)

in the same classroom!

Claudia Wow! I guess you're a lot alike in many
ways! Well, thanks, Alex and Andrew.
It's been great talking with you.

B Listen again and check your answers.

C Use the time line to complete the sentences about Alex and Andrew. Use the past perfect form of the verbs in the box.

| build | decide | graduate | ~~make~~ | record | start |

1995 — The twins are born.

2002 — The twins audition for the first *Spy Twins* movie.

2004 — They record their first pop song and make a TV movie.

2005 — The twins start a fashion company for young men's clothing.

2006 to 2012 — The twins make three more *Spy Twins* movies.

2013 — They graduate from high school; they start college.

2014 — The twins decide to stop acting.

2017 — They graduate from college.

2017 to present — They work as fashion designers for their clothing company.

1 By 2012, Alex and Andrew __*had made*__ four Spy Twins movies.

2 Before 2004, the twins _____ (not) a pop song.

3 By 2016, the twins _____ to stop acting.

4 The twins _____ (not) a fashion company yet in 2004.

5 The twins _____ from high school by 2015.

3 Past Perfect with Time Clauses

Grammar Presentation

The past perfect is often used with time clauses for events that occurred in an earlier time period leading up to a later event or time period.	*By the time Elyse discovered her sister, people had forgotten about the twin study.*

3.1 Order of Events

A Use time clauses to show two separate past time periods. Use the past perfect to signal an event that occurred in an earlier time period.	*Elyse had moved by the time the researchers called her.*
The time words *after*, *as soon as*, *before*, *by the time*, *until*, and *when* can introduce the time clauses.	*After they had met, they noticed their many similarities.* *Until Elyse started her research, she hadn't known about the twin study.*
B With *before* and *after*, the past perfect is not always necessary because the order is clear. In this case, the past perfect emphasizes the earlier time period.	*Elyse moved before she met her twin.* OR *Elyse had moved before she met her twin.*
C In time clauses with *when*, the use of the past perfect in the main clause usually shows a good amount of time between events.	*When Paula met Elyse, she had already learned about the research.* (She learned about the research. She met Elyse some time later.)
D The use of *as soon as* with the past perfect shows that one event happened very soon after the other.	*As soon as the researchers had learned about the public's reaction to the study, they stopped it.* (The scientists learned about the public's reaction to the study. They stopped the study very soon after that.)
The use of the simple past in both clauses shows that one event happened very soon after the other.	*When Paula met Elyse, she learned about the research.* (She learned about the research very soon after she met Elyse.)

Grammar Application

A Read the blog entry about twin studies. Underline the past perfect form of the verbs.

B Pair Work Discuss why the past perfect is used in each case in A. Then find a sentence with a time clause that describes two events that happened at the same time or almost the same time. What is the form of the verbs in this sentence?

TWIN WORLD by Cory Daniels

Before her twins were born, Kim Lee had read a lot about twin studies. After she had done a little research, Kim found an early reading study for twins. She contacted the researchers and learned that she had to wait until the twins were four years old. When she enrolled the twins in the study, she hadn't known that the twins needed to give a DNA sample. As soon as Kim learned this, she took the twins out of the study. Kim thought that taking a DNA sample was an invasion of her children's privacy.

Exercise 3.2 Time Clauses

Complete the article about siblings[1] who were separated as children. Circle the correct time word. Write the simple past or past perfect form of the verbs in parentheses. Sometimes more than one answer is possible.

[1] **sibling:** a brother or sister

[2] **family tree:** a drawing that shows all the members of a family, usually over a long period of time, and how they are related to each other

There are many stories of non-twin brothers and sisters who are separated for one reason or another and meet again as adults. Here are a couple.

Glenn Mint and Bruce Mathews are brothers. They had never met (until)/after (1) Glenn __started__ (start) working at the same company as Bruce. Bruce was surprised (2) because the new employee looked just like him. They started asking each other questions. Before/After they met, each man _____ (know) that he had a sibling. (3) (4) Before/As soon as Glenn _____ (discover) Bruce's birth date, (5) (6) he knew Bruce was his long-lost brother.

Quin Mara, 82, knew that she was adopted and that she had siblings, but she had never met them. After/Until a relative _____ (find) a family tree,[2] Quin (7) (8) learned the names of her siblings and started looking for them. Until/By the time she saw (9) the family tree, she _____ (not/know) that she was the youngest (10) of nine children. As soon as/Before she _____ (discover) that, (11) (12) she began to look for her brothers and sisters. She was very happy because five of her siblings were still alive. Before/After she _____ (meet) them, she (13) (14) didn't know that they had spent the last several decades looking for each other.

Exercise 3.3 Combining Sentences

Read the story about how environment affects personality. Combine the sentences with the time words in parentheses. Use the past perfect for the earlier event and the simple past for the later event.

1 Diego and Shannon were married for a few years.
Then they decided to have a baby.

(when) _When Diego and Shannon had been married_

for a few years, they decided to have a baby.

2 Diego and Shannon did not think much about the nature versus nurture debate. Then their first child, Mario, was born.
(until) _____

_____

3 Diego and Shannon didn't have much experience with music. Then they became parents.

(before) _____

_____

4 Three-year-old Mario saw an electronic keyboard in a shop. Then he asked his parents to buy him one.

(after) _____

_____

5 Diego and Shannon heard Mario playing the keyboard. Then they realized their son's musical talent.

(as soon as) _____

_____

6 Diego and Shannon realized Mario's talent. Then they enrolled him in piano classes.

(as soon as) _____

_____

7 Diego and Shannon enrolled Mario in piano classes. Then Mario became an excellent musician.

(after) _____

_____

8 Mario took a few years of piano classes. He started composing music.

(by the time) _____

_____

4 Past Perfect Progressive

Grammar Presentation

The past perfect progressive emphasizes the ongoing nature of a past activity or situation leading up to a more recent past time.	*Living with a roommate was hard for me in the beginning. I had been living alone for years.*

4.1 Forming Past Perfect Progressive

Form the past perfect progressive with *had + been + -ing* form of the verb. Form the negative by putting *not* between *had* and *been* or using the contraction *hadn't*.	*She knew Boston well when I visited her. She'd been living there for years.* *When my brother visited me, I had not/hadn't been living there long.*

4.2 Using Past Perfect Progressive

A Use the past perfect progressive for an action or situation that continued up to an event or situation in past time. This can show a reason or give background information.	*He looked tired because he had been working all night.* *My eyes were sore because I hadn't been wearing my contacts.*
B With some verbs such as *live, play, teach, wear,* and *work*, use either the past perfect or past perfect progressive. The meaning is similar.	*The twins had lived in different cities before they discovered each other.* or *The twins had been living in different cities before they discovered each other.*

Grammar Application

Exercise 4.1 Past Perfect Progressive

Complete the story about brothers who reconnected after many years. Use the past perfect progressive form of the verbs in parentheses.

Mark and Peter were brothers. Their parents could not take care of them. One family adopted Mark, and another family adopted Peter. Mark and Peter _had been dreaming_ (dream) of
(1)
finding each other since 2015. When they finally met, they were surprised by how much they had in common. For most of their adult lives, their jobs had been related, even though they _____ (not / work) in
(2)
the same business. Mark _____ (make) furniture, and Peter
(3)
_____ (sell) furniture. Mark _____
(4)   (5)
(interview) for jobs in furniture stores and decided to take a new position at Mark's store. Peter _____ (talk) to a friendly customer when he
(6)
saw a man who looked like him walk into the store. Peter quickly stopped what he
_____ (do) and introduced himself. That first day, Peter
(7)
and Mark talked for hours. They found out that they _____
(8)
(not / live) in the same city, but they had attended schools in the same district for most of their childhood. They _____ (cross) paths for many years
(9)
without ever meeting. They had never expected to have so much in common.

A Complete the interview with a woman who found her three siblings after many years. Use the past perfect progressive, the past perfect, or the simple past form of the verbs in parentheses. Use contractions when possible. Sometimes more than one answer is possible.

Vijay   Tell us how you found your family.

Paula   I **'d been looking** (look) for my sister all my life. I _____
(1)   (2)
(not / have) much luck, though. Then one day, I turned on the TV. A talk show was

on. The host of the show was interviewing three siblings – two brothers and a half

sister.[1] Different families _____ (adopt) the siblings many
(3)

years before.

Vijay   And?

Paula   They _____ (talk) about me before I turned on the program.
(4)
The siblings had recently reunited, and they _____ (search) for
(5)
a fourth sibling for the past several months. I called the TV station, and we all finally

_____ (meet).
(6)

Vijay   So, you _____ (look) for a sister all your life, and you found
(7)

three siblings!

Paula   Yes, it was wonderful! We all met at one of the network offices the following week.

After we _____ (speak) for a while, it was obvious to me that
(8)

they _____ (look) for me all their lives, too.
(9)

[1]**half sister:** a sister who is biologically related by one parent only

B Pair Work Discuss these questions with a partner.

■ Choose a sentence in A in which you can use either the past perfect or the past perfect progressive. Why are both possible here?

■ In which sentence in A is only the past perfect correct?

C Over to You Do an online search for twins, siblings, or other family members who reunited after many years. Write five sentences about their experiences. Use the past perfect and the past perfect progressive.

5 Avoid Common Mistakes ⚠

1 **Use the past perfect or past perfect progressive to give background information for a past tense event.**

had
I ~~have~~ never seen my sister in real life, so I was nervous the first time we met.

had been dreaming
I ~~have dreamed~~ about meeting her, and I finally did.

2 **Use the past perfect or past perfect progressive to give a reason for a past event.**

had been crying
Her eyes were red and puffy because she ~~cried~~.

3 **Use the past perfect (not the past perfect progressive) for a completed earlier event.**

arranged
They had ~~been arranging~~ a time to meet, but both of them forgot about it.

4 **Use the past perfect (not present perfect) to describe a completed event that happened before a past event.**

had
I ~~have~~ visited her in Maine twice before she came to visit me.

Editing Task

Find and correct seven more mistakes in the paragraphs about sibling differences.

had
    I ~~have~~ never really thought about sibling differences until my own children were born. When we had our first child, my husband and I have lived in Chicago for just a few months. We have not made many friends yet, so we spent all our time with our child. Baby Gilbert was happy to be the center of attention. He depended on us
5 for everything.

    By the time our second son, Chase, was born, we have developed a community of friends and a busier social life. We frequently visited friends and left the children at home with a babysitter. As a result of our busy schedules, Chase was more independent. One day I had just been hanging up the phone when Chase came into
10 the room. Chase picked up the phone and started talking into it. I thought he was pretending, but I was wrong. He had been figuring out how to use the phone!

    When my husband came home, he was tired because he worked all day. When I told him about Chase's phone conversation, though, he became very excited. Gilbert has never used the phone as a child. At first, we were surprised that Chase was so
15 different from Gilbert. Then we realized that because of our busy lifestyles, Chase had learned to be independent.

6 Academic Writing

Expository Writing

Brainstorm > Organize > **Write** > **Edit**

In Unit 3, you looked at essay structure and thesis statements. In this unit (4), you are going to write, revise, and edit your essay for the prompt below.

> *How has globalization changed your country?*

My Writing

Exercise 6.1 Planning Your Essay

Use your notes and writing from My Writing in Units 2 and 3 to complete the table. Note: If you have two body paragraphs in your essay, you will only have four paragraphs in your essay.

	A	B
paragraph 1		
paragraph 2		
paragraph 3		
paragraph 4		
paragraph 5		
thesis statement		

1 Decide the function of each paragraph: introduction, body, or conclusion. Write the functions in column A.
2 Think about the supporting details and examples you are going to include in each paragraph. Write notes in column B.
3 Write the thesis statement for your essay in the last row of the table.

Exercise 6.2 Writing Your First Draft

Write the first draft of your expository essay. Include an introductory paragraph with a hook, background information, and thesis statement; two or three body paragraphs with topic sentences and supporting ideas; and a concluding paragraph with a final thought, recommendation, or prediction.

Exercise 6.3 Revising Your Ideas

1 Work with a partner. Use the questions to give feedback on your partner's essay.

- Which of your partner's ideas seem strongest to you?
- Which of your partner's ideas need to be explained more clearly?
- What could your partner add or remove to make the essay easier to understand?

2 Use the feedback from your partner to revise the ideas and content of your essay.

Exercise 6.4 Editing Your Writing

Use the checklist to review and edit your essay.

Did you answer the prompt completely?	
Did you use the correct essay organization?	
Did you write a hook and background information in your introductory paragraph?	
Did you write an effective thesis statement?	
Did you write topic sentences that connect to your thesis statement in your body paragraphs?	
Did you develop your main ideas and include relevant evidence and supporting information in your body paragraphs?	
Did you summarize your main points in the concluding paragraph?	

Exercise 6.5 Editing Your Grammar

Use the checklist to review and edit the grammar in your essay.

Did you use the simple present and present progressive correctly?	
Did you use the simple past and past progressive correctly?	
Did you use time clauses correctly?	
Did you use *used to* and *would* correctly?	
Did you use the present perfect and present perfect progressive correctly?	
Did you use the past perfect and past perfect progressive correctly?	
Did you avoid the common mistakes in the charts on pages 14, 29, 46, and 65?	

Exercise 6.6 Writing Your Final Draft

Apply the feedback and edits from Exercises 6.3 to 6.5 to write the final draft of your essay.

Be Going To, Present Progressive, and Future Progressive

Looking Ahead at Technology

1 Grammar in the Real World

ACADEMIC WRITING

Comparison and contrast

A How is technology used today? Read the article about technology use in the future. What is one way that technology use will develop?

B Comprehension Check Answer the questions.

1 What are some ways technology will change in the future?

2 How will people in the future access the Internet?

3 What is "wearable tech"?

C Notice Find the sentences in the article and complete them.

1 Market research suggests that in the future we _____ on the Internet even more than we are now.

2 Scientists predict that ingestibles _____ the way we treat all sorts of diseases.

3 As technology changes, devices such as wearable tech

_____ more and more popular.

How many different verb forms in items 1–3 did the author of the reading use to talk about the future?

Looking AHEAD at Technology

Technology has become an essential part of everyday life for many people. We depend on the Internet, for example, for easy access to information and communication. Computers, cell
5 phones, and other handheld gadgets provide constant entertainment. No one knows for sure what technology **is going to bring** us in the future. However, there is no doubt that it **will continue** to drastically affect how we live and work.

10 Market research[1] suggests that in the future we **will be depending** on the Internet even more than we are now. Wearable tech is already here, with many people using bracelets and watches to track their health, activity, sleep, and fitness.
15 Smartglasses are popular too, connecting us to the Internet as we go about our day. The prediction, though, is that smartglasses **will** soon **include** "bone induction audio," allowing us to talk to our digital assistants or listen to music without needing
20 earbuds. Sound **will** simply **travel** through the bones in our heads instead.

Some people **will not want** their technology to be wearable, so what **is going to be** new and exciting for them? The answer is "ingestibles."

25 Ingestibles are smart tablets filled with sensors that you **will swallow** just like you swallow an aspirin. They **will allow** doctors to track what is happening inside your body. The sensors **will send** data about your body back to an external monitor. This way, doctors
30 **will** also **be able to check** that your medication is working correctly. Scientists predict that ingestibles **are going to change** the way we treat all kinds of diseases, from the common cold to cancer.

In the future, there **will be** many advances
35 in technology and many changes in the ways technology affects our lives. As technology changes, devices such as smart clothing **will become** more and more popular. In short, it is clear that almost everything we do **will happen**
40 with the help of technology.

Pill cam

[1]**market research:** the study of consumer behavior

2 *Be Going To*, Present Progressive, and Simple Present for Future

Grammar Presentation

Be going to and the present progressive are used to describe future plans. The simple present is used to describe a scheduled future event.

I'm *going to buy* some smartglasses someday.
My parents probably *aren't going to buy* smartwatches.
I'm *buying* a smartwatch tomorrow.

2.1 *Be Going To* vs. Present Progressive for Future Plans

A Use *be going to* + base form of the verb to express general intentions and plans for the future.	I'm *going to buy* a 3D TV someday.
You can use expressions like *probably, most likely, I think,* and *I believe* with this form.	My parents _probably_ *aren't going to buy* one. _I think_ they *are going to save* their money for a trip instead.
B Use the present progressive to express definite plans and arrangements for the future, especially when a time or place is mentioned.	I'm *buying* a 3D TV tomorrow. The class *is taking* a trip to the science museum next week.
C In many cases, both forms can be used to express the same idea.	I'm *watching* a movie this evening. I'm *going to watch* a movie this evening.

2.2 Simple Present for Scheduled Events

Use the simple present for scheduled events in the future and for timetables. Some common verbs for this use include *arrive, be, begin, finish, leave,* and *start*.	The conference *begins* on Monday and *ends* on Friday. Beginning June 10, all trains to New England *leave* from platform 14.

Grammar Application

A Complete the conversation about e-readers. Use *be going to* or the present progressive and the verbs in parentheses. Sometimes more than one answer is possible.

Mei I *'m going to buy* (buy) some smartglasses one of these days. Any suggestions?
(1)

Kyle Look at this ad. Big Buy _____ (have) a sale on the iSights next week.
(2)

Mei How much are they?

Kyle They _____ (lower) the price to $69.
(3)

Mei That's great. I _____ (visit) a friend near that area next week.
(4)
I'll stop by.

Kyle That's a great price.

Mei Yes, it's quite a deal. You know, I think companies _____ (give)
(5)
smartglasses away someday. They're getting less and less expensive. Soon they'll
be free!

Kyle I've got to go. I _____ (meet) some friends for dinner. What _____
(6)   (7)
you _____ (do) tonight?
(7)

Mei I _____ (go) straight home. I'm tired.
(8)

B Pair Work **Compare your answers with a partner. Discuss the reason for each of your answers.**

In the first sentence, one of these days *made the plan seem like an intention because he wasn't really sure, so* be going to *is correct.*

Look at the clues. Then complete the sentences about a new phone. Use *be going to*, the present progressive, or the simple present form of the verbs in parentheses.

1 Clue: definite plan
Best Product __*is launching*__ (launch) a new YouPhone next week.

2 Clue: scheduled event
The new YouPhone _____ (become) available in stores on Friday, January 15.

3 Clue: definite plan
All employees _____ (prepare) for a busy first day of sales.

4 Clue: definite plan

All stores _____ (open) at 8:00 a.m. that day.

5 Clue: definite plan

The stores _____ (give) away water and free coffee to customers in line.

6 Clue: scheduled event

School _____ (close) early that day because of a holiday.

7 Clue: future intention

The newspaper _____ (interview) Anne Green, a representative from BestProduct.

8 Clue: future intention

Ms. Green _____ probably _____ (speak) for a few minutes and then answer some questions.

Exercise 2.3 More *Be Going To*, Present Progressive, or Simple Present?

A Complete the article about a social networking site. Use *be going to,* the present progressive, or the simple present form of the verbs in parentheses. Sometimes more than one answer is possible.

CHANGES AHEAD for Youth Network

Youth Network, Inc., announced today that it __*is buying*__ (buy) FacePlace, the
                                            (1)
popular social networking website. FacePlace has already accepted Youth Network's offer
of $3.1 billion. The company has not made any definite plans, but it _____ probably
                                                                      (2)
_____ (start) asking people to pay for the site. It won't be free anymore.
              (2)
In addition, some people think that the network _____ (put) ads on
                                                            (3)
the site. Another possibility is that Youth Network _____ (show) its TV
                                                            (4)
programs on FacePlace. Next week, FacePlace technicians _____ (meet)
                                                                    (5)
with Youth Network technicians to help with the changes. They _____
                                                                          (6)
(plan) to shut down the old FacePlace website at 1:00 a.m. on Saturday, August 10. The new Youth
Network site _____ (go) live at 6:00 a.m. the next day.
                    (7)

B Pair Work Compare your answers with a partner. Discuss the reason for each of your answers.

In item 1, the plan *seems definite because the company made an announcement to the press, so the company arranged the action. The present progressive is correct.*

3 *Will* and *Be Going To*

Grammar Presentation

Will and *be going to* can both express future plans and predictions. They can also be used in other ways, for example, to make a promise or to express an expectation.	Smartglasses **will allow** us to connect to the Internet almost anywhere. Technology **is going to become** easier to use. **I'll help** you with your computer.

3.1 *Will* and *Be Going To* for Predictions and Expectations

A Use *will* and *be going to* for predictions, expectations, or guesses about the future.	People **will connect** to the Internet from almost anywhere. **I'm not going to have** Internet access while I'm on vacation.
B You can use *certainly, definitely, likely, maybe, perhaps,* and *probably* to show degrees of certainty.	Technology **will** <u>certainly</u> **be** more sophisticated in the future.
Use *certainly, definitely, likely,* and *probably* after *will* or after *be.*	There **will** <u>probably</u> **be** many people at the concert next week. Doctors **are** <u>definitely</u> **going to use** ingestibles in the future.
Use *maybe* and *perhaps* at the beginning of sentences.	<u>Maybe</u> **I'll get** a smartwatch this year.
C Use *be going to* to predict the future when there is present evidence.	My computer is behaving strangely. I think **it's going to crash**.
D Generally, in speaking, *be going to* is used for intentions and plans. However, in academic writing, *will* is used much more frequently.	By 2030, people throughout the world **will use** many types of wearable tech.

3.2 *Will* for Requests, Offers, and Promises

| Use *will* for requests, offers, and promises. | *Will you **help** me buy a computer?*
*I'll **research** the best buys for you.* |

3.3 *Will* for Quick Decisions

| Use *will* for decisions made at the time of speaking. | *"We need someone to take notes for our group."*
*"I'll **do** it."* (quick decision) |
| The same verb with *be going to* expresses a previous decision. | *"Bob **is going to do** it."* (previous decision) |

Grammar Application

Exercise 3.1 *Will* or *Be Going To?*

A Complete the phone conversation between an employee and a technician in the tech department. Circle *will* or *be going to*. If both are possible, circle both.

Bill Tech Department, Bill speaking.

Kate Hi, Bill. This is Kate in Business Development. My laptop is behaving very strangely this morning. It **will / ('s going to)** crash at any minute. **Will you / Are you going to**
(1)   (2)
send someone to look at it?

Bill Of course, I **will / am going to** .
(3)

Kate Soon?

Bill I promise. I**'ll / 'm going to** send Dave in five minutes.
(4)

Kate Bill, **will you / are you going to** send Silvia instead, please? She's fixed this same
(5)
problem before.

Bill Oh, OK. Then Silvia **will / is going to** be there in about five minutes.
(6)

Kate Thanks, Bill. Bye.

A few minutes later:

Silvia Hi, Kate. Are you having problems with your laptop again?

Kate Uh-huh. This is the fourth time! I think I**'ll / 'm going to** ask for a new computer.
(7)

Silvia I**'ll / 'm going to** look at it for you.
(8)

Kate Thanks, Silvia.

B Pair Work Compare your answers with a partner. Discuss the reason for each of your answers.

I chose be going to for item 1 because the speaker is making a prediction based on evidence. She said her computer was behaving strangely. That's evidence that it might be crashing.

Exercise 3.2 More *Will* or *Be Going To?*

A Listen to a discussion about education and technology. Complete the sentences with the form of the verbs you hear.

Ms. Ng ___*Will*___ everyone please ___*be*___ quiet? The noise
       (1)   (1)
_____ it hard to hear our speaker. And _____
                  (2)   (3)
someone please _____ the windows? The air
                                    (3)
conditioner isn't working well.

Alex I _____ it.
                          (4)

Ms. Ng Thanks. And _____ you all please _____
                              (5)   (5)
your smartphones? I promise I _____ you
                                              (6)
to do anything else except enjoy today's presentation. OK, today,
we _____ from an expert on education, Dr. Paul Bell.
              (7)
I'm sure you _____ all _____ him very interesting.
                  (8)   (8)

Dr. Bell Thank you. Well, it's clear that the world of the college student
_____ very different in a matter of a few years.
                  (9)
For example, we already know that colleges _____
                                                              (10)
more courses online. This _____ money for schools and
                                        (11)
for students. Students _____ money on transportation
                                    (12)
costs because they can learn anywhere. Online learning also means that
schools and individuals _____ fewer resources such
                                      (13)
as paper and fuel. But what _____ the consequences of online education
                                    (14)
_____?
          (14)

B Find an example of each meaning, and write the number of the item next to it.

   __1__ a request   _____ a promise
   _____ a prediction based on evidence   _____ an offer

C Group Work Make predictions or share expectations about the future of phones, TVs, movies, schools, cars, or something else. As a group, write five sentences. Use *will* and *be going to*. Share your sentences with the class.

4 Future Progressive

Grammar Presentation

The future progressive emphasizes an action that will be in progress at a specific time in the future.	We **will be treating** many diseases with technology in 10 years. Everyone **is going to be using** wearable tech in 2025.

4.1 Forming Future Progressive

A Form the future progressive with *will* or *be going to* + *be* + verb + *-ing*.	People **will be working** on mobile devices instead of laptops in five years. Consumers **are not going to be using** coins and paper money by the year 2025.
B Use the future progressive to describe or ask about an action in progress at a time in the future.	**Will** you **be working** tomorrow at noon?
Use *certainly*, *definitely*, *likely*, and *probably* after *will* or *be going to* to show degrees of certainty. Use them before *won't*.	I definitely **won't be watching** TV tonight. I'll probably **be working** on my project all afternoon.
C Sometimes *will* + base form and future progressive are very similar in meaning, especially when the future event will occur at an indefinite time.	I think the computer specialist **will arrive** later. I don't see her. I think the computer specialist **will be arriving** later. I don't see her.

4.2 Future Progressive and *Be Going To* Contrasted

The future progressive and *be going to* can both express plans and intentions. Use the future progressive for a more formal tone. Use *be going to* for a less formal tone.	Mr. Lee, **will** you **be coming** with me to the lecture on technology tomorrow? (more formal) Marie, **are** you **going to come** with me to the lecture tomorrow? (less formal)

Grammar Application

Complete the interview about the future of TV. Use the future progressive form of
the verbs in parentheses.

Claire   Mr. Reyes, you've been involved in the television industry for well over 30 years.
We know that the TV industry is changing rapidly. Tell us about its future.

Mr. Reyes   Certainly. The television industry *will be creating* (create) all of its own
(1)
shows in the future. It _____ (save) a lot of money this
(2)
way because it _____ (not/buy) the shows from other
(3)
producers. In addition, people _____ (watch) TV using
(4)
many different types of media.

Claire   What do you mean?

Mr. Reyes   I mean that we _____ (use) mobile devices instead
(5)
of televisions to watch TV shows. People _____
(6)
(not/watch) by themselves, either. They _____
(7)
(socialize) through social networks as they watch TV.

Claire   How will that work?

Mr. Reyes   Viewers _____ (send) messages, and they
(8)
_____ (chat) with others while they watch. In fact, they
(9)
are already doing so. This will affect marketing, too.

Claire   In what way?

Mr. Reyes   Advertisers _____ (ask) viewers to share their opinions
(10)
of the things they are viewing, such as products in ads or clothes worn
by actors.

Claire   It sounds as though advertising will become even more interactive.

Mr. Reyes   Exactly.

Claire   Thank you very much, Mr. Reyes, for taking the time to talk to us.

A Complete the formal announcement of a lecture on the future of movies. Use the future progressive form of the verbs in parentheses. Sometimes more than one answer is possible.

The Future of Movies

Presented by Dr. Maria Sanderson

Michaels Hall

8:00 p.m., Friday, January 7

What ___*will*___ people ___*be seeing*___ (see) at the movies 10 years from
     (1)   (1)
now? _____ we _____ (watch) only 3D movies? _____
      (2)   (2)   (3)
people _____ (watch) movies in theaters, or will theaters disappear?
           (3)
Dr. Sanderson _____ (discuss) the future of the movie industry and
                    (4)
the movie-going experience in general. She _____ (give) examples
                                   (5)
of past, present, and future film technology, and she _____ (take)
                                        (6)
questions from the audience.

B Complete the conversation between two students about the lecture in A. Use *be going to* or the future progressive and the verbs in parentheses. Sometimes more than one answer is possible.

Chao   ___*Are*___ you ___*going to go*___ (go) to the lecture?
         (1)   (1)

Verónica Yes, I _____ definitely _____ (attend). What about you?
              (2)   (2)

Chao   No, I _____ (not / go). I'm not interested. Why _____ you
                (3)   (4)
  _____ (go)?
      (4)

Verónica I'm taking film history, so it will help me with my class. I _____ (take)
                                                    (5)
  notes. I _____ also _____ (ask) questions.
         (6)   (6)

Over to You What will you be doing 20 years in the future? Where will you be living? What will you be doing for entertainment? Write five sentences about the way you imagine the future. Use the future progressive. Share your sentences with a partner.

5 Avoid Common Mistakes ⚠

1 **Use the future progressive to talk about actions that will be in progress at a future time.**

be working
You won't see me next week because I will ~~work~~ in Seoul.

2 **Use the simple present for scheduled events.**

starts
The video conference will always ~~start~~ at 4:00 p.m.

3 **Remember to use *be* with *be going to*.**

am
I ‸going to give a presentation on the twenty-fifth of next month.

4 **Use the present progressive (not *will*) when talking about definite plans.**

are traveling
We ~~will travel~~ to the home office at the end of the month.

Editing Task

Find and correct the mistakes in the email about travel plans.

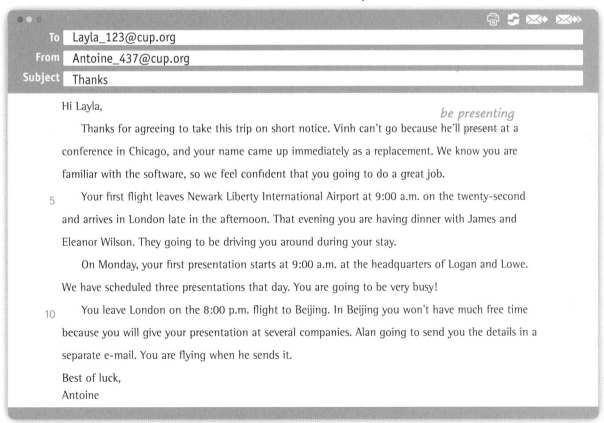

To   Layla_123@cup.org
From   Antoine_437@cup.org
Subject   Thanks

Hi Layla,

be presenting
Thanks for agreeing to take this trip on short notice. Vinh can't go because he'll ~~present~~ at a conference in Chicago, and your name came up immediately as a replacement. We know you are familiar with the software, so we feel confident that you going to do a great job.

5   Your first flight leaves Newark Liberty International Airport at 9:00 a.m. on the twenty-second and arrives in London late in the afternoon. That evening you are having dinner with James and Eleanor Wilson. They going to be driving you around during your stay.

On Monday, your first presentation starts at 9:00 a.m. at the headquarters of Logan and Lowe. We have scheduled three presentations that day. You are going to be very busy!

10   You leave London on the 8:00 p.m. flight to Beijing. In Beijing you won't have much free time because you will give your presentation at several companies. Alan going to send you the details in a separate e-mail. You are flying when he sends it.

Best of luck,
Antoine

6 Academic Writing

Comparison and Contrast

Brainstorm > Organize > Write > Edit

In this writing cycle (Units 5-8), you are going to write a comparison-and-contrast essay that answers the prompt below. In this unit (5), you will analyze an essay and use a graphic organizer to brainstorm and organize ideas about the topic.

Compare learning a language with studying math. How do you think the study of these subjects will change over time with new technology?

Exercise 6.1 Preparing to Write

Work with a partner. Discuss the questions.

1 What technology do you use the most today? Do you use it for education? If so, how?
2 In your opinion, how will technology change education in the future?
3 Is online learning as effective as face-to-face learning? Why or why not?

Exercise 6.2 Focusing on Vocabulary

Read the collocations and their meanings. Then complete the sentences with your own words.

> **core principle** (n) key value
> **credible alternative** (n) reliable substitute
> **distance learning** (n) general education from online instruction
> **modern phenomenon** (n) recent trend
> **online degree** (n) an academic qualification obtained from instruction on the Internet
> **significant difference** (n) important distinction
> **technological advance** (n) development in technology
> **virtual classroom** (n) online course

1 One interesting **modern phenomenon** in online education is _____

_____.

2 A subject that will probably not work well in the future for **distance learning** is _____.

3 One advantage of a real classroom over a **virtual classroom** is _____

_____.

4 One possible benefit of an **online degree** over a traditional degree will be

_____.

5 It is possible that a **credible alternative** to the Internet for doing research will be

_____.

6 Because of **technological advances**, in the next few decades it will become easier to

_____.

7 One of the **core principles** of many colleges is _____.

8 One **significant difference** between the classroom of today and the classroom of the future will be _____.

The **Future** of **Learning**

1 What is the future of learning in the 21st century? Will the physical classroom disappear and be replaced by the **virtual classroom**? Will universities worldwide soon compete for the services of the superstar professor who
5 will be teleporting[1] into their campuses and paid like professional athletes? At the moment, businesses are betting[2] a lot of money that online rather than face-to-face learning is the future of education. However, before answering these questions, it is important to compare
10 the two types of learning to decide which one will better prepare students for the world of work and life in general.

2 Although many people think it is a **modern phenomenon, distance learning** has been around for
15 at least 200 years in one form or another. Historical examples of long-distance learning include students being sent a series of weekly lessons by mail. Nowadays, distance learning means online learning, and the **technological advances** of the past 20 or so years have
20 meant that it is and will continue to be a **credible alternative** to face-to-face learning. Yet, while it is now possible to obtain a large variety of **online degrees**, are they worse than, equal to, or better than traditional college diplomas? A closer examination of this topic
25 will reveal that distance and traditional educational instruction will continue to have **significant differences** but also some similarities.

3 In comparing the two systems, the most obvious difference is going to be the way that instruction is
30 delivered. Distance learning is now heavily dependent on technology, particularly the Internet. In a face-to-face course, students will probably only require a computer for the purpose of writing an essay. In contrast, when learning remotely, technology will always be the
35 principal means of communication. Another difference is that face-to-face instruction must take place in real time and in one location. Conversely, distance learning can happen at any time and in any location, since the learning is not restricted by geography. This flexibility
40 means that students will be able to learn at their own pace, but it also means that learners will have to be well organized and self-disciplined. In other words, they must be more highly motivated in order to do well in distance-learning courses. Finally, with face-to-face learning,
45 the teacher and student will have the opportunity to develop a personal relationship. In a virtual classroom,

by contrast, the teacher may seldom or never actually meet the student, which could make it hard for teachers to understand their students' specific learning needs.

50 **4** Although the nature of the teacher-student relationship is going to be different in the two methods, they will still share the same **core principles**. Just as teachers are the "knowers" in a classroom, they are the ones who will be responsible for helping students understand the key
55 sections of an online course. The teachers need to decide how best to present the material to be learned and in which sequence the topics should be introduced. They will also create the assignments for the course and help the students know what resources (textbooks, websites,
60 and so on) will best support their learning. Likewise, the teacher will always have to provide student feedback in some way. For example, a language teacher in a classroom may be able to correct a student's grammar or pronunciation in the moment, whereas a distance-
65 learning teacher may need to provide written or recorded feedback to be delivered later. In any case, all the usual elements of the teacher's role are necessary, no matter what kind of instruction will be used.

5 In the end, it is difficult to state whether one form of
70 learning is better than another, since they are geared toward different learning situations. Online learning allows for greater flexibility, whereas the traditional classroom provides a more personal, dynamic learning environment. Nevertheless, both can produce positive results for the
75 student, which is the most important factor. Therefore, both systems are probably going to be part of our world for years to come. Perhaps in the future students themselves will be able to select elements of both systems to create a more flexible, complete, and personalized
80 educational path to success.

---

[1]**teleport** (v) to (cause to) travel by an imaginary very fast form of transport that uses special technology or special mental powers

[2]**bet** (v) to risk money on the result of a game or competition

Read the essay on page 81. Work with a partner. Discuss the questions.

1 Is distance learning a modern idea?
2 Does the writer generally approve or disapprove of online learning?
3 What is the writer's prediction about the future of learning?

Exercise 6.4 Noticing the Grammar

Work with a partner. Discuss the questions.

1 Underline the use of *will* in paragraph 1. How does the writer use this form?
2 Circle the present progressive form in paragraph 1. Is it used for the present or the future?
3 Highlight the use of *going to* in paragraphs 3, 4, and 5. How does the writer use this form?

Exercise 6.5 Noticing the Writing

Write the correct paragraph number(s) next to the description.

1 Similarities between the types of learning   Paragraph(s): _____

2 Differences between the types of learning   Paragraph(s): _____

3 General summary and conclusions   Paragraph(s): _____

4 History and background of the topic   Paragraph(s): _____

5 Thesis statement   Paragraph(s): _____

Exercise 6.6 Identifying Supporting Details

Are the supporting details about online learning, face-to-face learning, or both? Check the correct column.

	Online	Face-to-face	Both
1 Develops a strong teacher-student relationship			
2 Relies heavily on technology			
3 Takes place in real time			
4 Can be an effective way of teaching			
5 Requires a high level of motivation			
6 Not limited by geography			
7 Can suit many types of students			

Using Venn Diagrams

In comparison-and-contrast essays, writers look at the similarities and differences between two topics in order to present conclusions. They often use Venn diagrams to brainstorm and organize the differences and similarities.

Exercise 6.7 Applying the Skill

1 Work with a partner. Put the information from the chart in Exercise 6.6 in the Venn diagram below.
   - Write the details for online learning only in the left oval.
   - Write the details for face-to-face learning only in the right oval.
   - Write the shared details in the middle (overlapping) oval.

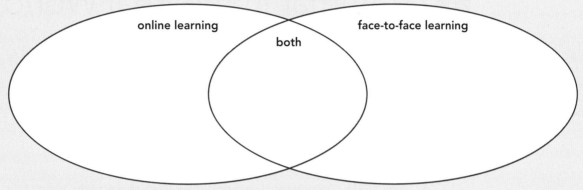

2 Think of two more supporting details for each learning type and add them to each outside oval. Then move any shared details to the middle.

My Writing

Exercise 6.8 Brainstorming Topics and Ideas

Work with a partner. Use a Venn diagram to brainstorm and organize your ideas for the prompt on page 80.

1 Compare and contrast studying a language with studying math. Think about:
   - level of interest
   - technology
   - possible jobs and salary
   - skills needed
   - level of education
   - future trends
2 Write details about studying a language in the left oval of your Venn diagram.
3 Write details about studying math in the right oval of your Venn diagram.
4 Write the shared details in the middle oval of your Venn diagram.

Exercise 6.9 Writing a Paragraph

Write a paragraph about learning a language <u>or</u> about studying math. Include reasons for someone to study the subject in college and some future benefits of studying it. Use the future forms you studied in Unit 5 correctly.

Future Time Clauses, Future Perfect, and Future Perfect Progressive

Business Practices of the Future

1 Grammar in the Real World

A What automatic technology do you use? Read the article about automation. What are the pros and cons?

B Comprehension Check **Answer the questions.**

1 What will many companies do in the future? Why?

2 What are some risks of automation?

C Notice **Complete these sentences from the article.**

1 By 2020, many companies _____ at least

some of their employees' jobs and **saved** large sums of money

because they _____ automation.

2 That figure _____ change **until**

people are confident that their jobs will be secure.

Look at the verbs that you wrote. There are three different forms for describing the future. Which form describes completed future events?

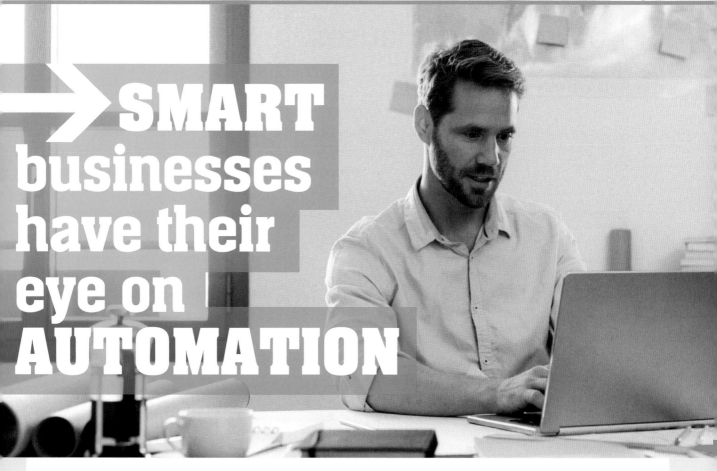

SMART businesses have their eye on AUTOMATION

For a long time, the world's businesses have been using mechanization. Mechanization is the term for using machines instead of animals or your own hands to do work. More and more
5 businesses are now thinking about automation. *Automation* is the term people use to describe the way information technology works automatically – without direction from a human, in other words. Instead of employing hundreds of people to
10 make, pack, send, deliver, or store things, you use technology and, sometimes, robots and other machines to do all of that for you.

By 2020, many companies **will have eliminated**[1] at least some of their employees' jobs and **saved**
15 large sums of money because they **will have been using** automation. **When these businesses move to automation**, we will see increasing numbers of drones delivering goods, robots serving coffee and pizza, bots organizing our calendars for us, and
20 refrigerators reminding us to buy fresh milk.

It sounds great at first. We will not need to do as much work because machines will do it for us. Automation has risks, however. Some people say that automation will lead to boredom
25 and unhappiness. Psychologists warn that the satisfaction humans get from making an effort to achieve a task will be lost, and that will make us unhappy. Seventy percent of Americans are already expressing concerns about automation
30 and the effect it will have on their lives. That figure probably will not change **until people are confident that their jobs will be secure**.

Although companies will save a lot of money by using the new technologies, one study
35 suggests that by the 2030s, about one job in five **will have been put** at risk from automation. However, estimates are not always reliable, so we watch and wait to find out.

[1]**eliminate:** remove or take away

2 Future Time Clauses

Grammar Presentation

Future time clauses show the order of future events.	*After people buy our phones, we'll use drones to deliver them.* *We're going to research robots before we choose one.*

2.1 Using Time Clauses for Future Events

A Use the simple present in the time clause. Use the future with *will* or *be going to* in the main clause.	*After I buy my new phone, I'll use the cloud to store my data.* *We're going to research cloud services before we choose one.*
You can also use the present perfect in the time clause to emphasize the completion of the event.	*Until business has improved, the company won't hire new employees.*
B Use time clauses with *after, as soon as, once,* and *when* when the event in the time clause happens first.	FIRST EVENT *As soon as / Once they use automation, their* SECOND EVENT *business will improve.* SECOND EVENT FIRST EVENT *I'll find a good job after I graduate.*
C Use time clauses with *before* and *until* when the event in the time clause happens second.	FIRST EVENT SECOND EVENT *I'll finish the report before I leave.*
Use *until* to show when the event in the main clause will stop or change.	 *I'll continue working on the report until she calls.*
In time clauses with *not ... until,* the action in the time clause happens first.	SECOND EVENT *We won't start using the software until all* FIRST EVENT *employees are trained.*
D The time clause can come first or last in the sentence. Use a comma when the time clause comes first.	*Once we start using automation, we'll save money.* *She is going to move as soon as she finds a better job.*

2.2 Using Time Clauses with *When* and *While* for Ongoing Events

A	Use *when* or *while* with the simple present in the time clause and *will* or *be going to* in the main clause to show two events that are happening at the same time.		*I'll be taking* my vacation *while* the company *moves* to its new office.
	You can also use the present progressive in the time clause to express an ongoing event.		*The staff is going to wait* outside *while/when* we're *discussing* our budget.
B	Use the simple present in the *when* clause to interrupt an ongoing event in the main clause.		*We'll be meeting when he arrives.* (The meeting will be happening. He will arrive during the meeting.)

Grammar Application

Exercise 2.1 Using Future Time Clauses

A Read the sentences about automation. Underline the time clauses, and circle the conjunctions in each clause. Double underline the main clauses.

1 (Once) a company starts using automation, <u>it will serve more customers</u>.

2 Companies will start saving a great deal of money as soon as they move to automation.

3 Companies are going to have difficulty competing until they begin to use bots and robots.

4 After companies have moved to automation, they will receive technological support and updates on new technology.

5 Once people believe that their jobs are secure, they are going to feel less anxious about automation.

B Complete the sentences from a meeting about automation. Circle the correct form of the verbs.

1 I think we **are going to attract** / attract more international customers once we **are going to start** / **start** using automation.

2 I'm concerned that our jobs **will not be** / is safe once we **begin** / will begin to use automation.

3 As soon as our company will start / **starts** using automation, we **are going to save** / save a lot of money. We will be able to eliminate our production department.

4 We **are going to save / have saved** up to $50,000 annually after we **will change / have changed** to using robots.

5 I'm pretty worried that the company **isn't going to save / hasn't saved** money until automation **will become / becomes** more reliable.

6 As soon as the company marketing department **will develop / has developed** faster drones, we **have / will have** better delivery services.

7 We **won't approve / approve** using drones until the manager **has approved / will approve** the budget.

Exercise 2.2 Time Clauses with *When* and *While*

Complete the conversation about social networking in advertising. Use the correct form of the verbs in parentheses. Sometimes more than one answer is possible.

Erin OK, everyone. We're going to have to find cheaper ways to market our products.

Bo I'm sure that while we **'re discussing** (discuss) the new budget next week, we'll
(1)
think of some inexpensive ways to market our products.

Erin We need to use social networking sites more than we do now.

Bo I agree. Let's prepare a presentation. Lisa can write some descriptions of our new
products. I'll do research on the most popular social networking sites while you
_____ (find) the budget figures.
(2)

Erin Sounds good. While we _____ (do) that, the art department will work
(3)
on some drawings for our profile page.

Bo OK. I'll investigate how other food companies market themselves on social
networking sites while the art department _____ (work) on
(4)
the drawings.

Erin Look for Dan's Imported Food. That's our biggest competitor.

Bo Right. I'm sure that when I _____ (study) Dan's page, I'll get some
(5)
good ideas. I'll take notes while I _____ (look) at it.
(6)

Erin While you _____ (analyze) Dan's page, I'll think about how we can use
(7)
apps for marketing as well.

Bo Great idea. While you _____ (think) about apps, I'll get some
(8)
information on the impact promotions can have.

Erin Good plan! Let's get moving!

Look at Jared's meeting agenda. Then complete the sentences about what is going to happen. Pay close attention to the sequence of events. Use *will* or the future progressive of the verbs in parentheses. Sometimes there is more than one correct answer.

	August 23	
8:00–8:20	Introduce new employees	
8:15	Sara arrives; introduce Sara	
8:20–10:00	Brainstorm for new budget	
10:00–10:20	Take break	
10:00	Print worksheets	
10:20	Return from break; hand out worksheets; put everyone into small groups	
10:20–11:30	Small-group discussions; walk around and take notes	
11:30	Vice president arrives; reassemble group	

1 I ___*will be introducing*___ (introduce) the new employees when Sara arrives.

2 When Sara arrives, I _____ (introduce) her.

3 I _____ (print) the worksheets when the group takes a break.

4 I _____ (hand out) the worksheets when the group returns from the break.

5 When people return from the break, I _____ (put) them into small groups.

6 When people work in small groups, I _____ (walk) around and _____ (take) notes.

7 When the vice president arrives, the groups _____ (finish) their discussions.

8 I _____ (reassemble) the group when the vice president arrives.

A Combine the sentences from Marta and Aaron's "to-do" list. Note that *M* is Marta and *A* is Aaron. Use *after, until,* or *when* with the present perfect in the time clauses. Sometimes more than one answer is possible.

1 Jan.–Feb. (M & A): Research and plan the business
  Mar. (M): Get a loan

  After Marta and Aaron have researched and planned the business, Marta
  will get a loan./Marta will get a loan after Marta and Aaron have
  researched and planned the business.

2 Mar.–Apr. (M & A): Get business training
  May–Jun. (M & A): Get management training

3 Apr. (A): Think of a name for the business
  May (M): Find a location for the business

4 Sept. (M): Get a tax identification number
  Oct. (M & A): Buy equipment for the business

5 Nov. (M & A): Promote the business
  Dec. (M & A): Open the business

6 First week of Dec. (M & A): Have a sale
  Dec. 25–31: Close for one week

B Pair Work Compare your sentences with a partner. What are some different ways to express the same ideas?

  A *I wrote "After Marta and Aaron have done some research, they will get a loan."*
  B *I wrote "Marta and Aaron won't get a loan until they have done some research."*

3 Future Perfect vs. Future Perfect Progressive

Grammar Presentation

The future perfect is used to describe events that will be completed at a time in the future. The future perfect progressive describes events that will be in progress at a time in the future. These forms are much more common in speaking than in academic writing.

By 2025, many companies *will have eliminated* some of their employees' jobs.

By 2025, our company *will have been using* bots for ten years.

3.1 Forming Future Perfect

Form the future perfect with *will +have +* the past participle of the main verb. Form the negative by putting *not* between *will* and *have*, or use *won't have*.

By May, we *will have opened* the new office.

Will the team *have finished* the project by next week?

By next week, the team *won't have finished* the project.

3.2 Forming Future Perfect Progressive

Form the future perfect progressive with *will + have + been +* the *-ing* form of the main verb. Form the negative by putting *not* between *will* and *have*, or use *won't have*.

By May, I *will have been working* here for a year.

How long *will you have been working* here by next month?

We *won't have been working* here for very long.

3.3 Future Perfect and Future Perfect Progressive Contrasted

A Use the future perfect for an event that will be completed by a time in the future.

I *will have made* my decision before tomorrow.

Will she *have told* you her decision by noon?

B Use the future perfect progressive for an event that will be in progress at a time in the future.

How long *will* he *have been working* in the computer industry on his fortieth birthday?

C You can introduce a particular future time with a preposition such as *before* and *by* (*by that time, by then*) or a time clause in the simple present.	**He'll have been working** for us for 10 years <u>by next June</u>. They just moved to Dallas, so they **won't have been living** there long <u>when you visit next month</u>.
You can use *already* to express certainty about future situations.	We can't change the plan. The managers **will** <u>already</u> **have had** their meeting by Monday. **They'll have** <u>already</u> **made** a decision by the time we get there.
D Use the future perfect, not the future perfect progressive, with stative verbs such as *have, hear,* and *know*.	She **will have known** about it by then. NOT She ~~will have been knowing~~ about it by then.

Grammar Application

Look at the schedules. Then complete the sentences with the future perfect. Use the negative when necessary.

> 10:45 a.m.: Katie will finish the report.
> 11:00 a.m.: The meeting will start.
> 11:15 a.m.: Kyle will arrive.

1 Katie *will have finished the report* by the time Kyle arrives.

2 The meeting _____ by the time Kyle arrives.

3 By 11:00, Kyle _____ .

> 12:30 p.m.: The meeting will end.
> 1:30 p.m.: Kyle and Katie will go out to eat lunch.
> 2:30 p.m.: Kyle and Katie will return from lunch.

4 By 12:40, the meeting _____ .

5 By 1:40, Kyle and Katie _____ .

6 By 2:15, Kyle and Katie _____ .

> 5:30 p.m.: Kyle's wife arrives home.
> 6:00 p.m.: Kyle leaves work.
> 7:30 p.m.: Kyle and his family will eat dinner.

7 Kyle's wife _____ before Kyle leaves work.

8 Kyle _____ by 6:15.

9 At 6:45, Kyle and his family _____ .

Exercise 3.2 Future Perfect Progressive

Read Eric's work schedule. Then complete the sentences with the information in the schedule. Use the future perfect progressive and *for*.

Tuesday	Wednesday	Thursday–Friday
8:30: Be at work 12:00: Lunch meeting with Mark at restaurant 1:00–4:00: Discuss new project 5:00: Meet with Japanese tutor; cancel tutoring sessions for Wed.– Fri. 6:15–7:15: Call from Japan	8:00: Pick up laptop from IT 9:00–5:00: Attend software training; bring lunch from home	9:00–5:00: Attend software training; bring lunch from home 6:00–8:00: Work out at the gym

1 By 4:30 on Tuesday, Eric / work / hours

   By 4:30 on Tuesday, Eric will have been working for eight hours.

2 By 4:00 on Tuesday, Eric / discuss the new project / hours

   _____

   _____

3 By 6:45 on Tuesday, Eric / talk on the phone / hour

   _____

   _____

4 By 4:00 on Wednesday, Eric / attend a software training / hours

   _____

   _____

5 By 5:00 on Friday, Eric / attend a software training / days

   _____

   _____

6 By 7:15 on Friday, Eric / work out at the gym / minutes

   _____

   _____

A A company is making its building energy-efficient and healthier for its employees. Read the time line. Then listen to questions about the time line. Circle *Yes* or *No*.

February 2015	Approve the building plans
March 2015	Find a temporary site for workers
April 2015	Move into the temporary site
May 2015	Construction firm starts construction; installs solar heating system
October 2015	Finish all construction; "green" interior designer arrives; install new workstations
February 2016	Move back into the building
June 2016	Water department inspects water quality
August 2016	Send report on building improvements to finance department
March 2017	New law starts that requires all buildings to have energy-saving features
August 2017	OSHA[1] (Occupational Safety and Health Administration) visit

[1]**OSHA:** a U.S. government agency that inspects companies' workplaces to make sure that the companies follow health and safety laws

1	Yes	(No)	**3**	Yes	No	**5**	Yes	No	**7**	Yes	No
2	Yes	No	**4**	Yes	No	**6**	Yes	No	**8**	Yes	No

B Listen again and check your answers.

C Over to You Answer the questions. Then share your answers with a partner.

- What year will it be in two years?
- What will you have accomplished by that time?
- What will you have been doing until then?

4 Avoid Common Mistakes ⚠

1   Use future forms in the main clause and present forms for the time clause.

We will buy it after we ~~will~~ get back from our trip.

2   Remember to use the future perfect when describing a future event that occurs before another future event.

     will have

They left by the time we get there, so we won't see them.

           have moved

By that time, you will ~~move~~.

3   Make sure you do not confuse the future perfect progressive with other forms.

         living

In June, we will have been ~~lived~~ in Texas for two years.

4   Remember to use *will* when forming the future perfect.

        will

By this time next year, she have gotten a better job.

Editing Task

Find and correct seven more mistakes in the paragraph about the future of health care.

                                                        have changed

         Experts say that in the next few years, the health-care industry will ~~change~~ in many ways because of technology and the Internet. I plan on working in this industry, so it is fascinating for me to know that by the time I graduate, the job market has changed dramatically. One change that interests me is in the doctor-

5   patient relationship. By that time, technology will empower patients because they will have been used the Internet to gather information and discuss information with others. Also, doctors will have been used smart medication for a few years, so the results of a patient's treatment will already be available to both the patient and the doctor. By the time a patient arrives for an appointment, the doctor and patient will

10   have been discussed many options. Also, when a patient will arrive at the office for his appointment, he will not have to fill out forms. The doctor have already seen the patient's information on screen. The whole health-care system will have improved, so more people will live in a state of good health.

5 Academic Writing

Comparison and Contrast

Brainstorm > Organize > Write > Edit

In Unit 5, you analyzed an essay, then brainstormed and organized ideas with Venn diagrams for the prompt below. In this unit (6), you will learn about the language and structure of a comparison-and-contrast essay.

> *Compare learning a language with studying math. How do you think the study of these subjects will change over time with new technology?*

Using Transitions to Show Comparison and Contrast

The ability to compare similar ideas or to contrast different ideas is an important skill in academic writing. This is especially true when writers are asked to discuss a subject before giving an opinion. Look at the following transitions.

Comparison: *Similarly, In the same way, Likewise*

Contrast: *However, In contrast, Conversely, On the other hand*

Exercise 5.1 Applying the Skill

Complete the sentences with your own ideas.

1 Academic subjects such as law can lead to high-paying careers. In contrast, _____
_____

2 The study of medicine involves both theory and practice. Similarly, _____
_____

3 Vocational training can be learned by taking special courses. Likewise, _____
_____

4 Science classrooms are often equipped with expensive equipment. Conversely, _____
_____

Comparison-and-Contrast Essay Structure

One common way to structure a comparison-and-contrast essay is to start with a discussion about the differences between the two subjects and then follow with a discussion about the similarities.

Introductory paragraph:
- gives some background on the two subjects of comparisons
- provides a thesis statement that explains whether the writer thinks that the differences or similarities are more important, or that they are equally important

Body paragraph 1: states the differences between subject 1 and subject 2

Body paragraph 2: states the similarities between subject 1 and subject 2

Concluding paragraph:

- restates the thesis
- includes a comment showing the writer's opinion
- may also end with a recommendation or prediction

Exercise 5.2 Applying the Skill

Work with a partner. Look at the excerpts from a comparison-and-contrast essay about modern work spaces. Complete the tasks that follow.

> **[Intro]** Thirty years ago the main electronic devices used in education were calculators, CD players, and overhead projectors. In contrast, today's college classrooms are wired to support interactive white boards and fast Internet access, and technology companies are investing heavily in e-learning. Experts say that by the end of 2025, the global value of e-learning will have reached more than $300 billion. However, will the college classroom of the future be better than the traditional college classroom? While e-learning may make tomorrow's education more convenient, the fundamental teaching in a college classroom is not likely to change very much in the near future.
>
> **[Body paragraph 1]** It is true that the future college classroom will look different from today's classroom …
>
> **[Body paragraph 2]** On the other hand, the basic formula for success in the classroom will continue to be the same …
>
> **[Conclusion]**

1 Underline the thesis statement. What subjects will the writer compare? Will the writer emphasize the differences of the subjects, the similarities, or both?

2 Which paragraph will discuss the similarities? What about the differences?

3 Circle the transition that shows comparison or contrast in the second body paragraph.

My Writing

Exercise 5.3 Writing Your Introductory Paragraph

1 Look at your Venn diagram from My Writing in Unit 5. Write three possible thesis statements for your essay.

2 Work with a partner. Discuss and revise your thesis statements.

3 Revise the topic sentences and supporting details you wrote in My Writing in Unit 5 to match one of the thesis statements.

4 Write your introductory paragraph. Include a hook, background information, and thesis statement.

Social Modals

Learning How to Remember

1 Grammar in the Real World

A Have you ever forgotten something important? Read the article about memory improvement. Which memory-improvement technique do you think works best?

B Comprehension Check Answer the questions.

1 What must you do to remember something, according to Gini Graham Scott?
2 What is visualization?
3 What are some ways to exercise your brain?

C Notice Find the sentences in the article and complete them.

1 You _____ **give** a class presentation, and you are terrified.

2 You _____ **brought** your notes with you, but where are they?

3 Scott says that you _____ first **take in** information in order to save it in your memory.

Which sentences tell you it is necessary to do something?

How to Improve Your Memory

Some people have excellent memories, but most of us struggle to remember at times. You know the feeling: You **have to give** a class presentation, and you are terrified. As you wait your turn, you repeat the information over and over in your mind, but you keep forgetting a
5 key point. You **should have brought** your notes with you, but where are they? You **can't remember**. If you are more forgetful than you would like to be, you **might want to follow** the advice of memory-improvement experts. Whether you want to memorize a speech or simply remember where you left your cell phone, these experts offer
10 tips to jumpstart[1] your brain.

Gini Graham Scott, PhD, is the author of *30 Days to a More Powerful Memory*. She points out that if you want to remember something, it is necessary that you pay attention. You **must observe** what you want to learn. People often forget things simply because
15 they weren't concentrating. Scott says that you **have to** first **take in** information in order to save it in your memory. Other experts agree that visualization is an effective technique forgetful people **should try**. Create a mental picture – a picture in your mind – of what you want to remember. The more unusual the image, the easier it will be to recall.
20 For example, if you want to remember the due date for a final project, you **could visualize** that date flashing in bold colors on a giant television screen. The scene **has to be** unusual and animated for the memory to stick. Memory specialists agree that the more you exercise your brain, the better you will be able to remember information. How
25 can you give your brain a workout?[2] You **might want to tackle** the daily crossword puzzle. Changing a daily routine **is** also **supposed to work**. In addition, you **could challenge** your brain by writing with your nondominant[3] hand or by taking a different route to school or work.

In today's multitasking[4] world, a good memory is crucial. Without
30 it, you **cannot maintain** order and priorities in your life. Fortunately, there are remedies[5] for forgetfulness. Practice careful observance, creative visualization, and mental exercise to improve your memory.

---

[1]**jumpstart:** start something more quickly by giving it extra help

[2]**workout:** a period of exercise

[3]**nondominant:** not as important, strong, or noticeable

[4]**multitask:** work on several tasks at the same time

[5]**remedy:** a substance or method for curing an illness, or a way of dealing with a problem or difficulty

2 Modals and Modal-like Expressions of Advice and Regret

Grammar Presentation

The modals and modal-like expressions *could*, *had better*, *might*, *might want to*, *ought to*, and *should* can be used to express advice and regret.

You **should try** to improve your memory.
I **should have** followed your advice.

2.1 Modals and Modal-like Expressions of Present and Future Advice

A Use *could* and *might* to offer advice and suggestions or to give choices.	He **could do** some puzzles to improve his memory. You **might try** some tips for improving your memory.
Might (*not*) is often used with *want to* to give suggestions.	You **might not want to** start with the most difficult math problem. Try this one – it's easier.
B Use *should* to say something is a good idea. Use *shouldn't* to say something is a bad idea.	Greg **should improve** his memory. Kate **shouldn't spend** so much time doing crossword puzzles.
Ought to is also possible, but less common. *Ought not* (*to*) is rare.	We **ought to take** a memory class together.
C Use *had better* (*not*) only in informal conversation to give strong advice, especially as a warning.	You**'d better pay** attention now. (Or you will be in trouble.)
There is often a negative consequence if the advice or warning is not followed.	She **had better not forget** my book again tomorrow. (Or I will never lend her anything again.)
Had is almost always contracted, and often omitted, in informal conversation.	He**'d better** remember to bring his ID next time.

▸▸ Modals and Modal-like Expressions: See page A3.

2.2 Modals and Modal-like Expressions of Past Advice and Regret

A Use *ought to have* or *should have* + the past participle for past events or situations that were advisable but did not happen.	*She **ought to have been** at the lecture, but she was sick.* (Being at the lecture was a good idea, but she wasn't there.)
	*You **should have made** an effort to improve your memory.* (Improving your memory was a good idea, but you didn't do it.)
B Use *shouldn't have* + the past participle for past situations in which bad decisions were made. It is often used to express regret.	*He **shouldn't have taken** that difficult class.* (But he did, and now he's frustrated.)
	*We **shouldn't have listened** to him.* (But we did, and now we're sorry.)
C *Should (not) have* may be used to criticize.	*You **should have followed** his advice.* (But you didn't, and now look at the trouble you're in.)

Grammar Application

Exercise 2.1 Present and Future Advice

A Complete the class discussion about improving memory. Circle the correct words or expressions.

Ms. Yost So, let's review our discussion about improving memory. What advice do experts give students? Sara?

Sara You (**should**)/ **'d better not** pay
(1)
attention to what you're learning.

Ms. Yost Right. So, for example, what's one good way to pay attention?

Sara Um, you **'d better / could** take notes while you're reading.
(2)

Manuel Or you **might / 'd better** take notes during lectures.
(3)

Ms. Yost Right. Do you have any other advice?

Manuel I think students **'d better / shouldn't** use a computer to take notes.
(4)
They **might not / should** use a pen and a piece of paper.
(5)

Ms. Yost Good idea. In fact, studies show that writing information by hand – instead of using a keyboard – helps you remember it better.

B Pair work Compare your answers with a partner. Discuss the reason for each of your answers.

I use had better not *for warnings. This isn't a warning. It's advice. So I chose* should *in number 1.*

Exercise 2.2 More Present and Future Advice

A Read the study tips from an article. Then complete the email to a friend. Use the tips and the modals in parentheses.

Study Tips

1 Try visualizing to remember dates and names.

2 Read your textbook two or three times.

3 Try teaching someone else the material.

4 Don't wait until the last minute to study.

5 Get plenty of sleep before a test.

● ● ●

Hi _____ ,

I know you're having trouble studying for tests. I just read some study tips online. Here's some advice:

1 (could) *You could try visualizing to remember dates and names.*

2 (ought to) _____

3 (might) _____

4 (should not) _____

5 (had better) _____

I hope this helps! Talk to you soon.

Best,

_____

B Pair Work Tell a partner which tips you use. Then think of two more study tips and share them with another pair.

Exercise 2.3 Past Advice and Regret

A Complete the conversation about Phoebe, a student who plagiarized. Use the correct form of the words in parentheses.

Jake   What happened to Phoebe? I heard she left college.

Sofia   She committed plagiarism. She really   *shouldn't have copied*   those articles
                                                          (1 not / should / copy)
from the Internet.

Jake I know. She _____ (2 should/take) notes on the web articles. Then she

_____ (3 ought to/summarize) her notes.

Sofia You're right. She

_____ credit (4 should/give) to the sources of the ideas, too. Why do you think she did that, anyway?

Jake Maybe she was under pressure or waited too long to start her paper. She _____ earlier. (5 ought to/start)

Sofia I agree. She _____ until the last minute. (6 should/not/wait)

Jake Or she _____ to the teacher if she was having (7 should/talk) problems. Maybe we _____ her. (8 should/help)

Sofia Yes, let's try to be more helpful the next time a classmate is stressed!

B Pair Work Compare your answers with a partner. Do you agree with the students' advice about Phoebe? What other advice would you give Phoebe?

C Group Work Think about a time when you made a decision you regret, or a time when a friend made a bad decision. What should you (or your friend) have done to make the situation better? Write five sentences with *should not have* + the past participle.

3 Modals and Modal-like Expressions of Permission, Necessity, and Obligation

Grammar Presentation

The modals and modal-like expressions *be allowed to*, *be required to*, *be supposed to*, *can*, *have to*, and *may* are used to express permission, necessity, and obligation in the present, past, and future.	We **weren't supposed to see** the answers for the memory test. They **will have to take** the test again. Students **may not take** the memory improvement class more than once.

3.1 Modals and Modal-like Expressions of Permission

A Use *can (not)* and *may (not)* to talk about permission in the present and future.	Students **can register** for the class now. You **may wait** until next week to register. I **can't miss** more than two classes. You **may not join** after the first class.
Use *could (not)* as the past form of *can (not)*.	We **could ask** questions at the end of the lecture, but we **couldn't interrupt** the lecture.
B You can also use *be (not) allowed to* for permission in the present, past, and future. For the future, add *will* before *be (not) allowed to*.	We **aren't allowed to talk** during the test. He **was allowed to talk** during the test, but he **was not allowed to use** his books. They **will be allowed to use** their notes tomorrow. She **won't be allowed to use** her notes.
You can use *permitted* instead of *allowed* in formal speech and writing.	Students **are not permitted to refer** to notes during examinations.

3.2 Modals and Modal-like Expressions of Necessity and Obligation

A Use *be required to*, *be supposed to*, *have to*, *must*, and *need to* to express necessity or obligation in the present and future. *Must* and *be required to* are more formal and are not often used in speaking.	You **are required to take** the class. Teachers **are supposed to hand out** the syllabus on the first day of class. Everyone **is required to work** hard. Applicants **must have** experience for this job.
Use *will be required to*, *will have to*, and *will need to* for future time.	You **will need to write** an essay for this course.
B Use *be not supposed to* or *must not* for the present and future to say that something is inappropriate or to express prohibition.	Students **are not supposed to take** their books into the exam room. (It is inappropriate.) You **must not talk** during the exam. (There is no choice.)
C Use *were required to*, *were supposed to*, or *had to* to describe necessity and obligation in the past.	The applicant **was required to take** a test. I **was supposed to stay** after class last week. We **had to arrive** at 7:00 a.m. for the exam.
There is no past form of *must*. Use *had to* instead.	He **had to reschedule** his exam yesterday. NOT He ~~must~~ reschedule his exam yesterday.

3.2 Modals and Modal-like Expressions of Necessity and Obligation *(continued)*

D The negative forms of *be required to*, *have to*, and *need to* describe choices or options.

*You **are not required to show** your ID.* (It is optional.)

*You **didn't have to remain** in the exam room after you finished.* (It was your choice.)

*Students **won't need to bring** their own pencils next time.* (It will be your choice.)

Grammar Application

Exercise 3.1 Present and Future Permission

A Complete the rules for a college Spanish class. Use the present or future form of the words in parentheses. Sometimes more than one answer is possible.

SPANISH 101 *CLASSROOM RULES*

DICTIONARIES

Students ___*can bring*___ monolingual dictionaries along to class, but they _____
　　　　　　(1 can/bring)　　　　　　　　　　　　　　　　　　　　　　　　　(2 not/may/use)

any bilingual dictionaries at all. Students _____ print dictionaries during tests.
　　　　　　　　　　　　　　　　　　　　　(3 can/use)

However, they _____ online dictionaries during tests.
　　　　　　　　(4 not/be allowed to/access)

LAPTOPS

You _____ laptop computers to class for note taking only.
　　　(5 be allowed to/bring)

You _____ laptops for Internet searches during class.
　　　(6 not/must/use)

COMPUTER LAB

Students _____ the lab until they have purchased the book.
　　　　　　(7 not/may/use)

B Rewrite the sentences about the students in the Spanish class. Use the rules in A and the correct form of the words in parentheses.

1 Emily wants to bring a bilingual dictionary to class. (be permitted to)

　　She isn't permitted to bring a bilingual dictionary to class.

2 Eric wants to use an online dictionary during a test. (be allowed to)

　　_____

3 Ann wants to use a print dictionary during tests. (may)

　　_____

4 Maria wants to bring a laptop to class. (can)

_____

5 James wants to check his email on his laptop during class. (be permitted to)

_____

6 David hasn't bought the textbook yet. He wants to go to the lab. (can)

_____

A Complete the conversation about classroom rules. Use the correct past form of the words in parentheses.

Ming   Last semester, I ___*could bring*___ a monolingual dictionary to class.
                                              (1 can/bring)

Danielle   Yes, but you _____ it during tests.
                                        (2 not/can/use)

Ming   That's right. And we _____ laptops to class,
                                            (3 be permitted to/bring)
            but we _____ the Internet during class.
                        (4 not/be allowed to/search)

Danielle   No, but we _____ on the Internet in the
                                    (5 be allowed to/go)
            computer lab after we finished our work.

Ming   _____ we _____ our own language at all during
            (6)   (6 be allowed to/speak)
            English class? I can't remember.

Danielle   No. We _____ that. We even had to ask
                            (7 not/be allowed to/do)
            our classmates questions in English.

B Over to You Think about a test or exam you took in the past. What could or couldn't you do? Write five sentences with *could* (*not*), (*not*) *be allowed to*, or (*not*) *be permitted to*. Then share your sentences with a partner.

Read the teacher's classroom rules and suggestions. Then rewrite the rules with the words in parentheses. Use the negative when necessary.

1 Read articles in English every day. It is an option. (have to)

   You don't have to read articles in English every day.

2 Don't be afraid to ask questions in class. (must)

_____

3 Turn in all your homework. I expect this. (be supposed to)

_____

4 Bring a flash drive next week. (must)

_____

5 Write an essay at the end of the semester. (be required to)

_____

6 Don't text during class. I expect this. (be supposed to)

_____

7 Send your writing assignments by email. It is an option. (need to)

_____

Exercise 3.4 More Present and Future Necessity and Obligation

A Listen to the psychology department announcement about a memory study. Circle *S* if the meaning of the sentence you read is the same as the one you hear. Circle *D* if the meaning of the sentence you read is different from the one you hear.

1 (S) D   Participants must attend two sessions.

2 S D   Sessions are not supposed to take more than one hour.

3 S D   Participants are not supposed to be younger than 18 years of age.

4 S D   Each participant must not have poor vision.

5 S D   Each participant is supposed to have normal hearing.

6 S D   Participants do not have to speak Mandarin.

7 S D   Participants are required to be students at the university.

8 S D   Participants must email the researcher by July 31.

B Listen again and check your answers.

Exercise 3.5 Past Necessity and Obligation

A Complete the story about an older person's learning experience. Use the correct forms of the words in parentheses.

When my grandmother was in high school, she ___*had to follow*___ a lot of rules
                                             (1 have to / follow)
and regulations, and she _____ very hard. There
                              (2 have to / work)
were no computers, so she _____ notes by hand. She
                                (3 have to / take)
_____ hundreds of textbook pages a week and write
     (4 be required to / read)
several papers each semester. She _____ any classes.
                                      (5 not / be supposed to / miss)
She _____ class every day in order to pass. Of course,
        (6 have to / attend)
there was no Internet then, so she _____ to the library
                                        (7 have to / go)
to do research. High school in her time was very different from how it is today!

B Over to You Write five sentences about some rules and regulations that you remember in a learning environment in the past, for example, in another school you attended. Share your sentences with a partner and discuss this question: How did the rules and regulations help you to learn?

4 Modals and Modal-like Expressions of Ability

Grammar Presentation

The modals *be able to* and *can* are used to express ability in the present, past, and future.	*I couldn't remember anything the professor said.* *I won't be able to pass the test.* *She can remember dates well.*

4.1 Modals and Modal-like Expressions of Present and Future Ability

A Use *be able to* and *can* to describe ability in the present.	*I am able to remember faces well, and I can usually remember names as well.*
Use *be not able to* and *can't / cannot* for negative statements in the present. *Be not able to* is more formal than *can't*.	*He isn't able to meet us today.*
B Use *can* and *will be able to* to describe ability in the future.	*We can meet the professor at noon tomorrow.* *He will be able to see us then.*
Use *can't* and *will not / won't be able to* for negative statements in the future. Notice that *not* comes before *be* in the future form.	*I can't go to the lecture on Friday.* *We won't be able to take the memory test until next month.*

4.2 Modals and Modal-like Expressions of Past Ability

A Use *could (not)* to describe general ability in the past. *Was / were (not) able to* is also possible, especially to talk about a particular ability or talent.	*When I was younger, I could be very persuasive.* *I could understand the lecture, but I couldn't remember all of the information.* *She was able to read by the time she was four.*

4.2 Modals and Modal-like Expressions of Past Ability (continued)

Use *was/were able to*, not *could*, to describe ability on a particular occasion in the past.	Once, I *was able to* convince my friend to memorize 100 new words in a week. NOT *Once, I could convince my friend to memorize 100 new words in a week.*
B Use *could have* + the past participle to describe situations in which a person had the ability to do something but did not do it.	I *could have taken* the memory test last Saturday, but I didn't sign up for it.
Use *couldn't have* + the past participle to describe situations in which a person didn't have the ability to do something.	Eric *couldn't have known* the answer to that question. He didn't study at all.

Grammar Application

Exercise 4.1 Past, Present, and Future Ability

Complete the story about memory loss. Use the past, present, or future form of the words in parentheses.

A few years ago, Alicia was a successful physician. She was very popular with her patients because she ___*could diagnose*___ their problems quickly and accurately.
(1 can/diagnose)

Alicia's favorite pastime was riding her bike. She _____
(2 can/ride)
her mountain bike for hours in the hills around her town. Then one day last year, a car came up behind Alicia while she was riding on a narrow road, and it hit her. The accident caused a serious brain injury, even though she was wearing a helmet.

Alicia is in full-time therapy now. Today, she _____
(3 be able to/do)
many things. However, when she finishes therapy, she _____
(4 not/be able to/return)
to her old job because of her memory loss. Therefore, Alicia is planning to help other people with her condition. Once Alicia is ready, she _____ of
(5 be able to/take care)
other patients.

Complete the sentences about Diana. Use *could have* and the correct form of the verbs in parentheses.

1 Diana had an accident like Alicia's. She was riding a bike in the hills when a car hit her. The driver ___*could have avoided*___ (avoid) hitting her, but he was driving too fast.

2 She went to a doctor, but he didn't think her injuries were serious. Diana didn't think the doctor _____ (make) a mistake about her diagnosis.[1]

3 Diana went to work after the accident, and her behavior seemed normal. Her co-workers _____ (not/imagine) that she had a brain injury.

4 The first clue that Diana was not well was when she went to a nearby store. She forgot how to get home. A neighbor had to help her. She _____ (not/remember) the way without help.

5 Finally, Diana found a specialist, Dr. Lee, who diagnosed her correctly and helped her get a service dog. Diana probably _____ (manage) fine by herself, but she was very thankful for the service dog because it made her life easier. Now she is in a memory rehabilitation program and doing well.

[1]**diagnosis:** when a doctor says what is wrong with someone who is ill

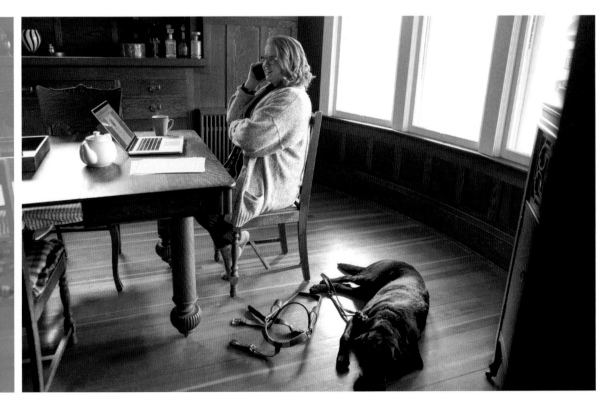

5 Avoid Common Mistakes ⚠

1   **When talking about advice and regret in the past, remember to use *have* + the past participle after a modal, not the simple past form of the verb.**

have
I should remembered her name, but I didn't expect her to be at the party, and I got confused.

2   **Remember to use a form of *be* in *be allowed to* and *be supposed to*.**

was
The president supposed to attend the 2 o'clock meeting, but he didn't show up.

3   **Use *did not have to* when talking about a choice in the past.**

did not have to email
I ~~must not have emailed~~ the office manager, but I wanted to be sure he was aware of the problem.

Editing Task

Find and correct six more mistakes in the paragraphs about multitasking.

is
Technology supposed to simplify life; however, in reality, it has led to people trying to do too many things at once. One example is driving while texting or talking on a phone. After an accident, drivers who are caught by the police admit that they should turned off their phones when they got in the car, but they did not. They must

5   not have called someone while driving, but they did.

Another issue is multitasking in the classroom. Many of my teachers have had a difficult time dealing with students who search the Internet while listening to lectures. One of my instructors said he ought to required a password last semester to log onto the Internet during class. Students must not have gone online, but they sometimes

10   checked email or visited websites instead of listening to the lecture. As a result, students were often distracted.

In contrast, my friend had an instructor who had the opposite view. My friend did not worry about taking notes because students not allowed to – even on paper! The professor thought all note taking was a form of multitasking; instead, he handed

15   out worksheets with highlights of his lecture. At the end of the semester, some students complained. They argued that the professor should not banned computers in class because students today are used to multitasking.

6 Academic Writing

Comparison and Contrast

Brainstorm > Organize > **Write** > Edit

In Unit 6, you learned about the language and structure of a comparison-and-contrast essay. In this unit (7), you are going to write the first draft of your essay for the prompt below.

> Compare learning a language with studying math. How do you think the study of these subjects will change over time with new technology?

Using Modals in Academic Writing

Writers often use modals and modal-like expressions to discuss possible effects, solutions, or recommendations in an essay.

Exercise 6.1 Applying the Skill

Re-read the concluding paragraph of "The Future of Learning" (page 81). Work with a partner. Discuss the questions.

In the end, it is difficult to state whether one form of learning is better than another, since they are geared toward different learning situations. Online learning allows for greater flexibility, whereas the traditional classroom provides a more personal, dynamic learning environment. Nevertheless, both can produce positive results for the student, which is the most important factor. Therefore, both systems might be part of our world for years to come. Perhaps in the future, students themselves will be able to select elements of both systems to create a more flexible, complete, and personalized educational path to success.

1 Underline two examples of modals or modal-like expressions in the paragraph. Why does the writer use them?
2 Why does the writer not use a modal or modal-like expression in the second sentence of the paragraph?

My Writing

Exercise 6.2 Planning Your Essay

Use the table on page 113 to plan your essay. Review your work in My Writing in Units 5 and 6, and follow the steps below.

1 Review the introductory paragraph you wrote in Unit 6, and make notes in the table. Include your thesis statement.
2 Make notes on the differences in body paragraph 1 in row 2.
3 Make notes on the similarities in body paragraph 2 in row 3.
4 Make notes on the concluding paragraph in row 4. Include your opinion.

Introductory paragraph	
Body paragraph 1	
Body paragraph 2	
Concluding paragraph	

Exercise 6.3 Writing Your First Draft

Write the first draft of your essay. Include:

- an introductory paragraph with hook, background information, and thesis statement
- a body paragraph about the differences of the topics
- a body paragraph about the similarities of the topics
- a concluding paragraph with your opinion and a final thought, recommendation, or prediction

1 Grammar in the Real World

ACADEMIC WRITING

Comparison and contrast

A How do you protect personal information like computer passwords? Read the article about hacking. What are some ways to prevent hackers from stealing personal information?

B Comprehension Check **Answer the questions.**

1 What age are many hackers?

2 What information do some hackers steal?

3 Is anyone's computer completely safe from hackers?

C Notice **Read the sentences. Check (✓) the box next to each sentence to show if the action or situation is possible or very certain.**

	Possible	Very Certain
1 Cyber hacking **can** happen to anyone.	☐	☐
2 In fact, it **might be** too easy.	☐	☐
3 There are other hackers who **must have** more malicious intentions because they steal credit card numbers and other personal information.	☐	☐
4 In short, if you act safely and responsibly, hackers **will** likely **have** a hard time breaking into your computer.	☐	☐

Which bold words in the sentences tell you that an action or situation is possible?

HACKING:
A Computer Crime on the RISE

Cyber[1] hacking **may be** the most common computer crime today. Cyber hacking occurs when a person accesses someone else's computer without permission and steals information. It **can happen** to anyone. It **might** even **have happened** to someone you know.

5　　The truth is that hacking is not difficult to learn. In fact, it **might be** too easy. Young adults tend to be skilled at using computers, so it **may not be** surprising to learn that a large number of computer hackers are teenagers. They **might hack** into other computers for the challenge – to see if they can do it and get away with it.

10　There are other hackers, however, who **must have** more malicious[2] intentions because they steal credit card numbers and other personal information.

Severe[3] penalties for these cyber crimes **should have stopped** hacking by now, but they have had little effect. It does not look like
15　cyber hacking **will go** away anytime soon. For protection against hacking, anyone who uses a computer or other technological device **should be** aware of hackers and **should be using** antivirus software. Another safety measure is to use complex[4] passwords, which **could prevent** attacks from being successful.

20　　In short, if you act safely and responsibly, hackers **will** likely **have** a hard time breaking into your computer. However, even these safety measures cannot guarantee that your information is safe.

[1]**cyber:** related to computers

[2]**malicious:** intended to harm or upset other people

[3]**severe:** extreme

[4]**complex:** having many connected parts, making it difficult to understand

2 Modals of Present Probability

Grammar Presentation

Modals of present probability are used to express how likely it is that something is happening now.	Your computer **may be** at risk of being hacked. He **must not be** worried about data security.

2.1 Modals of Present Probability

A Choose a modal depending on how certain you feel about something.

most certain ↕	can't, couldn't, have to, must (not)
certain	ought to, should (not)
least certain ↕	could, may (not), might (not)

Hackers **can't be** interested in my data.
Your password **must not be** secure.
Antivirus software **should protect** you.
It **shouldn't be** difficult to find good software.
Good antivirus software **could cost** a lot.
That software **might not be** good enough.

B Use *can't* and *couldn't* when you are almost certain something is not likely or not possible.

He **can't be** online now. His computer is broken.
Meg **couldn't be shopping** for a new laptop. Her old computer works perfectly.

You can also use *can't* and *couldn't* to express disbelief or surprise.

Your brand-new computer is broken? You **can't be** serious!

C Use *have to* and *must (not)* when you are mostly certain or when you think there is only one logical conclusion.

As a lawyer, he **has to know** that hacking into computers is illegal!
Large companies **must worry** about the security of their data.

In formal speaking and writing, *must* is much more common than *have to*.

People without antivirus software **must believe** they are not at risk.

D Use *ought to* and *should (not)* when you have an expectation based on experience or evidence. *Should* is more common than *ought to*. *Ought not to* is rare.

That computer **should be** available in the store because I saw it on the store's website.
You **shouldn't have** trouble figuring out my password because it's an easy one.

E Use *could*, *may (not)*, and *might (not)* when you are unsure or when you don't have much evidence.

I **could have** a virus on my computer because it isn't working normally.
I **might not buy** a new computer this year because my old one still works fine.

▸▸ Modals and Modal-like Expressions: See page A3.

Grammar Application

Exercise 2.1 Present Probability

A Complete the interview about hacking. Use the correct modals and the information in parentheses to help you. Sometimes more than one answer is possible.

Jason Today we are asking people: How secure is your computer or smartphone? Could you be the victim of a hacker?

Emily It's impossible. Hackers _can't/couldn't_ (1) be interested in my computer. I don't have anything valuable on it. **(impossible)**

Jason But you _____ (2) have some valuable information on your computer. Everyone does. **(a logical conclusion)**

Emily What do you mean?

Jason I'm sure you've bought things online at some point. Your credit card information _____ (3) be on your computer. **(a logical conclusion)**

Carlos Well, I'm certain that my phone is safe. It _____ (4) be of interest to anyone, especially a hacker. **(unlikely)**

Jason Oh, you _____ (5) have GPS – global positioning software – on your phone, then. Because if you did, you'd feel differently. **(a logical conclusion)**

Carlos But I *do* have GPS on my phone . . .

Jason Well, that _____ (6) make you a little less sure, then, because GPS is one of the things that hackers are interested in. It lets them see where you go every day. **(expectation based on evidence)**

Carlos My GPS? That _____ (7) be true! **(surprise)**

Belén You know, my computer _____ (8) be of interest to a hacker for some reason, I guess. **(unsure)**

Jason I'm afraid that's true.

B Pair Work Compare your answers with a partner. Take turns saying the sentences with other modals that have the same meaning.

Hackers can't be interested in my computer.

A Over to You Read the statements. Then respond with information that is true for you. Use modals of present probability to show how certain you feel that the statements are true for you. Explain why.

1 A person can hack into your computer or smartphone at any time.

  That can't be true. I have excellent security software.

2 It is very likely that a thief will steal your identity.

3 Your credit card number is not safe.

4 Your home is very safe. It's unlikely that a burglar can enter and take valuable items from you.

5 The downtown area of your city or town is dangerous at night. It's a bad idea to walk there alone at night.

6 It's very safe for children to walk to school alone in your neighborhood.

B Pair Work Take turns asking questions about each other's statements.

You say that it can't be true that a person can hack into your computer because you have good security, but good security is sometimes not enough. For example, banks tend to have good security, but hackers get into their computers.

3 Modals of Future Probability

Grammar Presentation

Modals of future probability with *could, may, might, ought to, should,* and *will* express the probability of something happening in the future.	*Your new computer should be here next week.* *I won't buy a new computer next year because my current one is still fairly new.*

3.1 Modals of Future Probability

A Choose a modal depending on how certain you are about something.

most certain	will (not)	Hackers **will be** interested in our company's financial data.
certain	should (not), ought to	Our new website **should be** ready by next week.
		The secure web page **ought to be** available soon.
least certain	may (not), might (not), could	She **could learn** a lot about Internet security in her course next month.

B Use *will* and *won't* to express strong certainty.

The company **will hire** very few people this year.

You can add words like *probably* and *likely* to weaken the certainty.

The company <u>probably</u> **won't hire** any students.

C Use *should (not)* and *ought to* when you have an expectation based on experience or evidence.

The software **should be** ready by Friday. (Because it is almost ready now.)

We **shouldn't expect** new passwords until Monday. (Because it usually takes a few days.)

D Use *could, may (not),* and *might (not)* when you are unsure or when you don't have much evidence.

The company **could start** storing personal data as early as next month.

A manager **might join** us next week.

You can also use these modals with a progressive form of the verb.

The class **may be** <u>starting</u> soon. There are a lot of students in the room.

Grammar Application

Exercise 3.1 Future Probability

A Complete the ad with *will* and the verbs in parentheses.

I-SAFE HOME SECURITY SYSTEM

The home of the future __will be__ (be)
(1)
safer. Homeowners _____ (be)
(2)
able to control everything in the home with the
new I-safe Home Security System.

Here are just a few of I-SAFE's features:

▶ You _____ (not / need) to worry about the new nanny. I-safe
    (3)
_____ (let) parents use their computers or smartphones at work to watch
    (4)
the nanny.

▶ I-safe _____ (allow) you to control appliances and heating and cooling systems
    (5)
from wherever you are.

▶ I-safe _____ (lock) the doors to your home for you.
    (6)

▶ The I-safe Home Security System _____ (be) available this spring.
    (7)

B Complete the conversation about the I-safe. The speakers are not very certain about the claims in the ad. Circle the correct words.

Customer   Are you going to sell the I-safe system next spring?

Sales clerk   It **will likely** / **will** be available next spring, but the manager isn't sure.
                 (1)

Customer   Can I use the I-safe to control the TV from my smartphone?

Sales clerk   You **will** / **should** be able to control the TV, but I'm not really sure.
                 (2)

Customer   I have a nanny. If I install I-safe cameras to watch her from time to time, she
            should / **may not** be happy about being on camera.
                 (3)

Sales clerk   You're right, there **shouldn't** / **could** be some concerns about privacy.
                 (4)

Customer   I use a tablet while I commute to work on the train. I haven't read anything
            about using the I-safe with my tablet. I-safe probably **won't** / **shouldn't** work
                 (5)
            with it, right?

Sales clerk   I'm not quite sure, but it **ought to** / **will** send images to your tablet.
                 (6)

Customer   OK. Thanks for your help.

C Pair Work Imagine that the I-safe company is going to give away its product for free for one month. Will you get an I-safe? Why or why not? Use modals in your answers.

A *I probably won't get an I-safe because I'm not very worried about home security.*

B *I might get one. I'm not sure because there could be some privacy issues with it.*

Exercise 3.2 More Future Probability

A Listen to the conversations about future probability. Write the missing words.

Conversation 1

Anne   Someone broke into the Lees' apartment, and now they're moving.

Martín   That's awful. Where are they going to go?

Anne   I'm not sure. __*They'll*__ probably move to the suburbs.
     (1)

Martín   But Joe Lee has a good job here in the city. _____ be able to
     (2)
move very far away.

Anne   I know. And the children are in school in the city. _____ want to
     (3)
change schools.

Martín   Well, I wish them luck.

Conversation 2

Truong   I spoke with Andrew Martinez yesterday. Guess what? _____ buy
     (4)
a home security system.

Ben   I know. We went to a home security show last week. He liked the system with
the cameras that send images to your phone. _____ be the
     (5)
system he's going to buy.

Truong   _____ learn a lot from Andrew when he puts in his system.
     (6)

Conversation 3

Reporter   The airport commissioner announced today that Bay City Airport will start
using cameras with sensors that will detect heart rate and body temperature.
_____ be ready by next year.
     (7)

Josh   I read about the cameras online as well. In fact, I heard that _____
     (8)
start using the cameras by the end of this year.

Katie   _____ be interesting to see what happens.
     (9)

B Listen again and check your answers.

4 Modals of Past Probability

Grammar Presentation

Modals of past probability with *can, could, may, might,* and *must* are used to make inferences or guesses about the past.	A hacker **couldn't have accessed** this computer! I have the best protection available. A hacker **might have found** a way to break into it.

4.1 Forming Modals of Past Probability

Form modals of past probability with modal + *have* + the past participle of the main verb.	The company **may have been** careless with security. I **must not have turned off** my phone.
Form the negative by putting *not* between the modal and *have*. Only use contractions with *could* and *can*.	She **could have changed** her password, but I'm not sure. It **couldn't have been** Joe's fault. He wasn't here.

4.2 Using Modals of Past Probability

A Choose a modal depending on how certain you are that something happened.

most certain ↑	couldn't, can't
certain	must (not)
least certain ↓	may (not), might (not), could

You **couldn't have chosen** a strong password. Kim guessed it immediately!

Someone **must have stolen** all the passwords because hackers have gotten into every computer.

The computer **may not have had** strong antivirus software because it was older.

B Use *can't have* or *couldn't have* when you are absolutely certain something was impossible or unlikely.

I **can't have entered** the wrong password! I've had the same one forever.

He **couldn't have hacked** our computers. He doesn't know how.

C Use *must (not) have* when you feel certain about something or when you believe there is only one logical conclusion.

I **must not have written** the password down. I can't find it anywhere.

You **must have received** the security email. Ms. Liu sent it to everyone.

D Use *could have, may (not) have,* or *might (not) have* when there isn't much evidence or when you are guessing.

He **may not have followed** the security advice because he didn't believe it was important.

He **might have changed** his password. I don't think he is still using his old one.

DATA FROM THE REAL WORLD

May (not) have, could (not) have, and *might (not) have* are the most common modals used for speculating about the past in speaking and writing. *Must (not) have* is less common. *Cannot/can't have* is relatively rare.

may (not) have	
could (not) have	
might (not) have	
must (not) have	
cannot/can't have	

 # Grammar Application

Exercise 4.1 Past Probability

Complete the article about credit card fraud. Use the correct form of the words in parentheses.

CREDIT CARD FRAUD: How Does It Happen?

There was a $10,000 charge from a jewelry store on Claudia's credit card statement.

She didn't buy any jewelry, so someone ___*must have stolen*___ her credit card number.
(1 must/steal)

Claudia said, "I _____ the victim of credit card theft."
(2 not/could/be)

However, someone obviously _____ her card information.
(3 must/obtain)

How _____ that _____? There are many ways a
(4)   (4 could/happen)

person _____ Claudia's credit card information. Someone
(5 might/steal)

_____ Claudia's credit card number when she used her card
(6 may/steal)

in a store or a restaurant. In addition, a thief _____ a credit card
(7 could/take)

account statement or a bill from her mailbox or her trash.

Exercise 4.2 More Past Probability

Write a response for each situation. Use the words in parentheses with modals of past probability to write guesses or logical conclusions. Sometimes more than one answer is possible.

1 Isabela can't find her wallet.

   ___*She may/might/could have lost it.*___
   (**guess:** she/lose/it)

2 There was a charge on Bo's bill that he didn't recognize.

   _____
   (**logical conclusion:** someone/steal/his credit card number)

3 Bo paid his credit card bill, even though he didn't recognize some of the charges.

_____
(logical conclusion: he / not / call / the credit card company)

4 The waiter took a long time to bring Hong's credit card back.

_____
(guess: he / copy / the card number)

5 Terry threw an unopened letter from her credit card company into the trash.

_____
(logical conclusion: she / not / think / it was important)

Exercise 4.3 Using Modals of Past Probability

Read the article about tips for avoiding identity theft. Then complete the sentences about examples of identity theft. Use the tips to write logical conclusions or guesses about what has happened. Sometimes more than one answer is possible.

HOW TO AVOID Identity Theft

Write to credit card companies. Tell them to remove your name from their mailing lists.

Check your credit card bill carefully each month. Make sure there are no incorrect charges on it.

Don't carry all of your credit cards with you.

Make scans of important documents, such as your passport, and keep the copies in a safe place in your home.

Check that emails from your bank and other businesses are authentic. Never give personal information in an email.

1 Fred gets a lot of credit card offers in the mail. He never opens them.

He must not have called the companies and asked them to remove his name from their mailing lists.

2 Sarah paid her credit card bill, but there were charges on it for things she did not buy.

_____

3 A pickpocket stole Luis's wallet while he was riding the bus. Now Luis has to cancel all of his credit cards.

_____

4 Wei went to Canada on a business trip and lost his passport. It took longer than usual for him to leave the country because he didn't know his passport number.

5 Nicole responded to an email that she thought was from her bank, and now she is missing money from her account.

5 Avoid Common Mistakes ⚠

1 Do not use *must* to talk about future probabilities.

will/may
It ~~must~~ be even more difficult to catch cyber criminals in the future.

2 Remember to use *be* + verb + *-ing* when using the progressive with modals.

be
He might ∧ working.

3 Use the correct word order when using modals of probability to talk about the past.

not
He must ∧ have ~~not~~ locked the computer because the thief was able to get his information.

Editing Task

Find and correct four mistakes in the paragraph about computer hackers.

What happens to computer hackers who decide to stop hacking? They might find that cyber crime can lead to interesting careers. For example, some companies hire a computer hacker with the hope that the former cyber criminal ~~must~~ become a brilliant *will* security consultant in the future. Although some say that these companies might
5 taking a risk by hiring these former criminals, the companies seem to believe that the risk is worth it. Adrian Lamo was breaking into computer systems for fun in high school. However, when he hacked into the *New York Times* in 2002, the newspaper must have not thought it was funny, because he was arrested. He now uses his skills for a different purpose and works as a consultant. Robert Tappan Morris might have ended his
10 chances for a good job when he created the Morris worm, a particularly bad computer virus, in 1988. However, he is now on the faculty of the famous Massachusetts Institute of Technology (MIT). Apparently, they believe that a reformed hacker must be able to stop future cyber crimes. In short, while computer hackers sometimes go to prison for their crimes, these days their career opportunities may increasing.

6 Academic Writing

Comparison and Contrast

Brainstorm > Organize > Write > Edit

In Unit 7, you wrote the first draft of your comparison-and-contrast essay. In this unit (8), you are going to review, revise, and edit your essay.

> Compare learning a language with studying math. How do you think the study of these subjects will change over time with new technology?

My Writing

Exercise 6.1 Revising Your Ideas

1 Work with a partner. Use the questions to give feedback on your partner's essay.

- Which of your partner's ideas seem strongest to you?
- Which of your partner's ideas need to be explained more clearly?
- What could your partner add or remove to make the essay stronger and easier to understand?

2 Use the feedback from your partner to revise the ideas and content of your essay.

Exercise 6.2 Editing Your Writing

Use the checklist to review and edit your essay.

Did you answer the prompt completely?	
Did you give background information and a thesis statement in your introduction?	
Did you have one body paragraph about the differences and another body paragraph about the similarities?	
Did you use examples to strengthen your arguments in the body paragraphs?	
Did you use transitions to show comparison and contrast?	
Did you summarize your main points and give your opinion in the concluding paragraph?	

Exercise 6.3 Editing Your Grammar

Use the checklist to review and edit the grammar in your essay.

Did you use *will*, *be going to*, and/or the present progressive for the future correctly?	
Did you use future time clauses correctly?	
Did you use social modals correctly?	
Did you use modals or modal-like expressions to discuss possible solutions, effects, or recommendations?	
Did you use modals of probability correctly?	
Did you avoid the common mistakes in the charts on pages 79, 95, 111, and 125?	

Exercise 6.4 Writing Your Final Draft

Apply the feedback and edits from Exercises 6.1 to 6.3 to write the final draft of your essay.

Nouns and Modifying Nouns

Attitudes Toward Nutrition

1 Grammar in the Real World

ACADEMIC WRITING

Opinion writing

A What makes a person healthy? Read the article about health habits today. Are people as healthy today as they were in the past?

B Comprehension Check Answer the questions.

1 Why does Michael Pollan argue that many modern food products are not truly food?

2 How did people stay active in the past?

3 What are some diseases related to obesity?

C Notice Look at the nouns in bold. Write **C** next to each noun that you can count and **NC** next to each noun that you can't count. Then look at the words that modify some of the nouns. Are they all adjectives? Circle the ones that are not adjectives. What part of speech are they?

1 green and brown **food**

2 heart **disease**

3 food **products**

4 the **elderly**

5 **obesity**

A HEALTH CRISIS

Obesity has become **a major problem** in the United States. According to recent National Institutes of Health studies, less than one-third of **Americans** over the age of 20 are at a healthy
5   weight. That means that two-thirds of the **adult population** is overweight, and one-third of all **adults** are obese.[1]

Modern U.S. society is partially responsible for this **alarming health trend**. Processed,
10   prepared, and packaged **food** has very little nutritional value. Michael Pollan, author of *Food Rules*, argues that **many modern food products** are not truly **food** at all. They contain a great deal of **fat** and refined[2] **sugar** but very little – or
15   no – nutrition.

One other cause of obesity is the unhealthy choices people are making in **their lifestyles**. **Exercise** used to be part of everyday **life**. It was a necessary part of a society where work depended

20   mostly on farming and physical labor.[3] Today, people often sit at a computer all day, watch hours of TV, use personal cars, and have little daily exercise.

Health experts have been studying ways to
25   reduce obesity because there is a link between obesity and other serious **diseases**, such as **diabetes**[4] and **heart disease**. **One way** is to eat more **green and brown food**, such as green **vegetables** and brown **rice** and **grains**. These
30   foods help people use calories, and they aid digestion.[5] In contrast, people who have a **diet** of mostly fast food, white sugar, white flour, and **fat** are at greater risk of obesity. **These diets** contain calories that easily become **fat** when people do
35   not use them for **energy** and exercise.

Experts recommend fewer **servings of** unhealthy food, bigger **portions of** healthy food, and a more active lifestyle.

---

[1]**obese:** extremely fat

[2]**refined:** made more pure by removing unwanted material

[3]**physical labor:** work that involves effort from the body

[4]**diabetes:** a disease in which the body cannot control the amount of sugar in the blood

[5]**digestion:** the ability of the body to create energy from food

Attitudes Toward Nutrition   **129**

2 Nouns

Grammar Presentation

| There are two types of common nouns in English: count and noncount. | COUNT NOUN
Vegetables are good for you.

NONCOUNT NOUN
Good *nutrition* is essential for good health. |

2.1 Count Nouns

Count nouns are nouns that you can count and make plural. Use a singular or plural verb with count nouns.	*This apple tastes great.* *Vegetables are very important and keep us healthy.*
Use a determiner such as *a / an*, *the*, *this*, and *his* with singular count nouns.	*Is a tomato a vegetable?* *There's an onion in the refrigerator.* *This banana doesn't taste ripe.* *His sandwich looks delicious.*
You can use a plural count noun with or without a determiner such as *a few*, *many*, *some*, *these*, and *those*.	*Some diets don't work very well.* *Diets often don't work very well.*

2.2 Irregular Plural Nouns

A Some plural nouns have irregular forms. These are the most common irregular plural nouns in academic writing.	*man – men* *woman – women* *child – children* *person – people* *foot – feet* *tooth – teeth*
B Some nouns have the same form for singular and plural.	*one fish – two fish* *one sheep – two sheep*
C Some nouns are only plural. They do not have a singular form.	*clothes* *headphones* *pants* *glasses* *jeans* *scissors*

2.3 Noncount Nouns

A Noncount nouns are nouns that cannot be counted. Use a singular verb with noncount nouns.

Here are some common categories of noncount nouns.

Abstract concepts: *health, nutrition*

Activities and sports: *dancing, exercise, swimming, tennis, yoga*

Diseases and health conditions: *arthritis, depression, diabetes, obesity*

Elements and gases: *gold, hydrogen, oxygen, silver*

Food: *beef, broccoli, cheese, rice*

Liquids: *coffee, gasoline, oil, tea*

Natural phenomena: *electricity, hail, lightning, rain, thunder*

Particles: *pepper, salt, sand, sugar*

Subjects: *economics, genetics, geology*

Areas of work: *construction, business, medicine, nursing*

Good **health** is very important.

Yoga has been my favorite activity for years.

Obesity has become a serious problem.

Oxygen is the most common element in the body by weight.

Broccoli isn't popular with my family.

Tea has many health benefits.

Hail consists of small balls of ice.

Too much **salt** isn't good for you.

I wasn't very good at **economics** in college.

She's studying **nursing**.

B You can use a noncount noun with or without a determiner. Use a determiner after you have already mentioned the noun and wish to give more information.

Cheese is one of my favorite foods, but I don't like *the* **cheese** on this pizza. It's too stringy.

C You can use *the* + certain adjectives to describe a group of people with the same characteristic or quality: *the dead, the disabled, the educated, the elderly, the living, the poor, the rich, the unemployed*. Use a plural verb.

The elderly sometimes *don't eat* well.

The poor *are* often *not able to buy* nutritious food.

The unemployed *are* especially *affected* by the poor economy.

▶▶ Noncount Nouns and Measurement Words to Make Noncount Nouns Countable: See page A5.

🌐 DATA FROM THE REAL WORLD

Some common noncount nouns in speaking and writing are:

advice	equipment	information	music	research	stuff
bread	evidence	knowledge	news	rice	traffic
cash	fun	luck	permission	safety	water
coffee	furniture	milk	progress	security	weather
damage	health	money	publicity	software	work

Grammar Application

A Complete the excerpt from a web article about nutrition. Circle the correct verbs.

A healthy diet **include /(includes)** a lot of fresh fruit and vegetables. Vegetables **is / are**
(1)   (2)
especially low in calories and high in nutrients such as vitamins and minerals. Therefore, it's a good

idea to add more fruit and vegetables to your diet if you want to improve your health.

Current nutrition guidelines **suggest / suggests** eating about four or five servings of fruit and
(3)
vegetables a day. One serving **is / are** about a half cup. Nutrition experts also **suggest / suggests**
(4)   (5)
choosing fruit and vegetables by color – dark green, yellow, red, and so on – and eating a variety

of colors each day. This is because fruit and vegetables with a lot of color often **contain / contains**
(6)
the highest amounts of nutrients. Half a cup of broccoli, for example, **has / have** 50 milligrams of
(7)
vitamin C and only about 15 calories.

Low-calorie fruit, such as tomatoes and berries, **is / are** also a good choice. A medium tomato
(8)
has / have only about 20 calories and 15 milligrams of vitamin C. Blueberries **has / have** 80
(9)   (10)
calories and 15 milligrams of vitamin C per cup. Intensely colored fruit and vegetables often

contain / contains antioxidants, chemicals that protect cells from disease. Antioxidants also
(11)
enhance / enhances the effects of vitamin C and protect the heart and your health!
(12)

B Over to You What else do you know about the benefits of fruit and vegetables?
Write five sentences about fruit and vegetables. Share your sentences with a partner.

Complete the statements about nutritional issues that affect different groups of people.
Rewrite the words in parentheses with *the* + adjective.

1 _The wealthy_ (People who are wealthy) tend to have a better diet than poor people
   do because they can easily shop for and buy whatever they need.

2 _____ (People who are poor) often do not have convenient access to fresh
   fruit and vegetables because there are few good supermarkets in poor neighborhoods.

3 There often are free food programs for _____ (people who are homeless) in
   large urban areas.

4 _____ (People who are elderly) sometimes have poor nutrition because they
   might suffer from diseases that cause a loss of appetite.

5 _____ (People who are young) are becoming less healthy in America because of too much junk food and a lack of exercise.

6 In Minneapolis and in many other parts of the country, farmers' markets are opening in areas that are easier for _____ (people who are disabled) to access.

7 _____ (People who are unemployed) in the United States can get help buying food by applying for SNAP, the government-sponsored Supplemental Nutrition Assistance Program.

8 We usually assume that _____ (people who are educated) make wise choices when they eat, but this is not always true.

Exercise 2.3 Count or Noncount Noun?

A Complete the magazine article about health. Add plural endings to the nouns in bold where necessary. If a noun does not have a plural, write **X** on the line.

Tips for a HEALTHY LIFE 🍎

Due to the worldwide epidemic of obesity, many people are concerned about their **health** _X_ . **Specialist** _____ who study how the body works have some **advice** _____ for
   (1)   (2)   (3)
you: exercise more and eat healthier food.

The Harvard School of Public Health recommends adding more exercise to your daily life. With the exception of some people who work in very active **occupation** _____
                                                                                    (4)
such as **construction** _____ or landscaping, many of us simply do not move enough
            (5)
throughout the day. **Exercise** _____ not only helps burn calories, it also lowers the risk
                       (6)
for many **illness** _____ such as **heart disease** _____ and diabetes. One way to increase
            (7)   (8)
activity is through aerobic exercise such as **swimming** _____ . Aerobic exercise increases
                                                (9)
your intake of **oxygen** _____ , which helps you burn fat faster. However, many physical
                  (10)
activities count as exercise, including **dancing** _____ and **gardening** _____ .
                                           (11)   (12)

The next step is changing our diet. Some **research** _____ shows that a plant-based
                                              (13)
diet is a good choice. People who eat less meat tend to be healthy. They do not usually eat processed food that is high in fat, sugar, and **salt** _____ . The Harvard School of Public
                                                        (14)
Health suggests that we follow a plant-based diet. They suggest eating fresh fruit and **vegetable** _____ and whole grains such as brown **rice** _____ . They also recommend
   (15)   (16)
preparing your food from fresh **ingredient** _____ .
                                   (17)

There is a lot of confusing **information** _____ about nutrition, but exercise and simple,
                               (18)
unprocessed food are all you really need to live a healthy life.

B Pair Work Make a list of the noncount nouns in A. Then work with a partner and identify which category the nouns in A are from: abstract concepts, activities and sports, diseases and health conditions, food, subjects, particles, or areas of work. Then think of one more noun for each category.

A Health *is an abstract concept.*

B *Right. And* kindness *is another abstract concept.*

3 Noncount Nouns as Count Nouns

Grammar Presentation

When we refer to noncount nouns as individual items, they can sometimes have a count meaning. They may also be made countable with measurement words describing specific quantities.

NONCOUNT NOUN
Light makes plants grow.
MEASUREMENT + COUNT NOUN
A bunch of lights were visible in the distance.

3.1 Making Noncount Nouns Countable

A Some noncount nouns can have a count meaning when we refer to individual items within a general category.	*I always put cheese on my pasta.* (general category) *English cheeses are very strong.* (individual kinds) *Food is essential to life.* (general category) *Some foods contain a lot of sugar.* (individual food items)
B Use measurement words to make noncount nouns countable. Here are common measurement words and expressions. Abstract concepts: *a bit of, a kind of, a piece of* Activities or sports: *a game of* Food: *a drop of, a grain of, a piece of, a serving of, a slice of* Liquids: *a cup of, a gallon/quart of, a glass of* Natural phenomena: *a bolt of, a drop of, a ray of* Particles: *a grain of, a pinch of* Subjects and occupations: *an area of, a branch of, a field of, a type of* Miscellaneous: *an article of* (clothing), *a bunch of* (people, objects), *a crowd of, a group of, a pack of* (wolves, dogs, wild animals), *a piece of* (furniture, equipment, news)	*Eight glasses of water are on the table.* *There is a piece of cake in the refrigerator.* *A bit of kindness goes a long way.* *I play five games of tennis a week.* *Would you like a piece of pie?* *The recipe calls for two cups of oil.* *A few drops of rain are enough to ruin a picnic.* *A pinch of salt makes food taste good.* *Two branches of medicine are cardiology and neurology.* *There were a bunch of people at the store.*

▶▶ Noncount Nouns and Measurement Words to Make Noncount Nouns Countable: See page A5.

Grammar Application

Exercise 3.1 Noncount Nouns with Count Meanings

A Complete the conversation about purchasing food through the Internet. Use the correct form of the nouns in parentheses. Sometimes more than one answer is possible.

Jake Do you have any __*experience*__ (experience) buying food online?
(1)

Emily Yes, I've bought different kinds of imported _____ (cheese), a
(2)
variety of _____ (coffee), and different sorts of _____ (tea).
(3) (4)

Jake I didn't know you liked _____ (cheese) so much.
(5)

Emily I don't. I bought all of those _____ (cheese) as gifts.
(6)

Jake Anyway, how was the shopping?

Emily I've had many good _____ (experience) with online shopping.
(7)
The prices were reasonable, and the items arrived in good condition.

Jake Did it take a long _____ (time) for the items to arrive?
(8)

Emily Not usually. Two _____ (time) they were late.
(9)

Jake Do you ever buy _____ (fruit) online?
(10)

Emily I don't think that's a good idea, but I have friends who buy _____
(11)
(fruit) like *cherimoya* and *durian* online without any problems.

Jake It's probably safe to buy _____ (coffee) and _____ (tea)
(12) (13)
online, right?

Emily Sure. I've also bought items like _____ (sugar) and
(14)
_____ (flour) online.
(15)

Jake Why would you do that?

Emily I buy hard-to-get _____ (sugar) such as *demerara* and *turbinado*
(16)
online because I can't find them in my local store.

Jake And there are special types of _____ (flour), too?
(17)

Emily Well, I have a friend who is allergic to wheat, so I get a few different gluten-free
_____ (flour) from a special diet site.
(18)

B Pair Work Compare your answers with a partner. Discuss the reasons for each of your answers.

I chose the noncount noun experience *in item 1 because the speaker is talking about an abstract concept.*

Exercise 3.2 Measurement Words with Noncount Nouns

Complete the sentences with the correct quantifier from the box. Add determiners and any other necessary words. Sometimes more than one answer is possible.

bit	cup	gallon	glass	piece	serving
can	drop	game	grain	pinch	slice

1 Let me give you _a bit of_ advice: Stop worrying about calories, and just eat food that's good for you.

2 Should we play _____ chess after dinner?

3 Please cut a very thin _____ bread for me.

4 _____ fruit is about a half a cup.

5 _____ tea has less caffeine than a cup of coffee.

6 Doctors recommend drinking 32 ounces of water a day, but it's hard to remember to drink four _____ water each day.

7 This sauce needs just _____ salt – not too much!

8 The cupboard is empty. There isn't even _____ rice left there!

9 Here's a bottle of soy sauce. Just put a tiny _____ soy sauce on the fish. We're trying to cut down on sodium.

10 The chocolate cheesecake that you baked looks absolutely delicious! Could you cut _____ for me?

11 I've brought you _____ chicken soup to help with your cold. It's not homemade, but I think it will help you feel better.

12 If you're going to the supermarket, could you pick up _____ milk? The children drink so much of it and we need a lot.

Exercise 3.3 More Measurement Words with Noncount Nouns

A Write the correct quantities of food in Luis's blog. Use the words in the box. Add any other necessary words.

1/bottle/water	~~quart/olive oil~~	2/piece/fish
1/box/pasta	2/loaf/bread	wedge/cheese

THE WANDERING GOURMET

by Luis Martinez

The highlight of my trip to San Francisco was the Ferry Plaza Farmers' Market. I spent a lot of money! My chef friend, Lisa, came with me. She made a delicious dinner from the ingredients. Here's what we bought:

1 *a quart of olive oil*

2 _____

3 _____

4 _____

5 _____

6 _____

B Pair Work Compare your answers with a partner. Then work together to think of more noncount nouns that you can use with each measurement word.

A *You can also say a quart of water.*

B *Or a quart of milk.*

4 Modifying Nouns

Grammar Presentation

Adjectives that modify nouns, including nouns acting as adjectives, follow a specific order.	*That was a **delicious green Washington** apple!* (opinion + color + origin) *I saw a **shocking government** report on nutrition.* (opinion + type)

4.1 Order of Modifiers

The order of modifiers is as follows:

Opinion/ Evaluation	Size	Age	Shape	Color	Origin	Material	Type
delicious traditional useful	large short small tall	antique new old two-year-old young	round square triangular	black green yellow	French imaginary scientific	cotton leather metal	dog government shoulder

▶▶ Order of Adjectives Before Nouns: See page A6.

4.2 Using Modifiers

A Do not use commas between two adjectives from different categories.	OPINION ORIGIN *That was a **delicious French** cake.* OPINION TYPE *It was a **disappointing medical** report.* SIZE MATERIAL *You'll need a **big metal** pan.*
B Use *and* or a comma between two adjectives of opinion.	OPINION OPINION *The food has an **interesting** and **memorable** taste.* *The food has an **interesting, memorable** taste.*
Use *and* between two colors or two materials used as adjectives.	COLOR + COLOR *She bought a **red** and **yellow** dress.* MATERIAL + MATERIAL *The **cotton** and **silk** tablecloth is new.*

Grammar Application

Complete the sentences with the adjectives in parentheses. Remember to use the correct order.

1 Wei got a ___new French glass___ (French / glass / new) coffeemaker for his 25th birthday.

2 Every other week, Mei's Kitchen will feature _____ (easy / Asian / new) recipes for you to try at home.

3 SNAP is a _____ (government / useful) food program for people who are out of work.

4 We went to the farmers' market in the city last Saturday and bought a lot of _____ (small / purple) potatoes.

5 The _____ (Thai / new) restaurant downtown has a _____ (rectangular / lovely) dining room area with _____ (red / beautiful) walls.

6 There were _____ (lovely / white) flowers in some _____ (glass / antique / tall) vases on the tables.

A On a separate sheet of paper, write five sentences about things in the picture. Use two or three adjectives in each sentence. Choose adjectives from the box, or think of your own adjectives.

antique	large	silver
beautiful	long	small
clean	metal	square
cotton	oval	tall
delicious	rectangular	white
enormous	round	wooden

There are clean white napkins in the tall clear glasses.

B Over to You Think of a party or wedding that you attended. Write five sentences to describe the decorations and the food. Use two or three adjectives in each sentence.

A Listen to a restaurant review. Complete the sentences with the missing words. Pay attention to punctuation and adjective order.

Last week, we ate at Le Bambou, an ___*elegant new*___ Vietnamese
(1)

restaurant in town. We ordered several _____
(2)

dishes. We highly recommend the _____ spring
(3)

rolls. They were a _____ appetizer, and they
(4)

were perfect for the _____ evening. The main
(5)

course was a _____ chicken dish served with
(6)

_____ vegetables.
(7)

We were especially impressed with Le Bambou's atmosphere. It has a

_____ dining room. The tables were covered
(8)

with _____ tablecloths, and they were all lit by
(9)

_____ candles in _____
(10)   (11)

holders. The walls were painted a lovely shade of blue, and the color gave the

restaurant a sense of calm. The serving dishes looked like _____
(12)

antiques. There were _____ dragons on the
(13)

plates.

All in all, Le Bambou was a _____ experience.
(14)

B Listen again and check your answers.

C Over to You Choose a restaurant that you know. Write a review of the restaurant similar to the review in A. Share your sentences with a partner.

Last month we went to the lovely, popular neighborhood restaurant called Buon Appetito …

5 Avoid Common Mistakes ⚠

1 **When a noun modifies another noun and a number comes before it, use the singular form of the noun.**

eight-year-old
An ~~eight-years-old~~ child should be able to pronounce all of the ingredients.

2 **When a noun is followed by a prepositional phrase, the verb agrees with the noun, not the object of the preposition.**

advertises
The company behind these products ~~advertise~~ to young children.

3 **Do not make noncount nouns plural.**

advice
The author has ~~advices~~ for shoppers.

4 **Remember to use the plural form of count nouns.**

vegetables
These ~~vegetable~~ taste good when they are served raw with salad dressing.

Editing Task

Find and correct seven more mistakes in the paragraphs about children's eating habits.

ten-year-old
What does a ~~ten-years-old~~ child eat in a day? Specialists in nutrition is finding out that the news is not good. As a result, they are looking for ways to improve children's eating habit. They are also involved in trying to help families make healthier choice.

5   Most experts suggest that a few key practices can help families. One of these practices are common sense: people should eat unprocessed food. When there is a choice between canned corn and fresh corn, people should choose the fresh corn. Secondly, people should read labels carefully. Because labels contain a lot of informations, people should familiarize themselves with the nutrition and calorie

10   content of their favorite products. Finally, people can boost the health content of certain kinds of food. For example, it is possible to substitute whole-grain flours for white flour in most recipes.

Parents and children live busy lives, but research shows that when a healthy child becomes a 40-years-old adult, that person can look forward to a healthy old age.

6 Academic Writing

Opinion Writing

Brainstorm > Organize > Write > Edit

In this writing cycle (Units 9-11), you are going to write an opinion essay that answers the prompt below. In this unit (9), you will analyze an essay, and then brainstorm and organize ideas about your topic.

> *Is disease prevention the responsibility of individuals and their families or of the government?*

Exercise 6.1 Preparing to Write

Work with a partner. Discuss the questions.

1 What are some significant health problems in your city or country?
2 Where do people go when they need health care?
3 How do people pay for health care today?

Exercise 6.2 Focusing on Vocabulary

Read the definitions. Complete the sentences with the correct form of the words in bold. Are the nouns count or noncount?

> **burden** (n) a duty or responsibility that is hard to bear
>
> **consultation** (n) a meeting with a doctor who is specially trained to give advice to you or other doctors about an illness
>
> **contribution** (n) money, support, or other help
>
> **labor** (n) practical work, especially work that involves physical effort
>
> **safety net** (n) something used to protect a person against possible hardship or difficulty
>
> **treatment** (n) the use of drugs, exercise, or other methods to improve the condition of a sick or injured person, or to cure a disease

1 When poor elderly people get sick, it can place a serious financial _____ on their adult children, who have to help pay for expensive medicine and treatments.

2 After six months of medical _____, the patient is cancer free.

3 It is a good idea to save some money as a(n) _____, just in case you lose your health insurance.

4 The doctor blamed my bad diet and lack of exercise when I went to her for a(n) _____ about my condition.

5 I gave a(n) _____ of $100 to an organization that gives bottles of clean water to people after natural disasters.

6 When you calculate the price of building a new hospital, you have to consider materials and the cost of _____.

Should Health Care
Be Free?

1 Who pays for health care? The answer varies from country to country. In the United States, people often receive their health insurance through their employer. In other places, health care is completely free for all citizens. There are also places where you can see a doctor only if *you* pay. Often, a patient has to choose between medium-quality, cheap care or high-quality, expensive care. Unfortunately, providing health care to an entire nation of citizens is a complicated matter. While different healthcare systems have various advantages and disadvantages, no system is perfect. However, the most important goal of a country's healthcare system should be to provide the public with basic, affordable health care.

2 There are many models of free public health care. In some countries, **consultations**, **treatment**, and medicine are free to all citizens. The government may pay for this directly, perhaps funded by the country's valuable natural resources that the government owns. Most countries collect money from citizens through taxes based on their income. Workers pay according to how much they earn, and employers also make a **contribution**. Hospitals and other medical services are then provided and run by the government. There may also be some private medical services that people can choose to buy. The advantage of systems such as these is clear: free basic health care for all, regardless of income. However, it is a very expensive system for governments, and as life expectancy and costs rise, many countries are facing either an unsustainable financial **burden**, or a drop in the quality of services and facilities provided.

3 In countries where citizens use private providers, health care is only available to patients who pay for it, and healthcare providers are commercial companies. In wealthier countries, most citizens can buy health insurance to cover their potential medical costs. However, not everyone can afford this, and some governments have programs that give financial assistance to those who need urgent medical care but cannot afford it. In other nations, there is no such **safety net**, and the poor or others who cannot pay simply do not get the health care they need. The disadvantages of this system are obvious: not only are individuals deprived of the medical attention they need, but also the lack of preventative medicine means that infectious diseases can quickly spread. One advantage, however, is that commercial organizations can sometimes provide higher-quality care than struggling government-funded ones, though it comes at a higher direct cost to the patient.

4 There are advantages to both private and public healthcare systems, and mixing these two systems might be the best option. In many countries, there is a mix of public and private funding. This system requires all citizens to have health insurance. The cost is deducted from salaries by the employer, who also makes a contribution for each worker. Citizens are able to choose either a public or private healthcare provider. In some countries, private companies are not permitted to make a profit from providing basic health care. Therefore, the mixed model provides more flexibility than either the public or private models and ensures access to health care for all. However, some people criticize this model for increasing the cost of **labor** more than in a public-only system. At the same time, most experts point out that the moral and economic cost of uninsured citizens, which is common in the private-only system, is more harmful to a country.

5 Most people would agree that no healthcare system is perfect. Both public and private healthcare systems have significant advantages and disadvantages. The challenge is to find a system that provides high-quality health care to all citizens, but which is also affordable and practical. Research suggests that a mixed system covers the most citizens at the lowest cost to the overall economy. However, changing from one system to another can be difficult. It will take strong leaders who truly have the best interests of all their citizens in mind to make progress in this area.

Read the essay on page 143. Work with a partner. Discuss the questions.

1 According to the writer, what is the main goal of a healthcare system?
2 Who pays for a public healthcare system? Who pays for a private healthcare system?
3 What system does the writer believe is the best healthcare system for people? Why?

Exercise 6.4 Noticing the Grammar and Writing

Look at the essay again, and complete the tasks.

1 Circle at least two adjectives the writer uses to describe a public healthcare system, a private healthcare system, and a mixed system.
2 Highlight the words *healthcare* and *health care* throughout the text. What is the difference?
3 Underline the topic sentences in paragraphs 2 and 3. What are the topics and main ideas?
4 Underline the first sentence in paragraph 4. What is the purpose of this sentence?

Exercise 6.5 Identifying Differences

Work with a partner. Look at paragraphs 2 and 3. Discuss the questions. Take notes on your answers.

1 What are the characteristics (costs, services, special features) of a public healthcare system?
2 What are the characteristics (costs, services, special features) of a private healthcare system?

Using T-Charts to Brainstorm and Organize Ideas

In opinion essays, writers look at several viewpoints on a topic and present their opinion on which viewpoint is better than the others. Writers often use graphic organizers called **T-charts** to examine the characteristics of two topics, and their advantages and disadvantages, or pros and cons.

Exercise 6.6 Applying the Skill

Use your notes from Exercise 6.5. Follow the steps to complete the T-chart.

1 Write the features of a public healthcare system on the left side.
2 Write the features of a private healthcare system on the right side.

Public	Private

My Writing

Work with a partner. Complete the tasks.

1 Brainstorm at least six ways to prevent illnesses.
2 If you think the ways to prevent diseases are the individual's or family's responsibility, write them in the first column of the T-chart.
3 If you think the ways to prevent diseases are the government's responsibility, write them in the second column of the T-chart.
4 Decide which side you think is more responsible for disease prevention. Explain your reasons.

Individuals	Government

Exercise 6.8 Writing an Opinion Paragraph

Write a paragraph. Use your T-chart in Exercise 6.7, and give your opinion on who is more responsible and why.

1 Choose a side to support.
2 Write a topic sentence that includes your opinion.
3 Write at least two reasons for your opinion with supporting details.
4 Write a concluding sentence.

Using Precise Nouns and Adjectives

Using precise nouns and precise adjectives will make your writing clearer. Look at the example:

Our healthcare system is expensive, so many people choose not to buy insurance.

Without a precise adjective, the reader does not know if you are referring to a *public*, *private*, or *mixed* healthcare system. Also, replace the general noun *people* with a precise noun like *adults*, *senior citizens*, or *students*.

Exercise 6.9 Applying the Skill

Review your paragraph. Add adjectives to make your nouns more precise, and replace general nouns with precise nouns.

1 Grammar in the Real World

ACADEMIC
WRITING

Opinion writing

A How does color affect your mood? Read the magazine article about the effects of color on mood. What is your favorite color? How does it affect your mood?

B Comprehension Check Answer the questions.

1 Why is it important to choose colors carefully when decorating a room?

2 What advice did the decorator give to the Wangs?

3 What are some examples of color-feeling associations?

C Notice Find the words in the article. Then circle the meaning of each set of words within the context.

1 bright orange walls
   a a group of walls in general   b specific walls

2 the orange walls
   a a group of walls in general   b specific walls

3 a sensitive person
   a one example from a category   b something in particular that was
      or group   previously mentioned in the text

4 the problem
   a one example from a category   b something in particular that was
      or group   previously mentioned in the text

Can you make a generalization about the use of *a / an*, *the*, and no article?

The **EFFECTS** of **COLOR** on **MOOD**

Research has shown that colors have **a** direct impact on our feelings. Therefore, it makes sense for people to surround themselves with colors that make them feel good. Successful decorating depends on making **the** right
5 color choices.

It is beneficial to choose colors that make people feel comfortable, happy, relaxed, energized, or whatever mood is desired. Bright orange walls in **a** bedroom, for instance, may keep **a** sensitive person awake, whereas light blue seems to
10 have **a** relaxing effect. Maya Romero of Omaha, Nebraska, suffered from chronic insomnia. **A** friend suggested that **the** orange walls in her bedroom might be contributing to **the** problem. Maya listened to her friend's advice and painted **the** walls light blue. Since then, she has had much less
15 trouble sleeping.

Color affects moods in a variety of ways. Yellow is **a** cheerful, uplifting color for **most** people. However, strong shades of yellow can be overwhelming when used for **an** entire room. Light yellow, on the other hand, can lift **a**
20 person's mood like **a** room filled with sunshine. Similarly, green can revive **the** spirit. This may be because green reminds us of nature.

Typically, people experience **the** color blue as comforting. However, it is better to avoid using too much blue in one
25 room. **A** room with blue walls and blue furniture can seem cold and overly formal. Christopher and Marie Wang of Duvall, Washington, moved into **a** new home and painted **the** walls in their living room blue. Then they filled the room with furniture of varying shades of blue. They loved it, but they noticed that
30 conversation died when they sat in **the** room with guests. They asked advice from **a** decorator to see if **the** problem was related to **the** decor. **The** decorator suggested that they replace their icy blue carpet with **a** carpet in warm colors, such as dark red or warm beige. She also recommended replacing
35 their classic-style furniture with more comfortable pieces. **The** Wangs report that, after they made **the** changes, **the** living room quickly became their favorite room for entertaining.

Clearly, **the** colors in an environment have **a** tremendous impact on **the** people who live or work there. Certain colors
40 can improve moods dramatically, while others can actually bring on feelings of sadness or loneliness. It is crucial to carefully consider color choices when decorating **a** living space or office.

2 Indefinite Article, Definite Article, and No Article

Grammar Presentation

The indefinite articles *a* and *an* and the definite article *the* come before singular count nouns. The definite article *the* can come before plural count nouns and noncount nouns.

*The color blue in **a** bedroom may relax people.*
*Choosing colors is **an** important part of decorating.*
***The** orange walls contributed to her insomnia.*

2.1 Indefinite Articles: *A/An*

A Use *a/an* before a singular count noun when the noun is part of a category or if it is a profession.	*Blue is **a** color.* *The power of color is **an** issue that many researchers study.* *Her sister is **an** interior decorator.*
B Use *a/an* to introduce a singular count noun when you first mention it.	***A** room with blue walls can seem formal.* ***An** orange bedroom can keep you awake.*
C Use *a/an* before a singular count noun to give definitions or make generalizations.	***A** decorator is a person who chooses colors and furniture for a room.* ***A** yellow room is more cheerful than a blue room.*

2.2 Definite Article: *The*

A You can use *the* before singular count nouns, plural count nouns, and noncount nouns.	*Where is **the** chair?* ***The** salespeople are very knowledgeable.* ***The** furniture in her house looks new.*
B Use *the* before a noun when you mention it a second time.	FIRST MENTION SECOND MENTION *I took **an** interesting class. **The** class was about the effects of color on people's moods.*
C Use *the* when a noun gives more information about a previously mentioned noun. The second noun is associated with the first noun.	*This is **a** good study on colors. **The** research makes some good points.* *That is **a** very interesting article. **The** information in it explains a lot about the power of color.*

2.2 | Definite Article: *The (continued)*

D Use *the* when the listener or reader can physically see or visualize the noun.	Push **the** button in front of you. Your class is in **the** room just below this one.
E Use *the* when the noun is unique.	The students are learning about **the** sun, **the** Earth, and **the** solar system.
F Use *the* before a singular noun used to represent a whole class or category. This is very formal.	**The** male robin is more colorful than the female.

2.3 | No Article

Use no article when a noncount noun or a plural count noun is used to make a generalization.	Research has taught us many things about the ways that we are affected by colors. Colors can affect our moods.

Grammar Application

Exercise 2.1 *A/An or The?*

Complete the textbook excerpt about color theory. Circle the correct articles. Sometimes more than one answer is possible.

CHAPTER 3: Color Theory

What is color theory? It is **a**/the tool and **a/the** guide for understanding colors. There are different
(1)   (2)
versions of color theory, but in **a/the** basic version, there are three primary colors. **A/The** colors
(3)   (4)
are blue, red, and yellow. As you can see by looking at **a/the**
(5)
color wheel, mixing equal parts of two primary colors produces
a secondary color. For example, if you mix blue and red, you get
purple. If you mix red and yellow, you get **a/the** color orange.
(6)

Tertiary colors are also created by mixing two primary colors.
However, to make **a/the** tertiary color, you use unequal amounts
(7)
of two colors. By doing that, you get colors like blue-green and
yellow-orange.

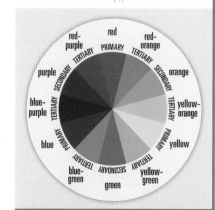

Fig. 8.1: Color Wheel

Now, look at **a/the** color wheel again. **A/The** colors that lie opposite each other on **a/the**
(8)   (9)   (10)
color wheel are called complementary colors. For example, **a/the** colors red and green are
(11)
complementary colors. So are **a/the** colors orange and blue. Look at **a/the** square below.
(12)   (13)
It contains **a/the** complementary colors red and green. Stare at it for
(14)
15 seconds, then stare at **a/the** white wall or **a/the** piece of white paper.
(15)   (16)

Did you notice that the "ghost" image (the image you see on the white
wall or paper) has the opposite colors? **A/The** green half of the square
(17)
becomes red and **a/the** red half becomes green. This is one characteristic
(18)
of complementary colors.

Exercise 2.2 *A/An, The,* or No Article?

A Listen to the web article about color harmony. Write *a/an, the,* or Ø for no article.

COLOR
Harmony

Some colors go together while some colors don't. Why?
Is there a way to understand why some colors work better
together than others? As many artists and designers know, __Ø__
(1)
color harmony is based on _____ color theory.
(2)

Let's think about _____ ways color harmony works in a room. One main rule of color
(3)
harmony is that one color must be stronger than _____ other colors in the room. In other
(4)
words, one color must be more intense than the others or cover a larger area than the others.

Another rule of color harmony is that you should not put two very intense colors next to each
other. For example, you should not have _____ bright red sofa on top of _____ bright
(5)   (6)
green rug. _____ human eye cannot focus on both colors at the same time, and _____
(7)   (8)
colors may seem to vibrate.

A third rule of color harmony is that the colors in a room should be related to each other
in some way. You can determine colors' relationships to each other by looking at _____
(9)
color wheel. Colors that are next to each other on the color wheel, such as red and red-orange,
will usually look good together. You can also put _____ complementary colors together.
(10)
These are colors that are on opposite sides of the color wheel, such as yellow and purple.
Color triads go well together, too. These are three colors that are the same distance from each
other on the color wheel. For example, _____ primary colors, red, blue, and yellow, form a
(11)
color triad. The secondary colors, green, purple, and orange, also form a color triad.

B Over to You **What is your favorite color combination? Write five sentences describing why you like this color combination and describing things that you own in these colors. Use nouns with *a/an*, *the*, and no article in your sentences. Then share your sentences with a partner.**

My favorite color combination is pink and orange. I like it because both colors are bright. I have a T-shirt with the colors pink and orange. The shirt was a gift from my sister. I also have a pair of pink and orange shoes.

3 Quantifiers

Grammar Presentation

Quantifiers are words such as *all (of)*, *some (of)*, and *a lot of* that describe an amount or number.	*All of the colors go well together.* *I have some information about colors.*

3.1 Quantifiers with Count Nouns and Noncount Nouns

A Quantifiers describe both large and small quantities or amounts. They are used with both count and noncount nouns.	**More** ↑ *all (of)* *many/a lot of* *quite a few (of)/a great deal of* *some (of)* *a few (of)/a little (of)* *few (of)/little (of)* *not a lot of/not many (of)/not much (of)* **Less** ↓ *not any (of)/none of/no*
B Use the following quantifiers only with count nouns: *quite a few (of), few, a few (of), not many (of)*	*Quite a few painters have studied at that art school.* *A few painters shared the paint.* *Few students have time for art classes.* *Not many students have found a summer job.*
C Use the following quantifiers only with noncount nouns: *a great deal of, a little, little, not much (of)*	*We have a great deal of work to do.* *I have a little information.* *She has little patience.* *There is not much time left to complete the work.*

3.1 Quantifiers with Count Nouns and Noncount Nouns (continued)

D Use *a few* to say there are some but not many.

There are always **a few** <u>students</u> who want to major in art.

Use *few* for a very small number.

There are **few** <u>scholarships</u> for international students.

E Use *a little* and *little* with noncount nouns.

Use *a little* to say there is some but not much.

I have **a little** money, so I can pay for it.

Use *little* for a very small amount.

I have **little** money. I don't have enough money.

3.2 Quantifiers That Are Used with Count Nouns and Noncount Nouns

The following quantifiers can be used with both count and noncount nouns:

Count Nouns	Noncount Nouns
All of the <u>students</u> in my class work hard.	I gave him **all of** the <u>money</u>.
She used **a lot of** <u>colors</u> in her painting.	I don't have **a lot of** <u>time</u> today to study.
Most of the <u>answers</u> are clear.	I knew how to use **most of** the <u>software</u>.
Some of the <u>students</u> don't know a lot about art.	I painted **some of** the <u>time</u> while I was on vacation.
I didn't take **a lot of** <u>notes</u> in class.	He didn't have **a lot of** <u>help</u> on the project.
We don't have **any** <u>solutions</u>.	They did**n't** put **any** <u>effort</u> into the job.
None of the <u>students</u> is absent.	**None of** the <u>work</u> is good.
There are **no** <u>excuses</u> for poor work.	That room has **no** <u>sunshine</u>.

3.3 Quantifiers and *Of*

A Use a quantifier without *of* when a noun is used in an indefinite or general sense.

Some students are late.

I was interested in **a few** art classes.

B Use a quantifier with *of* when the noun is specific and known to both the speaker and listener. Use *of* before a determiner such as *the, my, your, his, her, our, their, these,* or *those.*

Some of <u>the</u> students at my school are very smart.

A few of <u>the</u> activities in class require artistic ability.

C The quantifiers *a great deal of, a lot of,* and *none of* always include *of*.

A lot of people are interested in art.

NOT <s>A lot</s> people are interested in art.

Grammar Application

A Complete the article about color blindness. Circle the correct quantifiers.

COLOR BLINDNESS

Color blindness is a condition in which a person cannot see the difference between certain colors. **All of /(Many)** people think that color-blind people see **no / none** colors at all and only see black and
(1)   (2)
white. However, complete color blindness is very rare. **Not much / Not many** people are completely
(3)
color blind. However, **many / much** people do have some degree of color blindness. A large number
(4)
of the men in the world are color blind. Very **few / little** women, however, are color blind.
(5)

A great deal of / Quite a few people who suffer from weak color vision have red-green color
(6)
blindness. They cannot tell the difference between red and green. Think about the color purple. It is
made up of two colors: red and blue. If you have **a little / a few** red color blindness, and you look at a
(7)
bright purple flower, you may be able to see **a little / a few** red, but the flower will look almost blue.
(8)
If you have a more serious case of red color blindness, the flower may look completely blue to you.

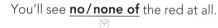

You'll see **no / none of** the red at all.
(9)
So why are some people color blind? We have red, blue, and
green cones in our eyes. You need to have **all / little** of the types
(10)
in order to see colors correctly. If you don't have **all / much** of the
(11)
types of cones, or if **few / some** of them are not working right, you
(12)
may see a red flower as green or a green vegetable as brown.

Look at this image. It is an Ishihara plate. Ishihara plates are
made up of different-colored dots. Do you see a number within
the circle? If not, you may have weak red-green color vision.

B Pair Work Work with a partner. Think about some activities (getting dressed, driving,
watching TV, reading, using a computer) that people with color blindness might have
trouble with. Write four sentences. Use different quantifiers in each sentence.

Many people with color blindness will have difficulty matching their socks.

A Complete the report about car sales. Use the quantifiers in the box and the chart below. Use each quantifier only once. Sometimes more than one answer is possible.

a great deal of	little	many of	no
few	many	most	quite a few

Anderson Auto Sales
Percentage of Sales by Color 2017 & 2018

	White	Silver	Black	Gray	Red	Blue	Brown	Green	Yellow	Other
% of Total Sales 2018	23	19	14	15	3	7	9	5	1	3
% of Total Sales 2017	19	32	12	9	12	9	2	0	2	3

1 In 2018, there was ___little___ demand for yellow cars.

2 In 2017, they had _____ success in selling green cars.

3 When Anderson Auto Sales created sales projections for 2019, they probably did not plan to sell _____ yellow cars.

4 _____ the cars sold in 2017 were white, silver, or black.

5 _____ of the cars sold in 2018 were white, silver, or black.

6 Compared to 2017, _____ the cars sold in 2018 were gray.

7 Compared to 2017, _____ customers favored red cars in 2018.

8 Compared to 2017, _____ customers bought brown cars in 2018.

B Rewrite five sentences from A using different quantifiers.

In 2018, there wasn't much demand for yellow cars.

1 _____

2 _____

3 _____

4 _____

5 _____

C Over to You Do Internet research to find out the most popular car colors this year or last year. Discuss your findings with a partner.

Exercise 3.3 Using Quantifiers with *Of*

Listen to the interview with the students about changes to their school. Complete the sentences with *of* or ✗ when *of* is not used.

CHANGES AT BAY CITY UNIVERSITY

Mark Recently, our university hired some __✗__ interior designers and color experts
(1)
to redesign the interior of the library at Bay City University. I asked a group of
students at the college what they thought about this. Here's what they said:

Josh Some __of__ my friends don't like it. They think the colors are too bright.
(2)
Some _____ people don't like to study at the library because the bright colors
(3)
make them uncomfortable.

Amy All _____ my friends love the new colors, but we know that some _____ people
(4)   (5)
don't like the color choices. You can never please all of the people when you
make a change, though.

Lynn A few _____ the people I know think it's great! They like being surrounded by
(6)
a lot _____ bright colors. I think a few _____ students would probably prefer to
(7)   (8)
have softer colors in the library, though.

Paulo None _____ my friends study in the library anymore. All _____ them study in
(9)   (10)
the dorms because they don't like the colors in the library. But I like the new
design. There were no _____ students studying on the first floor of the library
(11)
this morning, so I had the whole place to myself.

Exercise 3.4 More Quantifiers

A Over to You Interview some of your classmates. Have each student answer this question: *If you could make your room one color, which color would you choose and why?* Write the answers in the chart. Then write sentences about your classmates using quantifiers.

Name	Male (M) or Female (F)	Color
David	M	blue
Maria	F	beige (light brown)

Few of the male students chose blue. A lot of the female students chose beige.

B Group Work Share your sentences in a small group. What are the most popular colors for the women in your class? What are the most popular colors for the men in your class?

4 Avoid Common Mistakes ⚠

1 **Do not use *much* with plural nouns.**

                  many
We interviewed ~~much~~ interesting candidates, and we ended up hiring Ms. Stevens.

2 **Use an article before a singular occupation.**

      an
I am ⋀ assistant researcher.

3 **Write *a lot* as two words.**

        a lot
I have ~~alot~~ of friends.

Editing Task

Find and correct six more mistakes in this paragraph about color and memory.

Color and Memory

According to recent research, natural colors can help people remember things better. Felix A. Wichmann,ᵃ research scientist, and two of his colleagues conducted experiments on color and memory. In the first experiment, participants looked at 48 photographs of nature scenes. None of the photographs were of people. Half of the
5 photos were in black and white, and half were in color. Afterward, they looked at the same 48 photos mixed up with alot of new photos. They had to say which ones they had already seen. They remembered the color scenes much better than the black-and-white ones. None of the participants were sure about all of the photos. Another experiment involved much artificially colored photos. When artificially colored photos
10 were included in the set of 48 photos, participants forgot much of the photos. They did not remember the artificially colored photos any better than they remembered the black-and-white photos. These findings suggest that it is not just any colors that help to create alot of our memories. Only natural colors have that power.

Why is this research important? For one thing, advertiser may find these
15 results interesting. If advertiser uses natural colors in ads, consumers may be able to remember them better.

5 Academic Writing

Opinion Writing

Brainstorm > Organize > Write > Edit

In Unit 9, you analyzed an opinion essay and then used a T-chart to brainstorm and organize ideas for the prompt below. In this unit (10), you are going to learn ways to write stronger body paragraphs for your essay.

> Is disease prevention the responsibility of individuals and their families or of the government?

Using Transitions to Show Opposing Ideas

When you present an opinion, you often need to mention opposing ideas. You can introduce opposing views by joining sentences or clauses with certain phrases that show that there is a difference of opinion. Look at the following examples.

Many people believe that you are born with artistic ability. Other people claim artistic ability is developed.

⬇

Many people believe that you are born with artistic ability, **but** *other people claim artistic ability is developed.*

Many people believe that you are born with artistic ability. **However,** *other people claim artistic ability is developed.*

Despite / In spite of *the popular idea that you are born with artistic ability, some studies show that artistic ability is developed.*

Exercise 5.1 Applying the Skill

Join each pair of sentences. Write one sentence using the transition phrase in parentheses to show a difference of opinion.

1 Many people prefer bright colors. Other people feel they are not relaxing. (however)

_____

_____

2 Research indicates that color choice affects our mood. Some people say that they never notice room color. (but)

_____

_____

3 Color theory states that certain colors go together. Some artists create works with little thought of color combinations. (despite)

_____

_____

Adding Sentence Variety

Your writing will be stronger and more interesting if you vary the types of sentences that you use. To do this, you can combine longer, more complex sentences with shorter, more straightforward ones. Notice the difference between A and B.

A Many students do not like to study in our library. Our library has brightly colored walls. This is a problem. Bright colors may make people feel more excited. Students do not want to feel excited.

B Many students do not like to study in our library **because** the walls are brightly colored. This is a problem **because** bright colors make people feel excited. **However**, students want to feel calm and comfortable when they study.

Here are five techniques for adding sentence variety.

1 Vary the length of sentences in a text.

2 Use conjunctions to make compound sentences.

3 Begin sentences with prepositional phrases.

4 Use dependent clauses, like time clauses, to combine ideas and information.

5 Use transitions.

Exercise 5.2 Understanding the Skill

Work with a partner. Compare the two paragraphs. How did the writer add variety in the second paragraph?

(1)Color harmony is very important in interior design. People need to think about their color choices. One color should always be stronger than the other colors in a room. The strong color can be a focal point. Many living rooms are beige or white. In a beige room, you should add a bright color. You can have a bright chair or a bright rug. You should not have a bright chair and a bright rug in a brightly painted room. The room may seem too vibrant. Vibrant rooms are not very relaxing. You should have vibrant colors in bedrooms.

(2)Due to the importance of color harmony, people need to think about their color choices when they design a room. One color should always be stronger than other colors in order to make it a focal point. Although many living rooms are beige or white, you can still add a bright color with a chair or rug. However, when you have a bright chair or rug in a brightly painted room, the room may seem too vibrant. Vibrant rooms are not very relaxing, so avoid using them in bedrooms.

Follow the instructions to write sentences with the words provided. The first one is done for you.

1 Write two sentences: a longer one, and then a shorter one.

People / should / pay attention / their color choices/ in their bedrooms / bedrooms / should have / soft /colors/ better sleep

People should pay attention to their color choices in their bedrooms. Bedrooms should have soft colors for better sleep.

2 Write a sentence that includes a dependent clause.

Even though / my / kitchen / bright / I / feel / need /a color update.

_____

_____

3 Write a sentence that contains a relative clause.

The research / color theory / about / color / affect / mood / really interesting.

_____

_____

4 Write two sentences: a shorter one, and then a longer one.

Many people / suffer from / colorblindness / they / be / often / diagnose / red-green color blindness

_____

_____

My Writing

Work in a small group. Complete the tasks.

1 Review your paragraphs from My Writing in Unit 9. Who believes disease prevention is the responsibility of individuals and their families? Who feels disease prevention is the responsibility of the government?

2 Create a T-chart of the reasons your group members believe disease prevention is the responsibility of individual and their families or of the government.

3 Brainstorm with your group. Add at least two more reasons to each side.

4 Write down any ideas that you might use when you write your essay.

Structuring Opinion Essays

Opinion essays follow different models. They can present only reasons that support the writer's opinion in each body paragraph, without identifying what the opposing side may think. Or, they can present ideas held by the opposing side in the first body paragraph, and then focus the next paragraphs on the writer's opinion. In this opinion essay, you will use the second model.

Exercise 5.5 Applying the Skill

Write three body paragraphs for your opinion essay. Use your work from My Writing in Unit 9 and from Exercise 5.4 on page 160.

1 In the first body paragraph, write about an opposing opinion.
2 In the second body paragraph, present your opinion, and a reason with examples that support it.
3 In the third body paragraph, write about a different reason with examples that support your opinion.

Using Quantifiers and Pronouns to Hedge

In academic writing it is rare to use absolute quantifiers (*all*, *none of*, *not any*) or all-inclusive pronouns (*everybody*, *everyone*, *nobody*, *no one*) in academic writing. It is better to use indefinite quantifiers like *many*, *some*, *a few*, and *not much* to hedge, which means to indicate that the information is less certain because it might not be true in all cases.

Exercise 5.6 Applying the Skill

Work with a partner. Which sentences are more likely to be used in academic writing? Explain your answers.

1 All people feel the effects of color without knowing it.
2 Many people feel the effects of color without knowing it.
3 The majority of Americans support a public healthcare option.
4 No wealthy American wants to pay higher taxes for public health care.

Exercise 5.7 Editing Your Writing

Use the editing tips to improve your paragraphs.
- Use sentence variety.
- Use transitions to introduce opposing ideas
- Use quantifiers and pronouns to hedge.
- Avoid the common mistakes in the chart on page 156.

11 Pronouns

Unusual Work Environments

1 Grammar in the Real World

ACADEMIC
WRITING

Opinion writing

A What are the characteristics of a good workplace? Read the article about a unique workplace. How is this workplace unique?

B Comprehension Check **Answer the questions.**

1 What are some of the perks that SAS gives its employees?

2 What are some reasons SAS gives its employees these perks?

3 What does the voluntary turnover rate at SAS seem to show?

C Notice **Find the sentences in the article. What nouns do the words in bold refer to?**

1 Imagine **yourself** living the good life and working at the same time.

2 **Another** is a free health care facility.

3 These innovations also encourage employees to interact with **each other**.

THE COMPANY YOU KEEP

Imagine **yourself** living the good life[1] and working at the same time. Employees of SAS do that every day. The SAS Institute is a software development firm[2] in North
5 Carolina. For over twenty years, it has been on *Fortune* magazine's list of "Best 100 Companies to Work for in America."

In the late 1980s, SAS started giving its employees free candy. The perks[3] grew
10 from there. There is now a long list of on-site services at SAS. These include a fitness center, massage therapy, dry cleaning, and a beauty salon. **Anyone** can walk on the nature trails outside the offices at SAS and enjoy
15 gourmet food in the cafeteria. The perks reduce distractions so **everyone** can focus on work. These innovations[4] also encourage employees to interact with **each other**.

The company benefits[5] are impressive
20 as well. One benefit is a company child-care center. **Another** is a free health care facility. For employees and their families, there is also counseling and support for issues such as parenting, financial planning, and
25 stress management.

With a voluntary turnover rate[6] of only 2 percent, most employees seem satisfied with their jobs and are not considering leaving. This appears to show that the perks
30 and benefits are a success. While not all companies go to such extremes to keep their employees happy, it is clear that this strategy works well for SAS.

[1]**the good life:** a happy and contented life without financial problems

[2]**firm:** a company

[3]**perk:** a special, extra service that companies offer their employees, such as free or low-cost health club memberships

[4]**innovation:** something new or different

[5]**benefit:** a helpful service given to employees in addition to pay

[6]**turnover rate:** the percent of workers who leave a company

2 Reflexive Pronouns

Grammar Presentation

Reflexive pronouns are used to talk about actions when the subject and object of a sentence are the same person or people. They are often used for emphasis to say that the action is performed by that person and nobody else.

We should enjoy ourselves at work.
Sue herself determines how she is evaluated.
(Sue determines this, not someone else.)

2.1 Forming Reflexive Pronouns

There is a reflexive pronoun for each subject pronoun.	I you he she it	**myself** **yourself** **himself** **herself** **itself**	we you (plural) they	**ourselves** **yourselves** **themselves**

2.2 Using Reflexive Pronouns as Objects

A Use a reflexive pronoun when the subject and object of a sentence are the same.

SUBJECT   OBJECT
*They can get **themselves** treats during the workday.*

SUBJECT   OBJECT
*We introduced **ourselves** to the new staff.*

B Use a reflexive pronoun after an imperative in which you are directly addressing the reader or listener. The implied subject of the sentence is *you.*

*Imagine **yourself** living the good life and working at the same time.*
*Give **yourselves** a day off!*
*Ask **yourself** if this company is right for you.*

C Reflexive pronouns are often used with the following verbs:

be hard on
be proud of
believe in
blame
enjoy
feel good about
help
hurt
look at
push
remind
see
take care of
tell

*She was always hard on **herself**.*
*He was very proud of **himself** and his grades.*
*You have to believe in **yourself**. You can do it.*
*They blamed **themselves** for what happened.*
*We really enjoyed **ourselves** at the conference.*
*Eating well helps you feel good about **yourself**.*
*Please help **yourselves** to some food.*
*I hurt **myself** carrying those heavy boxes.*
*Look at **yourself** in the mirror.*
*She should push **herself** to work harder.*
*He reminded **himself** to get to work early.*
*The company saw **itself** as an innovator.*
*Take care of **yourself**. You're working too hard.*
*I tell **myself** that I am good at what I do.*

2.2 Using Reflexive Pronouns as Objects *(continued)*

D Use an object pronoun, not a reflexive pronoun, after prepositions when the meaning is clear without a reflexive pronoun. If the meaning isn't clear, use a reflexive pronoun.	*They took the candy home with* them. (They couldn't take the candy home with someone else.) *I'm very proud of* myself. (I could be proud of someone else.)

▶▶ Verbs That Can Be Used Reflexively: See page A6.

2.3 Other Uses of Reflexive Pronouns

A You can put the reflexive pronoun directly after a noun or pronoun for greater emphasis or at the end of the clause for less emphasis.	*The manager* **herself** *gave us candy.* (more emphatic) *I interviewed the candidates* **myself**. (less emphatic)
B Use *by* + a reflexive pronoun to mean *alone* or *without help.*	*I can work* by **myself**, *or I can work on a team.* *John completed the whole project* by **himself**.

⌨ Grammar Application

Exercise 2.1 Reflexive Pronouns

A Complete the statements about conditions at different companies. Circle the correct reflexive pronouns.

1 When the CEO and the head of Human Resources saw **himself/(themselves)** in the "100 Best Companies" article, they were surprised.

2 A pet cannot take care of **itself/ourselves** while its owner is on a business trip, so JM Corporation offers free pet care to its employees.

3 My company lets us take special days off, so I gave **itself/myself** a day off from work on my birthday.

4 The president helped to make the company a good place to work, so he was very proud of **herself/himself** when JM Corporation got the "100 Best Companies" award.

5 Susan and I own our company, so we can give **themselves/ourselves** a vacation anytime.

6 Before you go to your interview, you should ask **myself/yourself** why you want to work at JM Corporation.

7 Our new CEO introduced **ourselves/himself** to us at a meeting this morning.

8 Our manager said, "You and your team should congratulate **yourself/yourselves**. You all did a great job on the last project!"

B Over to You Answer the questions with information that is true for you.
Use reflexive pronouns.

- How do you take care of yourself?

- What should people tell themselves before a job interview?

- Think about a time when a friend or family member felt good about himself or herself.
  What happened?

Exercise 2.2 Reflexive Pronouns as Objects

Complete the excerpt from the Careers page of a company website. Write the correct
reflexive or object pronoun.

⌂   💬 ↻ ☰ ✉

⦚⦚⦚Work at JM CORPORATION!⦚⦚⦚

Imagine _____*yourself*_____ working at JM Corporation! Read these comments from our
(1)
happy employees and their families:

Jane Recognition makes JM a great place to work. If we challenge

_____ and take on special projects, we get rewarded. Also, I
(2)

can give _____ a day off whenever I want.
(3)

Manuel We love the benefits, such as child care. My wife couldn't imagine

_____ leaving the twins all day while she worked. Now, she
(4)

takes the twins to work with _____ every day.
(5)

Lisa The work-life balance is great here. At JM Corporation, I never take my

work home with _____ . For example, I can get everything
(6)

done by Friday and enjoy _____ on the weekends. Just ask
(7)

_____ : If you could have all this and a great salary, wouldn't you
(8)

want to work here, too?

Exercise 2.3 Other Uses of Reflexive Pronouns

A Complete the sentences with reflexive pronouns. Use the information in parentheses
to help you.

1 Bianca is a highly valued employee. She is able to handle difficult management crises
   _____*by herself*_____ (alone).

2 Bianca _____ (emphasis) always takes responsibility for any problems
   on a project.

3 I _____ (emphasis) think she would be a good candidate for promotion.

4 Robert is on Bianca's team, but he prefers to work _____ (alone).

5 Only Robert _____ (emphasis) can learn to become a better team player.

6 Two other team members would also rather work _____ (alone).

7 Bianca recognized this issue and suggested team-building training
_____ (emphasis).

8 Only the employees _____ (emphasis) can fix this problem, in my opinion.

B Group Work **Ask and answer the questions with your group members. Use reflexive pronouns. Then share your group's answers with the class.**

■ What kind of company do you imagine yourself working at someday?

■ What kind of job do you see yourself doing someday?

■ What kind of work tasks can you do by yourself?

Paulo imagines himself working at a big international company someday. He sees himself being the manager of a large group. He doesn't want to work by himself.

3 Pronouns with *Other/Another*

Grammar Presentation

Another, others, the other, and *the others* are pronouns that refer back to a noun. *Each other* and *one another* are reciprocal pronouns. They are used when two or more people do the same thing.	*Some employees are happy, but **others** are not.* *The fitness center is one benefit. **Another** is the dry-cleaning service.* *Employees help **each other**.*

3.1 Pronouns: *The Other, the Others, Others, Another*

A Use *the other* to describe the remaining member of a pair. Use *another* to describe an additional member of a group. It means *one more.*	*I have two favorite sports. One is swimming. **The other** is tennis.* (There are only two sports.) *Swimming is one of my favorite sports. **Another** is tennis.* (There are more than two sports.)
Use third-person singular verb forms with *the other* and *another.*	*One of my children goes to college and **the other** works.*

3.1 Pronouns: *The Other, the Others, Others, Another (continued)*

B Use *the others* for two or more remaining members of a specific group. Use plural verb forms with *the others*.

One of my children is in high school. The others <u>are</u> in college. (I have at least three children: the one in high school and at least two in college.)

C Use *others* (without *the*) for additional members of a group or to contrast these members with previous ones. Use plural verb forms with *others*.

Some people without jobs look for work every day. Others <u>look</u> once a week. (Two contrasting groups of people.)

3.2 Reciprocal Pronouns: *Each Other, One Another*

A *Each other* and *one another* are reciprocal pronouns. Use them when two or more people or groups do the same thing. There is no difference in meaning.

Each other is more common and more informal than *one another*.

The teacher and the student respect each other.

The teacher and the student respect one another. (The teacher respects the student. The student respects the teacher.)

The five employees in my company help each other.

The five employees in my company help one another. (Each employee helps the other four employees.)

🌐 DATA FROM THE REAL WORLD

Each other is more common than *one another* in conversation and academic writing. *One another* is slightly more common in academic writing than in conversation.

	Conversation	Academic Writing
Each other		
One another		

Reciprocal pronouns are less frequently used than personal pronouns (*I, you,* etc.).

Grammar Application

Exercise 3.1 *The Other, the Others, Others, or Another?*

A Complete the article about the benefits at two companies. Circle the correct words.

Vacation time is often a key benefit that attracts people to a company.

The others are / Another is child care. Although many companies today are cutting
     (1)

these types of benefits, **others are / the other is** still providing them.
          (2)

Two California companies offer great benefits for their workers. One is Amgen.

Others are/The other is Google. One of the benefits employees at Amgen enjoy is 17 paid
(3)
days off and three weeks of paid vacation each year. **The others is/Another is** the cafeteria.
(4)
Many companies have on-site cafeterias, but **the others don't/the other doesn't** tend to
(5)
offer take-out breakfasts and lunches like Amgen does.

Free food is one of the perks that Google employees really love, and rightly so.

Another includes/Others include four gyms, free laundry machines, and on-site doctors.
(6)
Google also provides new parents with vouchers for take-out meals for three months so they
don't have to cook when they get home.

Some employees appreciate the free food and laundry services at companies like Google.

Others are/The other is looking for long, paid vacations. When you are looking for a job,
(7)
be sure to consider the benefits offered by the company, and not just the salary.

B Over to You What benefits do you look for in a job? On a separate sheet of paper,
complete the sentences. Then share your sentences with a partner.

There are two major benefits that I look for in a job. One benefit is

_____ . The other is _____ . There are

other benefits that I think would be nice. One is _____ .

Others are _____ and _____ .

There are two major benefits that I look for in a job. One benefit is health insurance.
The other is paid vacation days. There are other benefits that I think would be nice.
One is help with child-care costs. Others are flexible hours and a gym.

Exercise 3.2 *The Other, the Others, Others, or Another?*

Complete the information from a company website. Use *the other, another, each other,* or
one another. Sometimes more than one answer is possible.

Do you want your employees to respect ____*each other/one another*____ ?
(1)
TeamBuilders has several programs to help you and your staff trust _____ more and
(2)
work more productively together.

Read some of our reviews from our customers:

JM Corporation: My staff participated in five TeamBuilders activities, and we really enjoyed

them. One great activity was the Blindfold activity. _____ was the
(3)

"Say It Out Loud!" activity. With these activities, all 12 people on my team learned how to communicate with _____ . Thanks, TeamBuilders, for giving us the tools we need to
(4)
help _____ get the job done!
(5)

Big Buy Stores: Our company did a couple of TeamBuilders activities. Even though we'd only planned to do one activity called "Build-It," we had so much fun that we decided to do _____ . We enjoyed both activities, but we preferred "Build-It"
(6)
to _____ activity.
(7)

4 Indefinite Pronouns

Grammar Presentation

| Indefinite pronouns (such as *everything, someone, anywhere, nobody*) are used when the noun is unknown or not important. | *The new boss wants to talk to everybody.*
Someone is moving into our office. |

4.1 Using Indefinite Pronouns

A Use *everybody, everyone, everything,* and *everywhere* to describe all members or things in a group. Use *everybody* or *everyone* for people. Use *everything* for things. Use *everywhere* for places.	*Everybody loves working here.* *Is everyone ready?* *He knows everything about this company.* *It seems you've looked everywhere for a job.*
B Use *somebody, someone, something,* and *somewhere* to refer to an unnamed person, place, or thing. Use indefinite pronouns with *some-* in questions to offer things or ask for things.	*Somebody is going to review our work today.* *Can I ask you something?* *I'd like to work somewhere really interesting.* *Would you like something to drink?*
C Use *anybody, anyone, anything,* and *anywhere* to refer to an unnamed person, place, or thing. Use indefinite pronouns with *any-* to ask questions and in negative sentences.	*"Can anybody receive financial help here?"* *"Sure. Anyone can ask for help."* *Do you need anything from the cafeteria?* *You can't take anything from this shelf.* *Have they advertised the product anywhere?* *I didn't go anywhere last night.*

4.1 Using Indefinite Pronouns (continued)

D Use *nobody, no one, nothing,* and *nowhere* to mean *none* or *not one* in affirmative statements.	*No one likes this company.* (= not one person) *She said nothing important in the meeting.* (= not one thing) *There is nowhere I'd rather work.* (= not one other place)

Grammar Application

Exercise 4.1 Indefinite Pronouns

Complete the interview between a career site and Ahn Nguyen, a corporate concierge for JM Corporation. Circle the correct indefinite pronouns.

INTERVIEW WITH A CORPORATE CONCIERGE

Interviewer First of all, what is a corporate concierge?

Ahn We're a lot like a hotel concierge, but instead of taking care of guests, we take care of employees. **(Everybody)/ Somebody** needs a little extra help sometimes,
(1)
especially people with high-pressure jobs.

Interviewer This is true **somewhere / everywhere**, not just at JM Corporation.
(2)

Ahn That's right. At JM, we're doing **something / anything** about it.
(3)
Somebody / Everyone at JM Corporation works very hard, and many travel a lot
(4)
for business. They can't take care of **something / everything** that they have to
(5)
do. I'm here to help.

Interviewer Can you give me some examples?

Ahn Sure. Imagine that **somebody / everyone** needs a suit cleaned for a business
(6)
trip. I'll take the suit to the dry cleaner and get it back in time for the trip.

Or **everyone / someone** might need a gift for a family member. I'll find
(7)
someone / something nice and have it wrapped and sent to the family member.
(8)

Interviewer Do you do **anything / nothing** else?
(9)

Ahn Sure. Let's say an employee wants to take a corporate guest

somewhere / everywhere nice for dinner. I'll recommend a restaurant and make
(10)
the reservations.

Interviewer Sounds like a fun job. Thanks very much for telling us a little bit about what the corporate concierge at JM Corporation does.

A Complete the conversation about vacations. Use *anyone*, *anything*, *anywhere*, *no one*, *nothing*, or *nowhere*.

Jane   Are you going _____*anywhere*_____ for your vacation this summer?
(1)

Adam   No, we aren't doing _____ . We're too busy at this time of year.
(2)

_____ takes a vacation in the summer at my company.
(3)

Jane   Wow! Does _____ complain about that?
(4)

Adam   No. _____ complains because we get three weeks' paid vacation each
(5)

year. It's just that _____ can take it in the summer.
(6)

Jane   Well, I wouldn't say _____ negative about that, either!
(7)

Adam   What about you? Are you going _____ ?
(8)

Jane   Well, _____ important happens at my company in the summer, so my
(9)

family is planning a two-week trip to the mountains. We went there last summer, too.

It's very beautiful and peaceful. There's _____ I'd rather be this summer
(10)

than in those mountains with my family.

Adam   Sounds great!

B Listen to a continuation of the conversation in A. Then answer the questions.

1 On average, how many paid vacation days do people in these places get?

European Union: _____*25–30 days*_____
Mexico: _____
The United States: _____
South Korea: _____
Japan: _____

2 Where do people get the most paid vacation time? _____

3 Where do people get the least paid time off? _____

C Pair Work Ask and answer the questions with a partner.

■ Are you going anywhere for vacation this summer?

■ Did you go anywhere last summer? If so, where did you go?

■ Are you doing anything special during your time off this year?

■ Does everyone in your family take off work at the same time for vacation?

5 Avoid Common Mistakes

1 **Use the plural pronoun *others* when talking about two or more people or things.**

others
Some managers value discipline; ~~other~~ believe in praise for good work.

2 **Use the object pronoun to form the reflexive pronouns *himself, itself,* and *themselves.***

themselves
Valuable employees can solve problems ~~theirselves~~.

3 **Indefinite pronouns with *any-, every-,* and *no-* (such as *anyone, everyone,* and *no one*) take singular verb forms.**

gets
Everyone in the company ~~get~~ a performance review once a year.

Editing Task

Find and correct six more mistakes in the paragraphs about management styles.

Management styles can vary widely. At one end of the extreme are the authoritarian managers who make all the decisions and are very strict. At the opposite
others
end, there are ~~other~~ who permit their employees to solve problems and suggest ideas theirselves. Permissive managers are most effective when innovation and
5 problem solving are part of the work process, for example, in technology. Stricter ones are effective when people are inexperienced or need a lot of guidance, or where there is high turnover of staff.

Mr. Jones is an example of an authoritarian manager. He relies only on hisself to make decisions at the restaurant where he works. Everyone are expected to follow
10 his orders exactly. His style works because employees are constantly changing, so nobody need to understand the rules and regulations.

Ms. Taylor is more democratic. The agents at her real estate agency manage their client accounts theirselves. Some of her agents focus on business while other work with private real estate accounts. It would be impossible for her to know
15 what each agent is doing at any given time, so Ms. Taylor's style works well for her company.

There are different kinds of management styles ranging from very controlling to very open. Effective managers have a style of managing that is appropriate to the needs of their companies.

6 Academic Writing

Opinion Writing

Brainstorm > Organize > Write > Edit

In Unit 10, you learned ways to organize your ideas and make your writing more interesting and cohesive. In this unit (11), you are going to write, revise, and edit your essay.

> Is disease prevention the responsibility of individuals and their families or of the government?

My Writing

Exercise 6.1 Planning Your Essay

Use your notes and My Writing paragraphs from Units 9 and 10 to complete the tasks.

	A	B
Body paragraph 1		
Body paragraph 2		
Body paragraph 3		
Thesis statement		

1 Write the main idea or topic sentence of each paragraph in column A.
2 Review the supporting details and examples for each paragraph. Write ways to improve them in column B.
3 Write the thesis statement for your essay in the last row of the table.

Exercise 6.2 Completing Your First Draft

Complete the first draft of your opinion essay. Include an introductory paragraph with a hook, background information, and thesis statement. Revise your three body paragraphs from Unit 10 as necessary. Write a concluding paragraph with a final thought, recommendation, or prediction.

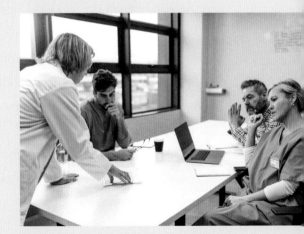

Exercise 6.3 Revising Your Ideas

1 Work with a partner. Use the questions to give feedback on your partner's essay.
   - Which of your partner's ideas seem strongest to you?
   - Which of your partner's ideas need to be explained more clearly?
   - What could your partner add or remove to make the essay stronger and easier to understand?

2 Use the feedback from your partner to revise the ideas and content of your essay.

Exercise 6.4 Editing Your Writing

Use the checklist to review and edit your essay.

Did you answer the writing prompt completely?	
Did you structure your opinion essay correctly?	
Did you write an effective thesis statement with a clear view?	
Do the topic sentences of your body paragraphs connect to your thesis statement?	
Did you present an opposing view in the first body paragraph?	
Did you use transitions when you mentioned the opposing view?	
Did you include details and examples to support your view in the second and third body paragraphs?	
Did you use sentence variety to make your writing stronger and more interesting?	

Exercise 6.5 Editing Your Grammar

Use the checklist to review and edit the grammar in your essay.

Did you use nouns and modifying nouns correctly?	
Did you use precise nouns and adjectives to make your writing clear?	
Did you use articles and quantifiers correctly?	
Did you use quantifiers and pronouns to hedge?	
Did you avoid the common mistakes in the charts on pages 141, 157, and 173?	

Exercise 6.6 Writing Your Final Draft

Apply the feedback and edits from Exercises 6.3 to 6.5 to write the final draft of your essay.

Getting an Education

1 Grammar in the Real World

**ACADEMIC
WRITING**

Summary-
response

A What can make attending college in the United States difficult? Read the article about the cost of attending college. What are some ways to make college more affordable?

B Comprehension Check **Answer the questions.**

1 Why do public colleges cost less than private colleges?

2 What is the difference between a grant and a loan?

3 What are two ways students can reduce or eliminate tuition costs?

C Notice **Find the sentences in the article and complete them.**

1 French students do not have to worry about _____ a lot for a college education because the government pays for it.

2 Some students want to avoid _____ loans, so they apply for grants, which they do not have to repay.

3 _____ a sport for a college team is one way to receive a scholarship.

What do the missing words have in common? In which sentence(s) does the missing word act as a subject? In which sentence(s) does the missing word act as an object?

The Cost of U.S. HIGHER EDUCATION

In many countries, the cost of a college education is not very high. In France, for example, university students pay an affordable $220 a year. French students do not have to **worry about paying** a lot for a college education because the government pays for it. In the United States, however, college tuition[1] is more expensive. Many students **have difficulty affording** it, especially at private colleges.[2] In 2010, the average cost per year of a private college in the United States was almost $37,000.

Public colleges[3] generally cost less because they depend on the government to help pay some of the expenses of education. However, if budget cuts reduce that money, tuition can increase. This can **prevent** students **from attending** even a public college.

The tuition at community colleges is the least expensive, costing about $3,500–$4,000 a year. Community colleges offer two-year programs with an associate's degree.[4] Other colleges and universities offer four-year programs and a bachelor's degree.[5] **Not attending** a four-year college right away is one option students use to save money. Many students attend a community college for the first two years of college and then transfer to a more expensive school for the last two years.

To help pay for college, many students apply for financial aid. Financial aid consists of loans, grants,[6] scholarships, and work-study programs. Students can apply for a student loan at a low interest rate. They must, however, **plan on repaying** the loan plus interest after they graduate. Some students want to **avoid repaying** loans, so they apply for grants, which they do not have to repay. Scholarships are another form of financial aid that students do not have to repay. **Playing** a sport for a college team is one way to receive a scholarship. Finally, students can apply for work-study programs. In these programs, students work at jobs at their school and receive a small salary to help pay for expenses.

For students **interested in getting** a higher education in the United States, the cost can be high; however, there are ways to make it less expensive. Once students resolve the issue of money, they can **concentrate on having** the exciting experience of college life.

[1]**tuition:** the money students pay for education
[2]**private college:** a school that does not receive its main financial support from the government
[3]**public college:** a school that depends on some financial support from the government
[4]**associate's degree:** a two-year degree at a community college
[5]**bachelor's degree:** a four-year degree at a college or university
[6]**grant:** money that a university, government, or an organization gives to someone for a purpose, such as to do research or study

2 Gerunds as Subjects and Objects

Grammar Presentation

A gerund is the *-ing* form of a verb that functions as a noun. It can be the subject or object of a sentence.	*Attending college is important these days.* *I enjoy learning.*

2.1 Using Gerunds as Subjects and Objects

A Use a singular verb form when the gerund is the subject of the sentence.	*Studying in the morning is difficult for me.* *Completing my application has taken hours.*
B Use a gerund as the object after the following verbs: Time: *delay, finish* Likes and dislikes: *appreciate, dislike, enjoy, mind* Effort and interest: *avoid, keep, practice* Communication: *defend, discuss, propose* Thinking: *consider, imagine, suggest*	*I finished working on the project last night.* *My sister dislikes working in a bookstore.* *I enjoy teaching.* *Practice interviewing with a friend.* *Discuss applying for a loan with your parents.* *He considered transferring to another school.*
C Use *not* before a gerund to make it negative.	*Not attending a four-year college is one option for students with little money.*
D Do not confuse a gerund with the present progressive form of the verb.	PRESENT PROGRESSIVE GERUND *I am considering working at home.*

▸▸ Verbs Followed by Gerunds Only: See page A7.
▸▸ Verbs followed by Gerunds or Infinitives: See page A7.

Grammar Application

Exercise 2.1 Gerunds as Subjects and Objects

A Students are commenting on the process of applying for college in the United States. Use the words to write sentences with gerund subjects and objects. Use the simple present for the main verbs.

1 complete the college application / take / a long time
   Completing the college application takes a long time.

2 find the money for college / be / a problem for me

3 my counselor/suggest/borrow money for college

_____

4 not get into a good college/worry/me

_____

5 I/enjoy/discuss my future plans with my friends

_____

6 not have enough money for tuition/be/a concern

_____

7 go to interviews at schools/make/me nervous

_____

8 teachers/suggest/start the application process early

_____

B Pair Work Discuss the gerunds in A with your partner. Which are subjects?
Which are objects?

Exercise 2.2 Gerunds as Objects

A Complete the web article about tips for starting the college application process.
Use the correct forms of the verbs in parentheses.

TIPS for GETTING a COLLEGE EDUCATION

Do you want a college education? First, ___*consider looking*___ (consider/look)
(1)
for the right college as soon as possible. If you are in high school or attending community

college, _____ (keep/study) hard so you'll have good grades.
(2)
Some schools require an essay on their college application. Many students in this position

_____ (dislike/write) the essay, but it's important, so
(3)

_____ (not delay/think about) it. Some schools require an on-site
(4)
interview, so _____ (practice/interview) with your friends or family.
(5)

Where will the money come from? Some students

_____ (consider/pay) for college
(6)
themselves. Other students _____
(7)
(not mind/borrow) money from their families, but not all families

can afford to pay for a college education. Sit down with your

family, and discuss all the options. _____ (discuss / work) at a part-time
(8)
job while you go to school, and _____ (imagine / work), studying, and
(9)
adjusting to a new lifestyle all at once. Is this really for you? If you think it is, then following these
tips will make the process easier.

B Group Work **Answer the questions. Use gerunds in your sentences. Then share your**
ideas with the group.

- What should people in high school keep doing as soon as they decide to go to college?

- What should people consider doing when they need money for college?

- What should people try imagining before they make the final decision to go to college?

Exercise 2.3 More Gerunds as Objects

Use the words to write sentences about students and tuition costs. Use gerunds as objects
and the present progressive form of the main verbs.

1 Jack / consider / go to a community college to save money
   Jack is considering going to a community college to save money.

2 Bo / think about / apply for financial aid instead of working

   _____

3 Jane / avoid / borrow money by getting a part-time job at school

   _____

   _____

4 My parents and I / not discuss / get a loan

   _____

5 Tom / not enjoy / work while he goes to college

   _____

6 My friend / delay / go back to school until he saves more money

   _____

7 Lisa and Henry / discuss / take part in a work-study program

   _____

   _____

8 Mei-ling / not consider / start college without a part-time job

   _____

   _____

9 Naresh / avoid / apply to too many different institutions

   _____

3 Gerunds After Prepositions and Fixed Expressions

Grammar Presentation

<table>
<tr>
<td>The gerund is the only verb form used after prepositions and in certain fixed expressions.</td>
<td>I am interested in studying art.
I'm not in favor of skipping a year of college.</td>
</tr>
</table>

3.1 Using Gerunds as Objects of Prepositions

<table>
<tr>
<td>Use a gerund as the object of prepositions after these common verb + preposition combinations:</td>
<td></td>
</tr>
<tr>
<td>Likes, dislikes, emotions: be afraid of, care for, be excited about, be interested in, worry about (or be worried about)</td>
<td>Are you afraid of failing?
Bryn is excited about applying to college.
I worry about not choosing the right school.</td>
</tr>
<tr>
<td>Interests and efforts: be interested in, learn about, be responsible for, be successful at, take care of</td>
<td>Many students are responsible for paying their own tuition.</td>
</tr>
<tr>
<td>Communication: complain about, hear of, insist on, talk about, be warned of</td>
<td>Some parents complain about having more than one child in college at the same time.
My friend insisted on visiting the school with me.
Did anyone talk about studying together tonight?</td>
</tr>
<tr>
<td>Thought: be aware of, believe in, concentrate on, dream of, forget about</td>
<td>I believe in sometimes staying up all night to study for a test.
My sister dreams of winning a scholarship.</td>
</tr>
<tr>
<td>Blame and responsibility: admit to, apologize for, confess to, be guilty of</td>
<td>We apologize for not contacting you sooner.</td>
</tr>
<tr>
<td>Other: apply for, depend on, plan on, be used to</td>
<td>I'm used to taking care of myself. I've lived alone for years.</td>
</tr>
</table>

▸▸ Verbs + Prepositions: See page A9.

A Use a gerund after certain common fixed verb + noun expressions: *have a difficult time/have difficulty/have trouble, spend time/spend money, waste time/waste money*	*She <u>had trouble</u> **finishing** her degree.* *I <u>spent a lot of time</u> **helping** in the library.* *Don't <u>waste time</u> **complaining**.*
B Use a gerund after certain common fixed noun + preposition expressions: *an excuse for, in favor of, an interest in, a reason for*	*There's <u>no excuse for</u> **being** late.* *He has <u>a reason for</u> **choosing** this school.*

▸▸ Expressions with Gerunds: See page A8.

Grammar Application

Exercise 3.1 Gerunds as Objects of Prepositions

A student is talking about his plans for going to college. Match the sentence parts.

1 Many students worry __c__

2 To pay for their education, they depend _____

3 I am very interested _____

4 I hope I will be successful _____

5 I'm not used _____

6 Fortunately, my parents want me to concentrate _____

7 They are planning _____

a in getting a college education.

b on applying for financial aid for me.

c̶ about being able to afford college tuition.

d on receiving scholarships and loans.

e on having an exciting college experience and not worrying about finances.

f at getting into the school of my choice.

g to studying and working at the same time.

Exercise 3.2 More Gerunds as Objects of Prepositions

A Complete the presentation on grants. Use the correct prepositions for the verbs in bold and the gerund form of the verbs in parentheses.

I know many of you are **excited** ___*about starting*___ (start) college soon. Also,
(1)

many of you are **worried** _____ (pay) for school. I'm sure you have
(2)

been **warned** _____ (take) out a lot of big loans. You have heard
(3)

some people **complain** _____ (owe) money for the rest of their lives.
(4)

Well, today, I'm going to **talk** _____ (apply) for three grants. Grants
(5)

aren't loans. You aren't **responsible** _____ (pay) them back.
(6)

The first type is the Pell Grant. The Pell Grant is for students who are

going to college at least part-time and need financial aid. If you're **interested**

_____ (ask) for a Pell Grant, **insist** _____ (talk)
(7)   (8)

with a guidance counselor to find out more about this program.

Are any of you **planning** _____ (major) in the areas of science
(9)

or mathematics? Then you might be **interested** _____ (try) for the
(10)

National Smart Grant. **Forget** _____ (get) this grant unless you
(11)

have maintained at least a 3.0 GPA in your first two years of college.

Finally, I know some of you are **dreaming** _____ (become)
(12)

teachers. The TEACH Grant is for students who **plan** _____ (teach)
(13)

at least four years in a low-income public or private school after graduation.

Now, are there any questions?

B **Read about each person's situation and complete the advice. Use the words in parentheses
with the correct preposition and the gerund form of the verbs.**

1 Chelsea wants to be an engineer, but she doesn't have a 3.0 GPA. She should not
  depend on getting (depend/get) a National Smart Grant.

2 Michael has completed two years of community college, but he doesn't
  have enough money to go to a four-year college. He should not
  _____ (be afraid/apply for) a Pell Grant.

3 Alison got a TEACH Grant, but she quit her teaching job after two years and got a
  high-paying job in computers instead. She must not _____
  (be worried/pay) back her loan.

4 Brandon goes to the community college, but he spends time partying and has a low
  GPA. He must not _____ (be interested/study).

5 Jorge got a TEACH Grant, taught for several years, and now is the head teacher at a
  private school. He must _____ (be successful/teach).

6 Sharon wants to major in computer science and get a National Smart Grant, but so
  far, her grades aren't that good. She should _____
  (concentrate/improve) her grades.

7 Rob's family can't help him pay for college, and he needs financial aid. He can
  probably _____ (depend/receive) a Pell Grant.

A Complete the conversations about college life. Use the correct forms of the fixed expressions in the box and the gerund forms of the verbs in parentheses.

(an) excuse for	have difficulty	in favor of	spend time
(an) interest in	have trouble	(a) reason for	waste time

Conversation 1

A I've heard some crazy _excuses for not handing in_ (not/hand in) papers.
(1)

B I don't think there's any good _____ (not/do) your
(2)
work once you're in college.

Conversation 2

A You _____ a lot of _____ (study). Does
(3)   (3)
it help?

B Yes, I would _____ (keep up) with my classes if I
(4)
didn't spend a lot of time studying.

Conversation 3

A A lot of people _____ (party) in college. What do you
(5)
plan on doing after you leave this school?

B I have _____ (get) a bachelor's degree, so I plan on
(6)
transferring to a four-year institution.

Conversation 4

A What type of student is the Joe Olinsky Foundation
_____ (give) grants to?
(7)

B We have money from a government fund that
we use for students who would otherwise
_____ (afford) a
(8)
two-year college.

 B Listen and check your answers.

C Group Work **Answer the questions. Use gerunds when appropriate. Then compare your sentences in your groups.**

■ What do you spend most of your time doing at school?

■ What do you have the most trouble dealing with at school?

■ What do you have an interest in doing after you leave this school?

Viet spends most of his time at school going to classes. I do, too. He has the most trouble dealing with parking. I have trouble dealing with the homework.

4 Gerunds After Nouns + *of*

Grammar Presentation

Gerunds are often used after nouns + of.	*The cost of getting an education is rising.* *I believe in the importance of studying hard.*

4.1 Nouns + *of* + Gerunds

The following nouns are often used in noun + of + gerund combinations:	
benefit of	A benefit of **going** to community college is cost savings.
cost of	The cost of **commuting** is rising because of gas prices.
danger of	There is a danger of **borrowing** too much money.
(dis)advantage of	What are some disadvantages of **taking** out loans for school?
effect of	The effects of **being** late are serious.
fear of	The fear of **being** jobless is what keeps me in school.
habit of	I'm in the habit of **not getting** up early.
idea of	The idea of **not going** to school is not an option.
importance of	It's impossible to underestimate the importance of **working** hard in school.
possibility of	The possibility of **not graduating** is worrisome.
problem of	The problem of **increasing** college costs affects a lot of students.
process of	He explained the process of **enrolling** in school.
risk of	She told me about the risks of **taking** out a loan.
way of	I'm thinking of a way of **paying** for school.

Exercise 4.1 Nouns + *of* + Gerunds

A Complete the conversations between Ms. Sparks, a community college counselor, and various families. Use the gerund form and the words in parentheses.

Conversation 1

Ms. Jones   We are concerned about _the cost of paying_ (the cost/pay) for our
(1)
son's education.

Ms. Sparks   I understand _____
(2)
(the fear/not be able to) afford college.

Ms. Jones   Of course, I want my son to have _____
(3)
(the possibility/get) the best education there is, but it's expensive.

Conversation 2

Mr. Allen   What are _____ (the advantages/go)
(4)
to a community college?

Ms. Sparks   _____ (the benefits/attend) a community
(4)
college are numerous. It's especially helpful for students who aren't sure of
their major.

Mr. Allen   Is there _____ (a possibility/get) in this semester?
(4)

Ms. Sparks   Yes, you can register today, if you like.

Conversation 3

Luisa   _____ (the process/apply) to college is long!
(4)

Ms. Sparks   I know it takes time, but you can reduce _____
(4)
(the risk/leave) something out by being organized. Here's a checklist to use.

B Over to You   Write four sentences on a separate piece of paper about your family's and
your thoughts about going to school. Use some of the noun + *of* expressions in the box with
gerunds. Then share your sentences with a partner.

| benefit of | effect of | habit of | idea of | possibility of | risk of | way of |

One benefit of going to school when you are older is that you know what you want to do.

5 Avoid Common Mistakes ⚠

1 **Remember to use a gerund after a preposition.**

getting
Students often worry about ~~get~~ into college.

2 **As a general rule, when you use a verb as a subject, use a gerund.**

Paying
~~Pay~~ for a private college can be very expensive.

3 **Always use a singular verb with a gerund subject.**

is
Interviewing at several colleges ~~are~~ time-consuming.

Editing Task

Find and correct seven more mistakes in the paragraphs about study habits.

studying
All students start the semester with the intention of ~~study~~ hard; however, find
time to study can be challenging. Finding good places to study are one challenge.
Another is finding enough hours in the day and creating a schedule. Successful
students face these problems realistically.

5   Different people have different purposes and needs when it comes to doing
college work. Study in a quiet library works well for some people. At the same time, a
coffee shop or cafeteria can also be a good place to work for those who get energy
from be in a stimulating environment.

      Then there is the question of time. Most students today are working, paying

10 bills, and taking classes at the same time, so they do not have the luxury of spend
many hours with their books. However, research offers hope. Studying for a few
minutes several times a day are a good way to learn new material.

      Learn what works for you is the key to academic success.

6 Academic Writing

Summary-Response

Brainstorm > Organize > Write > Edit

In this writing cycle (Units 12-13), you are going to write a summary and response for the prompt below. In this unit (12), you will focus on outlining and writing the summary paragraph.

> *Summarize the article "Creating a Successful Logo." Then choose a logo and analyze it in terms of the criteria in the article.*

Exercise 6.1 Preparing to Write

Work with a partner. Discuss the questions.

1 In the United States, colleges and universities market themselves to potential students. How is that marketing similar to normal business marketing? How is it different?

2 Companies often use logos to attract customers. Think of a company logo. What do you like about it? What do you dislike about it? Is it successful?

3 What do you use to evaluate a logo? Consider things like color and shape.

Exercise 6.2 Focusing on Vocabulary

Read the sentences. Match the words in bold to their definitions.

1 Providing all children with free, quality education is a basic **human right**.

2 The college admissions office uses clear, specific **criteria** to admit students.

3 Most of the campus is built in a traditional style, but the brand new art building is quite **contemporary**.

4 In the United States, colleges spend a lot of time asking former students for **donations** to support their athletic and academic programs.

5 The college first said that tuition would increase by 5%, but after students and teachers protested, a **subsequent** announcement reduced the increase to 3%.

6 One danger of **devoting** too much money **to** sports programs is that academics often suffer.

7 Some people think that it is not **appropriate** for college athletes with full scholarships to be paid.

8 Paying good employees a high salary is the best way to **retain** them, but company values are also important.

a _____ (adj) existing or happening in the present time

b _____ (n) fair and moral treatment that every person deserves

c _____ (adv) next; happening after something else

d _____ (n) money or goods given in order to help people

e _____ (n) standards used for judging something

f _____ (v) to keep; to continue having

g _____ (adj) correct or right for a particular situation

h _____ (v) to give a lot of time, effort, or money to something you support
or believe in

Creating a Successful Logo

In 2010, a group of world leaders got together to discuss bringing greater attention to human rights. They focused on branding, and they decided to hold a design competition for the purpose of choosing a logo that any organization that **devotes** itself **to human rights** could use.

5   A logo is an efficient visual form that conveys an organization's message. Logos may seem rather simple. After all, they are often just a name or very basic image. However, designing a successful logo takes a lot of time and thought, and meets a number of **criteria**. These criteria may differ depending on which graphic designer you ask, but there are some common themes.

10   First, good logos need to be clear and simple. Remembering simple logos is easy. In studies where participants were shown hundreds of unfamiliar logos, the ones they remembered later all had simple designs. For this reason, some designers advise using no more than two colors.

    A good logo also needs to be unique so that it will not be confused with the logo from another organization. For example, the logo for the Swedish furniture retailer IKEA is so familiar that any new logo in those shades of blue and 15 yellow would probably remind people of IKEA. With a unique logo, a designer hopes to arouse curiosity when people see it for the first time. It should make people want to know more about it. When tennis star Novak Djokovic started wearing shirts by the Japanese clothing manufacturer UNIQLO, people unfamiliar with the company became curious about the odd combination of letters that make up its logo.

    Next, logos should be flexible enough to adapt across time and placement. We all remember Apple's rainbow-20 colored design, which worked in the 1970s, but today would look retro. The **subsequent** gray and black Apple logo looks more **contemporary**, yet it **retains** the original design. Designers also need to consider where the logo will appear. Will it be on shopping bags? Coffee cups? Does it need to shrink down to a tiny icon on a digital device, like the Twitter bluebird or the Facebook "f"? Will people be able to recognize it from far away on the side of a truck?

    More than anything else, telling a story is the most critical criteria for a logo. A logo needs to convey the 25 company's identity and evoke an emotional response in the people who see it. But to be successful, the message and the response must be **appropriate** for the organization that the logo represents. The logo for the former Toys "R" Us toy store chain, with its childish handwriting and backwards R, conveyed a message of fun. It was childlike and playful. It worked for a toy company, but it probably would not work for a bank or insurance company. In contrast, the FedEx logo, with its block letters forming a forward-pointing arrow, looks like serious business. It attempts to inspire confidence: 30 We are a company you can trust your package to. An emotional response is particularly important for nonprofit organizations. The World Wide Fund for Nature (WWF) hopes that its iconic black and white panda will resonate with the public and encourage people to make a **donation** to support its global environmental conservation work on saving endangered species and their habitats as well as reducing people's footprint for a sustainable future.

    So, what logo did world leaders choose to convey an immediately recognizable and unmistakable message of 35 human rights? They selected Serbian designer Predrag Staki´c's logo, which combines the images of a bird and a human hand.

Read the article on page 189. Work with a partner. Ask and answer the questions.

1 What are three examples of successful company logos?

2 What sports figure is mentioned? Why?

3 Why did the WWF choose a panda as its logo?

Exercise 6.4 Noticing the Grammar and Writing

Work with a partner. Ask and answer the questions.

1 Circle the gerunds in the article. Which ones are subjects?

2 What is the main idea of the article? Underline it.

3 What are the main ideas of paragraphs 3-6? Highlight the sentences.

Using An Outline

You can use an outline to organize and sequence information. Main ideas provide the basic organization for an outline, with supporting details listed underneath them.

Exercise 6.5 Applying the Skill

1 Use the main ideas and details in the article to complete the outline.

Creating a Successful Logo

I. Introduction
  A Efficient form of visual _____
  B Meets specific _____

II. Criteria for a successful logo
  A Clear & _____
    1 Easy to _____
    2 Uses only a few colors (2)
  B _____
    1 Not easily confused with other logos - example: _____
    2 Arouses _____ - example: _____
  C _____
    1 Can adapt across time - example: _____
    2 Can adapt to _____ - example: _____
  D Tells a _____
    1 Conveys _____ - example: _____
    2 Evokes _____ - example: _____

---

2 Work with a partner. Compare your outlines.

3 What are the criteria the writer uses to determine if a logo is successful or not?

Summarizing

The summary paragraph includes the author's main idea and points. To write an effective summary, use your own words to avoid plagiarizing, but do not add to or change the author's ideas. The order of the ideas in the summary is the same as in the original article:

The **first sentence** introduces the summary by either restating the main idea (thesis) or giving a more general introduction to the author's ideas.

The **middle sentences** contain the main points and important details. Each main point usually has one or two details that briefly explain the point. Do NOT include all the details, only the most important ones.

The **last sentence** restates the main idea or states the author's ending comment.

Exercise 6.6 Applying the Skill

1 Reread the first paragraph of "The Cost of U.S. Higher Education" below. Then choose the best summary sentence.

   In many countries, the cost of a college education is not very high. In France, for example, university students pay an affordable $220 a year. French students do not have to worry about paying a lot for a college education because the government pays for it. In the United States, however, college tuition is more expensive. Many students have difficulty affording it, especially at private colleges. In 2020, the average cost per year of a private college in the United States was almost $37,000.

   a The author states that college in the United States is the most expensive in the world, and it is hard for all students to pay for it.

   b The author writes that college tuition in the United States is very expensive, and it is often difficult to afford.

   c The author claims that everyone wants to study in the United States, which is why college tuition is very high.

2 Work with a partner. Write summary sentences for paragraphs 2–4 of "The Cost of U.S. Higher Education" on page 177.

My Writing

Exercise 6.7 Writing Your Summary Paragraph

Write a summary paragraph of "Creating a Successful Logo" on page 189. Include the name of the article and its main idea. Then mention the main points and most important details. Conclude by restating the thesis or paraphrasing the writer's final comment. Use the outline in Exercise 6.5 and the grammar and writing skills in Unit 12 to help you.

Innovative Marketing Techniques

1 Grammar in the Real World

ACADEMIC WRITING

Summary-response

A What are some unusual types of advertising that you have noticed recently? Read the article on "guerrilla marketing." How do advertisers measure the success of a guerrilla marketing campaign?

B Comprehension Check **Answer the questions.**

1 What is guerrilla marketing? What is the purpose of guerrilla marketing?

2 How does guerrilla marketing get people's attention?

3 How is it different from traditional advertising?

C Notice **Find the sentences in the article and complete them.**

1 She wanted _____ it to raise money for her son's education.

2 The police tried _____ and destroy all of the signs.

3 A way to advertise with guerrilla marketing is _____ the environment in an unexpected way.

What do all the verbs you wrote have in common? Look at the words that come before these verbs. What kinds of words are they?

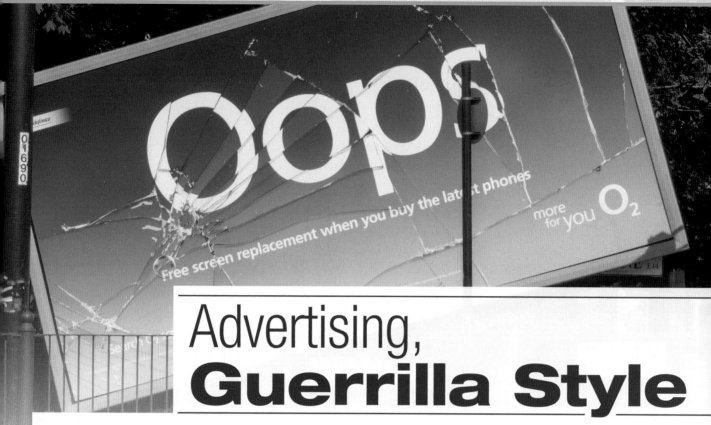

Advertising,
Guerrilla Style

Would you tattoo a website address on your body? One woman from Utah did just that. A company **got her to tattoo** its website address on her forehead for $10,000. She **wanted to**
5 **do** it to raise money for her son's education. The company **wanted her to do** it for cheap advertising space. They also got free publicity[1] because the story was on the news. This kind of extreme advertising – known as guerrilla
10 marketing – uses surprising ways to advertise a product and get people's attention.

A **way to advertise** with guerrilla marketing is **to use** the environment in an unexpected way. For example, a few years ago, a popular candy
15 company painted park benches so that they looked like giant chocolate bars. This creative ad[2] strategy got consumers' attention in a positive way.

For guerrilla marketing to be successful,
20 people must talk about the ads. A well-known sneaker company formed a partnership with Berlin's public transportation system. Every pair of sneakers was also a free pass to public transportation across the city for a whole year.
25 Anyone wearing the sneakers could ride the buses and trains at no extra cost. The news quickly spread on social media.

Not all guerrilla marketing works. A few years ago, an ad company **decided to place** signs with
30 flashing lights around different cities to advertise a television show. However, in Boston, the police thought the signs were bombs. The police **tried to find** and **destroy** all of the signs.

Unlike those who use traditional advertising
35 strategies, guerrilla marketers are not **afraid to shock** people. The idea is to **convince people to talk** about the products. However, it is **important** for companies **to consider** how people will react. Not all publicity is always good publicity.

---

[1]**publicity:** the attention received as a result of an activity meant to attract interest

[2]**ad:** advertisement; advertising

2 Infinitives with Verbs

Grammar Presentation

An infinitive is *to* + the base form of a verb. Some main verbs in a sentence are followed by an infinitive, not a gerund.	I decided *to learn* about advertising. The company planned *not to use* traditional advertising.

2.1 Verbs + Infinitives

Use an infinitive after the following verbs:

Time: *hesitate, wait*

Likes or dislikes: *care*

Plans or desires: *decide, hope, need, plan*

Efforts: *attempt, help, learn, manage*

Communication: *agree, offer, promise*

Possibility: *appear, seem, tend*

Use *not* before the infinitive to show the infinitive is negative.

We hesitated *to use* guerrilla marketing.

I don't care *to see* boring ads on TV.

The company is hoping *to buy* advertising space.

Guerrilla marketers attempt *to get* your attention.

Our company promised *not to waste* money.

Guerrilla ads tend *to shock* consumers.

▶▶ Verbs Followed by Infinitives Only: See page A7.

2.2 Verbs + Objects + Infinitives

A After some verbs, an object comes before the infinitive. The object performs the action of the infinitive. The following verbs are followed by an object + infinitive: *advise, allow, convince, encourage, get, persuade, prepare, teach, tell, urge,* and *warn.*

VERB + OBJ + INF

He got us *to try* a new advertising technique.

The company didn't tell the salespeople *to educate* consumers.

They urged the advertisers *not to surprise* people.

B Some verbs can be followed by either an object + infinitive or an infinitive only. These verbs include *ask, choose, expect, help, need, promise, want,* and *would like.*

VERB + OBJ + INF

My department chose Sally *to create* the new ads. (Sally will create the ads.)

VERB + INF

My department chose *to create* the new ads. (My department will create the ads.)

▶▶ Verbs + Objects + Infinitives: See page A8.

DATA FROM THE REAL WORLD

Research shows that these are the most common verbs + infinitives in academic writing:

appear, begin, continue, fail, seem, tend, try, want	Sales of the new product continued to rise last month. The boss failed to recognize the company's problems.

Grammar Application

Exercise 2.1 Verbs + Infinitives

Complete the homework assignment about guerrilla marketing with the correct forms of the words in parentheses. Use the simple present form of the main verbs.

GUERRILLA MARKETING

Guerrilla marketing ___*attempts to reach*___ (attempt/reach) consumers
(1)
in unexpected or unusual contexts, such as public places. Guerrilla marketers

_____ (hope/shock) or surprise potential consumers.
(2)
Why is guerrilla marketing so popular? One reason for this is that it

_____ (tend/cost) less than traditional marketing.
(3)
Guerrilla marketing usually _____ (manage/generate)
(4)
a lot of publicity for little money. It _____ (seem/be) effective
(5)
for most products; however, several experts think that people are getting tired of it.

I _____ (hesitate/admit) this, but I agree.
(6)

Exercise 2.2 Verbs + Objects + Infinitives

A Complete the conversation about a nontraditional type of advertising called reverse graffiti. Use the words in parentheses. Use the correct form of the main verbs according to the context.

Dae Ho Our advertising consultants ___*are advising us to try*___ (advise/us/try) a type
(1)
of guerrilla marketing called reverse graffiti.

Erin What's reverse graffiti?

Luis It's a way to write an image on a dirty public surface by removing the dirt.

It _____ (get/consumers/notice)
(2)
a product. Do you think the managers will like the idea?

Erin   Actually, I think the managers will _____
(3)
(tell / us / not do) it.

Dae Ho   Why? I think we can probably _____
(4)
(convince / them / try) it because it's cheap.

Luis   I bet we can _____ (persuade / them / do) it.
(5)

Dae Ho   OK. We'll need help, though.

Luis   I'll _____ (tell / Mike / create)
(6)
a presentation.

Erin   OK, Luis, but you should _____
(7)
(warn / him / prepare) for a lot of questions. Some people think it destroys
property, so it's vandalism. It might not be legal.

B Over to You   **Answer the questions with information that is true for you. Include the
verbs from A in your answers. Then share your sentences with a partner.**

■ What is your opinion of guerrilla marketing?

■ Does it work for you and your demographic (that is, people who are your age and
have similar likes and dislikes)? Why or why not?

*Guerrilla marketing tends to work well with people my age because my
generation likes innovative ideas.*

Exercise 2.3 Verbs + Infinitives and Verbs + Objects + Infinitives

**Complete the report on quick response (QR) codes.[1] Use the words in parentheses with the
simple present or simple past form.**

Last week, Steve Green ___*asked me to look into*___ (ask / me / look into)
(1)
QR codes, so I decided to interview people who use QR codes for marketing.

One way companies use QR codes is through smartphones. Consumers point
their smartphones at QRs, and the code takes them immediately to a company or
product website.

I _____ (choose / interview) two different people. Steve
(2)
_____ (urge / me / interview) the manager from Dan's Gourmet
(3)

Food for this report because his company uses QR codes. Dan said the QR codes

_____ (help/inform) consumers about the nutritional content of
           (4)

the product and _____ (help/them/use) the product correctly.
                              (5)

Dan also _____ (want/consumers/find out) about
               (6)

new products, so the QR code contains a link to Dan's company's website. The QR code

_____ (promise/become) an important marketing tool.
           (7)

　　After I interviewed the manager from Dan's, I _____

(prepare/visit) Liz Kurikova, the owner of a small flower shop. She was unable to meet
                              (8)

with me this week, but she _____ (encourage/me/contact)
                                          (9)

a friend of hers who runs a small ice cream shop. I spoke with Ned Searby at Astoria

Ice Cream. Currently, they _____ (not need/offer) this
                                          (10)

option to their customers. Once they start selling other products, however, they

_____ (expect/include) QR codes for products on the shelves.
           (11)

They _____ (would like/use) this technology to expand their
            (12)

business and promote their new products.

[1]**QR code:** an image like a bar code on products that contains links to text,
web addresses, and other types of information

3 Infinitives vs. Gerunds

Grammar Presentation

Some verbs can be followed by an infinitive or a gerund. Much of the time, the meaning is the same or very close, but sometimes there is a difference in meaning.	The woman *stopped to read* the ad. (The woman saw the ad as she was walking and stopped. She read the ad.) The woman *stopped reading* the ad. (The woman was reading the ad. Then she stopped.)

3.1 Similar Meanings of Infinitives vs. Gerunds

After some verbs, you can use either a gerund or an infinitive without any change in meaning. Verbs that can be followed by either an infinitive or a gerund include *begin, can't stand, continue, hate, like, love, prefer,* and *start.*	Broadcasters love *to get* free publicity. Broadcasters love *getting* free publicity.

3.1 Similar Meanings of Infinitives vs. Gerunds (continued)

When *begin*, *continue*, or *start* are in a progressive form, use an infinitive.	I'm beginning **to work** on the assignment now. NOT *I'm beginning ~~working~~ on the assignment now.*

3.2 Different Meanings of Infinitives vs. Gerunds

A The following verbs can be followed by either an infinitive or a gerund, but the meaning is different:

Infinitives	Gerunds
Did you forget **to tell** your assistant you'd be late today? (You never told your assistant.)	Did you forget **telling** your assistant you'd be late today? (You told your assistant, but you do not remember it.)
I regret **to tell** you that our sales have dropped. (I'm sorry that our sales have dropped, but I'm telling you about it.)	I regret **telling** you that our sales have dropped. (I told you our sales had dropped, but I wish I hadn't.)
They remembered **to email** the sales figures. (They almost forgot, but then they sent the email.)	They remembered **emailing** the sales figures. (They sent the email. Later, they thought about it again.)
People stopped **to look** at the colorful signs. (People stopped and looked at them.)	People stopped **looking** at the colorful signs. (People were looking at them but then stopped.)
The mayor tried **to change** the town's name, but the citizens didn't want to. (This was an experiment to see if he could do it. The mayor didn't succeed. He couldn't change the name.)	The mayor tried **changing** the town's name, but it didn't help tourism. (The mayor made an effort to do this, and he succeeded. He changed the name.)

B Note that the meaning of *tried* is only different in the past.

I tried **to pay** with a credit card, but the store only accepted cash. (I wanted to pay with a credit card, but they wouldn't let me.) ≠ I tried **paying** with a credit card, but I didn't like it. (I did pay with a credit card.)	I will try **to call** you tomorrow. = I will try **calling** you tomorrow. (= Tomorrow I plan to call you, but it may not work.)

▶▶ Verbs Followed by Gerunds or Infinitives: See page A7.

Grammar Application

Exercise 3.1 Meanings of Infinitives vs. Gerunds

A Rewrite the sentences about paying people to promote products through social media. Replace the infinitives in bold with gerunds. Replace the gerunds in bold with infinitives. Then label the sentence *S* (if the meaning is the same) or *D* (if the meaning is different).

1 Companies have begun **to pay** people to blog about their products.

   Companies have begun paying people to blog about their products.   *S*

2 LP Social Friends regrets **to tell** the media that they pay people to be "friends."

   _____   ____

3 I stopped **to read** the article about social media marketing.

   _____   ____

4 Alison forgot **mentioning** GamerWorld in her blog yesterday.

   _____   ____

5 Upside Energy Drinks continues **to pay** fans on social networking sites.

   _____   ____

6 People have started **questioning** Upside Energy Drinks' marketing strategy.

   _____   ____

7 A lot of people can't stand **reading** blogs that are full of ads.

   _____   ____

8 GamerWorld tried **to pay** me to write about them in my blog.

   _____   ____

9 I tried **changing** the privacy settings since I don't want messages from advertisers.

   _____   ____

B Pair Work In which sentences in A does the meaning change? Explain the difference in meaning to a partner.

Exercise 3.2 Infinitive or Gerund?

A Listen to a discussion of the results of a focus group.[1] The focus group watched a reality TV show called *Jake's Life* and tried to remember a product that they saw in the show. Match the sentence parts.

1 Bo regrets ___e___
2 Bo tried _____
3 Jocelyn doesn't regret _____
4 Participant 1 stopped _____
5 Participant 2 stopped _____
6 Participant 3 didn't remember _____
7 Nobody forgot _____
8 Jocelyn told Bo _____

a to push the button when Jake drank soda.
b to get a snack.
c to stop reading.
d seeing Jake drink anything.
e to say that the product placement isn't working.
f watching after the third episode.
g doing things differently this time.
h hiring Bo.

[1]**focus group:** a group of people whose opinions help marketers

B Listen again and check your answers.

4 Infinitives After Adjectives and Nouns

Grammar Presentation

| Infinitives can also follow some adjectives and nouns. | The consumers were **happy to see** some interesting advertising. |
| | The advertisers needed more **time to educate** the community. |

4.1 *Be* + Adjectives + Infinitives

Use infinitives after the following adjectives: *afraid, amazed, difficult, easy, embarrassed, fun, interesting, lucky, necessary, ready, sad, shocked, sorry, surprised, (un)likely, upset*.	Some companies are <u>afraid</u> **to use** new marketing techniques.
	The police were <u>ready</u> **to destroy** the ads.
	The advertisers were <u>sorry</u> **to cause** a problem.
It + *be* is frequently used with many of these words.	<u>It would be fun</u> **to surprise** people with guerrilla advertising.

▶▶ Be + Adjectives + Infinitives: See page A9.

4.2 Nouns + Infinitives

Use infinitives after the following nouns: *ability, chance, decision, time, way*.	Some ads have the <u>ability</u> **to excite** the public.
	It was a great <u>chance</u> **to learn** something new.
	It's <u>time</u> **to be** more creative in advertising.

Grammar Application

Exercise 4.1 *It + Be + Adjective + Infinitive*

Complete the article about tracking technology. Use the adjective + infinitive combinations in the box.

difficult / avoid	fun / go	necessary / use	~~surprising / know~~
easy / acquire	interesting / read	shocked / find out	unlikely / change

Who is watching you as you visit Internet pages? It may be

surprising to know that advertisers are following you as you surf
(1)

the Web. Many Internet users would be _____
(2)

how much companies know about them through tracking technology

such as cookies, which allow websites to identify visitors and

their web page preferences. Today, because of tracking technology, it is

_____ data on people's habits and tastes. Most websites
(3)

have this technology, so it is _____ . Companies believe
(4)

that it is _____ tracking because it helps consumers
(5)

find out about products that they like.

Here is an example of what companies can learn through tracking.

Maria thinks it is _____ to websites and comment
(6)

on movies she has seen. She also thinks it is _____
(7)

about health issues on several sites. She notices that ads pop up on topics

that she has done searches on, but she is _____ her
(8)

search habits because of this.

Complete the conversations about using nontraditional marketing. Use the words in parentheses to write sentences.

1 **A** We're going to do a survey on how well guerrilla marketing really works.

  B (that / be / a good way / get / information)

    That's a good way to get information.

2 **A** Our survey shows that product placement isn't working.

  B (it / be / time / do / something different now)

3 **A** Are you going to use QR codes or reverse graffiti?

  B (we / make / the decision / use / QR codes / yesterday)

4 **A** Why should I hire your advertising agency?

  B (we / have / the ability / attract / the 18- to 24-year-old demographic)

5 **A** Why are you considering paying sports bloggers to write about your product?

  B (it / be / a chance / introduce / our product to athletes)

6 **A** Why doesn't guerrilla marketing work, in your opinion?

  B (it / not / be / the best way / get / messages across / to older demographics)

7 **A** Why is the character holding the soda can so we can see the brand?

  B (it / be / a chance / sell / the product to viewers)

Group Work Think about the different types of marketing below. Evaluate each strategy in terms of how it works with children, teens, adults, and seniors (people over age 65). Compare and discuss your ideas with your group members. Use an infinitive + adjective and noun in each statement.

Guerrilla marketing may not be an effective way to attract seniors because it may be too shocking for some of them.

- Traditional advertising (TV commercials, magazine ads)
- Guerrilla marketing
- Product placement (placement of products in movies and TV shows)
- Viral marketing (paying bloggers and people with social networking sites)

Avoid Common Mistakes ⚠

1 **With the verb *want*, use verb + object + infinitive, not verb + *that* clause.**

The advertisers want ~~that~~ you ∧ buy their products.
(to)

2 **Use the correct word order when using the negative form of an infinitive.**

The company decided ∧ to ~~not~~ pay bloggers to write about their products.
(not)

3 **Do not confuse the preposition *to* with an infinitive *to*.**

PREP + GERUND

(seeing)
I look forward to ~~see~~ the new dragon movie.

VERB + INFINITIVE

(see)
Many people like to ~~seeing~~ familiar places and objects in a movie.

4 **Use an infinitive (*to* + the base form of verb), not *for* + base form of verb, where appropriate.**

(to)
It is important ~~for~~ make sure the advertisement targets the right audience.

Editing Task

Find and correct the mistakes in the paragraphs about advertising in movies.

Product placement in movies is a type of advertising that is popular today.
Advertisers want ~~that~~ consumers ∧ see their products in movies so that their products will *(to)*
seem more appealing. That's why advertisers pay filmmakers for place their products in
movies. For example, in one movie, a director arranged to using a pair of famous brand-
5 name sunglasses for make his characters appear fashionable. In another movie, the plot
required a certain type of luxury car. The filmmakers used the car in their film, but in this
case, they did not receive any money from the auto's manufacturers. For the automaker, it
was an easy way to not pay for advertising. Filmmakers seem to not mind the advertising
because they can earn extra money. Moviegoers do not seem to mind it, either.
10   In my opinion, product placement in movies is acceptable, but I want that
advertisers use product placement carefully. If directors expect to making a film that
is believable, then everything in the film must fit the story. Otherwise, the movie will
seem more like an advertisement. This would be terrible. I hope that filmmakers
continue to making wise decisions and use products that look natural on screen.

6 Academic Writing

Summary-Response

Brainstorm > Organize > Write > Edit

In Unit 12, you wrote a summary paragraph of "Creating a Successful Logo." In this unit (13), you will focus on planning and writing a response paragraph to the article. You will then review, revise, and edit your summary-response paragraphs.

> *Summarize the article "Creating a Successful Logo." Then choose a logo and analyze it in terms of the criteria in the article.*

Determining and Applying Criteria

Understanding criteria can help you organize an essay and ensure that you address the most relevant issues.

Exercise 6.1 Applying the Skill

1 Follow the steps to complete the chart below.

   a Choose a logo to analyze. It can be the logo of a school, business, or organization. Do not use any of the logos mentioned in the reading "Creating a Successful Logo."

   b Review your outline of the article on page 190. Write the four criteria for a logo.

   c Decide if your logo meets each of the criteria *completely*, *partly*, or *not at all*?

   d Briefly explain why your logo does or does not meet the criteria..

Your Logo:		
Criteria	**Does your logo meet the criteria?**	**Why or why not?**

2 Work with a partner. Discuss the questions.

   a Based on the information in your table, how successful do you think your logo is? Explain your answer.

   b Is your judgment based only on the criteria in the reading or were other criteria important to you?

Responding to an Article

One way to structure a summary-response essay is to write a summary paragraph followed by one or more response paragraphs. Here are some ways to respond to a writer's ideas. The examples are responses to "Advertising, Guerilla Style" on page 193.

1 Agree or disagree with the ideas.

I agree with the writer that when companies are creative in their marketing, they can attract new customers to their products.

I disagree with the writer that people have to discuss the ads for guerrilla marketing to be successful because people often just describe their purchases, not the ads themselves.

2 Find strengths or weaknesses in the article.

The writer **makes a strong/weak argument** that for guerrilla marketing to be successful, a company should consider partnering with another company. Some of the most effective ad campaigns, like movie tie-ins, involve multiple companies.

3 Connect the ideas to your personal experiences.

In my experience, ads that are shocking are very effective. For instance, I know people who purchased personal items because the ad was shocking and controversial.

My Writing

Exercise 6.2 Applying the Skill

Use the chart in Exercise 6.1 to write a response sentence for each of the criteria in "Creating a Successful Logo." Discuss your sentences with a partner.

1 _____

_____

2 _____

_____

3 _____

_____

4 _____

_____

Complete the tasks to plan your response.

1 Review your summary paragraph from My Writing in Unit 12. Is there anything you want to add, change, or delete?

2 If possible, include a picture of the logo you chose to analyze in your response as a visual reference for your reader.

3 Review your response sentences in Exercise 6.2. What details or examples could you add to support your ideas and develop them into paragraphs?

4 Make an outline to organize your ideas.

Exercise 6.4 Writing Your Response

Add a response to your summary paragraph to create a summary-response essay. Use your own words or include short quotes from the article so that you do not plagiarize.

1 Write one or more paragraphs explaining and applying each of the criteria for a successful logo to your choice.

2 Discuss any additional criteria that you think are important.

3 Conclude with an evaluation of the success of your logo based on the criteria and, if possible, something for your readers to think about and respond to.

Exercise 6.5 Revising Your Ideas

1 Work with a partner. Use the questions to give feedback on your partner's essay.

- Does your partner include all the main ideas from the reading in the summary paragraph? If not, what is missing?
- What criteria does your partner use to evaluate their logo? Do you agree with their conclusion?
- What could your partner add or remove to make their paragraphs stronger and easier to understand?

2 Use the feedback from your partner to revise the ideas and content of your paragraphs.

Exercise 6.6 Editing Your Writing

Use the checklist to review and edit your paragraphs.

Did you answer the writing prompt completely?	
Did you organize your essay clearly and correctly?	
Does your essay contain an effective summary of the article?	
Does your summary include the most important information from the article?	
Did you use your own words to summarize the points in the article?	
Did you apply the criteria from the article to a new logo?	
Did you identify any strengths or weaknesses in the article?	
Did you agree or disagree with any of the writer's ideas?	
Did you connect any of the writer's ideas to a personal experience or example?	
Did you draw a clear conclusion for your reader to think about or respond to?	

Exercise 6.7 Editing Your Grammar

Use the checklist to review and edit the grammar in your paragraphs.

Did you use gerunds correctly?	
Did you use any noun + *of* + gerund constructions?	
Did use infinitives correctly?	
Did you use any verb + infinitive and adjective + infinitive constructions?	
Did you include objects before infinitives when necessary?	
Did you avoid the common mistakes in the charts on pages 187 and 203?	

Exercise 6.8 Writing Your Final Draft

Apply the feedback and edits from Exercises 6.5 to 6.7 to write the final draft of your paragraphs.

1 Grammar in the Real World

ACADEMIC
WRITING

Argumentative
writing

A Have you moved very often in your life? If so, why did you move?
Read the interview about geographic mobility. What are some of the
reasons why people move?

B Comprehension Check **Answer the questions.**

  1 What are some reasons why people move long distances?

  2 What are some reasons why people stay nearby when they move?

  3 Why is the mobility rate in Russia lower than in the United States?

C Notice **Find the sentences in the article and complete them.**

  1 Professor, you **have been** interested in geographic mobility for

     a long time, _____ you?

  2 Mobility **isn't** easy to explain, _____ it?

  **Look at the verbs you wrote and the verbs in bold. What do you
  notice about the use of *not*?**

Geographic Mobility
ACROSS CULTURES

Interviewer Today we're speaking with two specialists in geographic mobility. They will discuss some reasons why people move from one place to another. Professor O'Neill is from
5 Carlow University in the United States, and Professor Tabenkin is from Zala University in Russia. Let's start with Professor O'Neill. Professor, you have been interested in geographic mobility for a long time,
10 **haven't you**?

O'Neil Well, yes. When I was a boy, my best friend moved away, and that affected me deeply. As I grew older, I saw more people move away. I noticed that the population
15 decrease affected local businesses. As a result, I got interested in the choices people make about moving.

Interviewer People are very mobile and are moving a lot. But most people aren't moving long
20 distances, **are they? Isn't** that curious?

O'Neil Yes. That's interesting. In fact, I've been studying the connection between moving and distance recently. Every year, about 11.6 percent of people in the United States
25 move, and of these, about 14.8 percent move to a different state.

Interviewer **Doesn't** that surprise you?

O'Neil No, not really. Often, people who change jobs have to move long distances. On
30 the other hand, people looking for better housing usually stay near their original home. And people who relocate[1] for family reasons may move far away or stay nearby.

Interviewer So, I guess it depends on the situation,
35 **doesn't it**?

O'Neil That's right. It's more complicated than you may think. For example, my wife was living in California when we met. When we got married, she moved a long distance to live
40 with me in Chicago. Now her sister, who lives near Chicago, is expecting a baby. She and her husband plan to move a short distance to be closer to us.

Interviewer Professor Tabenkin, people in Russia have
45 the same issues, **don't they**?

Tabenkin To a certain extent, yes. It's harder to find housing in Russia, so people tend to move less frequently. In fact, the mobility rate in Russia is less than 2 percent. In my
50 research, I found that young people often decide not to move because available, affordable housing would take them further from family.

Interviewer OK. But **don't** people sometimes have to
55 move long distances for economic reasons?

Tabenkin Yes, that's true. Personally, I had to move a very long distance ten years ago because there were no jobs nearby. However, my experience doesn't seem to be the norm.[2]

Interviewer 60 Mobility isn't easy to explain, **is it**? Thank you both for your thoughts on this issue.

---

[1]**relocate**: move to a new place   [2]**norm**: an expected situation or a situation considered to be typical

2 Negative Questions

Grammar Presentation

Negative questions are similar to *Yes/No* questions in that they begin with an auxiliary verb, a modal, or a form of *be*.	*Haven't you moved recently?* *Aren't there many reasons why people move?*

2.1 Forming Negative Questions

A Negative questions usually begin with a contraction.	*Don't you live around here?* *Can't you help me move?* *Wasn't he living in Chicago?*
B The full form of *not* in negative questions is very formal. The word *not* comes between the subject and the main verb.	*Were they not living in Chicago?* *Have you not moved recently?*
C With a contraction, use *are* instead of *am* with *I*. Use *am* when you use the full form.	*Aren't I correct?* *Am I not correct?*

2.2 Using Negative Questions

A Use negative questions when you think the information is true and you expect people to agree.	*Don't people often move when they change jobs?* (My experience tells me people often move when they change jobs.) *Isn't it unusual for people to move in Russia?* (I've read that it's unusual to move in Russia.)
B Use negative questions to show surprise or disbelief.	*"Tom has changed his major to English."* *"Really? Isn't he still planning to work at a bank?"*
C Use negative questions to show annoyance or anger.	*Didn't you say you would call me?* (I'm angry that you didn't call me.) *Shouldn't Bob have finished that report by now?* (I'm annoyed because Bob hasn't finished the report.)

2.3 Answering Negative Questions

Respond to a negative question just as you would a regular *Yes/No* question. Typically, we answer negative questions with *yes* or *no* and an explanation.	*"Don't you want to move?"* (Do you want to move?) *"Yes, I do. I'd like to live somewhere else."* *"No, I don't. I really want to stay here."*

Grammar Application

Exercise 2.1 Negative Questions

A family is packing for a big move. Complete the negative questions with the correct form of the words in parentheses.

1 _____*Didn't I tell*_____ (I told) you to be careful with that lamp?

2 _____ (you have been listening) to what I've been saying?

3 _____ (you can stop) texting and help me?

4 _____ (you should have bought) bigger boxes?

5 _____ (I am) correct that you promised to help?

6 _____ (you were going to take) the baby to the neighbor's?

Exercise 2.2 More Negative Questions

Read the sentences about moving and migration. Then write negative questions with the information in parentheses. Use contractions when possible.

1 A lot of people left Ireland in the 1800s.
   Didn't a lot of people leave because of a famine?
   (You heard that a lot of people left because of a famine.)

2 Hope of employment brings a lot of immigrants to rich countries.
   _____
   (You heard that good schools have made rich countries more attractive, too.)

3 Some people move great distances.
   _____
   (You heard that some people move great distances to reunite with family members.)

4 Some corporations require their employees to move to another country.
   _____
   (You think that this is happening more because of globalization.)

5 People are able to move around more freely because of globalization.
   _____
   (You heard that the laws are changing to allow even more movement.)

Pair Work Read the chart on migration in the United States. Study it for 30 seconds. Then cover it. What details can you remember? Ask your partner negative questions. Then switch roles and answer your partner's negative questions.

A *Haven't 60 percent of men moved?*

B *Yes, that's right.*

A *And haven't 50 percent of college graduates moved?*

B *Actually, no, 77 percent of college graduates have moved.*

People Who Move: Percentages of people who have moved at least once in their lifetimes

	% of People Who Have Moved	% of People Who Have Never Moved
Total	63	37
By Gender		
Men	60	40
Women	65	35
By Education		
College graduates	77	23
High school graduates	56	44

▶▶ www.pewsocialtrends.org/2008/12/17/who-moves-who-stays-put-wheres-home

3 Tag Questions

Grammar Presentation

Use tag questions to confirm information or ask for agreement.	*You're a professor, aren't you?* *He hasn't been studying, has he?*

3.1 Forming Tag Questions

A The verb in a tag question is an auxiliary verb, a modal, or a form of *be*.	*Your parents have never moved, have they?* *She got the job, didn't she?* *You can't stay, can you?*

3.1 Forming Tag Questions *(continued)*

B The pronoun in a tag question agrees with the subject.	*The students will be on time, won't they?* *Your sister lives close by, doesn't she?*
Use *it* when the subject is *that* or *something*.	*That's amazing information, isn't it?*
Use *they* when the subject is *someone* or *everyone*.	*Someone recorded the interview, didn't they?* *Everyone respects the professor, don't they?*
C Use an affirmative tag with a negative statement.	NEGATIVE STATEMENT AFFIRMATIVE TAG *They don't live in Chicago,* *do they?* *You're not from Russia,* *are you?*
Use a negative tag with an affirmative statement.	AFFIRMATIVE STATEMENT NEGATIVE TAG *Geography is interesting,* *isn't it?* *Her sister moved to Chicago,* *didn't she?*

3.2 Answering Tag Questions

A In negative tags, we expect the listener to answer *yes*, but it is possible to answer *no*.	*"They moved from Miami to Chicago, didn't they?"*
	   "Yes, they got jobs in Illinois." (That's right, they moved.)
	   "Actually, no." (That's not right. They didn't move.)

B In affirmative tags, we expect the listener to answer *no*, but it is possible to answer *yes*.	*"They didn't move from Miami to Chicago, did they?"*
	   "No, they decided to stay." (You're right, they didn't move.)
	   "Yes, they had to move for work." (Actually, they did move.)

C You cannot answer *Yes . . . not.*	*"They didn't move from Miami to Chicago, did they?"* *"Yes, they did."* OR *"No, they didn't."* NOT *"Yes, they didn't."*

Grammar Application

Exercise 3.1 Tag Questions

Match the statements and tags about a friend who is moving.

1 Erica and her family are moving overseas, __d__   a do they?

2 You knew about their move, _____   b didn't you?

3 Erica's company is relocating to London, _____   c aren't you?

4 Erica's husband won't get a new job, _____   d aren't they?

5 They don't have a place to live yet, _____   e don't I?

6 Erica will get an international driving permit, _____   f isn't it?

7 I have a lot of information about their move, _____   g will he?

8 You're giving them a going-away party, _____   h won't she?

Exercise 3.2 Tags

Complete the questions about the stresses of moving. First underline the subject and circle the auxiliary verb in each sentence. Then write the correct tag.

1 <u>Moving</u> (can) be stressful as well as expensive, __can't it__ ?

2 People can sometimes deduct moving costs from their income taxes, _____ ?

3 Things have sometimes disappeared from a moving truck, _____ ?

4 Your friends will give you boxes, _____ ?

5 Everyone should read reviews of a moving company before hiring one, _____ ?

6 Marta has been disorganized since the move, _____ ?

7 Vinh and Ahn weren't moving today, _____ ?

8 It's been a stressful time for you, _____ ?

Exercise 3.3 Statements in Tag Questions

Complete the questions about people who are moving. Use the words in parentheses with the correct verb forms.

1 _____ *Mary is retiring to Florida* _____ , isn't she?
  (Mary / retire / Florida)

2 _____ , hasn't he?
  (Raul / relocate / London)

3 _____ , didn't she?
  (Annette / attend school / France)

4 _____ , won't they?
  (Miriam and Amir / turn down the promotion / New York)

5 _____ , did you?
(You / like / the air quality / Hong Kong)

6 _____ , will he?
(Bernard / take the children / with him / Texas)

Exercise 3.4 Answering Tag Questions

Complete the conversations with the expected answers.

Conversation 1

Paolo I'm interviewing for a job in New York.

You grew up there, didn't you?

Luis _____ Yes, I did _____ . What do you want
            (1)
to know?

Paolo Well, I'm worried about housing. Apartments

aren't cheap there, are they?

Luis _____ . They're also hard to find.
              (2)

Conversation 2

Phoebe You've read the article on migration patterns for class today, haven't you?

Alex _____ . It was interesting.
             (3)

Phoebe Oh, good. You don't have time to tell me about it before class, do you?

Alex _____ . But I can send you a link to the article.
             (4)

Conversation 3

Claudia I heard the company is moving to Dallas, Texas. Some of us will have to move,

won't we?

Jun _____ . I'll know exactly who next week.
            (5)

Claudia You have family there, so you won't mind moving, will you?

Jun _____ . My family's excited.
            (6)

Conversation 4

Fen There are a lot of new families moving into the neighborhood, aren't there?

Bin _____ . I'm glad to see new faces.
            (7)

Fen It's nice to see a lot of young children around again, isn't it?

Bin _____ . It's wonderful!
            (8)

Use rising intonation in the tag when you are not certain your statement is true.	*"Moving wasn't difficult, was it?"* *"Yes, it was!"* *"There won't be a quiz tomorrow, will there?"* *"No, there won't."*
Use falling intonation when you expect the listener to agree with you.	*"His research is really boring, isn't it?"* *"Yes, it is."* *"You didn't go to class, did you?"* *"No, I didn't."*

A Listen and repeat the questions in the chart above.

B Listen to the conversations about a student moving far away to attend college. Draw the intonation pattern above the tag. Then write *U* if the speaker is uncertain of the information or *E* if the speaker is expecting agreement.

Conversation 1

1 You're not still thinking about going to college in Pennsylvania, are you? _U_

2 But that college doesn't offer the major you want, does it? _____

Conversation 2

3 Your son is thinking of going to college far from home, isn't he? _____

4 Duquesne University is in Pittsburgh, isn't it? _____

Conversation 3

5 You're excited about moving to Pennsylvania for college, aren't you? _____

6 You're not worried about moving so far from home, are you? _____

Conversation 4

7 Your son is worried about moving so far from home, isn't he? _____

8 But you and your wife feel OK about him moving so far away, don't you? _____

C Pair Work Find out information about your partner by asking tag questions. Use both intonation patterns. Use rising intonation when you are uncertain and falling intonation when you expect agreement.

A   *You're from Egypt, aren't you?*

B   *Yes, I am. You're studying culinary arts, aren't you?*

A   *Actually, no. My major is geography.*

4 Avoid Common Mistakes ⚠

1 **In negative questions, use the auxiliary verb + _not_.**

Didn't she
~~She no~~ call you?

2 **Answer negative questions the same way as regular _Yes/No_ questions.**

"Aren't you coming with us?"

No, I'm not.   *Yes, I am.*
"~~Yes.~~" (I'm not coming.)   "~~No.~~" (I'm coming.)

3 **In tag questions, remember to use an auxiliary verb + a pronoun in the tag.**

wasn't it
The research was old, ~~no~~?

4 **In the tag, use an auxiliary verb that agrees with the main verb + the correct pronoun for the subject.**

aren't they
They are still living in their hometown, ~~isn't it~~?

Editing Task

Find and correct six more mistakes in the conversation about economic mobility.

A   That article on economic mobility in America was really interesting, ~~no~~? *wasn't it*

B   It sure was. Some of the facts were surprising, isn't it? I was especially surprised that there is more economic mobility in countries like France and Germany.

A   I was, too. I thought there was more mobility here. By the way, don't you have a class

5   right now?

B   Yes. I'm finished for today. I'm free for the evening.

A   But you're working tonight, no?

B   No, I quit my job.

A   Really? Why? You no like it?

10 B   The job was fine. The truth is I'm moving to Florida with my family at the end of the semester, so I'm really busy.

A   You're kidding! Why? Your family no like it here?

B   They like it here, but there aren't many good jobs. We're moving where the jobs are.

A   But you only have one semester left, isn't it?

15 B   That's right, but I have to go with them.

5 Academic Writing

Argumentative Writing

Brainstorm > Organize > Write > Edit

In this writing cycle (units 14-16), you will write an argumentative essay that answers the prompt below. In this unit (14), you will analyze an argumentative text and start brainstorming ideas about your topic.

> *Which is more important when choosing a home: location or size?*

Exercise 5.1 Preparing to Write

Work with a partner. Discuss the questions.

1 Why might people move from one location to another?
2 What are the most beautiful buildings in your country? Describe them.
3 How do you feel about modern architecture? Give an example.
4 In your opinion, which is more important in architecture, beauty or function?

Exercise 5.2 Focusing on Vocabulary

Read the sentences and choose the best definition for the words in bold.

1 The **function** of an architectural drawing is to show what a building will look like after construction.
   a complexity or detail
   b purpose

2 Box-like buildings without windows or unique features can seem very **depressing**, can't they?
   a making you feel unhappy and without hope
   b making you feel physically weak and less active

3 When you see a magnificent work of art, such as a painting or a beautiful building, the creativity behind it can be **inspiring**.
   a causing eagerness to learn or do something
   b informative or educational

4 Not taking care of public parks and buildings **reflects** badly **on** a city and its government.
   a reacts to
   b damages

5 That architect has a wonderful **reputation** in her field; she is widely admired by many other architects.
   a the general opinion that people have about someone
   b a collection of works

6 He **demonstrated** the new construction technique for the public.
   a criticized or disapproved of something
   b showed how to do something; explained

Form or Function?

At the start of the twentieth century, Louis Sullivan, one of the creators of modern architecture, said that "form follows **function**." The term *functionalism* is used to suggest that the
5   idea behind architecture focuses primarily on the purpose or use of a building. That seems to mean that the look of a building is unimportant, doesn't it? On the contrary, many people feel that beauty is the most important factor in architectural design.
10 In the modern world, it seems that most architects try to combine the two ideas, aiming to create buildings that are both functional and **inspiring** in their beauty. This goal is often difficult to achieve, however. Don't we create buildings to serve the
15 needs in our lives? If so, the role that function plays should always be prioritized over form.

   Many people believe that architects have a wider responsibility to society than just designing functional buildings. Beautiful, well-constructed
20 buildings are a symbol of a civilized[1] society, and they **reflect** well on the **reputation** of a business or owner. Ugly public buildings, on the other hand, can project a negative image of the organization. Don't you agree? People say
25 that living or working in an ugly place creates a **depressing** and uninspiring environment. In contrast, an attractive building can make people feel happier and increase their motivation to work.

   The beauty of a building is important; however,
30 the reason for creating a building in the first place—its use—is even more important, isn't it? When building an airport terminal, for example, you need to think of the needs of passengers as well as planes. Passengers want to get to
35 their plane as quickly as they can, and planes need to be parked in a way that maximizes their ease of use. A solution to this challenge is that many airport terminals have a circular shape with satellite areas. Residential homes need to have
40 enough space for a family, art galleries need wall space to show pictures, and factories need to produce goods as efficiently as possible. Each type of building has a different function, and, therefore, it has a different form.

45   There is no reason that architecture cannot be both functional and beautiful, is there? Yet in practice, this can cause problems. The International Style of the 1920s and 1930s, an example of which is the Guggenheim Museum in
50 New York, was supposed to combine beauty with function. Many consider the museum's white spiral ramp beautiful, but there have been complaints that it is impractical, as it is difficult to stand back to view the art. Also, the ramp is so narrow that it
55 can become overcrowded. The Farnsworth House by Ludwig Mies van der Rohe is another icon of beautiful design that **demonstrate**s the idea that "less is more." However, critics have attacked it for a lack of privacy because of the huge glass
60 windows. It also has a leaky flat roof and has been repeatedly flooded. It seems that even these two celebrated designs have problems with functionality.

   If architects focus only on function, buildings
65 may be cold, ugly, and uninteresting. There is no doubt that a building with a beautiful form is something we can all appreciate. However, an attractive design that does not consider the practical needs of the people who live or work in
70 the building is also problematic. For this reason, shouldn't functional needs be addressed before visual ones? This issue of practicality is the most important feature of the buildings we live in, work in, and visit. Therefore, function must outweigh
75 form when an architect plans a building.

[1]**civilized:** having a well-developed way of life and social systems

Read the text on page 219. Work with a partner. Discuss the questions.

  1 What is the main idea of the reading?

  2 What are two examples of buildings that are beautiful but not completely practical?

  3 What are two problems that may occur when a building only focuses on function?

Exercise 5.4 Noticing the Grammar and Writing

Work with a partner. Complete the tasks.

  1 Highlight six questions in the text.

  2 Underline the last sentence in the first paragraph. What is the purpose of this sentence?

  3 What is the writer's view about architecture?

  4 What reasons and examples does the writer give to support this view?

  5 Where might this text appear? Explain your answer.

Negative and Tag Questions in Academic Writing

Negative questions and tag questions are not common in academic writing. They are generally found in less formal writing, like editorials, blogs, or popular magazines.

Exercise 5.5 Applying the Skill

Revise two negative questions and two tag questions in the text to make them appropriate for academic writing. You may need to combine more than one sentence when you revise the negative questions.

  1 _____

  2 _____

  3 _____

  4 _____

Argumentative Essays

In an argumentative essay, a writer looks at several viewpoints on a topic and attempts to give reasons to persuade the reader that one of those viewpoints is better than the others.

Exercise 5.6 Identifying Arguments and Reasons

1 Work with a partner. Review the text on page 219, and complete the T-chart.

2 In each column, which reason is the most persuasive? Which is the least persuasive? Why?

Writer's Argument:	Opposing Argument:
Reasons:	Reasons:

My Writing

Exercise 5.7 Brainstorming and Organizing

Work with a partner. Complete the tasks.

1 Many people choose a home based on its location or size. Why are these important considerations when selecting a home?

2 Write the reasons for considering location in the first column of the T-chart.

3 Write the reasons for considering size in the second column of the T-chart.

4 Look at your T-chart. Which do you feel is more important? Explain your answer.

Location	Size

Exercise 5.8 Writing an Argumentative Paragraph

Use your answers in Exercise 5.7 to write a paragraph about the importance of either location or size. Include a topic sentence, at least two reasons for your argument with supporting details, and a concluding sentence.

1 Grammar in the Real World

ACADEMIC
WRITING

Argumentative
writing

A Is it possible to identify "typical" American values? Theories exist about the values Americans hold today – and why. Read the article about one view of American values. Do you agree with the writer's point of view?

B Comprehension Check Match the two parts of the sentences.

1 According to some historians, the difficulty of living on the frontier led to _____

2 Survival under difficult circumstances may have led to _____

3 The lack of towns and traditions may have led to _____

a optimism.

b the value of hard work.

c individualism.

C Notice Find the sentences in the article and complete them.

1 Many Americans _____ they must work hard in order to be happy.

2 Traditionally, American children _____ they are responsible for their own lives.

3 Not all historians _____ frontier life influenced modern American values.

How many subjects are in each of these sentences? What word connects the two clauses?

U.S. Cultural Values

Values are beliefs held in common by members of a group. They often come from shared experiences. For example, some historians assert[1] **that the settlement of the American**
5 **West in the nineteenth century shaped many American values. These include the importance** of hard work, optimism, and individualism.

Countless U.S. children have learned in school **that hard work is essential**. In fact,
10 many Americans believe **that they must work hard in order to be happy**. How did this belief develop? According to some researchers, as Americans moved deeper into the continent, they discovered **that the West was mostly**
15 **wilderness**.[2] Their lives were difficult, and they had to work hard to survive. Some historians are convinced **that their success helped form a general belief in the value of hard work**.

Furthermore, many Americans believe **that**
20 **they should have a positive view of the future**. A few historians suggest **that this perspective helped put men on the moon**. What is the origin of this optimism? Some research suggests **that struggles on the frontier**[3] **encouraged this**
25 **attitude**. People found **that they could survive, even in difficult situations**.

Another common belief about Americans is **that they are individualistic**. Traditionally, American children have learned **that they are**
30 **responsible for their own lives**. This way of thinking supports the idea **that every person can succeed through hard work**. In addition, Americans tend to believe **that they can start over when they make mistakes**. Why
35 do they feel this way? It is the belief of some historians **that this idea developed as a result of frontier life**. Because there were few towns and traditions, settlers created their own rules. Each new settlement developed its own ways
40 of getting things done. When settlements faced problems, they had no choice but to try new and different approaches.

Not all historians agree **that frontier life influenced modern American values**.
45 Furthermore, the United States is becoming more and more culturally diverse all the time. Undoubtedly, this is already affecting the values held by its citizens. In what way might American values change?

---

[1]**assert:** to state an opinion

[2]**wilderness:** an area of land that has not been farmed or had towns and roads built on it

[3]**frontier:** the western area of the United States that did not have many white settlers from the eastern part of the United States

2 That Clauses

Grammar Presentation

Noun clauses function like nouns in sentences. They often begin with the word *that*.	*Many people believe that they must work hard in order to be happy.*

2.1 Forming *That* Clauses

A *That* clauses have their own subject and verb.

MAIN CLAUSE		THAT CLAUSE	
SUBJECT	VERB	SUBJECT	VERB

Many Americans think that anyone can succeed.

B In conversation and informal writing, *that* is often omitted. In academic writing, *that* is usually not omitted.

Most people recognize cooperation is important. (informal)

Most people recognize that cooperation is important. (formal)

2.2 Using *That* Clauses

Use *that* clauses after the following verbs that express mental activity:

assume, believe, decide, discover, expect, feel, find (out), guess, hear, hope, imagine, know, learn, notice, read, realize, recognize, say, see, show, suppose, think, understand

Can we <u>assume</u> that the core values have remained basically the same?

Some people <u>believe</u> that hard work brings happiness.

I've <u>discovered</u> that some cultures don't have a positive view of the future.

I <u>read</u> that American values developed during the colonial period.

Grammar Application

Exercise 2.1 Forming *That* Clauses

Combine the sentences about employees in the United States. Use *that* clauses.

1 Many Americans notice something. They are working harder but have less money.

   Many Americans notice that they are working harder but have less money.

2 In fact, recent research has found something. Hard work doesn't always lead to wealth.

   _____

   _____

3 Many older Americans are realizing something. They are unable to retire after working hard all their lives.

_____

_____

4 Many employees assumed something. Their companies would reward them for their hard work.

_____

_____

5 Researchers recently reported something. Job satisfaction has declined in recent years.

_____

_____

6 Employers are beginning to understand something. It is important to give people some freedom at work.

_____

_____

Exercise 2.2 Using *That* Clauses Without *That*

Over to You Do you believe that money makes people happy? Why or why not? Write five sentences. Use *that* clauses but do not use *that* in your sentences. Then share your sentences with a partner.

A *I don't think money makes people happy because having money causes many problems.*

B *I disagree. I believe you need a certain amount of money to feel secure, and this makes people happy.*

Exercise 2.3 Using *That* Clauses

A Write statements with *that* clauses using the words in parentheses.

1 Europeans work fewer hours than Americans. (I / understand)

   I understand that Europeans work fewer hours than Americans.

2 The average European gets about two months' vacation every year. (Michael / read)

_____

3 The average American works 46 weeks per year. (international labor statistics / show)

_____

4 Culture may be one reason for the difference in attitudes toward work. (some experts / believe)

_____

5 Europeans tend to value leisure more highly than Americans.
(a group of scholars / found)

_____

6 Americans tend to value earning money more highly than Europeans.
(some scholars / believe)

_____

7 Many Americans seem to use possessions as a measure of success.
(a professor at Gradina University / wrote)

_____

B Group Work **As a group, talk about differences between Americans and Europeans.
You may also include another culture that you know about. Discuss the following questions,
or use your own ideas.**

- How much vacation time do Americans usually get?
- How much vacation time do Europeans usually get?
- How much vacation time do people from other cultures usually get?
- Who tends to relax on vacation?
- Who tends to bring work to do on vacation?

Use the following verbs in your discussion:

believe	hear	imagine	read	see	suppose	think

A _I've heard that Americans get less vacation time than Canadians._
B _I think that's true. My brother lives in Canada, and he told me the same thing._

3 Agreement Between *That* Clauses and Main Clauses

Grammar Presentation

Use a past form in a *that* clause when the verb refers to a past event. When it refers to a present event or state, use a present form.

Some historians believe that American values developed a long time ago. (present belief about a past action)

Some historians believe that early American history explains certain American values. (present belief about a present state)

3.1 *That* Clauses in Sentences with Present Verbs in the Main Clause

A When the main clause is in the present, use a present form in the *that* clause to express a fact or general truth.

Many Americans feel that nothing is impossible.

Some cultures think that cooperation is very important.

B When the main clause is in the present, use a past form in the *that* clause to describe a past event.

Some historians don't think that early American history influenced American culture.

C When the main clause is in the present, use a future form in the *that* clause to describe a future event.

I assume that you are going to do more research.

3.2 *That* Clauses in Sentences with Past Verbs in the Main Clause

A When the main clause is in the past, use a past form in the *that* clause to describe an event or idea that happened at the same time as the event in the main clause.

Nineteenth-century Americans knew that hard work was necessary.

My professor noticed that many students were writing about the nineteenth century.

B When the main clause is in the past, use a present form in the *that* clause to express a universal truth or a fact that applies to the present.

Who discovered that the Earth is round and not flat?

Scientists discovered that DNA holds the code for life.

When I started living on my own, I found out that life is sometimes very hard.

C Use the past perfect or past perfect progressive when the event in the *that* clause happened before the event in the main clause.

I discovered that she had been copying my history research for years!

I heard that she had failed the test.

D Use *would* or *was/were* going to when the event of the *that* clause happened after the event of the main clause.	*I* <u>heard</u> that a famous historian <u>would be speaking</u> at the conference. *We* <u>discovered</u> that we <u>were going to study</u> twentieth-century history.

Grammar Application

Complete the sentences about the influence of Latin American cultures on mainstream U.S. culture. Use a *that* clause with the correct verb form. Sometimes more than one answer is possible.

1 Anthropologists agree / there be / links between Latin American cultures and U.S. culture (present for general truth)

   Anthropologists agree that there are links between Latin American cultures and U.S. culture.

2 Research / shows / contemporary Latin American cultures / have / roots in African, European, and indigenous cultures (present for general truth)

   _____

3 Sociologists / believe / Latin American cultures / influence / world culture as well as U.S. culture (past event)

   _____

4 Many musicologists / agree / modern U.S. music / be / derived in part from Latin American cultures (present for general truth)

   _____

5 Many language experts / assert / Spanish speakers / contribute / a great many words to the English language (past event)

   _____

6 Most sociologists / agree / Latin American cultures / continue / to influence U.S. culture (future for future action)

   _____

Listen to part of a lecture on westward movement in nineteenth-century North America. Complete the sentences with the words you hear.

In the nineteenth century, many people __*believed that*__ Americans __*had*__ the right
                                              (1)   (2)
to expand across the continent. John Quincy Adams, the sixth president of the United States,

_____ one large country _____ good for all Americans.
        (3)   (4)

However, some people _____ the westward
(5)
expansion _____ some negative consequences.
(6)
For example, some people _____ westward
(7)
expansion _____ a negative impact on Native
(8)
American culture. In fact, some Americans at the time

_____ the U.S. government _____
(9)   (10)
Native American land unfairly. They also _____
(11)
westward expansion _____ many wars, such as the Mexican-American War of
(12)
1836. Most people _____ Americans _____ native plants and
(13)   (14)
wildlife as well.

Exercise 3.3 Agreement Between *That* Clauses and Main Clauses

Group Work Do Internet research on how a culture, such as Irish-American or Latin American culture, has influenced culture in the United States or Canada. Write statements with *that* clauses. Use simple present for general truths, simple past for past events, and future for future action. Share your sentences with your group members. Use the following phrases in your sentences:

- I learned / discovered / found that . . .
- For example, . . .
- Another area that . . .
- A recent study showed / found that . . .

I learned that Indian culture has influenced American culture. One area that Indian culture has influenced is entertainment. Many film specialists agree that Bollywood movies are influencing American movies.

4 *That* Clauses After Adjectives and Nouns

Grammar Presentation

That clauses can follow some adjectives and nouns.	*I'm sure that a cultural group shares at least some values.* *I have the feeling that our values are quite different.*

4.1 *That* Clauses After Adjectives

A You can use a *that* clause after adjectives that express certainty or emotion.	*I'm certain that I haven't read enough about American culture.* *The conference organizers were pleased that he accepted the invitation.*

B You can use *that* clauses after *It + be +* certain adjectives. These adjectives often express emotions or degrees of certainty. They include:

certain, clear, evident, (un)fortunate, interesting, (un)likely, surprising, understandable

<u>It is evident</u> *that many other cultures have influenced U.S. culture.*

<u>It is unfortunate</u> *that many students don't know more about their country's history.*

<u>It is unlikely</u> *that we'll finish the unit by the next class.*

<u>It is understandable</u> *that historians disagree about the development of cultural values.*

4.2 *That* Clauses After Adjectives

A You can use *that* clauses after nouns that express thoughts and ideas, such as *belief, feeling, impression,* and *possibility.*

It was our <u>impression</u> *that the historian was wrong.*

There was no <u>possibility</u> *that he was going to convince us.*

B You can use noun *+ be + that* clauses with these commonly used nouns: *concern, difference, hope, idea, impression, point, problem, saying,* and *views.*

The <u>concern was</u> *that we would never find out the truth.*

The <u>point is</u> *that the United States is a very large country.*

The <u>problem is</u> *that very individualistic people can find it hard to work in a group.*

DATA FROM THE REAL WORLD

Research shows that the following nouns frequently occur with *that* clauses:

assumption, belief, claim, conclusion, doubt, fact, hope, idea, impression, possibility, report, suggestion, view

Is it your assumption *that we cannot find jobs in other companies?*

We came to the conclusion *that he would never understand our point of view.*

Grammar Application

Exercise 4.1 *That* Clauses After Adjectives

Complete the magazine interview with a cultural studies expert. For each item, use the words in parentheses with the correct form of *be* and a *that* clause.

U.S. CULTURE AND THE WORLD

Interviewer Some experts are studying culture, and they have expressed some concerns. What are they concerned about?

Dr. Green *They are concerned that U.S. culture may have a negative impact on global culture.*

(1. they / concerned / U.S. culture may have a negative impact on global culture)

Interviewer Why are they worried?

Dr. Green _____

_____

(2. some people / worried / Americanization is making everything the same)

Interviewer Why do they think this?

Dr. Green _____

_____

(3. they / aware / Hollywood and fast-food chains are influencing culture)

Interviewer What's your opinion?

Dr. Green _____

(4. I / convinced / culture is a two-way street)

Interviewer Why do you think that?

Dr. Green _____

_____

_____

(5. I / positive / other cultures influence U.S. culture as much as U.S. culture influences them)

Interviewer Can you give some examples?

Dr. Green _____

(6. a lot of people / surprised / the French invented movies)

Interviewer What else?

Dr. Green _____

_____

(7. they / surprised / the British invented one of the original fast foods, fish and chips)

Interviewer So what can we conclude?

Dr. Green _____

(8. I / sure / we all benefit from global cultural exchange)

A Group Work **Complete the answers to these questions about the spread of U.S. culture worldwide. Explain your answers.**

1 Is the exportation of U.S. culture to the rest of the world a good thing?

It is my belief that *the exportation of U.S. culture is in some ways a good thing and in some ways a bad thing* .

2 Survey your group members: Do you think that most people outside of the United States have a favorable opinion of U.S. popular culture?

It is our feeling that _____

_____ .

3 Does your group think that most people outside of the United States have good feelings about American fast-food restaurants opening up in cities around the world?

It is our group's impression that _____

_____ .

B Over to You **Read the results of a survey about the exportation of U.S. culture. Write three sentences about the survey results. Use the following adjectives:** *amazed, disappointed, glad, pleased, relieved, surprised.* **Discuss your reactions with a partner.**

What is your opinion of U.S. popular culture, such as music, TV shows, and movies?

Very favorable	21%
Somewhat favorable	39%
Somewhat unfavorable	25
Very unfavorable%	14%
No Answer	1%

I'm not surprised that most people have mixed feelings about U.S. culture.

5 Avoid Common Mistakes ⚠

1 **Do not use a comma before a *that* clause.**

Their parents are pleased, that they are getting married.

2 **Remember that *that* clauses need a complete verb.**

was
I noticed that she ˄ leaving.

3 ***That* clauses must have a subject.**

many settlers
Records show that ˄ hoped to return east later.

4 **In academic writing, do not omit *that*.**

that
Some cultures believe ˄ individuals should put other people first.

Editing Task

Find and correct six more mistakes in the paragraphs about a famous American of the mid-nineteenth century.

Settlers from the east who traveled across the American West in the
that
mid-nineteenth century understood ˄ they faced a difficult journey across deserts and

mountains. They knew, that the trip would take years and that some people lose their

lives. However, they were optimistic.

5   Michael T. Simmons was one of those determined travelers. Someone told him

to go to the Pacific Northwest for new opportunities. He sold his business to pay

for the supplies that he and his family needed. He knew that the area was largely

unknown. He also knew that was dangerous. This did not stop him.

When Simmons and his group reached Oregon, he announced that was

10   going to continue north. The Hudson's Bay Trading Company heard the news, and

they discouraged him. However, Simmons was certain, that the trip going to be

successful, and he did not listen. Instead, he continued north as planned. After he

arrived, he helped to establish the first settlement in the territory that is now known

as Washington State. Documents show that Simmons built the first mill using water

15   from the Tumwater waterfall for power. For this, he is sometimes called the father of

Washington industry.

6 Academic Writing

Argumentative Writing

Brainstorm > Organize > Write > Edit

In Unit 14, you analyzed a text and brainstormed ideas for the prompt below. In this unit (15), you will continue brainstorming and start organizing your ideas by connecting information and supporting arguments.

> *Which is more important when choosing a home: location or size?*

Connecting Information

When you present an argument, you need to connect the information clearly and logically. To do this, there are several ways to refer back to a previous sentence with the same topic.

Countless U.S. children have learned that **hard work** is essential. In fact, many Americans believe that they must **work hard** in order to be happy.

Work hard in the second sentence is a rewording of *hard work* in the first sentence. **Rewording** connects the sentences and helps avoid unnecessary repetition.

Writers also use reference words such as *this, that, these, those*, or reference phrases like *that is why, for this reason*, or *in spite of this* to connect information and avoid repetition.

Traditionally, American children have learned that they are responsible for their own lives. **This** way of thinking supports the idea that every person can succeed through hard work.

Exercise 6.1 Applying the Skill

Complete the paragraph with the correct words and phrases from the box.

for this reason	in spite of	this	those

U.S. culture has spread all over the world. (1)_____ concerns many people for a number of reasons. North American movies, music, and TV programs often give a false impression of life in the U.S. (2)_____, some experts warn that this "Hollywood culture" does not accurately reflect American society and can lead to misunderstandings of U.S. citizens. (3)_____ who say it is inaccurate believe that Hollywood portrays a glamorous life in which everyone is beautiful, rich, and happy. Others argue this is not a real concern. (4)_____ the portrayal of America in popular movies, people around the globe are well aware of the struggles many Americans encounter.

Supporting Arguments

Writers need to think about how to support an argument by following it with specific facts or observations that can persuade the reader.

Point of view: Working hard is the most important value that Americans have.

Not a specific fact or observation → not very persuasive: This is because it is good to work hard.

A specific observation → much more persuasive: People who work hard are more financially secure and contribute more to their community.

Exercise 6.2 Understanding the Skill

Read the numbered sentences. Choose the follow-up sentence that sounds more persuasive.

1 Having an optimistic view of the future is an important value.
   a This is because you will be happier.
   b If you are positive, you are likely to accomplish more things.

2 People need to know the history of their country.
   a It is sad that people do not know their country's history.
   b When you understand your country's history, you better understand its values.

3 The exportation of American culture is positive.
   a It is good because people want to know more about American culture.
   b When a culture is exported, people learn and understand more about others.

Exercise 6.3 Applying the Skill

Work with a partner. Read the opinions. Think of a supporting statement for each one.

1 The best way to learn about American culture is to watch movies.

2 People who are very individualistic do not work well with others.

3 Americans place too much importance on work, and not enough on family.

My Writing

Exercise 6.4 Organizing Ideas

1 Work in a small group. Review your paragraphs from My Writing in Unit 14. Who believes choosing a home for size is more important? Who believes choosing a home for location is more important?

2 Create a new T-chart about the advantages of the size and location of a home. Write all the reasons that you can think of in each column.

3 As a group, organize the reasons from strongest to weakest.

4 Write down any ideas that you can use in your essay.

16 Noun Clauses with *Wh-* Words and *If/Whether*

Inventions They Said Would Never Work

1 Grammar in the Real World

ACADEMIC WRITING

Argumentative writing

A Have you ever thought of inventing something? If so, what was it? Read the article about inventors. What obstacles did Edison and the Wright brothers face?

B Comprehension Check **Answer the questions.**

1 Why did people doubt Thomas Edison?
2 How did Edison convince the world of his accomplishment?
3 What were the obstacles the Wright brothers faced?

C Notice **Find the sentences in the article and complete them.**

1 No one knew exactly _____ .

2 Second, the success of inventors often depended on

_____ .

3 He could not predict _____ .

Look at the sentences again. Answer the questions.

1 In sentence 1, what type of question is the missing clause similar to?

  a an information question   b a *Yes/No* question

2 In sentences 2 and 3, what type of question is the missing clause similar to?

  a an information question   b a *Yes/No* question

INVENTIONS PEOPLE SAID WOULD NEVER WORK

Throughout history, new ideas have often faced skepticism[1] from society. Skepticism, however, has never stopped the creation of new inventions. Three important American inventors, Thomas Edison and
5 Orville and Wilbur Wright, faced strong public doubt, but they persevered,[2] and the results were the invention of the electric light bulb and the airplane.

While Edison may now be considered a brilliant inventor, in his lifetime he faced much criticism. Most
10 inventors in his day would not announce an invention until they had a model. Edison, however, stated that he had invented the light bulb, but he had no actual evidence for it. Thus, scientists doubted **what he said**. Also, most inventors had a schedule
15 for their projects, but Edison did not. No one knew exactly **when he would complete it**. Moreover, his experiments failed repeatedly, and this added to the skepticism. However, in 1882, Edison succeeded in lighting up an entire New York neighborhood,
20 and the world finally understood **what he had accomplished**.

Many inventors in the early 1900s wondered **whether it was possible to fly**. The Wright brothers proved **what others doubted** by inventing the first
25 airplane. However, they faced many obstacles along the way. First, most inventors were highly educated, but the Wright brothers had little formal education. Second, the success of inventors often depended on **whether they had financial support**. The
30 Wright brothers had none. Finally, most inventors publicized their research, but the Wright brothers did not. No one knew exactly what they were doing. Consequently, the public did not believe that the Wright brothers would succeed. Wilbur himself was
35 not sure **what would happen**. He could not predict **if their airplane would fly or not**. Then, in 1903, the Wright brothers flew their airplane for 12 seconds in Kitty Hawk, North Carolina. No one could believe **what they were seeing**. Five years later in France,
40 they flew another plane higher and longer.

Inventors almost always face public disbelief. Some people have trouble believing that new ideas are possible, but they certainly are. No one can be sure about **what the future holds**.

---

[1]**skepticism:** doubting the truth or value of an idea or belief
[2]**persevere:** continue doing something in a determined way despite difficulties

2 Noun Clauses with *Wh-* Words

Grammar Presentation

Noun clauses with *wh-* words can act as subjects, direct objects, or objects of prepositions.	*What they wanted* was financial support. The inventor understood *how we should build the machine.* I learned about *how many inventions are made every year.*

2.1 Forming Noun Clauses with *Wh-* Words

A Noun clauses with *wh-* words use statement word order (subject + verb).	I've just realized *what he did!* I don't know *when Edison invented the light bulb.*
B When noun clauses with *wh-* words *who*, *what*, and *which* act as subjects, they take a singular verb.	*What happened next* <u>is</u> going to surprise you.

2.2 Using Noun Clauses with *Wh-* Words

A Noun clauses with *wh-* words often appear after the following verbs: Thoughts and opinions: *consider, know, remember* Learning and perception: *figure out, find out, see, understand, wonder* Emotions: *care, doubt, hate, like, love*	I don't <u>remember</u> *who invented the airplane.* We need to <u>figure out</u> *why our invention failed.* Our professor <u>cares</u> *how we do our work.*
B Noun clauses with *wh-* words often follow verbs + prepositions, including *care about, decide on, find out about, forget about, know about, learn about, read about,* and *see about.*	We shouldn't <u>forget about</u> *which inventions succeeded and which didn't.* I <u>read about</u> *where Edison grew up.*

2.3 Reduced Noun Clauses with Infinitives

Noun clauses with *wh-* words can often be reduced to *wh-* word + infinitive. Common infinitives used this way include *to ask, to consider, to decide, to figure (out), to find (out), to forget, to know, to learn, to remember, to say, to see, to show, to understand, and to wonder.*

We're not sure who/whom[1] *to ask* for *information.*
= *We're not sure* who/whom[1] *we should ask for information.*

I don't know what *to say about your invention.*
= *I don't know* what *I can say about your invention.*

[1]The use of *whom* is infrequent, except in very formal writing.

Grammar Application

Exercise 2.1 Noun Clauses with *Wh-* Words

A Listen to the conversation among a group of students doing Internet research on recent inventions and inventors. Complete the sentences with the noun clauses you hear.

Peter	OK, let's start with Randi Altschul.
Larry	I don't know ___*who Randi Altschul is*___ . (1)
Paula	Neither do I. I don't know _____ . (2)
Peter	I know _____ . She invented the disposable (3) cell phone.
Paula	I'm impressed! I wonder _____ . (4)
Larry	I don't know.
Peter	Got it! It says here her cell phone wasn't working well, and she felt like throwing it away.
Larry	Let's find out _____ . (5)
Peter	It says here she got a patent for it in 1999.
Larry	I just found out _____ at the (6) time. It was Florida.
Paula	I wonder _____ . (7)
Peter	It says here that it was only 2 inches by 3 inches – kind of like a credit card.
Larry	I wonder _____ . (8)
Peter	It was made of recycled paper.

PHONE-CARD-PHONE™
Working Model

B Pair Work With a partner, talk about what you know or don't know about other inventions. Use the verbs in A with *wh-* noun clauses.

I know when the smartphone was invented. It was in 2007. I remember what company first made it, but I don't know who invented it.

Exercise 2.2 Reduced Noun Clauses with *Wh-* Words + Infinitives

Some college students are talking to a business adviser about their new product. Rewrite the sentences with *wh-* words + infinitives.

1 We don't know where we should start.

   We don't know where to start.

2 Amy wonders where she could find a good patent lawyer.

   _____

3 I don't know how I can find a manufacturer for our product.

   _____

4 Binh is wondering who he can ask for money for our invention.

   _____

5 I'll figure out who we can contact for financial advice.

   _____

6 I wonder what we should charge for our product.

   _____

3 Noun Clauses with *If/Whether*

Grammar Presentation

Noun clauses can begin with *if* or *whether*. These noun clauses are similar in some ways to *Yes/No* questions, but they follow statement (subject + verb) word order.	I'm not sure *if the Wright brothers invented the airplane*. He doesn't know *whether we will get money for our experiment*.

3.1 Forming Noun Clauses with *If / Whether*

A Use statement word order (subject + verb) for noun clauses with *if/whether*.	I don't know **if the public will accept our idea.** I don't know **whether Edison really invented the light bulb.**
B You can use the words *or not* at the end of both *if* and *whether* clauses.	The scientist didn't know **if/whether you would understand her invention <u>or not</u>.**
Or not can immediately follow *whether*, but not *if*.	The scientist didn't know **whether <u>or not</u> you would understand her invention.** NOT *The scientist didn't know if ~~or not~~ you would understand her invention.*
C You can use *if/whether* to introduce two options.	We don't know **whether the new phone <u>or</u> the new tablet will come out first.**

3.2 Using Noun Clauses with *If / Whether*

A You can use noun clauses with *if/whether* after the following verbs: Thoughts and opinions: *decide, know, remember* Learning and perception: *figure out, find out* Emotions: *care, doubt, matter, mind*	I <u>haven't decided</u> **if I'm going to write a report about the Wright brothers.** He can't <u>find out</u> **if Edison first tried the light bulb in New York.** They <u>doubted</u> **whether anyone would steal their idea.**
B You can also use noun clauses with *whether* after verbs + prepositions, including *care about, decide on, find out about, forget about, know about,* and *read about*. You cannot use *if* after prepositions.	You should <u>forget about</u> **whether you'll make a lot of money with that invention.** NOT *You should forget about ~~if you'll make a lot of money with that invention~~.*
C You can use an infinitive with *whether*. You cannot use an infinitive with *if*.	He didn't know **whether <u>to share</u> his discovery.** (= He didn't know whether he should share his discovery.) NOT *He didn't know ~~if to share his discovery~~.*

 DATA FROM THE REAL WORLD

Noun clauses with *if* are much more frequent than noun clauses with *whether. Whether* is more frequent in writing than in speaking.

Combine the sentences. Use a noun clause with *if* or *whether*. Sometimes more than one answer is possible.

1 Scientists have not decided something. Is time travel possible?

  Scientists have not decided whether time travel is possible.

2 Many people don't know something. Do some robots think like humans?

  _____

3 Many people don't know this. Can we invent a non-polluting fuel?

  _____

4 We can't remember this. Has anyone invented a self-cleaning house?

  _____

5 Many people don't know about this. Are hybrid cars good for the environment?

  _____

6 Scientists haven't figured this out. Are there other planets humans can live on?

  _____

A Read the inventor's list of questions about her invention. Rewrite the questions as sentences. Use noun clauses with *if* or *whether*.

1 Can I really invent a solar-powered car?

  I don't know if I can really invent a solar-powered car.

2 Will it take a long time to invent it?

  _____

3 Am I smart enough to do it by myself?

  _____

4 Do people really want solar-powered cars?

  _____

5 Will a solar-powered car work on cloudy days?

  _____

6 Is my car going to be too expensive?

  _____

B Read more questions from the inventor in A. Rewrite the questions as sentences. Use *whether or not* with an infinitive.

1 Should I get some help?

  I can't decide whether or not to get some help.

2 Should I take out a loan from the bank?

_____

3 Should I patent my idea first?

_____

4 Should I see a lawyer?

_____

4 Noun Clauses in Direct and Indirect Questions

Grammar Presentation

Wh- noun clauses and noun clauses with *if* and *whether* can be used in direct and indirect questions.	*Do you know when New York got electricity?* (direct question) *I was wondering when New York got electricity.* (indirect question)

4.1 Forming Direct and Indirect Questions

A Direct questions with noun clauses have question word order and end with a question mark. Common phrases include: *Do you know . . . ? Can you tell me . . . ? Would you know . . . ?*	*Do you know who invented the first calculator?* *Are you trying to find out if Edison was born in this country?* *Can anyone tell me if Edison was born in Scotland?*
B Indirect questions with noun clauses have statement word order and end with a period. Common phrases include: *I want to find out . . . I'd like to know . . . I don't know why . . .*	*I have been wondering what a patent is.* *My group really needs to find out if the Wright brothers had financial support for their invention.* *I'd like to know if people need to get patents for their inventions.*

▶▶ Verbs and Fixed Expressions that Introduce Indirect Questions: See page A10.

Grammar Application

Exercise 4.1 Direct and Indirect Questions

Complete the interview with artist and inventor Crispiano Columna. Rewrite the questions in parentheses as noun clauses in direct and indirect questions. Sometimes more than one answer is possible.

| ArtOnline | I'm wondering *if you are both an artist and an inventor* .
(1 Are you both an artist and an inventor?) |

Crispiano Columna   Yes, I'm both.

ArtOnline   I'd like to know _____ .
(2 What is your most famous invention?)

Crispiano Columna   I make sculptures that you can wear as gloves.

ArtOnline   I was wondering _____ .
(3 Can you show us an example?)

Crispiano Columna   Yes, I'm wearing a pair right now.

ArtOnline   I was wondering _____ .
(4 Did you study art in college?)

Crispiano Columna   No. In fact, I studied literature.

ArtOnline   I'd like to know _____ .
(5 How did you become an artist?)

Crispiano Columna   I taught myself. I learned about color and drawing from books.

ArtOnline   I'd like to know _____ .
(6 What was your first invention?)

Crispiano Columna   I invented a toy airplane for my nephew when I was a teenager.

Exercise 4.2 More Indirect Questions

A Look at the pictures of inventions. Write one indirect question about each picture. Use the following phrases:

I wonder / I'm wondering . . .   I'd like to know . . .   I'm interested in knowing. . .

| The hair protector | The food cooler | The baby mop | The butter stick |

I wonder who invented the hair protector.

1 _____

2 _____

3 _____

4 _____

B Pair Work Take turns reading your questions.

5 Avoid Common Mistakes ⚠

1 **Remember that a noun clause with a *wh-* word follows statement word order.**

No one knows what ~~will~~ the next great invention ‸be.
will (above "will")

2 **Be careful to spell *whether* correctly.**

The success of the invention depended on ~~wether~~ people would buy it.
whether (above "wether")

3 **Do not confuse *whether* and *either*.**

The newest electronic devices will always tempt us, ~~either~~ we like them or not.
whether (above "either")

Editing Task

Find and correct the mistakes in the paragraphs about the importance of the Internet.

Many inventions make life more convenient, but the Internet is the most essential one today. The Internet is a part of daily life. Although some people worry about ~~wheather~~ this fact is harmful or not, many agree that they do not know what would they do if they could not go online.
whether (above "wheather")

5 First of all, the Internet helps people communicate instantly with family and friends who are far away. In the past, people had to write a letter or pay for a long-distance call to find out how were they doing. While they waited, they worried about whether their loved ones were all right. Now there are many ways to contact people and find out if they are well.

10 In addition, the Internet helps people find information. If we want to know what is the temperature in Seoul today, we only have to type the question. Also, it is very easy to look for employment, research solutions to a problem, and even find out wether a movie is playing nearby.

It is too early to tell either the Internet causes serious long-term problems for
15 society or not. To me, it seems extremely valuable because it connects me to people I care about and to information I need.

6 Academic Writing

Argumentative Writing

Brainstorm > Organize > Write > Edit

In Unit 15, you learned ways to connect information and support your arguments for the prompt below. In this unit (16), you will write, revise, and edit your essay.

> *Which is more important when choosing a home: location or size?*

Register in Academic Writing

The types of language used in informal writing and in formal, academic writing are very different. Academic writers use more precise, technical words and more formal phrases and linking words.

They usually avoid slang, colloquial expressions, first-person pronouns, contractions, exclamation points, abbreviations like *etc.*, and negative and tag questions.

Exercise 6.1 Applying the Skill

Replace the informal words and phrases in bold in the paragraph with academic words and phrases from the box.

a great deal of	benefits	critical	fundamentally	reduce	undoubtedly

    I'm sure that the greatest invention of all time is the microwave. The microwave **basically** makes our lives easier. It has a number of **good things**. First, with a microwave, we can prepare **lots of** food in a very short time. Microwaves **cut down** our meal preparation time, which is useful in our busy lives. Next, microwaves are small, and this is **really important** if you have a small kitchen.

Argumentative Essay Structure

Argumentative essays often follow the structure below.
- **Introductory Paragraph**
- **Body Paragraph 1**: Argument #1 in favor of your choice being more important
- **Body Paragraph 2**: Argument #2 in favor of your choice being more important
- **Body Paragraph 3** (if necessary): Argument #3 in favor of your choice being more important
- **Concluding Paragraph**

My Writing

Exercise 6.2 Applying the Skill

1 Write your point of view.

2 Review your notes and T-charts from My Writing in Units 14 and 15. Choose the 2–3 strongest arguments for your body paragraphs. Think of reasons and support for them.

3 Write your thesis statement.

4 Write the first draft of your argumentative essay.

Exercise 6.3 Revising Your Ideas

1 Work with a partner. Use the questions to give feedback on your partner's essay.

- Which of your partner's ideas seem the strongest to you?
- Which of your partner's ideas needs to be explained more clearly?
- What could your partner add or remove to make the essay stronger and clearer?

2 Use the feedback from your partner to revise the ideas and content of your essay.

Exercise 6.4 Editing Your Writing

Use the checklist to review and edit your essay.

Does your essay answer the prompt completely?	
Does your essay follow the argumentative essay structure?	
Does your essay support your point of view with persuasive language and ideas?	
Did you connect information clearly and logically?	
Did you support your argument with specific examples and information?	
Did you use the correct register for an academic essay?	

Exercise 6.5 Editing Your Grammar

Use the checklist to review and edit the grammar in your essay.

Did you use *that* clauses correctly?	
Did you use noun clauses correctly?	
Did you avoid the common mistakes in the charts on pages 217, 233, and 245?	

Exercise 6.6 Writing Your Final Draft

Apply the feedback and edits from Exercises 6.3 to 6.5 to write the final draft of your essay.

1 Grammar in the Real World

ACADEMIC WRITING

Argumentative writing using graphs and tables for support

A What makes people work hard at their jobs? Read the article about employee motivation. What type of reward is particularly effective in motivating workers?

B Comprehension Check **Complete the chart. Check (✓) whether each reward is external or internal.**

	External Reward	Internal Reward
1 Pay raise		
2 Feeling successful		
3 Freedom to work independently		
4 Good salary		
5 Good grades		

C Notice **Find similar sentences in the article and complete the sentences below.**

1 Lionel Messi _____, "Money is not a motivating factor… My motivation comes from playing the game I love."

2 Daniel Pink, the author of a book on motivation, _____ an audience once that Google was a great example of a company that supported autonomy.

3 Pink _____ the audience that Google News and Gmail had been created during this free time.

Each sentence tells what someone says. Which sentence gives the actual words of the speaker? How do you know?

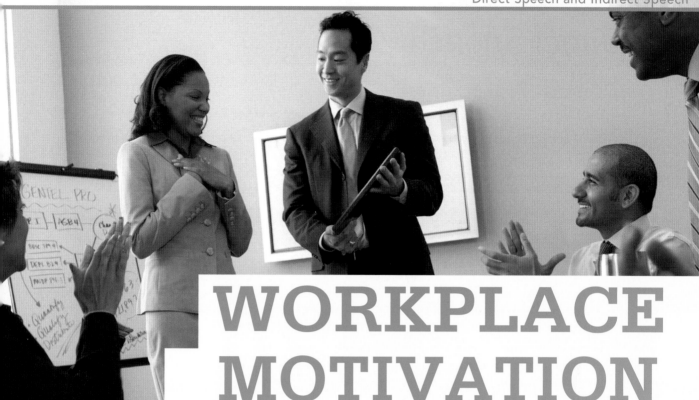

WORKPLACE MOTIVATION

Motivation is the desire to do something. Soccer star Lionel Messi **said**, "Money is not a motivating factor... My motivation comes from playing the game I love." Messi meant that he enjoys playing soccer more
5 than making millions of dollars. Can that be true? What other factors are important in motivating people?

Many psychologists believe that there are two types of rewards that affect motivation: external rewards and internal rewards. External rewards are rewards that
10 someone gives you. A pay raise is a common external reward. A good grade at school is also an example of an external reward. Internal rewards are connected to the feelings people have about the work they do. The satisfaction you get when you do something well is
15 an internal reward. Researcher Frederick Herzberg (1923–2000) studied motivation in the workplace for many years. Herzberg **said that** employers must think about factors that affect employees' feelings of satisfaction. Herzberg **explained that** working
20 conditions and relationships among co-workers affect workers' motivation. Therefore, employers need to create an environment that makes employees feel safe, valued, and accepted.

Some studies on workplace motivation have
25 focused on autonomy, which is the freedom to work independently. This is an important internal reward. Daniel Pink, the author of a book on motivation, **told** an audience once **that** Google was a good example of a company that supported autonomy. One day each
30 week, Google engineers focus on their own ideas. Pink **informed** the audience **that** Google News and Gmail had been created during this free time.

Research also shows that appreciation is a powerful reward. In his book *The 1001 Rewards and*
35 *Recognition[1] Fieldbook*, Bob Nelson described a study on the effects of appreciation on motivation. The study **asked**, "What motivates you?" Workers ranked the importance of 65 motivating factors. Nelson **indicated that** appreciation for their work ranked first for
40 the workers.

The subject of worker motivation is complex. People expect fair pay for their work. However, research **shows that** people find internal rewards more meaningful than a high salary.

---

[1]**recognition:** special positive attention

2 Direct Speech

Grammar Presentation

Direct speech repeats people's exact words.	Lionel Messi said, "Money is not a motivating factor. … My motivation comes from playing the game I love."

2.1 Forming Sentences with Direct Speech

A Direct speech consists of a reporting clause and a person's exact words.	REPORTING CLAUSE *Lionel Messi said, "Money is not a motivating factor."*
The most common reporting verb is *said*. Use a comma after the verb.	*Our manager said, "Treat the customers like family, and they will come back."*
To quote speech, use quotation marks and a capital letter to begin the direct speech. End the direct speech with punctuation inside the quotation marks.	*My colleague said, "We are going to lead the company in sales next year!"*
B The reporting clause can also come at the end or in the middle of direct speech. Notice that the verb can also come before the subject in the reporting clause when the reporting clause comes at the end or in the middle.	*"The company pays its workers fairly," the president said.* *"We didn't do well this year," said Liz, "so we won't get a sales bonus."*
C Use the verb *asked* to quote a question.	*Mr. Smith asked, "What do you hope to accomplish in this job?"*

Grammar Application

Exercise 2.1 Statements in Direct Speech

A Rewrite the quotations about motivation as direct speech. Sometimes more than one answer is possible.

1 in my experience, there is only one motivation, and that is desire –Jane Smiley

   Jane Smiley said, "In my experience, there is only one motivation, and that is desire."

2 the ones who want to achieve and win championships motivate themselves
–Mike Ditka

_____

_____

3 the ultimate inspiration is the deadline –Nolan Bushnell

_____

_____

4 motivation is the art of getting people to do what you want them to do because
they want to do it –Dwight D. Eisenhower

_____

_____

5 I'm a great believer in luck, and I find the harder I work, the more I have of it
–Thomas Jefferson

_____

_____

6 great work is done by people who are not afraid to be great –Fernando Flores

_____

_____

7 nothing great was ever achieved without enthusiasm –Ralph Waldo Emerson

_____

_____

8 you miss 100 percent of the shots you don't take –Wayne Gretzky

_____

_____

9 the journey of a thousand miles begins with a single step –Lao Tzu

_____

_____

B Over to You Choose two of the quotations, and write a sentence that explains what
each one means.

_When Jane Smiley said, "In my experience there is only one motivation, and that
is desire," she meant that the only real motivation is wanting to do something._

C Pair Work Share your sentences with a partner. Discuss whether you agree or disagree
with your partner's interpretation.

A Read the transcript of an online discussion about motivating employees. Then rewrite each question as a direct speech question. The information in parentheses tells you where to put the reporting clauses – at the beginning or end of the sentences.

⌂   💬   ↻   ☰   ✉

Working Today

Today, motivational expert Camila Valdez is here to answer your questions.

Claire   **Is money the best way to get employees to work harder?**
(1)

Camila   No. Studies show that appreciation and recognition are the best ways.

Pedro   **Do you have guidelines for rewarding employees?**
(2)

Camila   Try to match the size of the reward to the size of the accomplishment.

Roxana   **When should you give the rewards?**
(3)

Camila   It's really best to give them as soon as possible after employees have

accomplished something.

Hong   **What are some ways to motivate employees?**
(4)

Camila   Give rewards that fit your employees' working style.

Chelsea   **Can you give an example of what you mean?**
(5)

Camila   Certainly. For example, give a more flexible schedule to working parents.

They will feel more focused at work because they will be able to take care

of their home-related responsibilities.

---

1 (beginning) *Claire asked, "Is money the best way to get employees to*

work harder?"

2 (end) _____

3 (beginning) _____

4 (end) _____

5 (beginning) _____

B Over to You   Ask two classmates these questions: Would money motivate you to work harder? Why or why not? Then write a short report on your interviews with direct speech statements and questions.

I talked to Anne and Mike. I asked, "Would money motivate you to work harder?" Anne said, "No, it wouldn't." I asked, "Why not?" Anne said, "I work to please myself. That's my reward." Then I asked Mike, "Would money motivate you to work harder?" Mike said, "Yes, it would."

3 Indirect Speech

Grammar Presentation

Indirect speech tells what someone says in another person's words. Indirect speech is also called reported speech.	Lionel Messi said, "Money is not a motivating factor." (direct speech) Lionel Messi said that money was not a motivating factor. (indirect speech)

3.1 Forming Indirect Speech

An indirect speech statement consists of a reporting verb such as *say* in the main clause, followed by a *that* clause. The word that is optional and is often omitted when speaking.	She said, "The boss is angry." (direct speech) She said (that) the boss was angry. (indirect speech)

3.2 Tense Shifting in Indirect Speech

A After a past verb in the reporting clause, the verb form in indirect speech usually changes. The verb shifts to express a past time.

DIRECT SPEECH	INDIRECT SPEECH
She said, "The boss *is* angry."	She said that the boss *was* angry.
He said, "She *is enjoying* the work."	He said that she *was enjoying* the work.
They said, "The store *closed* last year."	They said that the store *had closed* last year.
The manager said, "The group *has done* good work."	The manager said that the group *had done* good work.

B The following forms usually change in indirect speech.

DIRECT SPEECH	INDIRECT SPEECH
He said, "The department *will add* three new managers."	He said that the department *would add* three new managers.
She said, "They *are going to hire* more people soon."	She said that they *were going to hire* more people soon.
The teacher said, "The students *can work* harder."	The teacher said that the students *could work* harder.
Their manager said, "Money *may not be* very important to them."	Their manager said that money *might not be* very important to them.

C The forms of *should, might, ought to,* and *could* are the same in direct and indirect speech.

DIRECT SPEECH	INDIRECT SPEECH
The boss said, "He should go home."	*The boss said that he should go home.*

D Do not change the form of verbs in general truths or facts.	*She said, "Martin Luther King, Jr. was a great man."* *She said (that) Martin Luther King, Jr. was a great man.* NOT *She said that Martin Luther King Jr. ~~had been~~ a great man.*

▶▶ Tense Shifting in Indirect Speech: See page A11.

Grammar Application

Exercise 3.1 Tense Shifts in Indirect Speech

Read the quotes about a psychology course. Then rewrite each quote as indirect speech. Sometimes more than one answer is possible.

1 The professor said, "Psychology 101 includes a unit on motivation."

   The professor said that Psychology 101 included a unit on motivation.

2 A student said, "The class is discussing motivation and personality this week."

   _____

   _____

3 The professor said, "The class is reading about Abraham H. Maslow's theories on motivation."

   _____

   _____

4 One student said, "I'm learning a lot in the class."

   _____

   _____

5 Another student said, "I don't understand the lectures."

   _____

   _____

6 The teaching assistant said, "The readings have great practical value."

   _____

   _____

Exercise 3.2 Modals and Future Forms in Indirect Speech

Read the excerpt from a lecture on how to motivate adult learners. Then complete the email. Rewrite each sentence from the lecture as indirect speech. Sometimes more than one answer is possible.

Welcome to Motivating Adult Learners. This class is for people who teach adults. Participants in the course are going to learn all about motivating adult learners. The course will rely heavily on participants' own experiences. Students should come to class prepared to discuss their own experiences. We may occasionally have guest speakers. The course will include presentations, homework, and weekly quizzes. There will be three papers and two oral presentations. Participants can substitute an oral presentation for one of the papers.

To	jake15@cambridge.org
From	marta34@cambridge.org
Subject	First Class Meeting

Hi Jake,

   Here's what happened in class today. The instructor welcomed us, and then she said Motivating Adult Learners was for people who teach adult learners.

1 *She said that participants in the course were going to learn all about motivating adult learners.*

2 _____

3 _____

4 _____

5 _____

6 _____

4 Indirect Speech Without Tense Shift

Grammar Presentation

Indirect speech usually includes a shift in verb tense. However, in some cases the form of the verb does not change.	*The president announced that she **was going** to start an employee program next year.* *The president announced that she **is going** to start an employee program next year.*

4.1 Keeping the Original Tense in Indirect Speech

You may use the tense in the original direct speech clause when you report statements that are still true now, such as: Facts or general truths	*He said, "A pay raise **is** a common reward."* *He <u>said</u> that a pay raise **is** a common reward.*
Habits and routines	*Leo said, "Our meetings always **begin** on time."* *Leo <u>said</u> that their meetings always **begin** on time.*
Actions in progress	*Eve said, "I**'m studying** hard for the exam.* *Eve <u>said</u> that she **is studying** hard for the exam.*

▸▸ Tense Shifting in Indirect Speech: See page A11.

4.2 Using Present Tense Reporting Verbs

Use a present tense verb in the reporting clause when what was said relates to the present and is still important at the moment of speaking. Keep the same tense as in the quote.	*Everybody always **says**, "Employees **need** to be motivated."* *Everybody always **says** that employees **need** to be motivated.*

Grammar Application

Exercise 4.1 Keeping the Original Tense in Indirect Speech

Read the quotes from a business meeting. Then rewrite the quotes as indirect speech. Use the same tense as the direct speech. Sometimes more than one answer is possible.

1 "We are trying to improve our new marketing plan."
  –the marketing manager

  The marketing manager said that we are trying to improve our new marketing plan.

2 "The client loves it." –the manager

_____

3 "We have always solved these problems in the past." –Janet

_____

4 "Staff satisfaction has been very important." –Janet

_____

5 "Tomorrow, we are going to have a half-day training session on giving constructive feedback." –Rodrigo

_____

_____

6 "We will all work together, as a team." –Rodrigo

_____

_____

Exercise 4.2 Using Present Tense Reporting Verbs

A Complete the sentences. Use the correct form of the verbs in parentheses.

1 My father always says that money _**makes**_ (make) the world go round.

2 My friend Amanda insists that a good night's sleep _____ (be) more important than studying.

3 My aunt says that she _____ (enjoy) doing the work more than making money.

4 My friend says that he _____ (enjoy) having autonomy at work.

5 My colleague says that it _____ (not/be) always easy to stay motivated.

6 My manager says that you _____ always _____ (should/ask) questions if something is not clear.

B Pair Work Discuss the sentences in A. Do you agree with the statements?

5 Other Reporting Verbs

Grammar Presentation

Although *say* is the most common reporting verb, many other verbs can introduce indirect speech.

The president **explained** that our company's workers deserved higher pay.

The president **told us** that our company's workers deserved higher pay.

5.1 Other Reporting Verbs

A *Tell* is a common reporting verb. Always use a noun or object pronoun after *tell*.

The president **said** that he was doing a great job.

The president **told him** that he was doing a great job.

B You can use these verbs in place of *say*: *admit, announce, complain, confess, exclaim, explain, mention, remark, reply, report, state,* and *swear*.

"The workers need recognition," **said** the manager.

The manager **admitted** that the workers needed recognition.

When used with an object, the object comes after *to*.

He **swore** to us that he'd be on time in the future.

C You can use these verbs in place of *tell*: *assure, convince, inform, notify,* and *remind*. Always use a noun or object pronoun with these verbs.

The president **told the managers**, "All workers need to be creative."

The president **reminded them** that all workers need to be creative.

▶▶ Reporting Verbs: See page A11.

 DATA FROM THE REAL WORLD

Commonly used reporting verbs in formal writing include *claim, explain, find, show, state,* and *suggest*.

The author **claimed that** internal motivation was more effective than external motivation.

The results of the study **showed that** money was not always an effective way to motivate employees.

Grammar Application

Complete the excerpt from an email about a presentation on cultural differences in motivation. Circle the correct verbs.

Wei **said** /**told** me that he had attended a presentation on the cultural
(1)
differences that affect motivation. He **said** / **told** that an expert on motivation
(2)
gave the presentation. He **said** / **told** me that the expert was Dr. Ghosh.
(3)
He **reminded** / **mentioned** me that we had read one of her articles in class.
(4)

Anyway, Dr. Ghosh **said** / **informed** the group that the typical workplace
(5)
included people with various cultural backgrounds. She **explained** / **reminded**
(6)
that these workers had different expectations. She **informed** / **explained** the
(7)
group that these workers often had different motivations.

At the same time, Dr. Ghosh **reminded** / **remarked** that there was no one
(8)
way to motivate all workers. She **admitted** / **reminded** that in multicultural
(9)
settings, it was even more complicated.

She **stated** / **reminded** the group that managers shouldn't make
(10)
generalizations about cultures. She **assured** /**remarked** that the "human touch,"
(11)
getting to know employees as individuals, was the best way to motivate them.

A Listen to the conversation about a presentation on cultural differences in classrooms.
Complete the sentences with the words you hear.

David   What happened in class today?

Mira   We had a guest speaker. He _told us_ about the importance of motivation in
(1)
the language classroom. He _____ there are two kinds of
(2)
motivation: intrinsic and extrinsic.

David   Right. Last week, the professor _____ there were two different
(3)
types, and she gave examples.

Mira   Yes. So anyway, the speaker _____ he had done a study of
(4)
students in Japan and students in the United States. He _____
(5)
both groups had native-speaking English teachers. He _____
(6)
the purpose of the study was to see whether the teachers' remarks had a negative
effect on the motivation of the Japanese students.

David   What did he find out?

Mira   He _____ the study found four ways in which the teachers'
(7)
behavior had a negative effect on Japanese students' motivation.

David   Did he give any examples?

Mira   He _____ classroom discussion is one area where there are
(8)
key differences. He _____ in the Japanese classroom, students
(9)
generally listen more and talk less.

David   And as we know from our reading, Porter and Samovar _____
(10)
in the U.S. classroom, some students speak up spontaneously, and that a lot of
teachers encourage discussion.

Mira   Right. So, he _____ when a teacher criticizes a Japanese group
(11)
for not participating, it has a bad effect on motivation.

B Listen again and check your answers.

C Over to You Compare the behavior of American and Japanese students to students from another culture that you are familiar with. Use sentences with indirect speech.

The speaker said that in the Japanese classroom, students listen more and talk less. That is true in my culture, too. Students show respect that way.

6 Avoid Common Mistakes ⚠

1 For verbs such as *admit*, *announce*, *complain*, *explain*, and *mention*, the object pronoun comes after the preposition *to*.

                      to us

He explained ~~us~~ the objective.

2 **Change the form of the verb in indirect speech in most cases.**

                    had

He claimed that they followed the directions.

3 **Use beginning and ending quotation marks with direct speech.**

The director said, ˇ All designers may work from home on Fridays. ˇ

Editing Task

Find and correct the mistakes in the paragraphs about a memorable event.

       One of the highlights of my life happened through an experience at work.
                                      to us
It started when my manager announced ~~us~~ some interesting news. He said, I am
starting a company band. Then he asked, "Who wants to join?" I mentioned him that
I had played guitar for many years. He said, You should definitely try out.

5   On the day of tryouts, I was a little nervous because everyone played extremely
well. After I auditioned, the manager thanked me and explained me that he will let
me know soon.

     I forgot about it, so I was very surprised when I got a phone call from my
manager a few days later. He said, You can play lead guitar. I said, Wow! That's great!

10 After that, the band practiced a few times a week. A few months later, we played
at the company party. We were nervous, but we played well. The president of the
company spoke to me later and said I have a lot of talent. I was embarrassed by his
compliment, but I said I am proud to play for the company. I will never forget
that experience.

7 Academic Writing

Argumentative Writing Using Graphs and Tables for Support

Brainstorm > Organize > Write > Edit

In this writing cycle (Units 17-20), you will write an argumentative essay that uses graphs or tables to answer the prompt below. In this unit (17), you will analyze an essay with graphs and then brainstorm ideas about the topic.

> *Using what you know about the job market, what is a good choice for a career path with a secure future? Include information from graphs or tables to support your choice.*

Exercise 7.1 Preparing to Write

Work with a partner. Discuss the questions.

1 Is it important to have a college degree? Why or why not?

2 College tuition in the United States is very expensive. Do you think the benefits of a degree outweigh the costs? Why or why not?

3 A founder of Netscape, an early Internet search company, has said that people who earn a degree in a non-technical field like literature will probably be working in a shoe store upon graduation. Do you agree or disagree? Why or why not?

Exercise 7.2 Focusing on Vocabulary

Read the sentences. Then match the words in bold to the definitions.

1 Steve Jobs, one of the **founders** of Apple Inc., said that quality was more important than quantity.

2 Business leaders **disputed** the government's claim that the number of jobs had grown.

3 The successful campaign against buying the corporation's products **illustrates** the power of the consumer.

4 There is some **ambiguity** in the law, so it is difficult to know if the company did anything wrong.

5 This new technology has the **potential** to change how students learn about science.

6 According to economists, the more you consume something, the more your enjoyment of it will **diminish**. In other words, you will never enjoy it as much as you do when you first buy it.

7 The consequences of the economic crash **extend** beyond the city to the whole country.

    a _____ (v) to disagree with

    b _____ (n) the state of being unclear or having more than one possible meaning

    c _____ (n) people who establish an organization

    d _____ (v) to decrease in size or importance

    e _____ (v) to go further

    f _____ (n) the possibility to develop and succeed

    g _____ (n) an example that explains something

What Is the Value of a College Education?

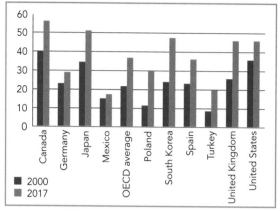

Benjamin Franklin, one of the founding fathers of the United States, once said, "An investment in knowledge pays the best interest." These days, a college education is a significant investment, so it makes sense to consider carefully whether it is worth the time and money. In good economic times and bad, and in spite of
5 its rising cost, the answer appears to be "yes." Figure 1, from the Organization for Economic Cooperation and Development (OECD), shows that around the world the number of people getting a college education is rising steadily.

A college education has a broad and positive impact. People with a college degree are by far the most likely to enter and remain in the labor force. In OECD
10 countries, average participation in the labor force for those who never completed high school is about 59%. The OECD reports that for those with a high school degree, the figure is about 76%, and for college graduates, it is about 84%. They also state that college graduates earn more than those with only a high school degree. In the United States, a new high school graduate earned on average
15 less than $30,000 per year in 2017, whereas those with a college degree made over $52,000. Over a lifetime, that difference adds up to about a million dollars. Figure 2 **illustrates** that the impact of a college degree on income in selected OECD countries can be dramatic.

The consequences of getting—or not getting—a college education **extend**
20 beyond income. There is a strong association between education and health. Chronic[1] diseases, such as heart disease and diabetes, pose the greatest risks to public health in developed countries today. These diseases are caused, at least partly, by lifestyle choices, such as poor diet or smoking. In general, people with higher levels of education make healthier lifestyle choices and have greater access
25 to high-quality healthcare.

It is evident that a college degree provides an economic advantage, but not all degrees have the same earning power. Most analysts suggest that degrees in STEM fields (science, technology, engineering, and math) have the greatest **potential** impact on future income. In the United States, a college graduate with, for example,
30 a chemical engineering degree can expect to earn about $70,000 annually, whereas a graduate with a literature or art degree may be lucky to get $36,000 for an entry-level position. Marc Andreessen, the **founder** of the internet company Netscape, once declared that someone who studies a non-technical field like literature will probably end up "working in a shoe store."

Yet, technical knowledge alone may not be sufficient for success. Steve Jobs, one of the founders of Apple, famously claimed, "It's
35 technology married with liberal arts ... that yields the results that make our hearts sing." Other major employers in the technology field agree. Industry leaders say that employees from the liberal arts are often good at managing **ambiguity**, unlike engineers, who tend to see situations in black and white. Liberal arts graduates can see a problem from multiple perspectives.

It is interesting to note that the income gap between liberal arts and STEM graduates gradually **diminishes** as they continue in their careers. In fact, liberal arts degrees are quite common among the world's most highly paid workers. About one-third of the directors of Fortune 500
40 companies have a liberal arts background. Students, parents, politicians, and industry leaders may argue over which are the most valuable degrees, but the value of a college degree in general cannot be **disputed**.

Figure 1 Percentage of Population (25–64) with a College Education

Source: Organization for Economic Cooperation and Development (OECD), Online Education Database, retrieved September 13, 2019, from https://stats.oecd.org/Index.aspx. See Digest of Education Statistics 2018, table 603.20.

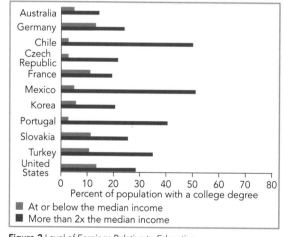

Figure 2 Level of Earnings Relative to Education

Source: OECD (2019), Education and earnings: Level of earnings relative to median earnings, by educational attainment, OEC.Stat, https://stats.oecd.org/Index.aspx?DataSetCode=EAG_EARNINGS, accessed on August 1, 2019.

[1] **chronic** (adj) lasting for a long time, especially something bad

Exercise 7.3 Comprehension Check

Read the text on page 263. Work with a partner. Discuss the questions.

1 Summarize the main argument of the text.
2 What benefits of a college degree are mentioned in the text?
3 According to Figure 1, what three countries had the highest percentage of citizens with a college education?

Exercise 7.4 Noticing the Grammar and Writing

Work with a partner. Complete the tasks.

1 Underline the first sentence. Why does the writer use a quote to introduce the topic?
2 Find another quote in the text. How does the writer introduce the quote?
3 Look at Figure 1. What is the writer's purpose in using this graph?
4 Look at Figure 2. What is the writer's purpose in using this graph?
5 What is the source of the information in the graphs?

Understanding and Using Graphs and Tables

Information in academic texts is often presented through graphs and tables. Writers include these to support their ideas or argument. It is important to understand and interpret the information in your graphs and tables, and to draw inferences and conclusions for your reader.

Exercise 7.5 Applying the Skill

Work with a partner. Ask and answer the questions about the information in Table 1.

Table 1. The 100 Best Jobs in the U.S., with Median Salary

Rank	Job Title	Median Salary
1	Software Developer	$101,790
4	Dentist	$165,120
14	Surgeon	$208,000
28	IT Manager	$139,220
42	Lawyer	$119,250
62	Hairdresser	$24,850
66	Medical Assistant	$32,480
76	High School Teacher	$59,170
88	Massage Therapist	$39,990

Source: U.S. News and World Report 2018

1 What information does the table present?
2 What can you infer from the table?
3 In addition to salary, what other factors do you think make a job a "best job"?

My Writing

Argumentative Essays with Graphs or Tables as Support

In argumentative essays, writers present their position, reasons, and supporting evidence. Evidence used in graphs and tables should come from credible sources, such as educational or research institutions, government websites, and respected news organizations.

Exercise 7.6 Brainstorming Topics and Ideas

1 Work with a partner. Make a copy of the chart and complete it.

- Column 1: Write the names of three careers.
- Column 2: Write relevant information from the reading, Table 1, and other credible sources you find. Include the name of the source in parentheses.
- Column 3: Make notes about the career and the information you found.

Career	Information (Name of Source)	Notes

2 In your opinion, which of the careers is the best choice for a financially secure future? Why?

Using Reporting Verbs to Introduce Evidence

Writers use reporting verbs to introduce evidence. Reporting verbs also show readers how the writer feels about the evidence. **Neutral reporting verbs** show a more neutral feeling towards the evidence.

The report **said** that the number one skill employers are looking for is flexibility.

Strong reporting verbs show a strong feeling towards the evidence.

The report **asserted** that the number one skill employers are looking for is flexibility.

Neutral reporting verbs: *advise, accept, acknowledge, recognize, encourage, interpret, analyze, examine, investigate, consider, evaluate*

Strong reporting verbs: *argue, assert, convince, emphasize, indicate, persuade, refute, show, state, stress, support, warn*

Exercise 7.7 Applying the Skill

Use the information from Exercise 7.6 to write a paragraph that asserts which career would best lead to a secure future. Include a topic sentence, at least two reasons for your argument with supporting details and evidence, and a concluding sentence. Use at least one reporting verb to introduce evidence.

Creative Problem Solving

1 Grammar in the Real World

**ACADEMIC
WRITING**

Argumentative
writing using
graphs and tables
for support

A When you have to solve a problem, what strategies do you use? Read the article about brainstorming. Would you prefer traditional brainstorming or "brainwriting"?

B Comprehension Check **Answer the questions.**

1 What are the four rules of brainstorming?

2 Why does Michalko believe that brainwriting may be more productive than brainstorming?

3 According to the writer, who can use brainstorming?

C Notice **Find the sentences in the article and complete them.**

1 First, he told participants _____ other people's ideas.

2 Therefore, he asked participants _____ even unusual ideas.

What are the forms of the missing verbs?

BRAINSTORMING
as a Problem-Solving Tool

There is more than one way to solve a problem. One method many people use is brainstorming. Brainstorming is an activity designed to produce a number of ideas in a short time. Alex Osborn

5 invented the word in 1939. In his book *Unlocking Your Creative Power*, Osborn said that the word *brainstorm* means using the brain to solve a problem creatively. Although he **said that groups should brainstorm** in a particular way, variations

10 on his technique have also become popular.

Osborn's original brainstorming method had four rules. First, he **told participants not to judge** other people's ideas. Second, he welcomed all ideas, even wild ideas. Osborn said that crazy

15 ideas could get people thinking along new lines and could lead to effective solutions. Therefore, he **asked participants to shout out** even unusual ideas. Third, Osborn **asked group members to produce** a large number of ideas. He thought that

20 the group would find a few really good ideas if many different ones were available. Finally, Osborn **asked the brainstorming group if they could improve** the ideas that had been suggested.

One alternative to brainstorming is

25 brainwriting. Brainwriting is a silent version of brainstorming. With brainwriting, participants write down their ideas instead of shouting them out. In his book *Thinkertoys*, creativity expert Michael Michalko suggests that brainwriting may be more

30 productive than traditional brainstorming. This is because people often think of additional ideas as they write. He also asserts that this method is better for quieter individuals because they do not have to express their ideas out loud.

35 Brainstorming and brainwriting are flexible methods. Anyone can use them because they do not require a lot of training or expensive materials. These processes are all effective tools for creative problem solving in professional, academic, and

40 personal situations.

2 Indirect Questions

Grammar Presentation

Indirect questions tell what other people have asked. There are two kinds of indirect questions: *Yes/No* questions and information questions.

He asked, "Are your jobs satisfying?"
He asked *if our jobs were satisfying*.
The director asked, "Which technique do you prefer?"
The director asked *us which technique we preferred*.

2.1 Forming Indirect Questions

A Use *asked* in the reporting clause and *if* to introduce an indirect *Yes/No* question.	"Will we start attending brainstorming sessions?" Mia *asked*. Mia *asked if* we will/would start attending brainstorming sessions.
Use *asked* in the reporting clause and the same *wh-* word to introduce an indirect information question.	"*When* will the training begin?" our manager *asked*. Our manager *asked when* the training will/would begin.
B Use statement word order in the indirect question.	He asked if *Rita was* one of our most productive employees.
C After *ask*, you can use a direct object. The direct object can be a noun or pronoun.	She *asked the students* if they understood. She *asked me* when I wanted to leave the company.

Grammar Application

Exercise 2.1 Forming Indirect Questions

Read the interview between Joanna and Dr. Martin, a critical thinking expert. Then rewrite each of Joanna's questions as an indirect question.

Joanna	Dr. Martin, why is creative thinking in the business world so important?
Dr. Martin	Companies need very creative people to help design and market new products.
5 Joanna	Why will creative thinking be even more important in the future?
Dr. Martin	Competition is getting stronger. You have to be creative to stay competitive.
Joanna	What techniques have worked to get people to think creatively?
Dr. Martin	One technique that really works is to move the body. I tell people who are sitting at a desk to move into the conference room or take a walk outside.

10

Joanna	How does moving promote creativity?
Dr. Martin	Moving stimulates the brain.
Joanna	Are there any other ideas like this?
Dr. Martin	Of course. Try putting colorful pictures on the wall. Never try to be creative in an empty room.
Joanna	Do objects and colors stimulate creative thinking?
Dr. Martin	They definitely do.

15

1 What did Joanna ask Dr. Martin about creative thinking in the business world?

Joanna asked Dr. Martin why creative thinking in the business world was important.

2 What did Joanna ask Dr. Martin about the future?

3 What did Joanna ask about creative techniques?

4 What did Joanna ask about moving?

5 What did Joanna ask about other ideas?

6 What did Joanna ask about stimulating creative thinking?

Exercise 2.2 More Forming Indirect Questions

Read the conversation about a company's creativity exercises. Then rewrite each of Ahmet's questions as an indirect question.

Ahmet	How was your creativity session yesterday?
Irina	It was fun, and we had some really good ideas, too.
Ahmet	Was the session here?
Irina	Yes, it was here.
Ahmet	Who was your leader?
Irina	It was Dr. Martin, a creativity expert. She gave us a problem to solve. Then she gave us large pieces of white paper and markers in a lot of different colors.
Ahmet	What did you do with the paper and the markers?
Irina	We drew pictures of things that we wanted to say, that is, the solutions we had for the problem.
Ahmet	Interesting. How long were you drawing pictures?

5

10

Irina	We did that for about an hour. Then we had a thing called "incubation." We stopped working, had lunch, and then watched a TV show!
Ahmet	Why did you watch TV in the office?
15 Irina	The idea was to forget about everything and then come back to the problem. When we went back to work, we then found the best solution.

1 What did Ahmet ask Irina about yesterday?

He asked her how her creativity session was.

2 What did Ahmet ask Irina about the location?

_____

3 What did Ahmet ask Irina about the leader?

_____

4 What did Ahmet ask Irina about the paper and the markers?

_____

5 What else did Ahmet ask Irina about the activity with the paper and markers?

_____

6 What did Ahmet ask Irina about watching TV in the office?

_____

Exercise 2.3 Using Indirect Questions

Group Work **Ask and answer the questions about creativity with two students. Then share your answers with the whole class.**

■ What are some situations in which people have to be creative?

■ Why is creativity difficult for some people?

■ When you have to be creative, do you have any techniques to stimulate your thinking? What are they?

3 Indirect Imperatives, Requests, and Advice

Grammar Presentation

| Imperatives, requests, and advice are usually made indirect with an infinitive. | *"Please sit down."* He asked us to sit down. *"Would you please turn off your phones?"* He asked us to turn off our phones. |

3.1 Indirect Imperatives, Requests, and Advice

A Use an infinitive in indirect imperatives. Use *not* + infinitive in negative indirect imperatives. You can use *tell* or *say*.	*"Don't make a lot of noise,"* said Mr. Jung. Mr. Jung said *not to make* a lot of noise.
Use an infinitive in indirect requests. You can use *ask*, *tell*, or *say*.	*"Please turn off your phones,"* said Mr. Cho. Mr. Cho told us *to turn off* our phones.
Use an infinitive to report advice given with modals such as *should*. Use *not* + infinitive to report advice with *should not*. You can use *tell* or *say*.	*"You shouldn't reject any ideas,"* Carl said. Carl told us not to reject any ideas.
B Always use an object after *tell*.	Ms. Ali told *us* to work quietly. NOT ~~Ms. Ali told to work quietly.~~
Use a pronoun or noun after *ask* to show the person who is the object of the request.	Sam asked *her* to share her ideas with the group.

Grammar Application

Exercise 3.1 Indirect Imperatives and Requests

Read the directions that a trainer gave to a group of employees. Then rewrite the steps with infinitives and the words in parentheses.

1 "Get into groups of three or four."
2 "Don't get into a group with someone you usually work with."
3 "Cut out pictures from magazines that show your ideal working environment."
4 "Don't criticize your group members' choices."
5 "Present your picture to the other groups."
6 "Comment on the other groups' pictures, but don't criticize people's choices."
7 "Discuss the emotions that the pictures suggest."

> I attended a problem-solving session with Dr. Martin yesterday. The goal was to help us get along better with each other. She helped us a great deal. Here's what she did:
>
> 1 (First/she/tell) *First, she told us to get into groups of three or four.*
> 2 (Then/she/say) _____
> 3 (She/tell) _____
> 4 (Dr. Martin/say) _____
> 5 (Then/she/tell) _____
> 6 (After that/she/say) _____
> 7 (Finally/Dr. Martin/say) _____

Exercise 3.2 Indirect Requests and Advice

Listen to the marriage counseling session. Then answer the questions. Use the words in parentheses and *ask*, *say*, or *tell*.

1 What did the therapist tell the husband and wife to do?

The therapist told them to take a pad
of paper and a pencil.
(take a pad of paper and a pencil)

2 What did the husband ask?

_____

_____
(take a different pencil)

3 What did the wife ask?

_____
(use her own pen)

4 What did the therapist say?

_____
(write for 15 minutes without stopping)

5 What did the therapist tell the clients?

_____
(not look at each other's writing during the activity)

6 What did the therapist say?

_____
(not talk to each other)

7 What did the therapist tell the clients?

_____
(be prepared to read their descriptions to each other)

8 What did the husband ask?

_____
(have a little more time to write)

Exercise 3.3 Indirect Advice

A Over to You Think of some good and bad advice you or people you know have received. What was the advice? Write six sentences.

Good Advice

My father's doctor told him not to eat meat and to exercise more.

1 _____

2 _____

3 _____

Bad Advice

Economists told Americans in 2015 to buy real estate because prices would increase.

4 _____

5 _____

6 _____

B Group Work **Compare your answers with your group members. Discuss why the advice was good or bad. Take notes on your group members' answers.**

A *My father's doctor told him not to eat meat and to exercise more. This was good advice because it helped him to get into better shape.*

B *Many economists told their clients to buy real estate because prices would increase. This was bad advice because real estate prices went down.*

4 Avoid Common Mistakes ⚠

1 **Use infinitives in indirect imperatives.**

        to

The leader asked us ~~that we~~ write for 5 minutes about the topic.

2 **In indirect *Yes/No* questions, remember to use an *if* clause.**

    if   *wanted*

He asked me ~~did I want~~ to be the group leader.

3 **Remember to use an object pronoun or noun after *tell*.**

    them

I told∧my ideas, and we ended up using two of them in the project.

Editing Task

Find and correct the mistakes in the paragraph about a brainstorming session.

                                     if   *wanted*

        When my psychology professor asked our class ~~did~~ we ~~want~~ to try brainstorming as part of our next group project, I had no idea that the experience would be so challenging or successful. First, when we started, one of our members asked many unimportant questions. When the team leader asked her that she asks the questions

5   later, that person began complaining. Then the team leader asked the person did she want to be the group leader. The rest of us told this was a bad idea, and there was an argument. A different problem arose when we met the second time. The leader asked one student that he takes electronic notes, but he forgot. As a result, when we met the third time, the leader had to tell the information again. She asked me that

10   I write the notes this time, and I did. Aside from these minor problems, the group generated a lot of ideas and finally came up with a successful proposal for a project. So, if someone asked me do I want to work as a group again, I would say yes because even though it is hard to work as a group, the outcome can be better.

5 Academic Writing

Argumentative Writing Using Graphs and Tables for Support

Brainstorm > Organize > Write > Edit

In Unit 17, you analyzed an essay with graphs and brainstormed ideas for the prompt below. In this unit (18), you will focus on incorporating information from graphs into your writing, and you will write a thesis statement and body paragraphs for your essay.

> *Using what you know about the job market, what is a good choice for a career path with a secure future? Include information from graphs or tables to support your choice.*

Analyzing Information in Graphs and Other Visuals

Academic writing involves including evidence. Evidence includes direct or indirect speech from experts, survey and research results, and visuals, such as graphs, tables, diagrams, and charts. The most common types of these visuals are bar graphs, line graphs, and pie charts. It is important to connect the information in the visual with the information in the text.

Exercise 5.1 Applying the Skill

1 Work with a partner. Look at the bar graph that ranks the most important interpersonal skills for workplace success. Take turns explaining each of the skills listed.

2 Think about the career you are going to write about. Which skills are critical for that career? Rank the skills that are important for that career. Explain your rankings to your partner.

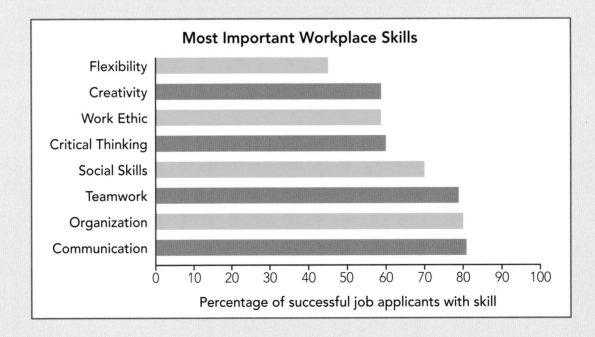

Making and Evaluating Claims

In an argumentative essay, a writer makes a claim and then provides support for that claim. The claim is delivered in the thesis statement. Use the following criteria to evaluate the effectiveness of a thesis statement:

- Does my thesis statement make a claim that my readers can argue about?
- Does it give readers an idea of what my essay will be about?
- Is the claim specific enough to be effectively supported in a short essay?

Exercise 5.2 Applying the Skill

Work with a partner. Read three possible thesis statements for an essay about the importance of problem-solving in the workplace. Evaluate each one using the criteria you learned.

1 Brainstorming is one of the most popular tools when solving workplace problems.
2 According to the graph, being able to solve problems is the top skill for employers.
3 Brainstorming is an effective technique when solving problems because it gives everyone an opportunity to share their ideas.

Adding Indirect Advice from Experts

To strengthen their claims, writers often include indirect advice from experts. Indirect advice often appears directly after the writer's idea.

Exercise 5.3 Applying the Skill

Read the first two sentences of a paragraph about brainwriting. Underline the writer's claim. Circle the source and expert's name. Highlight the indirect advice.

Brainwriting is the most effective type of brainstorming. In his book, *Thinkertoys*, creativity expert Michael Michalko suggests that brainwriting may be more productive than traditional brainstorming because people think of additional ideas as they write.

My Writing

Exercise 5.4 Organizing Your Claims and Evidence

Work in a small group. Review your paragraph from My Writing in Unit 17. Discuss the questions.

1 What career did you choose to write about? Why?
2 What evidence do you have to support your claim? What could you add to strengthen it?
3 How could you better connect the evidence to your ideas?

Exercise 5.5 Writing Body Paragraphs

Write a thesis statement and two body paragraphs for your essay. Include a graph, table, or indirect advice as support.

The Passive (1)

English as a Global Language

1 Grammar in the Real World

ACADEMIC WRITING

Argumentative writing using graphs and tables for support

A Should everyone speak English? Why or why not? Read the article on the use of English around the world. Why is English important to learn?

B Comprehension Check **Answer the questions.**

1 Where is English being spoken?

2 When do people around the world speak English?

3 What might be some disadvantages of English being a global language?

C Notice **Match the sentences in A with the sentences in B that mean the same thing.**

A	**B**
_____ 1 International companies **ask** their employees to learn English for their jobs.	a How **is** English **used** by nonnative speakers?
_____ 2 In addition, English **dominates** the Internet.	b Employees of international companies **are** often **asked** to learn English for their jobs.
_____ 3 How do nonnative speakers **use** English?	c In addition, the Internet **is dominated** by English.

Look at the forms of the verbs in bold in each of the matched sentences. How are the verbs in column B different from the verbs in column A?

ENGLISH IS SPOKEN HERE

An Italian businesswoman in Russia speaks English in meetings. Teenagers from Argentina, Turkey, and Japan chat online – in English. Learning English is clearly important in today's world. David
5 Crystal, a linguist[1] who studies the English language, believes that English has become a global language, although it is not an official language in many countries. According to Crystal, no other language **has been spoken** in so many countries and by so
10 many speakers. Currently, over 360 million people speak English as a first language around the world, and approximately one billion speak it as a second language. This means that there are more nonnative speakers of English than native speakers. How **is**
15 English **used** by nonnative speakers? Employees of international companies **are** often **asked** to learn English for their jobs. In addition, the Internet **is dominated**[2] by English. Some experts say that more than half of the information on the Internet is
20 in English. Also, English **has** long **been viewed** as a common language among travelers from different countries. The use of English worldwide appears to have clear benefits for everyone.

Does this increase in the use of English worldwide
25 have any disadvantages? Some say that cultures
may lose some of their identity if people use English instead of their native languages. For example, much of a culture's identity **is reflected** in its music and literature. Would these songs and stories be
30 as effective in English? Others say that the English language itself could change. In fact, this is happening now. When English **is spoken** by a group of people whose native language is not English, words from the native language **are** sometimes **mixed in**, and
35 the pronunciation of words is different from British or American English. This means that dialects[3] and different forms of English **are being spoken** in various areas around the world. Sociologists **are** currently **studying** this phenomenon. The loss of
40 cultural identity and the creation of varieties of English are two areas of interest for sociologists and linguists.

English **is being used** worldwide more and more, and for many people, learning it is necessary for their personal and professional lives. There are obvious
45 advantages to learning English. The disadvantages remain unclear. It is clear that varieties of English will continue to evolve. How will this affect how English is **taught**? In the future, will greater numbers of people have to decide which variety of English they learn?

---

[1]**linguist:** someone who studies languages and their structures

[2]**dominate:** control a place or person, want to be in charge, or be the most important person or thing

[3]**dialect:** a local variety of language that differs in its pronunciation and word usage

2 Active vs. Passive Sentences

Grammar Presentation

A passive sentence and an active sentence have similar meanings, but the focus of the sentences is different. In the passive sentence, the focus is on the action or on the person or thing receiving the action.	The president asked the employees to speak English. (active) The employees were asked to speak English. (passive)

2.1 Passive Sentences with By + Agent

A In active sentences, the agent (or doer of the action) is in subject position. In passive sentences, the object of the active sentence becomes the subject. The word *by* comes before the agent.

AGENT   OBJECT

People spoke English at the meeting. (active)

English was spoken by people at the meeting. (passive)

B The agent is not always necessary.

English was spoken at the meeting. (We assume people were doing the speaking.)

C Use the *by* + agent phrase if the agent is important or if the meaning of the sentence would be unclear without it.

The Internet is dominated by English.

NOT The Internet is dominated. (By who or what?)

2.2 Present and Past Forms of the Passive

A For the simple present form of the passive, use the present form of *be* + the past participle of the main verb.

Some international companies ask their employees to learn English. (active)

Employees are asked to learn English by some international companies. (passive)

B For the present perfect form of the passive, use *has / have + been* + the past participle of the main verb.

The company has told the employees to speak English. (active)

The employees have been told to speak English. (passive)

C For the present progressive form of the passive, use the present form of *be + being* + the past participle of the main verb.

These days, people around the world are speaking many dialects of English. (active)

These days, many dialects of English are being spoken by people around the world. (passive)

2.2 Present and Past Forms of the Passive *(continued)*

D For the simple past form of the passive, use the past form of *be* + the past participle of the main verb. This form is the most common.	*Years ago, people did not consider English a global language.* (active) *Years ago, English was not considered a global language.* (passive)
E For the past progressive form of the passive, use the past form of *be* + *being* + the past participle of the main verb. This form is rare.	*Ten years ago, fewer people were using English online.* (active) *Ten years ago, English was being used by fewer people online.* (passive)
F In passive sentences, do not use a form of *do* in questions and negative statements in the simple present and simple past.	*Do most travelers speak English?* (active) *Is English spoken by most travelers?* (passive) *Turkish teenagers didn't use English to chat online two decades ago.* (active) *English wasn't used by Turkish teenagers to chat online two decades ago.* (passive)

🌐 Research shows that the simple present, present perfect, and simple past forms of the passive are much more frequent than the present progressive, past progressive, and past perfect forms of the passive.

▶▶ Irregular Verbs: See page A1.
▶▶ Passive Forms: See page A12.

DATA FROM THE REAL WORLD

Research shows that in academic writing, these are the most common verbs used in the passive:	*analyze, calculate, carry out, collect, determine, expect, find, measure, observe, obtain, prepare, see, set, show, test,* and *use*

Grammar Application

Exercise 2.1 Active and Passive Sentences

A Complete the online interview with a reporter from BusinessTimes Online and the CEO of an international company. Circle the correct verb forms.

⌂   💬 ↻ ☰ ✉

Reporter I would like to ask some questions about your use of English here at BR

Corporation. **Do people speak English /** (**Is English spoken**) by most executives?
(1)

CEO Yes, most executives **speak / are spoken** English at this branch.
(2)

Reporter	Do only executives speak English? I mean, do lower level employees **use / are used** English here, too?

(3)

CEO	No, English **isn't used / doesn't use** by them much.

(4)

Reporter	Why is English necessary for some employees?
CEO	English **is needed / needs** by executives who travel. Also, we

(5)

are expected / expect them to read technical documents in English.

(6)

Reporter	**Does BR Corporation support / Is BR Corporation supported** English

(7)

language learning?

CEO	Yes, BR Corporation **is offered / offers** onsite English courses.

(8)

Reporter	**Are the courses taught / Do the courses teach** by native English speakers?

(9)

CEO	Yes, native speakers **are conducted /conduct** all of our English classes.

(10)

Reporter	Thank you for speaking with me today.

B Pair Work Which sentences in A are in the passive? Rewrite them as active sentences.
Do most executives speak English?

C Group Work Rewrite the active sentences in A as passive sentences. In which sentences is the *by* + agent phrase necessary? Share your answers with the group.

Exercise 2.2 Present Forms of the Passive

Complete the article about foreign-language teaching. Use the simple present or present perfect form of the passive with the verbs in parentheses. Sometimes more than one answer is possible.

●●●

English *has been taught* (teach) in many countries all over the world for years.
(1)

It _____ currently _____ (speak), at least to some degree, by
(2)   (2)

one–quarter of the world's population. Schools in the United States also recognize the

importance of learning other languages. For some time, languages other than English

_____ (include) in these schools' programs. Recently, a growing number of
(3)

languages has become available. Which languages _____ (offered) by U.S.
(4)

high schools nowadays? The results may surprise you.

French is one of the most popular foreign languages for high school students.

It _____ (teach) in most U.S. high schools for many years. Arabic
(5)

is becoming more and more popular. In fact, Arabic _____ (offer) at many
(6)

Massachusetts public schools these days. Chinese is also beginning to gain popularity.

An increase in the number of students learning Chinese _____
(7)

(report) for several years in various states across the country. It _____
(8)

(estimate) that more than 200,000 U.S. school children are now enrolled in

Mandarin Chinese classes.

Exercise 2.3 Past Forms of the Passive

A Read the active sentences about language. First underline the object in each sentence. Then rewrite the sentences as passive sentences. Sometimes more than one answer is possible.

1 At one time, many people used Latin as a global language.

   At one time, Latin was used as a global language by many people.

2 The ancient Romans spoke Latin.

   _____

3 Ancient Roman authors wrote many important manuscripts.

   _____

4 For many centuries, the Romans conquered neighboring nations.

   _____

5 These conquered groups spoke versions of Latin.

   _____

6 Conquered people from Britain to Africa used Latin.

   _____

7 People were still speaking Latin after the Roman Empire fell.

   _____

8 Scholars and scientists were using Latin until the eighteenth century.

   _____

B Read the sentences in A again. In which sentences are the agents not important? Discuss the reasons for your answers with a partner. Then rewrite these sentences in the passive without the agent.

   A *In the first sentence,* many people *isn't important because we know that only* people use language.

   B *You're right. The sentence could be* At one time, Latin was used as a global language.

3 Verbs and Objects with the Passive

Grammar Presentation

Transitive verbs (verbs that take an object) can occur in the passive. Intransitive verbs (verbs that do not take an object) cannot occur in the passive.	*Someone **saw** her at the conference.* (transitive) *She **was seen** at the conference.* *I **fell** asleep.* (intransitive)

3.1 Transitive and Intransitive Verbs

A Some common transitive verbs that occur in the passive are *call, concern, do, expect, find, give, know, left, lose, make, put, see, take,* and *use*.	*Improvement of your language skills **is expected**.* *I **was given** a new English textbook.* *The reasons for his success **were not known**.*
B *Born* is the past participle of *bear. Born* is used almost exclusively in the passive.	*I **was born** in a small town.* *Where **were** you **born**?*
C Some common intransitive verbs, which have no passive form, include *appear, arrive, come, die, fall, go, happen, live, look, occur, sit, smile, stay, wait,* and *walk*.	*When **did** your symptoms first **appear**?* NOT *When were your symptoms first appeared?* *Globalization of some languages **happens** over time.* NOT *Globalization of some languages is happened over time.*

3.2 Passive Forms with Direct and Indirect Objects

Some verbs, such as *give, offer, show,* and *tell,* can have two objects: a direct and an indirect object. In passive sentences, either the direct object or the indirect object can become the subject. Use *to* before an indirect object that is not in subject position.	INDIRECT OBJ DIRECT OBJ *The team gave the manager the report.* *The manager **was given** the report by the team.* *The report **was given** to the manager by the team.*

Grammar Application

Read the sentences about "dead" languages. Underline the verb in each sentence. If the sentence can occur in the passive, write the passive sentence on the line. Do not use an agent. Write ✗ if a passive form is not possible.

1 People in Ancient Rome spoke Latin.
  Latin was spoken in Ancient Rome.

2 People don't use Latin for everyday communication today.
  _____

3 Some languages die.
  _____

4 This occurred with Dalmatian.
  _____

5 People spoke Dalmatian in Croatia. _____

6 Dalmatian speakers lived in coastal towns of Croatia. _____

7 Groups in different regions developed dialects of Dalmatian.
  _____

8 Native speakers didn't record the grammar of Dalmatian.
  _____

A Over to You Answer the questions about a language you know. Use the underlined verbs in your answers. Use passive sentences when possible. Use the indirect object as the subject of the passive sentence when possible. Write sentences that are true for you.

1 What is a computer called in this language?
  A computer is called "bilgisayar" in Turkish.

2 What English words are used in this language?
  _____

3 Do any other foreign words occur in this language? If so, what are they?
  _____

4 Is this language spoken by more people or fewer people than it was 50 years ago?
  _____

5 What advice is frequently given by teachers to people learning this language?
  _____

6 Do speakers of this language tell their children traditional stories?
  _____

B Group Work Share your sentences with your group members.

A Read the sentences about Esperanto, a language that was created as a global language. Underline the agents.

1 The first book about Esperanto was published by a company in 1887.

2 Esperanto was invented by L. L. Zamenhof.

3 Esperanto was created by its inventors to be a very easy language to learn.

4 The grammar was designed by Zamenhof to be simple and clear.

5 It is spoken by about 10,000 people.

6 It is being used by people in about 115 countries.

7 It has not been recognized as an official language by any country.

8 The language is used by some international travelers.

B Pair Work Read the sentences in A again. Circle the direct objects. Compare your answers with a partner.

4 Reasons for Using the Passive

Grammar Presentation

The passive is used to describe processes and to report news events. The agent is not important. The focus is on the action or on the person or thing receiving the action.	*First, the students were shown a video in English.* *A "dead" language has been brought back to life in one community.*

4.1 Reasons for Using the Passive

A Use the passive to describe a process or a result. Common verbs to describe a process or a result are *compare, develop, examine, make, measure, study,* and *test*.	*First, the information was studied.* *Then recommendations were made.* (process) *Therefore, English was made the official language of the company in 2010.* (result)
B Use the passive when you don't know who performed the action. You can also use the passive to avoid directly blaming or criticizing someone.	*The report was poorly written.* (We don't know, or we don't want to say, who wrote the report.)
C Use the passive to report news events.	*Recommendations for the teaching of languages were published today.*

Grammar Application

Exercise 4.1 Describing Processes and Results

A Listen to a report on a language study of English as a Second Language (ESL) students. Then complete the answers to the questions. Use the passive and the words in parentheses.

1 How many groups of students were there? (put into)

   The students *were put into two groups*   .

2 What was the assignment at the beginning of the semester? (give)

   Students in each group _____ .

3 What did group 1 study? (teach)

   Group 1 _____ .

4 What did group 2 study? (teach)

   Students in group 2 _____ .

5 Who read the essays? (read)

   The first and final essays _____ .

6 What did the judges do with all of the final essays? (put)

   All of the final essays from group 1 and group 2 _____

   _____ .

7 How did the judges rate all the final essays? (rate)

   The essays _____ .

8 What rating did the essays produced by group 1 receive? (give)

   Most of the final essays produced by group 1 _____ .

9 What did the results seem to indicate? (include)

   ESL students' writing improves when grammar and writing instruction

   _____ .

B Listen again and check your answers.

Read the sentences about preserving two Native American languages. Then rewrite each sentence in the passive. Do not use an agent. Sometimes more than one answer is possible.

1 In 2009 in Minnesota, the legislature established a volunteer group to preserve Native American languages.

   In 2009 in Minnesota, a volunteer group was established to preserve Native American languages.

2 The legislature recognized the importance of preserving the Native American languages.

   _____

   _____

3 The volunteer group collected data on the use of the Ojibwe and Dakota languages.

   _____

4 In Minnesota, many Native American people no longer spoke the Ojibwe and Dakota languages.

   _____

5 The volunteer group developed a strategy to teach the Ojibwe and Dakota languages in schools.

   _____

6 The group is developing teacher-training programs.

   _____

7 In 2011, a nonprofit business released software for teaching the Ojibwe language.

   _____

8 The preservation of the languages will strengthen the Native Americans' cultural identities.

   _____

Read each classroom scenario and pretend you are the teacher. Then write passive statements to avoid directly blaming or criticizing someone. Use the underlined sentences in your answers. Sometimes more than one answer is possible.

1 <u>Someone stole some valuable equipment from the classroom.</u> You think that someone in the class is responsible, but you aren't sure. You tell the class:

   Some valuable equipment was stolen from the classroom.

2 One student's essay contained plagiarized material. <u>The student copied some material in his essay from the Internet.</u> You tell the student:

   _____

3 A hacker broke into the school's e-mail system last night. No one knows who is responsible, but you must inform the students. You tell the class:

_____

4 A student hands in the second draft of an essay. You see a lot of grammar mistakes. The student did not edit the paper carefully. You tell the student:

_____

5 Avoid Common Mistakes ⚠

1 **Remember to use a form of _be_ in passive sentences.**
        is
English∧spoken at most airports.

2 **Always use the past participle form of the verb in passive sentences.**
            translated
The words have been ~~translating~~ into Spanish, Arabic, Chinese, and Urdu.

3 **Do not use the passive form when the subject is the doer of the action.**
        studying
I have been ~~studied~~ English for five years.
Most students have ~~been~~ used an English dictionary.

4 **With questions, remember to put _be_ before the subject.**
  was
Why∧he ~~was~~ given an award?

Editing Task

Find and correct the mistakes in the paragraphs about English spelling.

Even good writers will tell you that English spelling has ~~been~~ confused them at one time or another. The same sound spelled many different ways. For example, the words _lazy_ and _busy_ are pronouncing with a /z/ sound, but they are not consistent in their spelling because of strange rules that are being related to the vowels.

5 Why English is written this way? English is an ancient language that contains old spelling rules. Also, other languages have been contributed many words to English.

Some experts who have been studied the English language for years would like to see English spelling simplified. They ask important questions: Why so much time is wasted on spelling lessons? Why is literacy lower in English-speaking countries than

10 in countries with simplified spelling? They point to the fact that many other languages simplified successfully. They suggest that in places such as Sweden, France, and Indonesia, changes to the written form have helped make learning to read easier.

6 Academic Writing

Argumentative Writing Using Graphs and Tables for Support

Brainstorm > Organize > **Write** > Edit

In Unit 18, you wrote the first draft of your thesis statement and body paragraphs for the prompt below. In this unit (19), you will focus on the introductory paragraph and then complete the first draft of your essay.

> *Using what you know about the job market, what is a good choice for a career path with a secure future? Include information from graphs or tables to support your choice.*

Making a Logical Appeal in the Introductory Paragraph

In an argumentative essay, writers try to create a connection with readers from the beginning that will persuade them to agree with the essay's thesis or possibly to take some action. Writers do this by making a logical appeal. A hook, such as a surprising statistic, interesting story, or powerful quote, can help make a strong logical appeal.

Exercise 6.1 Understanding the Skill

Read two possible introductory paragraphs (a-b) for an essay about the importance of learning English. Work with a partner. Discuss the questions.

a   English is everywhere. When people can speak English, they are able to travel anywhere, watch movies, and listen to music. English is a world language. People who speak and understand English have more opportunities than those who do not. Experts say that the number of people who speak English is growing every day. People should learn English.

b   Diana, who lives in Chile, chats with Hiro, who lives in Japan. Marc works for Amazon customer service and lives in Spain. Hoda takes classes from an American university while she is living in Iran. What do all these people have in common? They are communicating in English. Our world is growing smaller, and English is becoming a world language. More people are using English for work, school, and entertainment. Learning English opens up new opportunities, and can make a person a more marketable professional.

1 What kind of hook does each paragraph use?
2 What background information is included in each paragraph?
3 Which introduction makes the most successful logical appeal to you? Why?

My Writing

Exercise 6.2 Applying the Skill

Use your work in My Writing in Units 17 and 18 to answer the questions.

1 What is your thesis statement?
2 What is the main idea of each body paragraph?
3 Using the information in 1–2, what logical appeal can you make to your reader?
4 Write the introductory paragraph of your essay.

Using Active and Passive Voice to Discuss Visuals

When writers discuss figures (graphs, charts, diagrams), they use specific words and phrases, sometimes in the passive voice.

To introduce a trend by discussing a figure, the active voice is usually preferred.

English is now spoken by over 360 million people. Figure 1 **shows** where these speakers live.

Use the passive to focus on the information, not the *who* or the *where*.

Speakers of English, who do not reside in an English speaking country, learn English in a number of ways. The most common ways **are presented** in Figure 2.

The following verbs are frequently used to discuss figures in academic writing:
demonstrate, depict, display, illustrate, indicate, portray, present, reveal, show

Exercise 6.3 Applying the Skill

Work with a partner. Complete the tasks.

1 Review the body paragraphs of your essay. Identify where you included a figure.
2 How did you introduce it? Did you use a frequently used verb?
3 Revise your paragraphs if necessary.

Exercise 6.4 Writing Your Essay

Use your work in My Writing in Units 18 and 19 to write the first complete draft of your essay. Include:

- An introductory paragraph with your thesis statement
- 2-3 body paragraphs with information from graphs or tables for support
- A concluding paragraph that summarizes your thesis and reasons, and that includes a final thought, recommendation, or prediction

20

The Passive (2)

Food Safety

1 Grammar in the Real World

ACADEMIC WRITING

Argumentative writing using graphs and tables for support

A What do you know about genetically modified food? Read the article about genetically modified food. What are some genetically modified foods?

B Comprehension Check **Answer the questions.**

1 What are genetically modified foods?

2 What are some advantages of genetically modified foods?

3 What are some concerns about genetically modified foods?

C Notice **Find the sentences in the article and complete them.**

1 For example, those in favor of GM foods believe that crops _____ to resist insects.

2 Opponents insist that the problem of world hunger _____ by producing more food.

3 However, _____ extra care _____ until the long-term risks are known?

What verb comes after modals in passive verb forms?

GENETICALLY Modified Food

Genetically modified[1] (GM) foods come from plants that **have been changed** in a laboratory. This technology alters the genes[2] of the plants. It was developed so that food could have specific, desirable traits. For example, the first GM crop in the United States consisted of tomatoes that were genetically changed to stay firmer longer.

Many people have strong opinions about the potential[3] benefits and risks of GM agriculture. For example, those in favor of GM foods believe that crops **should be designed** to resist insects. They point to the example of sweet corn. They say that sweet corn **used to be destroyed** by pests. This created serious problems. Farmers lost money. Crops **got damaged** and **could not be eaten**. Therefore, they say that a great benefit **can be found** in GM sweet corn, which has been modified to resist insects that cause damage. People who oppose GM foods see the issue differently. They cite[4] a study that links GM corn to organ[5] damage in rats. They claim that the safety of these crops has not been tested adequately.[6]

GM supporters see GM soybeans as another beneficial crop. These crops are not harmed by a powerful weed-killing chemical. This chemical kills weeds the first time it is applied, so farmers use less of it. Supporters say that this improves air and water quality since fewer pollutants enter the environment. Critics argue that the weeds are no longer affected by the weed killer, and new "superweeds" are growing. Therefore, farmers have to use more chemicals to save their crops.

Finally, those in favor of GM foods say that better control of pests and weeds has made it possible for GM crops to produce more food in a shorter time. They believe this increased production will help feed a world population which is expected to grow to 9 billion by 2050. Opponents insist that the problem of world hunger **will not be solved** by producing more food. They argue that farmers grow enough food now and that global hunger is a result of unequal food distribution, not the result of a food shortage.[7]

Clearly, there are pros and cons to this debate. GM foods seem to have the potential to benefit the world. However, **should** extra care **be taken** until the long-term risks are known?

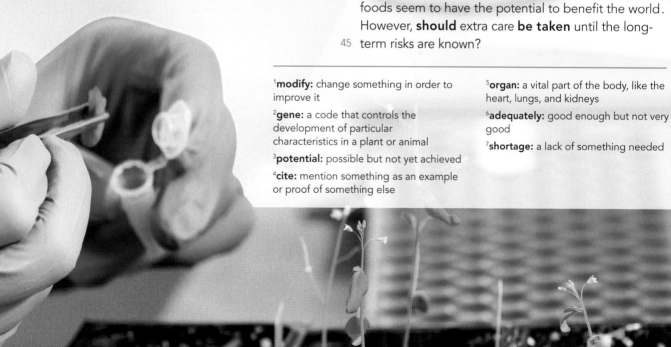

[1]**modify:** change something in order to improve it

[2]**gene:** a code that controls the development of particular characteristics in a plant or animal

[3]**potential:** possible but not yet achieved

[4]**cite:** mention something as an example or proof of something else

[5]**organ:** a vital part of the body, like the heart, lungs, and kidneys

[6]**adequately:** good enough but not very good

[7]**shortage:** a lack of something needed

2 The Passive with *Be Going To* and Modals

Grammar Presentation

You can use the passive with *be going to* and modals.	GM foods *will replace* natural foods. (active) Natural foods *will be replaced* by GM foods. (passive)

2.1 Forming the Passive with *Be Going To* and Modals

A For the passive with *be going* to, use *be going to* + *be* + the past participle of the main verb. *Not* comes before *be going to* in the negative form.	*Only natural foods are going to be served in our house.* *The food is not going to be eaten immediately.* *Is more GM food going to be grown in the future?*
B For the passive with modals, use a modal + *be* + the past participle of the main verb. *Not* follows the modal in the negative form.	*People could be harmed by GM food.* *People must be informed.* *Food should not be eaten if it isn't fresh.* *Will questions about GM food be answered by scientists?*

▶▶ Passive Forms: See page A12.

⌨ Grammar Application

Exercise 2.1 The Passive with *Will* and *Be Going To*

Complete the interview about plans for a food conference. Circle the passive form of the verbs.

> **Reporter** A conference called **The Future of Food** will hold /(will be held) at
> Bay City Tech next week. Issues concerning the food industry
> (1)
> **will be discussed / will discuss** by experts from a variety of fields.
> (2)
> We interviewed two participants, Dr. Fred Bell, a biologist, and Deniz
> Martin, the president of the Traditional Food Society. First, what major
> issues **are going to address / are going to be addressed** at next week's
> (3)
> conference?
>
> **Dr. Bell** Policies on food aid **are going to debate / are going to be debated** in
> (4)
> one session.
>
> **Reporter** What are the issues there?

Dr. Bell Well, GM plants **are going to be promoted/are going to promote**
as the main solution to hunger in poor nations.
(5)

Reporter World hunger is a serious problem. What's your opinion as a biologist?
Will the situation **improve/be improved** by GM plants?
(6)

Dr. Bell No, the problem of world hunger **will not solve/will not be solved** by GM
crops, in my opinion.
(7)

Reporter Don't some experts believe that GM food will help increase crop production?

Dr. Bell In my opinion, crop production **will not be increased/will not increase** by
GM plants. In fact, there is no proof of this so far.
(8)

Reporter Ms. Martin, what Traditional Food Society issues
will be presented/will present at the conference?
(9)

Ms. Martin The issue of sustainable food production – growing food without
harming people or the environment – **will address/will be addressed** .
For example, ways to improve organic farming methods
(10)
will be demonstrated/will demonstrate .
(11)

Reporter Thank you both for your time.

Exercise 2.2 The Passive with Modals

A Read the facts that a student collected for a report on pesticides.[1] Rewrite the facts as
passive sentences. Sometimes more than one answer is possible.

1 Pesticides can harm humans, animals, and the environment.

   Humans, animals, and the environment can be harmed by pesticides.

2 Pesticides can cause air pollution.

   _____

3 In the United States, scientists can find pesticides in many streams.

   _____

4 Pesticides may have harmed some farm animals.

   _____

5 Pesticides may have affected meat from farm animals.

   _____

6 Pesticides in water could affect fish.

   _____

7 In some cases, pesticides can affect humans.

   _____

[1]**pesticide:** a weed-killing chemical

B **Pair Work** Compare your sentences with a partner.

Complete the web article about a government recall. Rewrite the steps as passive sentences with modals. Use the indirect object as the subject of the passive sentence when possible. Sometimes more than one answer is possible.

NOTICE to Purchasers of Sunny Farm Eggs

We regret to inform you that Grade A eggs from Sunny Farm sold in the last two weeks have been making customers sick. If you have recently purchased eggs or are concerned about the situation, you can take the following steps:

1 You must check the date and plant number on the container first.

   The date and plant number on the
   container must be checked first.

2 You must not open the package.

   _____

3 You must not consume the product.

   _____

4 You can return the product for a refund.

   _____

5 Store management may ask you questions about the product you bought.

   _____

6 Store management might offer you a similar product.

   _____

Group Work **Discuss the questions about GM food. Use passive sentences with modals.**

- Should food be genetically modified? Why or why not?

- In your opinion, can people be harmed by eating genetically modified food? If yes, in what ways?

- Should genetically modified food be labeled in the United States? Why or why not?

A *In my opinion, food should not be genetically modified because we don't know the dangers.*

B *I disagree. I think food should be genetically modified because it's the best way to end world hunger.*

3 Get Passives

Grammar Presentation

Passive sentences with *get* instead of *be* are more informal and are often used to express stronger emotions.	*The storm destroyed the crops.* (active) *The crops got destroyed by the storm.* (passive)

3.1 Forming *Get* Passives

A For the *get* passive, use a form of *get* + the past participle of the main verb.	*He is getting transferred to the research department.* *Our orange trees got damaged last night.*
B For negative statements and questions in the simple present and simple past, use a form of *do* + *get* + the past participle of the main verb.	*In my opinion, food doesn't get inspected carefully enough.* *Did your crops get damaged in the hurricane?*

3.2 Using *Get* Passives

We often use *get* passives to talk about negative situations or situations we think are beyond our control.	*Some food companies are getting fined for using unsafe equipment.*

DATA FROM THE REAL WORLD

The *get* passive is more common in speaking than in general writing. In formal academic writing, the *get* passive is very infrequent.

speaking
general writing
formal academic writing

Say: *"She got arrested and charged with murder."*
Write: *She was arrested and charged with murder.*

 Grammar Application

Exercise 3.1 *Get* Passives

Complete the interview about food contamination. Write *get* passives with the words in parentheses. If there is a line through the agent, do not use it in the passive.

Alternative **REVIEW**

Interviewer There's been another case of contaminated[1] lettuce. How does this happen? An anonymous lettuce grower agreed to be interviewed if we did not mention his name. So, I hear _you're getting investigated by the FDA_
(1 the FDA[2] is investigating you)
for problems with food safety. What happened?

Grower _____ .
(2 ~~Something~~ contaminated our lettuce)

Interviewer _____ ?
(3 Did the FDA recall the lettuce)

Grower Yes, _____ .
(4 ~~The FDA~~ recalled it)

Interviewer What happened, exactly?

Grower I'm not sure. As you know, _____
(5 ~~workers~~ pick our produce)
right here on the farm. _____ here.
(6 ~~Workers~~ also pack it)

_____ . This can cause contamination.
(7 ~~Workers~~ sometimes mishandle it)

[1]**contaminated:** less pure and potentially harmful | [2]**FDA:** Food and Drug Administration, a U.S. government agency

| Interviewer | Don't you have strict procedures? |

| Grower | Yes, but it's been very hot lately. Working conditions have been difficult. |

Perhaps _____ .
(8 ~~something~~ distracted the workers)

| Interviewer | _____ before it goes to |
(9 Doesn't ~~someone~~ check your produce)

the stores?

| Grower | No, _____ . That's our responsibility, |
(10 ~~people~~ don't inspect it)

and my company is very sorry that we didn't catch it.

| Interviewer | I see. Well, thank you very much for agreeing to be interviewed. |

Exercise 3.2 More *Get* Passives

A Over to You **Look at the following statements about food safety. Check (✔) the statements you agree with.**

☐ **1** When a restaurant gets inspected, the results should be posted on the restaurant's front door.

☐ **2** Food recalls get publicized too much. This hurts farmers, and a lot of perfectly good food gets thrown away.

☐ **3** If a supermarket sells spoiled food, the manager should get fired.

☐ **4** If a restaurant gets temporarily shut down for food safety problems, no one should ever eat there again.

☐ **5** All foreign fruit and vegetables should get inspected before entering the country.

B Group Work **Compare your answers with your group members. Discuss your reasons. Use *get* passives.**

A *I think that when a restaurant gets inspected, the results should be posted on the restaurant's front door.*

B *I disagree. If a restaurant gets inspected and receives a low rating, it's bad for business.*

4 Passive Gerunds and Infinitives

Grammar Presentation

Gerunds and infinitives can occur in the passive.	Some people worry about genetically modified food *harming* them. (active)
	Some people worry about *being harmed* by genetically modified food. (passive)
	Consumers should expect food companies *to give* them accurate information about their food. (active)
	Consumers should expect *to be given* accurate information about their food. (passive)

4.1 Forming Passive Gerunds

A To form passive gerunds, use *being* + the past participle of the main verb.	Consumers are afraid of food companies *harming* them. (active)
	Consumers are afraid of *being harmed* by food companies. (passive)
B Common verbs that are followed by passive gerunds include *avoid, consider, dislike, enjoy, like, miss, quit,* and *remember.*	I remember *being given* information about GM foods in the supermarket.
C Common verbs + prepositions that are followed by passive gerunds include complain *about, keep on, succeed in,* and *worry about.*	The restaurant worried about *being closed* by the food inspectors.
D Common adjectives + prepositions that are followed by passive gerunds include *afraid of, aware of, concerned about, content with, interested in, tired of,* and *worried about.*	The company was interested in *being seen* as a socially responsible company.

▶▶ Verbs Followed by Gerunds Only: See page A7.
▶▶ Verbs Followed by Gerunds or Infinitives: See page A7.
▶▶ Verbs + Prepositions: See page A9.
▶▶ Adjectives + Prepositions: See page A10.

4.2 Forming Passive Infinitives

A To form passive infinitives, use *to be* + the past participle of the main verb.	*Food companies are not likely to solve the problem of world hunger.* (active) *The problem of world hunger is not likely to be solved by food companies.* (passive)
B Common verbs followed by passive infinitives include *ask, expect, hope, manage, refuse, seem,* and *want*.	*The manager of the restaurant expected to be told that the restaurant passed the inspection.*

▸▸ Verbs Followed by Infinitives Only: See page A7.

▸▸ Verbs Followed by Gerunds or Infinitives: See page A7.

 # Grammar Application

Exercise 4.1 Passive Gerunds and Infinitives

Complete the sentences about restaurant food safety. Circle the correct passive forms of the verbs.

1 Customers at Corner Café recently complained about (being)/to be served undercooked food.

2 The manager of the café was concerned about **to be / being** inspected.

3 The owners were afraid of **to be / being** told they must close the cafe if the problems were not corrected.

4 The owners expected **being / to be** cited by the county food safety bureau.

5 The staff hoped **to be / being** paid for the time that the restaurant was closed.

6 The manager was not happy about **being / to be** told to close the restaurant.

Exercise 4.2 More Passive Gerunds and Infinitives

A Listen to an interview with consumers about food labeling. Write the passive gerund or infinitive forms you hear.

Reporter	Hello to everyone. Today I'll be asking people their thoughts on food labeling. First, let's talk to Andrew. Andrew, do you read food labels?
Andrew	I refuse ___*to be forced*___ to do so much work when I go shopping! I just want _____ decent, healthy food. No, I don't read them. (2)
Reporter	I can understand that. Al and Mei?

| Al | We expect _____ the truth by food companies, |
| | (3) |

but we know labels aren't always accurate.

| Mei | You have to inform yourself. All consumers have to start _____ |
| | (4) |

better _____ , so we always read them.
(4)

| Reporter | OK. And you, Roxana, do you read food labels? |

| Roxana | Yes, because I'm a pretty informed consumer. I'm not too concerned |

about _____ by food companies, but I'm not
(5)

interested in _____ , either!
(6)

| Reporter | Thank you, Roxana. And finally, Jessica. What do you think? |

| Jessica | It's sometimes easy _____ by product labeling, so I |
| | (7) |

don't read them much because they don't matter. Take the word

natural, for example. You expect it _____ for food that
(8)

has few or no artificial ingredients. However, the word *natural* can be

used for genetically modified food products.

| Reporter | Thanks to you all. It appears that consumers are tired of |

_____ by food companies.
(9)

B Over to You Complete the sentences about food labeling with passive gerunds or infinitives and the verbs in the box. Write sentences that are true for you.

| ~~confuse~~ | give | lie to | tell |
| do | inform | sell | use |

1 I'm tired of _being confused by food labels_____ .

2 I expect _____ .

3 I'm (not) concerned about _____ .

4 I hope _____ .

5 It's (not) easy _____ .

C Pair Work Compare your answers with a partner.

A *I'm tired of being confused by food labels. I don't want to be told something is "organic" when it really isn't.*

B *Well, I know what you mean, but actually, I'm tired of being told to eat organic and healthy food all the time. Why can't I enjoy a candy bar once in a while?*

5 Avoid Common Mistakes ⚠

> **1** **In passive sentences, use a past participle after *be*, not the base form of the verb.**
>
> produced
> Unintended side effects can be ~~produce~~ by new technologies.

> **2** **Don't forget to use *be* + the past participle to express a passive meaning.**
>
> be caused
> An allergic reaction can ~~cause~~ by many different kinds of foods.

Editing Task

Find and correct seven more mistakes in the paragraph about some GM food concerns.

> made
> It is certain that many advances in technology will be ~~make~~ in the twenty-first century. Although many of these advances will improve our future, others may do as much harm as good. GM foods are one example. Currently, many new foods are creating by scientists. For instance, many people suffer from food allergies. Certain
>
> 5   GM foods may help avoid this problem; the food's DNA has been change so that the food no longer causes allergic reactions. Also, one day, the world's growing population may be feed with GM foods that grow quickly. This will make it possible for more food to be produce. These new foods can be use to feed more people. However, GM foods have another side. Because these foods have not existed very
>
> 10   long, scientists do not know all their effects. For example, some people fear that cancer can cause by GM foods. This is especially troubling because GM foods might not mark as such, so consumers may not know what they are buying. When they develop new foods, scientists should be aware of the concerns that consumers have. In my view, we should be careful with any new technology.

6 Academic Writing

Argumentative Writing Using Graphs and Tables for Support

Brainstorm > Organize > Write > **Edit**

In Unit 19, you wrote the first draft of your essay to answer the prompt below. In this unit (20), you will review, revise, and edit your essay.

> *Using what you know about the job market, what is a good choice for a career path with a secure future? Include information from graphs or tables to support your choice.*

My Writing

Using the Passive Voice in Academic Writing

Academic writers often use the passive voice to avoid repetition or when the focus is on a process or action rather than who did the process or action. However, in academic writing it is important to avoid using *get* passives.

Exercise 6.1 Applying the Skill

Review the essay you wrote in My Writing in Unit 19.

- Find at least one place to use the passive voice to avoid repetition.
- Find at least one place to use the passive voice to focus is on a process or action rather than who did the process or action.
- Edit any sentences in which you used a *get* passive.

Exercise 6.2 Revising Your Ideas

1 Work with a partner. Use the questions to give feedback on your partner's essay.

- Which of your partner's ideas seem strongest to you?
- Which of your partner's ideas need to be explained more clearly?
- What could your partner add or remove to make the essay stronger and easier to understand?

2 Use the feedback from your partner to revise the ideas and content of your essay.

Exercise 6.3 Editing Your Writing

1 Use the checklist to review and edit your essay.

Did you answer the writing prompt completely?	
Did you organize your essay correctly?	
Does your introduction make a successful logical appeal?	
Does your thesis statement make a claim that people could argue about?	
Do your body paragraphs have topic sentences that connect to your thesis statement and support your claim?	
Did you include and analyze at least one graph or other visual?	
Did you use reporting verbs to introduce evidence?	
Did you add indirect advice from an expert?	

Exercise 6.4 Editing Your Grammar

Use the checklist to review and edit the grammar in your essay.

Did you use direct and indirect speech correctly?	
Did you include indirect advice correctly?	
Did you use active and passive voice correctly?	
Did you avoid *get* passives?	
Did you avoid the common mistakes on pages 261, 273, 287 and 301?	

Exercise 6.5 Writing Your Final Draft

Apply the feedback and edits from Exercises 6.2 to 6.4 to write the final draft of your essay.

Subject Relative Clauses (Adjective Clauses with Subject Relative Pronouns)

Alternative Energy Sources

1 Grammar in the Real World

ACADEMIC WRITING

Expository writing

A What are some alternative sources of energy (other than oil or coal)? Read the article about one type of alternative energy. Is "people power" an efficient energy source? Why or why not?

B Comprehension Check **Answer the questions.**

1 What are some ways that people can make energy?

2 How can "people power" help the environment?

3 What are some problems with people power?

C Notice **Find the sentences in the article and complete them. Then draw an arrow from each missing word to the word that it refers to.**

1 Professional athletes, _____ **exercise routines** can last for several hours, could help power a house!

2 This heat, _____ **is sent** to a nearby building, cuts the energy bill by 25 percent.

3 However, people _____ **support** green energy are confident that this technology will catch on in the near future.

Look at the words in bold that follow the words you wrote. What parts of speech are the words in bold?

EXERCISING for ELECTRICITY

Much of the world's energy comes from sources like oil and coal, **which cannot be replaced when used up.** Renewable sources – water, wind, and the sun – are better for the environment. However, these alternative
5 sources of energy have not always been sufficiently explored for political and economic reasons. People **who care about the environment** are looking for more alternative sources that might appeal to people who make decisions about these things. One source **that is**
10 **becoming popular** uses energy **that is generated by humans**, sometimes called "people power."

With people power, people create electricity through exercise. People exercise in green gyms, **which contain special treadmills**. These machines
15 convert human energy into electricity that helps run the lights and air-conditioning. People power also helps prevent air pollution. Someone **who exercises for one hour** can feel good about the fact that he or she is helping prevent carbon dioxide from going into the air.
20 Professional athletes, **whose exercise routines can last for several hours,** could help power a house!

Exercise is not the only way people can make energy. One company has created surfaces **which are powered by humans.** People dance or walk on special

25 dance floors and sidewalks. This movement generates electricity, **which can light up the dance floor or power street lamps.** Body heat is used for power, too. One system in Sweden gathers the body heat from commuters in a train station. This heat, **which is sent to**
30 **a nearby building,** cuts the energy bill by 25 percent.

People power is not perfect, though. Large gyms need a lot of energy to run. People power, **which only generates a part of the total electricity needed,** does not lower the gym's electric bill much. Also, the use
35 of this technology is moving slowly. Business leaders, **who must focus on making a profit,** do not always want to be the first to create new products. They are afraid to spend money on technology **which might not be successful.** However, people **who support green**
40 **energy** are confident that this technology will catch on in the near future.

People power is not a major energy source yet, but it could be soon. Meanwhile, this "green energy" encourages people to exercise, and it makes people
45 more aware of the environment. It is one kind of technology **that helps people and the planet** at the same time.

2 Identifying Subject Relative Clauses

Grammar Presentation

Relative clauses modify – define, describe, identify, or give more information about – nouns. In a subject relative clause, the relative pronoun is the subject of the clause. An identifying relative clause gives essential information about the noun it modifies.	SUBJECT *I go to a gym. The gym creates its own electricity.* RELATIVE PRONOUN *I go to a gym that creates its own electricity.*

2.1 Forming Identifying Subject Relative Clauses

A The subject of an identifying subject relative clause is the relative pronoun. The relative pronoun refers to the noun before it. Use *who* or *that* for people, and *which* or *that* for things.	NOUN RELATIVE PRONOUN *Nowadays, people often drive cars that don't use a lot of gas.*
Do not add a second subject to the clauses.	*People that exercise can use special machines to create electricity.* NOT *People that they exercise can use special machines to create electricity.*
B The information in an identifying subject relative clause is essential. Do not add a comma before this type of clause.	*People who care about the environment often recycle their garbage.* (The relative clause tells which people.) *The school uses the electricity that comes from the exercise machines in the gym.* (The relative clause tells which electricity.)
C The verb in the relative clause agrees with the noun that the relative pronoun modifies.	SINGULAR NOUN SINGULAR VERB *Someone that supports the environment recycles.* PLURAL NOUN PLURAL VERB *Many people that support the environment recycle.*

▸▸ Relative Clauses: See page A13.

2.2 Using Identifying Subject Relative Clauses

A Use an identifying relative clause to give essential information about a noun. These clauses are also called restrictive subject clauses.	*People power is a kind of energy.* (What kind of energy? What is important about it?) *People power is a kind of energy **that creates electricity**.* (The relative clause gives essential information.)
B Use an identifying relative clause in definitions, especially with words such as *anyone, people, someone,* or *something*.	*Green energy is something **which doesn't hurt the environment**.* *Environmentalists are people **who care about the environment**.*

Grammar Application

Exercise 2.1 Subject Relative Pronouns

A Complete the article about people power. Use *who* or *which* and the simple present form of the verbs in parentheses.

Silvia is a student at Bay City University (BCU) <u>who works out</u> (work out) at the (1) campus gym every day. Today, she is exercising on a bike _____ (connect) (2) to a power grid. Silvia is possibly producing the energy _____ (keep) the (3) gym lights on or _____ (power) a professor's laptop in another part of the (4) campus. BCU and Bay City Tech are just two educational institutions _____ (5) (use) human energy as power.

We interviewed Mark Sandoval, a BCU employee _____ (run) campus (6) operations. He said, "This is not a program _____ (save) the university (7) money. It's more of an experiment _____ (illustrate) to the (8) students how they affect their environment." GreenGo is a Bay City human energy company _____ (provide) BCU with the exercise equipment. Rita Crane, a GreenGo (9) spokesperson, said, "We enjoy working with students and faculty_____ (take) (10) their impact on the environment very seriously."

B Listen to the article and check your answers.

A Complete the energy definitions with *who* or *that* and the correct form of the verbs in parentheses. Sometimes more than one answer is possible.

1 Geothermal energy is heat _____*that comes*_____ (come) from inside the earth.
2 Renewable energy is something _____ (not/disappear).
3 Ecologists are people _____ (study) the relationship between organisms and the environment.
4 A green politician is someone _____ (put) environmental issues ahead of other issues.
5 A sustainable engineer is anyone _____ (design) objects to protect the environment.

B Complete the energy definitions with subject relative pronouns and the words in the box.

chemicals/trap/heat in the atmosphere ~~fuel/come/from vegetable oil or animal fat~~ people/be/part of a political group focused on good environmental policy someone/work/to protect the environment structures/not have/a large negative impact on the environment	a type of energy/come/from human exercise a type of energy/use/the sun as its source a vehicle/use/two sources of power to run

1 Biodiesel is a kind of _*fuel that/which comes from vegetable oil or animal fat*_ .
2 A conservationist is _____ .
3 "Greens" are _____ .
4 Greenhouse gases are _____ .
5 A hybrid car is _____ .
6 Solar energy is _____ .
7 People power is _____ .
8 Green buildings are _____ .

A Combine the sentences from an alternative energy company's advertisement. Use *who*, *that*, or *which* in subject relative clauses. Sometimes more than one answer is possible.

1 GreenGo is a company. It develops renewable energy systems.
   *GreenGo is a company that/which develops renewable energy systems.*
2 GreenGo developed a technology. The technology turns exercise machines into power generators.

   _____

   _____

3 GreenGo builds machines like exercise bikes. These exercise bikes let exercisers generate electricity from their workouts.

_____

_____

4 The electricity connects to a power grid. The power grid covers a large geographic area.

_____

_____

5 Sachiko Hanley is the woman. The woman invented this technology.

_____

6 Many GreenGo clients are colleges and other institutions. The institutions have on-site gyms.

_____

7 GreenGo provides an energy source. The energy source is good for the environment.

_____

8 "We are proud to work with institutions. They have the same environmental goals that we do."

_____

_____

B In each of the sentences you wrote in A, underline the subject relative clause and draw an arrow from the relative pronoun to the noun in the main clause it refers to.

GreenGo is a company that develops renewable energy systems.

3 Nonidentifying Subject Relative Clauses

Grammar Presentation

Nonidentifying subject relative clauses have the same form as identifying clauses. Unlike identifying clauses, nonidentifying clauses provide additional, not essential, information about the nouns they modify.	*Biodiesel fuel, which often comes from plants, is an economical source of energy.* (Where the fuel comes from is extra information. It is not essential information about *Biodiesel fuel*.)

3.1 Forming Nonidentifying Subject Relative Clauses

A Like identifying subject relative clauses, the subject of a nonidentifying subject relative clause is the relative pronoun. The relative pronoun refers to the noun before it.

Use *who* for people and *which* for things. Do not use *that* in a nonidentifying clause.

People power, which is a way to create energy, is popular.

NOT *People power, ~~that~~ is a way to create energy, is popular.*

B Use commas before and after the nonidentifying subject relative clause. The commas indicate that the information is not essential to the meaning of the noun. It is extra information.

Hybrid cars, which are better for the environment, use less gas.

3.2 Using Nonidentifying Subject Relative Clauses

A Use a nonidentifying subject relative clause to give nonessential information about a noun. These clauses are also called nonrestrictive clauses.

People power, which is a way to create energy, is popular with environmentalists.

B Nonidentifying relative clauses are more common in writing and formal speaking than in informal speaking.

3.3 Identifying vs. Nonidentifying Subject Relative Clauses

A Identifying relative clauses provide essential information about the noun. The information in the clause identifies or distinguishes the noun.

Renewable energy that comes directly from the sun is called solar energy. (The information identifies a particular type of renewable energy – not all types of renewable energy.)

My sister who lives in Maine loves being outside. (The information distinguishes this sister from the other or others; it implies there is more than one sister.)

B Nonidentifying clauses give extra information about a noun. The information is not essential. In speaking, use a short pause before and after the clause. In writing, separate the clause between commas.

Renewable energy, which releases fewer greenhouse gases, is becoming more popular. (The information does not identify the type of renewable energy; it gives more information about it.)

My sister, who lives in Maine, loves being outside. (The information is extra, not essential; it also implies the speaker has only one sister.)

Grammar Application

Exercise 3.1 Identifying or Nonidentifying?

A Read the news report on building affordable green homes in New Orleans. Underline the relative clauses. Label each of the relative clauses *I* (for identifying) or *NI* (for nonidentifying).

As the environment changes, hurricanes and other severe storms have become a serious problem in the United States and Latin America. Hurricanes, <u>which primarily attack</u> *NI* <u>southern and southeastern parts of the United States</u>, have been increasing in severity. The hurricane that did the most damage in recent history was Hurricane Katrina. Since

5 then, a great number of Americans, including many celebrities, have helped the people of New Orleans rebuild their homes.

The celebrity who is best known for building homes in New Orleans is Brad Pitt. Pitt, who created a foundation called Make It Right, helps build new "green" homes in New Orleans. The goals of this foundation are admirable. Make It Right volunteers, who work for

10 free, want to build 150 new green homes in the Lower 9th Ward.

The foundation is not simply providing new homes. Make It Right homes have many features which are environmentally sound. For example, Make It Right homes have metal roofs which absorb heat and keep them cool. It is possible that Make It Right homes will inspire new home builders not only in New Orleans but around the world as well.

B Pair Work Compare your answers with a partner. Discuss the reason for each of your answers.

The relative clause which primarily attack southern and southeastern parts of the United States *is nonidentifying, because it is not essential to understanding the sentence. You can say* Hurricanes have been increasing in severity, *and the idea is complete.*

Exercise 3.2 Nonidentifying Subject Relative Clauses

Combine the facts and the additional information about green architecture. Use nonidentifying relative clauses.

1 Fact: Green architecture is becoming more common.

Additional Information: Green architecture considers both design and the environment.

　Green architecture, which considers both design
　and the environment, is becoming more common.

2 Fact: The Turning Torso building uses only renewable energy.
Additional Information: The Turning Torso building is located in Malmö, Sweden.

3 Fact: The Turning Torso building was inspired by a sculpture of a twisting human being.
Additional Information: The Turning Torso building is the tallest building in Sweden.

_____

_____

4 Fact: The Burj al-Taqa will be a wind- and solar-powered green skyscraper.
Additional Information: The Burj al-Taqa will be in Dubai.

_____

_____

5 Fact: Eckhard Gerber has also designed a green building in Riyadh.
Additional Information: Eckhard Gerber designed the Burj al-Taqa.

_____

_____

6 Fact: Architect Eric Corey Freed believes that people will pay more for green buildings.
Additional Information: Eric Corey Freed has written several books on building green structures.

_____

_____

4 Subject Relative Clauses with _Whose_

Grammar Presentation

Subject relative clauses that begin with the pronoun _whose_ show possession.	_In Sweden, there are train commuters. The commuters' body heat supplies energy for a building._
	In Sweden, there are train commuters **whose** body heat supplies energy for a building.

4.1 Forming Relative Clauses with _Whose_

A The pronoun _whose_ shows a possessive relationship between the noun before and after it.	_They are the scientists **whose research** has won awards._ (The research belongs to the scientists.)
	That is the product **whose inventor** attended this college. (The product is related to the inventor.)

4.1 Forming Relative Clauses with *Whose* (continued)

B The verb in the relative clause agrees with the noun following *whose*.

WHOSE + SINGULAR NOUN + SINGULAR VERB
He's the scientist whose newest idea is often quoted.

WHOSE + PLURAL NOUN + PLURAL VERB
He's the scientist whose ideas are often quoted.

4.2 Using Relative Clauses with *Whose*

Relative clauses with *whose* can be identifying or nonidentifying subject relative clauses.

IDENTIFYING RELATIVE CLAUSE
They are the journalists whose articles have explained green energy. (The information in the clause identifies which journalists.)

NONIDENTIFYING RELATIVE CLAUSE
Brad Pitt, whose movies are well known, gives a lot of money to environmental causes. (The information about his movies is not essential to identifying Brad Pitt.)

Grammar Application

Exercise 4.1 Subject Relative Clauses with *Whose*: Identifying or Nonidentifying?

A Read the article about a human-powered vehicle. Underline the subject relative clauses. Add commas when necessary.

Meet Charles Greenwood, the inventor of a new type of car. Greenwood, <u>whose human-powered car can go up to 60 miles per hour,</u> is an engineer. This inventor whose dream is to sell the cars to the public has also started a business to manufacture it. A car whose power source is human energy is obviously good for the environment. How does

5 it work? The car whose main power source is human-operated hand cranks[1] also runs with a battery. It's not expensive, either. The car – the HumanCar Imagine PS – will sell for about $15,000. A hybrid car whose selling price will only be about $15,000 should be very popular with energy-conscious consumers.

10 There are other benefits to a human-powered car. A car whose power source is human energy might also help drivers stay fit. In addition, owners expect to save money operating the HumanCar. The HumanCar whose main source of power is human-operated hand cranks gets the

15 equivalent of 100 miles to the gallon of gas in a regular car.

[1]**crank:** a handle or bar on a machine that you can turn to make another part turn

B Pair Work Compare your answers with a partner. Discuss whether each subject relative clause is identifying or nonidentifying.

The relative clause whose human-power car can go up to 60 miles per hour *is nonidentifying because it is not necessary for identifying Greenwood.*

Exercise 4.2 *That, Who, or Whose?*

Complete the article about green awards. Use *that*, *who*, or *whose*. Sometimes more than one answer is possible.

AWARDS for Being Green

There are many organizations ___*that*___ offer awards to companies _____ practices
(1)   (2)
help the environment and society. Some organizations recognize the work of companies
_____ focus on environmentally responsible practices. The Evergreen Award program
(3)
honors companies _____ create environmentally friendly products. An award in 2010
(4)
went to Play Mart Inc., a maker of plastic playground equipment _____ products were
(5)
made from jugs and bottles from landfills.

The One Show is another awards organization, _____ Green Pencil award
(6)
celebrates environmentally conscious advertising. In 2009, Häagen-Dazs received the
award for their advertisements _____ raised awareness about the disappearance of
(7)
honeybees. Häagen-Dazs, _____ ice-cream is well known, also donates money to
(8)
research _____ studies honeybees. People _____ buy certain flavors of
(9)   (10)
Häagen-Dazs ice-cream help support this research.

Exercise 4.3 Subject Relative Clauses with *Whose*

Pair Work Answer the questions. Use subject relative clauses with *whose* in your sentences. Then compare your answers with a partner.

- What are the benefits of human-powered vehicles and flying machines?
- What are the disadvantages to these inventions?

A *I said, "A vehicle whose power source is human energy is good for the environment."*
B *I said, "A vehicle whose power source is human energy probably won't go very far or very fast."*

Unit 21 Subject Relative Clauses (Adjective Clauses with Subject Relative Pronouns)

5 Avoid Common Mistakes ⚠

1 Use *which* or *that* for things, not *who*.

Scientists are looking for new energy sources ~~who~~ *which/that* don't harm the environment.

2 Use *who* or *that* for people, not *which*.

Governments support researchers ~~which~~ *who/that* are trying to develop alternative approaches to energy.

3 Don't use *who's* when you mean *whose*.

An inventor ~~who's~~ *whose* innovative technology solves the energy crisis will help all of us.

4 Don't include a second subject in the relative clause.

A fuel that ~~it~~ is renewable will help solve the world's pollution problems.

Editing Task

Find and correct eight more mistakes in the paragraph about an alternative renewable energy source.

People think renewable energy only comes from water, wind, or the sun, but there is another renewable energy source: biofuels. Biofuels are fuels ~~who~~ *which/that* are derived from oils in plants. Farmers who's fields were once planted with food crops can now grow energy on their land. The most commonly used example of this is ethanol, a biofuel who
5   is usually made from corn and added to gasoline. However, ethanol has been criticized. Some critics say that the world, who's population continues to grow, needs all of its corn for food production. Others have argued that it takes too much energy to produce corn ethanol. Recently, scientists which do biofuels research have been working to overcome these problems. For example, some scientists have produced a genetically modified
10   tobacco that it contains more oil than usual. Other scientists have produced genetically modified tobacco plants that they produce a lot of oil. This oil can be made into ethanol. In fact, some scientists have produced ethanol from inedible grass that it grows in the wild. The scientists which made these inventions hope that biofuels will become an important part of our renewable energy future.

6 Academic Writing

Expository Writing

Brainstorm > Organize > Write > Edit

In this writing cycle (Units 21–23), you will write an expository essay that answers the prompt below. In this unit (21), you will analyze a text, and then brainstorm and organize ideas about the topic.

> *Explain the advantages and disadvantages of three types of renewable energy and decide which would work best in your country or region.*

Exercise 6.1 Preparing to Read

Work with a partner. Discuss the questions.

1 What can we do to protect our natural resources like air and water?
2 What will happen if important resources that we use, like water, fresh food, and oil disappear?
3 What do you think the slogan, "Reduce, Reuse, Recycle" means?
4 What are some other things that you do to be "green"?

Exercise 6.2 Focusing on Vocabulary

Read the definitions. Complete the sentences with the correct form of the words in bold.

> **adopt** (v) to accept or begin to use something
>
> **alarming** (adj) causing worry or fear
>
> **catastrophic** (adj) causing sudden and very great harm or destruction
>
> **resistant** (adj) not wanting to accept something, especially change or new ideas
>
> **urgent** (adj) needing immediate attention
>
> **vital** (adj) necessary or extremely important for the success or continued existence of something

1 Finding solutions to climate change is a(n) _____ issue that must be addressed now.

2 Global warming is _____ to most people because the future of the planet is in danger.

3 Scientists warn us that not reducing our use of fossil fuels will have _____ effects on our environment and will likely lead to the extinction of many species.

4 Over one hundred United Nations delegates signed a document to _____ new environmental standards in order to slow down climate change.

5 Experts say that it is _____ to stop pollution caused by factories for the survival of certain plant and animal species.

6 Manufacturers are often _____ to using "green" production methods that cost more, so we need new laws that force them to do it.

Maintaining Our Natural Resources

The world's natural resources are being used at an **alarming** rate—not only fossil fuels such as coal, oil, and gas, but also water, wood, metals, and minerals. This has many potential consequences for the billions of people who live on Earth. In
5 recent years, both individuals and governments have become more interested in better management of the world's resources. An immediate way for individuals to improve the situation is for everyone to reduce, reuse, and recycle products. Alternative energy solutions, which are equally essential to our future, are
10 generally the responsibility of governments, though they are not always practical for various reasons.

Each of us must learn to use fewer natural resources on a daily basis. We can start by reducing the number of electrical items that we leave plugged in, using less water, and avoiding fossil fuel-powered transportation. In our homes, we can use only energy-saving light bulbs and install water meters. Parents need to train children from an
15 early age to turn off lights that they are not using. It is sometimes difficult to persuade people to use less energy and water or to waste less food, but an effective way to motivate people to **adopt** less-wasteful practices is to make these important commodities more expensive. As a result, many cities now tax carbon emissions, which is a step in the right direction.

Another effective way to help the environment is by encouraging people to reuse or restore old, unwanted
20 objects. When people reuse, they reduce waste. Additionally, items like glass bottles can be cleaned and reused without having to be broken and remade. Reusing objects is an efficient process that consumes less energy than recycling. It does, however, often require a lot of planning and administration, which can increase costs. For example, there are concerns regarding reused medical equipment and food-storage items because of safety and hygiene issues. Still, the benefits of reusing many items are clear.

25 Most of us know that materials such as paper and plastic can be recycled into new products, but this process depends on individual and community action. It is true that sorting through used materials before recycling them can be a dirty job, and breaking up electronic equipment to recycle rare metals is time-consuming and potentially dangerous. However, as long as we understand the work and potential dangers involved, the necessity of recycling on a community scale is evident.

30 In recent years, a lot of attention has been paid to the dangers of relying on fossil fuels. For this reason, the use of alternatives to coal, oil, and gas are becoming more and more common. Alternative energy sources can be recovered or produced without emitting carbon dioxide and without contributing to global warming. They can decrease air pollution, which is better for our health, as it diminishes instances of asthma. They are often sustainable resources as well, which means they will not get used up.

35 There are many examples of alternative energy sources including hydropower, solar energy, biomass[1], and geothermal energy, though each has its limitations. Hydropower, which utilizes the power of moving water, is a good choice for places with waterfalls and rivers. Wind power is most productive in areas with sustained wind, like hilltops and open water. Places that receive constant sunlight during the day, like deserts, are the best candidates for solar energy. The burning of biomass can be used to create steam and is available everywhere, but only if
40 government or companies are willing to invest in it. Finally, geothermal energy, which uses the heat within the earth to produce electricity and heat buildings, is limited to countries like Iceland that are situated above this kind of energy source. Clearly, particular types of alternative energy may work best for particular regions. The other side of this reality is that some of these energy sources may not be available at all to some people because of where they live. However, these are not reasons for governments to do nothing.

45 Clearly, individuals, governments, and businesses must work together to avoid a **catastrophic** depletion of **vital** natural resources in the future, and **urgent** action is required now. Alternative energy production is certainly essential, but it can be expensive and time-consuming to install the required elements. Some developing areas of the world may simply be unable to pay for it. In other places, corporations and taxpayers may be **resistant** to it. The "reduce, reuse, recycle" strategy, at least for the present, seems to be a manageable one that can be
50 practiced by both individuals and organizations. People who may be resistant to the idea of changing their ways by "going green" need to see that it is crucial to do this for the future of the planet.

---

[1]**biomass (n)** dead plant and animal material suitable for using as fuel

Read the text on page 317. Work with a partner. Discuss the questions.

1 What is the writer's main idea?
2 What are two suggestions that the writer offers for using fewer natural resources on a daily basis?
3 What are three advantages of alternative energy sources?
4 What are two disadvantages of alternative energy sources?

Exercise 6.4 Noticing the Grammar and Writing

1 Highlight two examples of *that* in paragraph 2. How does the writer use these relative clauses?
2 Highlight two examples of *which* in paragraph 6. How does the writer use these relative clauses?
3 Look at paragraph 3. Circle the advantages. Underline the disadvantages. How is the paragraph organized?
4 Read the last sentence of paragraphs 2-7. How do they support the writer's main idea?

Organizing Ideas in a Table

A **table** is a graphic organizer that helps writers visualize and organize ideas, relationships, and concepts before writing. Tables are especially helpful when examining the advantages, disadvantages, and other characteristics of multiple items.

Exercise 6.4 Applying the Skill

1 Use information from the reading on page 317 to complete the table.

	What are the benefits?	What are the drawbacks?	Is it effective for my country? What is the impact of producing it?
hydropower			
solar energy			
wind power			
biomass energy			
geothermal energy			

2 Compare your answers with a partner, and discuss the differences.

My Writing

Expository Essays

In expository essays, writers explain, illustrate, or clarify ideas about a topic. When you explain ideas, it is important to discuss both the advantages and disadvantages. This will help readers better understand your thesis.

Exercise 6.6 Brainstorming Topics and Ideas

Work with a partner. Complete the tasks.

1 Review the alternative energy sources you discussed in Exercise 6.4. Decide which three would work best in your country.

2 Complete the table below. Use ideas from the reading on page 317 to help you.

Rank	Type of Energy	Reason
1		
2		
3		

Using Relative Clauses to Add Information and Avoid Repetition

As you learned in this unit, relative clauses add information about nouns. Relative clauses are often formed by combining two sentences. When you combine two sentences with a relative clause, you avoid repetition, which makes your ideas clearer and more fluent. Look at these examples:

My university has solar panels. The **solar panels** were made in Germany.

My university has solar panels **that** were made in Germany.

In the first example, the term *solar panels* is repeated. Repeating a term or phrase can make your writing choppy. The second example flows better and is more concise.

Exercise 6.7 Writing a Paragraph

Write a paragraph about one of the alternative energy sources in Exercise 6.6. Include a topic sentence, at least two advantages and two disadvantages, and a concluding sentence. Use the grammar and writing skills you learned in this unit to improve your writing.

Object Relative Clauses (Adjective Clauses with Object Relative Pronouns)

Biometrics

1 Grammar in the Real World

ACADEMIC WRITING

Expository writing

A What are some techniques that the police use to solve crimes? Read the article about how the police analyze evidence. What are some modern techniques for analyzing evidence?

B Comprehension Check Answer the questions.

1 What are some types of forensic evidence?
2 What is one way that police can identify someone?
3 Why can forensic evidence sometimes be inaccurate?

C Notice Match the first part of the sentence from the article on the left with the second part on the right.

A	B
1 The victim shows the police the room _____	a **that** thieves leave behind.
2 Traditional forensic techniques include collecting and analyzing evidence _____	b in **which** the theft occurred.
3 This evidence includes dust, hair, or fibers _____	c **that** police find at the crime scene.

Do the words in B in bold act as the subjects or objects of the clauses they are in?

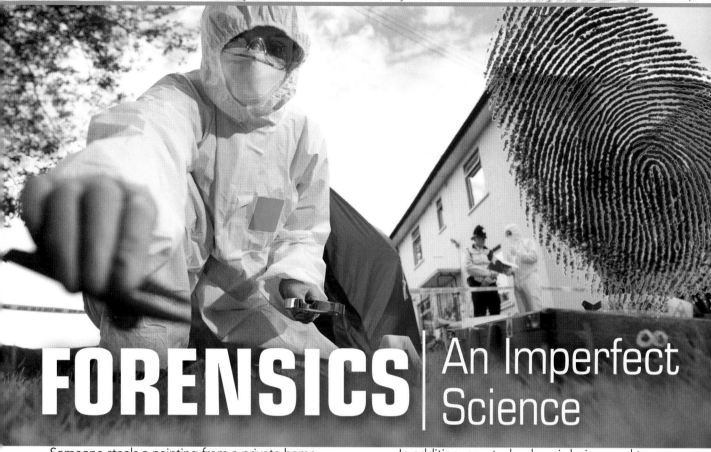

FORENSICS | An Imperfect Science

Someone steals a painting from a private home. The victim shows the police the room **in which the theft occurred**. Police collect clothing fibers and dirt left on the carpet. Experts then use the fibers
5 and dirt to identify the thief. The thief is caught, and the art is returned. The use of scientific tests to investigate crimes like this one is called forensics. Traditional forensic techniques include collecting and analyzing evidence **that police find at the crime**
10 **scene**. This evidence includes dust, hair, or fibers **that thieves leave behind**. Police sometimes use dogs to investigate a crime. Scents **that dogs are trained to recognize** include the scents of people, drugs, and explosives. Police also look for fingerprints, **which**
15 **they often find on hard surfaces**. Unfortunately, fingerprints are often incomplete. However, new techniques use computer programs to help police identify suspects or missing people. Computer programs can produce a list of matches for partial
20 fingerprints. This kind of list, **which police use to narrow a large field of suspects**, helps investigators work efficiently.

In addition, new technology is being used to analyze other evidence. New video cameras can
25 automatically identify a face **whose image police have on film**. Police can compare the faces of suspects to the image of the criminal and find the actual person more quickly. There is also a new way **in which police can identify someone who may be**
30 **a "missing person."**[1] This new technology compares a digital image of the person's iris[2] with the irises of people who are listed as missing in a database.

Forensic evidence **that police collect** is not always accurate. For example, fiber matching is inconclusive.[3]
35 Currently, fibers **that investigators analyze** can only be matched to a type of cloth. The fibers may not be from clothes **that the suspect owns**. Another concern is that there are no strict training standards for forensic dogs. Therefore, agencies like the FBI have only a few
40 dog teams **whose work they trust.**

Combining technology with traditional methods is changing the way **that criminal investigations are done.** Forensic science is not perfect, but it is still an important tool in investigations.

---

[1]**missing person:** someone who has disappeared
[2]**iris:** the colored part of the eye

[3]**inconclusive:** not leading to a definite result or decision; uncertain

2 Identifying Object Relative Clauses

Grammar Presentation

In an object relative clause, the relative pronoun is the object of the clause. An identifying object relative clause gives essential information about the noun it modifies.	OBJECT *Evidence is sometimes inaccurate. Police collect this evidence.* RELATIVE PRONOUN *Evidence that police collect is sometimes inaccurate.*

2.1 Forming Identifying Object Relative Clauses

A The object relative pronoun follows the noun it replaces and comes at the beginning of the relative clause. In an object relative clause, the relative pronoun is the object of the clause.	*Humans aren't aware of smells. A dog can recognize smells.* RELATIVE NOUN PRONOUN *Humans aren't aware of smells that a dog can recognize.*
B Use the relative pronouns *who*, *that*, or *whom* with people. Use *which* or *that* for things.	*Detectives are people who/that/whom I respect tremendously.*
These pronouns are frequently omitted in speaking, but not in formal writing.	*Forensic evidence is something which/that police count on.* (in writing) *Forensic evidence is something police count on.* (in speaking)
When referring to people, *that* is more common than *who*. The pronoun *whom* is very formal and is much less common than *that* or *who* in conversation.	least formal *Detective Paula Cho is a person that I admire very much.* *Detective Paula Cho is a person who I admire very much.* *Detective Paula Cho is a person whom I admire very much.* most formal
C Use *whose* + a noun to show possession. *Whose* cannot be omitted.	*The person whose car the thieves stole was a friend of mine.*

▶▶ Relative Clauses: See page A13.

2.2 Using Identifying Subject Relative Clauses

Use an identifying relative clause to give essential information that defines or identifies the noun it modifies.	*Evidence that criminals leave at the crime scene is called forensic evidence.* (*That criminals leave at the crime scene* identifies the evidence.)

🖥 Grammar Application

Complete the sentences about forensic technology. Use *who* or *which* and the verbs in parentheses.

1 *Biometrics* refers to the techniques __*which*__ people __*use*__ (use) to identify individuals by their physical or behavioral characteristics.

2 Biometric information _____ experts _____ (analyze) includes DNA, fingerprints, eyes, and voice patterns.

3 People _____ the police _____ (suspect) of a crime can be excluded with the use of biometrics.

4 Biometric technology can match fingerprints with ones _____ the police _____ (have) on file.

5 One type of biometric technology _____ people _____ (utilize) for security is the fingerprint scanner.

6 For example, people _____ Disney World _____ (admit) to the park must have their fingerprints scanned.

7 The fingerprint scanners _____ Disney World _____ (use) help to stop people from entering the park without a proper ticket.

Complete the web interview about forensic technology. Rewrite the sentence pairs in parentheses as single sentences with object relative clauses. Sometimes more than one answer is possible.

Reporter: I understand that our police department has some new forensic technology.

Mayor: *Yes, it has a new system that it uses to analyze DNA.*
(1 Yes, it has a new system. It uses the system to analyze DNA.)

Reporter: What does it look like?

Mayor: _____
(2 It's a hand-held device. Officers bring it to the crime scene.)

_____
(3 It helps the police to analyze data. They find the data at the scene.)

Reporter: I understand that not everyone is happy about this device.

Mayor: _____
(4 The device has privacy issues. Some people are concerned about these privacy issues.)

Reporter	Why is this a concern?
Mayor	_____
	(5 Well, the DNA might get the person in trouble. The device collected this DNA.)
	_____
	(6 For example, many people have health issues. They want to keep these issues private.)
Reporter	Oh, I see. This is certainly a lot to think about. Thank you for the interview.

Exercise 2.3 Sentence Combining

A Rewrite the reporter's notes on local crimes. Use identifying object relative clauses with the relative pronouns in parentheses.

Recent Crime Reports

1 A man was arrested for theft. Police raided his house last night. (whose)

A man *whose house police raided last night was arrested for theft* .

2 The detectives made their report. The police sent the detectives to the crime scene. (whom)

The detectives _____ .

3 Several valuable items had been stolen. The police recovered the items. (that)

Several valuable items _____ .

4 The man has not been identified. Burglars invaded the man's home. (whose)

The man _____ .

5 Detectives have visited the house. The thief broke into the house yesterday. (which)

Detectives _____ .

6 The man is in good condition. A car hit him last night. (that)

The man _____ .

B Pair Work In which sentences in A can you omit the pronoun? Discuss the answer with a partner. Then rewrite the sentences with the pronoun omitted.

3 Nonidentifying Object Relative Clauses

Grammar Presentation

Nonidentifying object relative clauses have the same form as identifying clauses. Unlike identifying clauses, nonidentifying clauses provide additional, not essential, information about the nouns they modify.	Evidence from crimes, *which we call forensic evidence*, can help police solve cases. (*Which we call forensic evidence* is extra information. It is not essential to understanding *Evidence from crimes*.)

3.1 Forming Nonidentifying Object Relative Clauses

A Use *who* or *whom* for people. Use *which* for things. Use *whose* for possessive people and things.	*The Sherlock Holmes stories were written by the Scottish author Arthur Conan Doyle, who/whom many people think was English.*
Do not use *that* in nonidentifying relative clauses.	*Forensic science, which Sherlock Holmes used, has been recognized as science since the 1800s.* NOT *Forensic science, ~~that~~ Sherlock Holmes used, has been recognized as science since the 1800s.*
Do not omit the relative pronoun in nonidentifying object clauses.	*The character Sherlock Holmes, who Arthur Conan Doyle created, was a fictional detective.* NOT *The character Sherlock Holmes, ~~Arthur Conan Doyle created~~, was a fictional detective.*
B Use commas before and after the nonidentifying object relative clause.	*Arthur Conan Doyle, whose medical clinic not many patients attended, had time to write his stories.*

Grammar Application

Exercise 3.1 Nonidentifying Object Relative Clauses

Read part of a presentation on a forensic science program. Underline the nonidentifying clauses. Add commas.

Forensic science, <u>which many of you know about from popular TV shows</u>, has become a popular career. Forensic science courses which many colleges are offering today prepare students for careers in crime scene investigation. The University of Central Florida (UCF) which I attended has a forensic science program. Your area of
5 specialization which you choose during your time here depends on your interests and skills. The area that I chose was forensic biochemistry because I wanted to study

odontology. Forensic odontology which the police use to analyze teeth is challenging and fascinating. Forensic analysis which focuses on chemistry and analysis of different kinds of evidence is also available. Introduction to Forensic Science which you take

10 after other preliminary courses will help you decide on the area of specialty. I wish you all the best of luck!

Exercise 3.2 Using Nonidentifying Object Relative Clauses

Read the sentences about a TV show that popularizes forensics. Combine the sentences with nonidentifying object relative clauses. Add commas when necessary.

1 *NCIS: Naval Criminal Investigative Service* is an American TV series. Donald Bellisario and Don McGill created it.

NCIS: Naval Criminal Investigative Service, _which Donald Bellisario and_ _Don McGill created, is an American TV series._ .

2 The program became a hit in 2011. CBS first showed it in 2003.
The program _____ .

3 *NCIS* has been on the air for many years. The entertainment industry has awarded it several awards.
NCIS _____

_____ .

4 The program is shown in Australia, New Zealand, Canada, the UK, and Poland. Over 22 million people watched season 10.
The program _____ .

5 "NCIS Theme" is the show's theme tune. CBS records first released it in 2009.
"NCIS Theme," _____ .

_____ .

6 *NCIS: The Game* was popular. CBS released it in 2010.
NCIS: The Game _____

_____ .

4 Object Relative Clauses as Objects of Prepositions

Grammar Presentation

The relative pronouns in object relative clauses can be the object of prepositions.	OBJ. OF PREP. *There's the police officer. I spoke to <u>her</u>.* RELATIVE PRONOUN *There's the police officer to <u>whom</u> I spoke.* *There's the police officer <u>who</u> I spoke to.*

4.1 Object Relative Clauses as Objects of Prepositions

A The prepositions in object relative clauses can come at the end of the clause in informal speaking and writing.	The police examined the chair *that/which I was sitting <u>on</u>*. The witness, *who/whom I spoke <u>to</u> yesterday*, will appear in court.
In identifying relative clauses, use the relative pronouns *who*, *that*, or *whom* for people and *that* or *which* for things. You can also omit the relative pronoun.	IDENTIFYING RELATIVE CLAUSE The police examined the chair *(that/which)* I was sitting on. The police officer *(who/that/whom)* I met with was robbed.
In nonidentifying relative clauses, use the relative pronouns *who* or *whom* for people and *which* for things. You cannot omit the relative pronoun.	NONIDENTIFYING RELATIVE CLAUSE The door, *which I entered through*, was broken during the crime. The witness, *who/whom I spoke to yesterday*, will appear in court. NOT *The witness, ~~I spoke to yesterday~~, will appear in court.*
B In more formal spoken and especially in written English, the preposition comes before the relative pronouns *whom* or *which*. Do not use *that* or *who*.	The police examined the chair <u>on which</u> I was sitting. NOT *The police examined the chair on ~~that~~ I was sitting.* The witness, <u>with whom</u> I spoke yesterday, will appear in court. NOT *The witness, with ~~who/that~~ I spoke yesterday, will appear in court.*
You cannot omit the relative pronoun.	NOT *The police examined the chair ~~on I was sitting~~.* NOT *The witness, ~~with I spoke yesterday~~, will appear in court.*

 # Grammar Application

Exercise 4.1 Prepositions and Object Relative Clauses

A Listen to a detective describe a crime scene. Complete the sentences with the words you hear.

I arrived at the crime scene at 11:00 a.m. The crime had taken place in a restaurant. The room __*that*__ the crime occurred __*in*__ was the kitchen.
                         (1)   (1)
The back door was open. The back wall was covered in graffiti. I found a spray can

under a table. The spray can, _____ I found fingerprints _____ , matched
                                  (2)   (2)
the color of the graffiti. I asked the kitchen staff to talk to me as a group. The group,

_____ the chef was the only one missing, was very nervous. I learned that the
       (3)
chef had a lot of enemies. I spoke to a cleaning person _____ the chef had argued
                                                             (4)

_____ (4) last week. I also interviewed several waitresses _____ (5) the chef had gone out _____ (5) . One waitress showed me the chef's locker, _____ (6) I found more spray cans _____ (6) .

B Listen again and check your answers.

Exercise 4.2 Using Prepositions and Object Relative Clauses

A Combine the sentences from a crime scene investigator. Use identifying object relative clauses with a preposition at the end of the clause. Sometimes more than one answer is possible.

1 The room was the office. I found broken furniture in it.

The room _which/that I found broken furniture in_ was the office.

2 I found fibers on the floor. The broken furniture was lying on the floor.

I found fibers on the floor _____ .

3 The neighbors said they heard nothing. I spoke to them.

The neighbors _____ said they heard nothing.

4 The house was unlocked. The crime took place in it.

The house _____ was unlocked.

5 There were fingerprints on the door. The criminal entered through it.

There were fingerprints on the door _____ .

6 The lab matched the fingerprints immediately. I sent the evidence to it.

The lab _____ matched the fingerprints immediately.

B Rewrite your answers in A as formal sentences.

1 _The room in which I found broken furniture was the office._

2 _____

3 _____

4 _____

5 _____

6 _____

5 Avoid Common Mistakes ⚠

1 Use *who/whom/that*, not *which*, for people and *which/that* for things.

who/whom/that
The investigator is someone ~~which~~ he respects.

that/which
NCIS is a crime show ~~who~~ I watch.

2 Remember to omit the object pronoun after the verb in object relative clauses.

The evidence that the police found ~~it~~ was used to find the suspect.

3 Do not use a comma before an identifying object relative clause.

The TV crime program, that people thought was the most popular, worked closely with the police to develop its stories.

4 Do not use *what* in relative clauses.

The crime ~~what~~ I am talking about happened yesterday.

Editing Task

Find and correct six more mistakes in the paragraphs about eyewitness testimony.

A victim who police have taken ~~her~~ to the police station gives testimony. She looks at a man in a police lineup and says, "That's the person which I saw in my car." During the trial, the woman gives her testimony in front of the jury, and the jury makes a decision. Soon, the man goes to jail. However, it is possible the woman whose testimony
5 was used is wrong. Researchers now claim that the eyewitness stories what courts often rely on are not always reliable.

Psychologists have conducted experiments who revealed some surprising results. They played a crime-scene video for participants and then asked the participants to remember details. Results showed that participants often described events, which
10 they knew nothing about and had not seen in the video. Similarly, the suspect what participants chose out of a police lineup was rarely the actual criminal.

Psychologists who courts have hired them have testified that eyewitness testimony is not as accurate as was once assumed. As such, psychologists have developed new rules to guide the use of eyewitness testimony.

6 Academic Writing

Expository Writing

Brainstorm > Organize > Write > Edit

In Unit 21, you analyzed an essay and used a table to brainstorm and organize ideas for the prompt below. In this unit (22), you will develop your ideas, learn ways to make your writing clearer and more coherent, and write the first draft of your expository essay.

> *Explain the advantages and disadvantages of three types of renewable energy and decide which would work best in your country or region.*

Introducing Advantages and Disadvantages

You can use a range of phrases that introduce advantages and disadvantages of ideas or solutions to problems.

One major advantage of … is …	The most serious disadvantage of … is …
The most obvious advantages of … are …	A distinct disadvantage of … is …
Another apparent advantage of … is …	One other potential disadvantage of … is …

When a criminal leaves hair at the scene of a crime, the police can use it to find the criminal. This **is one major advantage of** forensic science.

A **distinct disadvantage of** forensic science is that evidence is not always useful. For example, fingerprints may be incomplete.

Exercise 6.1 Understanding the Skill

Work with a partner. Use the prompts to create sentences. Use phrases from the skill box to introduce advantages and disadvantages.

1 advantage, eyewitness, identify criminal
2 disadvantage, eyewitness, misidentify criminal
3 advantage, study, chemistry and forensics
4 disadvantage, study, chemistry and forensics

Exercise 6.2 Applying the Skill

Look at your paragraph from My Writing in Unit 21. Identify the sentences in which you have listed an advantage or disadvantage. Rewrite the sentences with phrases you have learned.

Building Coherence

It is important to make the relationship between different ideas in a text clear to your reader. The ideas should flow in a logical way. This is called **coherence**, and it makes your writing easier to follow. For example, if you are referring back to an idea already presented, the reader should understand that clearly. Use the following to build coherence in your writing.

- Pronouns that refer back to an idea already introduced: *they, them, it, one*, etc.
- Conjunctions and connectors: *however, therefore, in contrast, although*, etc.
- Determiners: *this, that, these, those*, etc.
- Transition words and phrases: *for example, in the same way*, etc.

Exercise 6.3 Applying the Skill

Complete the paragraph with words from the box. You will not use all the words.

For example	However	That	Them	They	Those

   Many students are interested in studying forensic science due to the large number of programs that feature it. (1)_____, *Forensic Cops* is a popular TV show that follows crime scene investigators in Los Angeles. (2)_____ are employed by a police department and help conduct the investigation. (3)_____, the forensic team does not physically find the criminal. (4)_____ job is for the police team.

My Writing

Ordering Ideas in an Essay

Writers often present several ideas related to the main topic in an expository essay. The most important or useful idea generally comes last to leave the readers with a powerful idea. Therefore, when writing about your energy sources, put the energy source that is most likely to be successful in your country at the end.

Exercise 6.4 Planning Your Essay

Work in a small group. Complete the tasks.

1 Compare your paragraphs from My Writing in Unit 21. Which energy sources are the most popular? Why?
2 Discuss the advantages and disadvantages of each source you listed in the brainstorming table on page 319. Revise and edit your ideas based on your discussion.
3 Order the energy sources you are going to write about. Put the most important one last.

Exercise 6.5 Writing Your First Draft

Review your notes. Write an introductory paragraph and three body paragraphs. Use the grammar and writing skills you learned in this unit to improve your writing.

1 Grammar in the Real World

ACADEMIC WRITING

Expository writing

A Do you know anyone born after 1995? Some studies suggest that individuals born during this time have similar traits, such as a high level of independence. Read the article about Generation Z, a term for these individuals. How might these people be different from other, older people in the workplace?

B Comprehension Check Answer the questions.

1 When was Generation Z born?

2 Why are Gen Zers so hard-working and entrepreneurial?

3 Why is Generation Z so comfortable with technology?

C Notice Read the sentences. What words could you add to the words in bold to make them relative clauses? Are the new clauses subject or object relative clauses?

1 David Stillman, **a Generation Z expert**, believes this is the result of the way they were raised.

2 **Gen Zers working a regular job** often have their own income-generating projects on the side.

Generation Z in the Workplace

Generation Z, **also known as iGen or Gen Zers**, are people born between 1995 and 2012. There are over 65 million of them in the United States alone, **where they are now entering the workplace**. It is
5 hard to generalize about such a large group, but these young workers often share certain traits.

This group is hard-working, pragmatic, and entrepreneurial. David Stillman, **a Generation Z expert**, believes this is the result of the way they
10 were raised. They were raised at a time **when many parents lost their jobs in the Great Recession**. Therefore iGen values job security more than previous generations.

In the workplace, their entrepreneurial spirit shows
15 up in several ways. Gen Zers are willing to work very hard, and they prefer to work alone. They also expect to be able to spend time on their own projects at work. **Gen Zers working a regular job** often have their own income-generating projects on the side.
20 These "side hustles" include selling things online and providing services via social media.

Generation Z, **raised in the era of YouTube, social media, and smartphones**, are the first real digital natives. They have never known life without Wi-Fi.
25 They are totally comfortable with technology in the workplace. They are multi-tasking experts. They can watch an online video, comment on Instragram, and listen to music at the same time.

However, their work habits can sometimes serve
30 as distractions. Working on their own side projects can cause moments of inattentiveness, **during which serious errors can occur**. Some members of Generation Z are known for being distracted on the job. Older colleagues may find this trait annoying.

35 This generation of employees will use technology and their own entrepreneurial spirit to make the workplace more efficient. They want to work hard and succeed. Generation Z is ambitious, independent, and tech savvy. These are the traits **already helping them**
40 succeed in workplaces around the country.

2 Relative Clauses with *Where* and *When*

Grammar Presentation

The adverbs *where* and *when* can be used in relative clauses. *Where* is used to modify nouns of place, and *when* is used to modify nouns of time. In these cases, we call these words relative adverbs.

The computer lab is a place where many young students feel comfortable.

Night is a time when many students study for exams.

2.1 Relative Clauses with *Where*

A Use *where* in relative clauses to modify a noun referring to a place. Common nouns include *area*, *country*, *house*, *place*, and *room*.	*This is the only <u>area</u> where you can find Wi-Fi outside of the office.* *The United States is a <u>country</u> where a lot of research on young people is done.* *The office is a <u>place</u> where workers often compete.*
B Do not use a preposition before *where*. Use *which* instead. The use of preposition + *which* is common in academic writing.	*It's a city <u>in which</u> you can find Wi-Fi almost everywhere.* NOT *It's a city ~~in where~~ you can find Wi-Fi almost everywhere.*

▸◂ Relative Clauses: See page A13.

2.2 Relative Clauses with *When*

A Use *when* in relative clauses to modify a noun referring to a time. Common nouns include *day*, *moment*, *period*, *season*, *time*, and *year*.	*The <u>day</u> when you graduate is the <u>day</u> when you will need to find a job.* *Spring is the <u>time</u> when most students graduate.* *The late 1990s and early 2000s are the years when many young people in the workforce were born.*
B Do not use a preposition before *when*. Use *which* instead. The use of preposition + *which* is very formal.	*Summer is the time <u>during which</u> many jobs become available.* NOT *Summer is the time ~~during when~~ many jobs become available.* *The day <u>on which</u> you start your new job will be very busy.* NOT *The day ~~on when~~ you start your new job will be very busy.*

2.2 Relative Clauses with *When* (continued)

C You can omit the relative adverb *when* in identifying relative clauses.	*Ricardo remembered the moment he met his boss.* = *Ricardo remembered the moment when he met his boss.*

 DATA FROM THE REAL WORLD

Research shows that in writing, nonidentifying relative clauses with *where* and *when* are much less common than nonidentifying relative clauses with *which*. Clauses with *when* are the least common and are used in rather formal writing.

Grammar Application

Exercise 2.1 Object Relative Clauses with *Where* and *When*

Complete the sentences about Generation Z. Circle the correct words. Note Ø means no relative adverb.

1 Gen Zers believe America is a place **(where)/ when** anyone can be successful.

2 They were born at a time in **which / where** technology was a part of everyday life.

3 They had childhoods **when / in** which everyone had a smartphone.

4 They are entering the workplace during a period **when / which** Wi-Fi.

5 They expect a work environment **Ø / where** people can work independently.

6 They grew up during a period **when / where** the Great Recession was an issue.

7 The day **Ø / where** they graduate from school is a time of both joy and anxiety.

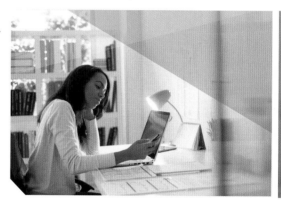

Exercise 2.2 More Object Relative Clauses with *Where* and *When*

A Listen to an interview with a Millennial who is helping to change the world in a positive way. Circle the answers to the questions.

1 Where did Sean go?

   a To Haiti   **b** To Florida

2 When did Sean go?

   a After a rainstorm   **b** After an earthquake

3 Why did Sean go?

    a To help people   **b** To take a break from school

4 What did he do there?

    a Work in a large city to give basic medical care   **b** Work in small towns to give basic medical care

B Listen again. Complete the interview with the words you hear.

Interviewer Some people think that members of the Millennial generation only think about themselves, but there are a lot of young people who are making a difference. They are helping others and trying to make the world a better place. One of these young people is Sean Green. Sean is a medical student in Florida. He went to Haiti at a time ___*in which*___ they needed him the most.
(1)
Sean, tell us your story.

Sean Sure, I'd be happy to. I went to Haiti at a time _____ many
(2)
people were suffering – right after the 2010 earthquake.

Interviewer Why did you go?

Sean Haiti is a place _____ there aren't enough doctors. I'm in
(3)
medical school now. So it seemed like a good opportunity for me to get experience and to help people as well.

Interviewer What did you do there?

Sean I worked in small towns _____ the earthquake destroyed
(4)
the homes of many people. I lived in a town _____ a lot of
(5)
people were hurt, and helped give basic medical care. It was the season
_____ there is a lot of rain. There was mud everywhere. It was a
(6)
challenge to keep things clean.

Interviewer Tell us a little about the people you worked with.

Sean The people in the town _____ I worked gave us a lot of help.
(7)
They were very friendly and welcoming. It was an amazing experience.

Interviewer Thank you for your time, Sean.

C Listen again and check your answers.

Exercise 2.3 Relative Clauses with *When*

Look at the information in the chart. It shows three important generations in the United States and the major events or influences in their lifetimes. Then write sentences about the years in parentheses. Use relative clauses with *when, in which,* and *during which*. Sometimes more than one answer is possible.

	Name of Generation	Years Born	Important Lifetime Events or Influences
	Baby Boomers	1946–1964	President Kennedy dies, 1963 Vietnam War ends, 1975
	Generation X (Gen Xers)	1965–1981	The Berlin Wall falls, 1989
	Millennials	1980–2000	The Great Recession occurs, 2007–2009

1 (1946–1964)

The years 1946–1964 are the years when the Baby Boomers were born.

2 (1963)

_____

3 (1975)

_____

4 (1965–1981)

_____

5 (1989)

_____

6 (1980–2000)

_____

7 (2007)

_____

3 Reduced Relative Clauses

Grammar Presentation

Relative clauses with *be* can often be reduced to phrases. There are three types of reduced relative clauses: participle phrases, prepositional phrases, and appositives.	RELATIVE CLAUSE *The expert who is giving tomorrow's talk on Generation Z is very well known.* REDUCED RELATIVE CLAUSE *The expert giving tomorrow's talk on Generation Z is very well known.*

3.1 Forming Reduced Relative Clauses

A Reduce a subject relative clause by omitting the relative pronoun (*that, which, who*) and *be*.	*My brother, a Gen Zer, likes a fast-paced environment.* *= My brother, who is a Gen Zer, likes a fast-paced environment.*
B Do not shorten a subject relative clause with *be* + a single adjective. Instead, move the adjective before the modified noun.	*I know a lot of people who are self-confident.* *I know a lot of self-confident people.* NOT *I know a lot of people self-confident.*
C Do not reduce object relative clauses.	*Our new assistant, who I am meeting tomorrow, is a Gen Zer.* NOT *Our new assistant, meeting tomorrow, is a Gen Zer.*

3.2 Reduced Relative Clauses with Participle Phrases

A Participle phrases are a reduced form of relative clauses with a verb that includes a form of *be*.	*Students concerned with the environment should get involved in environmental groups on campus.* *= Students who are concerned with the environment should get involved in environmental groups on campus.*
B This verb can be in the form of verb + *-ing* (present participle) or the past participle form. This includes progressive verbs and passive verbs.	VERB + -ING *He is the person designing the best software.* PAST PARTICIPLE *She did the things not expected of her.* *This is the intern known to be the hardest working.*

3.3 Reduced Relative Clauses with Prepositional Phrases

A You can omit the relative pronoun and the verb *be* when they are followed by a prepositional phrase in identifying relative clauses.	PREP. PHRASE *The computers in our classroom are fast.* = *The computers that are in our classroom are fast.*
B An adjective can also come before the prepositional phrase.	ADJ. + PREP. PHRASE *Young workers low in self-esteem are unusual.*

3.4 Reduced Relative Clauses with Appositives

A You can omit the relative pronoun and the verb *be* when they are followed by a noun phrase in nonidentifying relative clauses. This is called an appositive.	*Jan Smith, an expert on Generation Z, will be speaking at noon today.* = *Jan Smith, who is an expert on Generation Z, will be speaking at noon today.*
Often the position of the modified noun and the appositive is interchangeable.	*An expert on Generation Z, Jan Smith, will be speaking at noon today.*
B Appositives begin and end with commas.	*Résumés, brief documents that summarize an applicant's work background, are necessary for all job applications.*
In academic writing, appositives often occur in parentheses, instead of commas.	*Résumés (brief documents that summarize an applicant's work background) are necessary for all job applications.*

Grammar Application

Exercise 3.1 Reducing Relative Clauses

A Read the sentences about different generations. Check (✓) the sentences that can be reduced.

☑ 1 Young people who are entering the workforce are different from other generations.

☐ 2 In general, Millennials, who attentive parents raised, are confident workers.

☐ 3 Gen Zers who are in the workforce tend to be independent and hard-working.

☐ 4 Generation X, which is another large group in the workforce, does not tend to equate age with respect.

□ 5 Baby Boomers who work with Millennials often think they do not show enough respect.

□ 6 Baby Boomers, who are loyal employees, have started to retire from their jobs.

□ 7 Millennials, who were hurt by the recession, still tend to be optimistic.

□ 8 Baby Boomers who were graduating from college in the 1960s lived in prosperous times.

□ 9 Most Millennials who are not attending school say they intend to go back.

□ 10 Many Gen Zers who are in the office also have side jobs.

□ 11 Gen Zers that dress casually at work sometimes upset older workers.

B Rewrite the sentences in A with reduced relative clauses. If a sentence cannot be reduced, write ✗.

1 *Young people entering the workforce are different from other generations.*

2 ✗ _____

3 _____

4 _____

5 _____

6 _____

7 _____

8 _____

9 _____

10 _____

11 _____

C Pair Work Compare your answers with a partner. Discuss what kind of reduced relative clause each sentence is. If a sentence couldn't be reduced, say why not.

A *The reduced relative clause in number 1 is a participle phrase, so it can be reduced.*

B *That's right, but the relative clause in 2 can't be reduced because it is an object relative clause.*

Exercise 3.2 Relative Clauses with *Be* + Prepositional Phrases and *Be* + Adjectives +
Prepositional Phrases

Combine the sentences from a company website about the type of employees it seeks.
Use relative clauses. Then rewrite the sentences using reduced relative clauses.

1 People are at JP Corporation. They represent every generation.

 People *who are at JP Corporation* represent every generation.

 People at JP Corporation represent every generation.

2 People are good with technology. They have an advantage here.

 People _____ have an advantage here.

 _____

3 Workers are familiar with soical media. They will be able to use these skills here.

 Workers _____ will be able to use these skills here.

 _____

4 Employees are good at multitasking. They will enjoy our fast-paced environment.

 Employees _____ will enjoy our fast-paced

 environment.

 _____

5 Employees are high in self-esteem. They do well here.

 Employees _____ do well here.

 _____

6 People are interested in advancement. They will find it here.

 People _____ will find it here.

 _____

7 Employees are in our training programs. They appreciate learning new skills.

 Employees _____ appreciate learning new skills.

 _____

8 People are accustomed to a dynamic environment. They will be happy here.

 People _____ will be happy here.

 _____

Read the advice for managers who work with Generation Z. Rewrite the sentences that you can shorten. If you can't shorten the sentence, write **✗**.

1 Managers should encourage Gen Zers who are hard-working.

   Managers should encourage hard-working Gen Zers.

2 Workers who are Generation Z seek independence from their managers.

3 Even Gen Zers who are confident appreciate feedback.

4 Gen Zers appreciate work schedules that are flexible.

5 Employees who are Generation Z want their managers to listen to them.

6 It's important to provide challenges for Gen Zers who are successful.

7 Managers must not underestimate GenZers who are self-educated.

8 Managers who are Millenials might expect Gen Zers to work 9 to 5.

9 Employees who are Gen Zers sometimes need less direction than older workers.

10 Gen Zers who are unemployed don't always have a lot of experience in job interviews.

Pair Work With a partner, discuss the work styles of people at your school, such as students, teachers, and administrators. Write five sentences with relative clauses. Then write shortened versions without relative clauses. Use the words in the box or your own ideas.

appreciate feedback	are family oriented	enjoy team work
appreciate work-life balance	are self-assured	have a "can-do" attitude

Students who are at this school tend to have a "can-do" attitude.
Students at this school tend to have a "can-do" attitude.

4 Avoid Common Mistakes ⚠

1 **Do not use a preposition before *when*.**

There was a period ~~in~~ when people did not change jobs often.

2 **In clauses with *where*, remember to use a subject.**

          he
The place where ^works is very busy.

3 **When shortening relative clauses to appositives, be sure to omit both the pronoun and *be*.**

My mother, ~~is~~ an office manager, often works late.

Editing Task

Find and correct eight more mistakes in the paragraphs about the separation between younger and older technology users.

Digital Natives vs. Digital Immigrants

There was a time ~~in~~ when my mother always complained about my use of technology. She did not understand why I had to constantly text friends and go online. My mother, is a digital immigrant, grew up without a lot of tech gadgets. As a result, she is uncomfortable using technology at the office where works. On the other hand, my

5 brothers and I, are all digital natives, are happy to use technology all the time.

Digital natives, are lifelong technology users, use mobile devices instinctively. These people do not remember a time in when they were not connected to the Internet. In fact, they find it annoying when they go to places where cannot connect to the Internet. Digital immigrants, in contrast, remember a time in when there was no Internet.

10 As a result, some of them see the Internet as useful but not essential. In addition, digital immigrants sometimes find it difficult to figure out how to use technology. For example, when my mother first began uploading information, she had to call someone for help. Lately, however, my mother has found a social media site where often goes in her free time to stay in touch with friends and family members.

5 Academic Writing

Expository Writing

> Brainstorm > Organize > Write > Edit

In Unit 22, you learned how to make your writing clearer and more coherent, and you wrote your introduction and body paragraphs for the prompt below. In this unit (23), you will write the conclusion, and then you will revise and edit your essay.

> *Explain the advantages and disadvantages of three types of renewable energy and decide which would work best in your country.*

My Writing

Concluding Paragraphs

Concluding paragraphs restate the writer's main ideas and leave the reader with a final thought. The first sentence, or topic sentence, should summarize your thesis. Do not repeat your thesis exactly; instead, restate it. The end of your conclusion should leave the reader with a final thought, recommendation, or call to action.

Exercise 5.1 Applying the Skill

Review your paragraphs from My Writing in Unit 22. Complete the tasks.

1 Write your thesis statement. _____

_____

2 Restate your thesis. _____

_____

3 What three renewable energy sources did you discuss? _____

4 What source did you think would work best for your country? _____

5 What do you want your readers to do or think about in your conclusion? ___

_____

Exercise 5.2 Writing Your Conclusion

Use the information in Exercise 5.1 to write your conclusion. Add it to the rest of your essay.

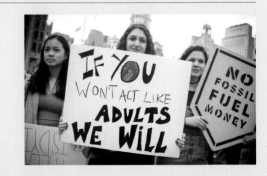

Exercise 5.3 Revising Your Ideas

1 Work with a partner. Use the questions to give feedback on your partner's essay.
- Which of your partner's ideas seem strongest to you?
- Which of your partner's ideas needs to be explained more clearly?
- What could your partner add or remove to make the ideas easier to understand?

2 Use the feedback from your partner to revise the ideas and content of your essay.

Exercise 5.4 Editing Your Writing

Use the checklist to review and edit your essay.

Did you answer the prompt completely?	
Did you organize your essay correctly?	
Did you use relative clauses to add information and avoid repetition?	
Did you use academic phrases to introduce advantages and disadvantages?	
Did you use several methods to build coherence in your essay?	
Did you put your ideas in a logical order that leaves your reader with a strong understanding of your thesis?	
Did you summarize your thesis and main points, and offer your readers a final thought, recommendation, or call to action in your concluding paragraph?	

Exercise 5.5 Editing Your Grammar

Use the checklist below to review and edit the grammar in your essay.

Did you use relative clauses to avoid repetition and make your writing clearer and more concise?	
Did you use identifying subject relative clauses to help identify or clarify any nouns you discussed?	
Did you use relative clauses to provide background information or to add information?	
Did you form reduced relative clauses correctly?	
Did you avoid the common mistakes in the charts on pages 315, 329, and 343?	

Exercise 5.6 Writing Your Final Draft

Apply the feedback and edits from Exercises 5.3 to 5.5 to write the final draft of your essay.

Real Conditionals: Present and Future

Media in the United States

1 Grammar in the Real World

A Do all the news sources you read (websites, magazines, newspapers, etc.) have similar viewpoints about current topics and issues? Read the article about the news media in the United States. What is the writer's view of the media?

B Comprehension Check **Answer the questions.**

1 How do some political analysts describe the behavior of Americans toward media?

2 What is an example of how media sources reinforce someone's political views?

3 Why might people become even more isolated in their beliefs in the future?

C Notice **Read the sentences from the article. Which sentence describes a present situation? Which sentence describes a future situation?**

1 On the other hand, if people mostly disagree with the president's policies, they often choose to watch news shows that criticize the president.

2 If predictions of increased Internet use are correct, people will likely become even more isolated in their beliefs.

The Influence of **MEDIA** on Public Opinion

The media[1] provide news from a wide of sources with a variety of viewpoints. Some sources provide a more balanced look at the issues than others. These more balanced news sources offer
5 a deeper understanding of the issues without the influence of the views of political parties. This unbiased[2] view of the news may appear to align[3] with the values of Americans, but is it, in fact, what Americans really want? Some political analysts
10 claim that many Americans tend to read, watch, and listen to the news media that reflect their own views. **If people surround themselves with media that reflect only their beliefs,** they may not be exposed to opposing ideas. The media, in
15 this case, are not informing people, but reinforcing that their view of the world is right.

One example of this occurs during an economic crisis. **If people watch certain TV news stations,** they will hear mostly positive things
20 about the president's solutions. **If they support the president's policies,** they may also choose to read online news pages with a similar view. These websites likely explain how the crisis was caused by politicians from the opposing party.
25 **If those people read only these websites,** they might be convinced that the crisis was the fault of the opposing party. They might conclude that the president was doing a wonderful job. On the other hand, **if people mostly disagree with the
30 president's policies,** they often choose to watch news shows that criticize the president. They might also visit websites and read blogs that do not support the president's policies. **When they rely only on these news sources,** they come to a
35 different conclusion. They are convinced that the president is failing.

If predictions of increased Internet use are correct, people will likely become even more isolated in their beliefs. This is because links in
40 blogs and web pages will connect people with information that supports only their views. How might this affect politics in the future? **If we don't address this issue today,** could the isolation of beliefs become problematic in our political future?

---

[1]**media:** newspapers, magazines, television, and radio, considered as a group
[2]**unbiased:** not influenced by personal opinion
[3]**align:** agree with and support something or someone

2 Present Real Conditionals

Grammar Presentation

Present real conditionals describe situations that are possible now and their results. They describe general truths, facts, and habits.	*If people share beliefs*, they often get along better. *I usually believe something when I read it in a good newspaper.*

2.1 Forming Present Real Conditionals

A Use an *if* clause to describe a possible situation. The *if* clause is the condition. The main clause describes the result. It expresses what happens when the condition exists.	IF CLAUSE (CONDITION) MAIN CLAUSE (RESULT) *If I like a reporter, I read her articles.*
Use the simple present in the *if* clause and in the main clause.	*If I have time in the morning, I read the newspaper.*
B You can use *when* or *whenever* in the *if* clause. The meaning does not change.	*When you trust people, you tend to believe them.* = *If you trust people, you tend to believe them.*
C You can put the *if* clause or the main clause first, but the punctuation is different. If the *if* clause is first, a comma follows it. If the main clause is first, do not use a comma. Usually the *if* clause comes first.	IF CLAUSE MAIN CLAUSE *If you control the media, you control public opinion.* MAIN CLAUSE IF CLAUSE *You control public opinion if you control the media.*
D You can use conditionals in questions. Use question word order only in the main clause.	IF CLAUSE MAIN CLAUSE *If you see something on the news, do you always believe it?*

▶▶ Conditionals: See page A14.

2.2 Using Present Real Conditionals

A Use present real conditionals to describe: Facts and general truths Habits and routines	*If a website is popular, people talk about it.* *I always read the news online if I wake up early.*
B You can emphasize the result by putting the *if* clause first and using *then* to introduce the main clause. Using *then* is more common in speaking.	*If you only read one news website, then you never get the full story.*

Grammar Application

Complete the article about news habits. Use present real conditionals with the verbs in parentheses. Add commas when necessary.

CITY VOICES: The News and You

City Voices talked to several area residents. Here's what they had to say.

"When I _____ *am* _____ (be) in the car, I _____ (listen) to the radio.
(1)   (2)

My husband _____ (watch) the comedy news shows if he _____
(3)   (4)

(stay) up late." – Alexa, 28, office manager

"If a friend _____ (text) me about something interesting I generally
(5)

_____ (check) out other websites to find out more information." – Su Ho, 32, engineer
(6)

Complete the interview with a foreign correspondent. Use the conditions and results in the chart.

Condition	Result
1 I hear about a story	I get on the phone
2 I hear about a good story	I try to go beyond the basic facts
3 I feel like I'm getting emotionally involved in a story	I drop it
4 A story is important	Many people talk about it
5 My editor calls and tells me to investigate a story	I move quickly

CAREERS MAGAZINE

Careers   Today, we are talking to our foreign correspondent, Mercedes Rivera. Ms. Rivera, how do you get a story?

Mercedes   If *I hear about a story, I get on the phone* . I make
(1)

appointments to interview people connected with the story.

Careers	What makes your reporting special?
Mercedes	If _____ . I look
	(2)
	at all the details to give both sides of the story.
Careers	How do you avoid bias?
Mercedes	If _____ . I give
	(3)
	it to another reporter.
Careers	What is difficult about your job?
Mercedes	There's a certain amount of pressure. _____
	(4)
	when _____ . I have to work fast in the digital
	(4)
	age. _____ if _____ .
	(5) (5)
Careers	Well, thank you for talking to us today, Ms. Rivera.

Exercise 2.3 Emphasizing the Result in Present Real Conditionals

A Read the tips on how to detect bias in the media. Then rewrite the tips as present real conditionals with the words in parentheses and *probably (not) be*. Emphasize the result by using *then*.

How to Detect BIAS in the MEDIA

To detect bias in the media, be aware of the following conditions. These conditions often indicate bias.

1 A newspaper, website, or TV station ignores important stories.
2 A newspaper prints sensational headlines.
3 A newspaper prints an important story in the back of the newspaper.
4 A magazine prints an unflattering[1] photo of a politician.
5 A reporter uses words with negative connotations[2] instead of neutral terms.

[1]**unflattering:** making someone look less attractive or seem worse than they usually do
[2]**connotation:** a feeling or idea that is suggested by a word in addition to its basic meaning

1 (impartial) *If a newspaper, website, or TV station ignores important*
stories, then it probably isn't impartial.

2 (accurate) _____

_____

3 (balanced) _____

_____

4 (biased) _____

_____

5 (fair) _____

_____

B Pair Work Discuss other ways that the media show that they are biased or fair. Write two sentences using *if* clauses and the expressions with *probably (not) be* in A.

Exercise 2.4 Present Real Conditionals

A Over to You Answer the questions with information that is true for you. Write present real conditionals on a separate piece of paper. Use the phrases in the box or your own ideas.

get the news online	pay attention to the news
know a story is accurate	read a newspaper
listen to news on the radio	watch TV news

■ Do you pay attention to the news?

■ How do you get the news?

■ How do you know a news story is accurate?

If there's a big story in the news, I watch one of the TV news channels, but I don't pay attention to the news much in general.

B Pair Work Interview your partner. Ask and answer the questions in A. Do not look at your sentences when you answer. Look at your partner.

3 Future Real Conditionals

Grammar Presentation

Future real conditionals describe possible situations in the future and the likely results.	*If you don't like a politician, you won't like his or her policies.*

3.1 Forming Future Real Conditionals

A Use the simple present in the *if* clause and a future verb form in the main clause.	*If you arrive early tomorrow at the debate, you will get a good seat.*

3.1 Forming Future Real Conditionals *(continued)*

B Use a comma after the *if* clause only when it begins the sentence.	*We will have a more balanced view if we read a variety of news websites.* *If Sandra doesn't agree with a politician's ideas, she will not vote for him.*

3.2 Using Future Real Conditionals

A Use future real conditionals to describe: Plans Predictions	*If the TV media don't cover the debate tonight, I'll read about it online.* *If you read this article, you won't be disappointed.*
B Use *even if* when you believe the result will not change. *Even if* means "whether or not."	*Some people will believe the news even if it isn't true.* (The news may or may not be true. Some people will believe it either way.)
Use *unless* to state a negative condition more strongly. It often has the same meaning as *if . . . not*.	*Unless a reporter interviews many people, she won't find out the truth.* = *If a reporter does not interview many people, she won't find out the truth.*
C When an *if* clause has many results, use the *if* clause only once.	*If people believe everything they hear, they won't know the truth. They will be easily fooled.* NOT *If people believe everything they hear, they won't know the truth. If people believe everything they hear, they will be easily fooled.*

Grammar Application

Exercise 3.1 Future Real Conditionals for Predictions

Complete the sentences about being well informed about political viewpoints. Circle the correct verb forms. Add commas when necessary.

1 If a person (studies)/ will study history, she understands /(will understand) political issues better.

2 You **are / will be** a better critical thinker if you **listen / will listen** to opposing viewpoints.

3 You **become / will become** a more informed voter if you **understand / will understand** the issues.

4 You **make / will make** better choices in future elections if you **learn / will learn** about the candidates' voting records.

5 If a person **learns / will learn** about economics he **makes / will make** wiser financial decisions.

6 If people <u>get/will get</u> the news from several sources they <u>have/will have</u> a more complete picture of an issue.

Exercise 3.2 Future Real Conditionals for Predictions and Plans

A A newspaper is having financial difficulties. Write future real conditionals with the information in the chart.

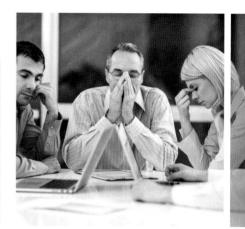

Proposals	Predictions and Plans
1 fire 10 reporters	be able to stay in business
2 stop home deliveries	lose money
3 charge for online access	increase revenue
4 not find new advertisers	not make more money
5 put more articles online	attract new readers

1 *If we fire 10 reporters, we'll be able to stay in business.*

2 _____

3 _____

4 _____

5 _____

B Read what members of the staff have to say about the proposals in A. Circle the correct meaning for each opinion.

1 Even if we fire 10 reporters, we won't be able to stay in business.

  a Firing reporters will help.   **b** Firing reporters won't help.

2 Unless we fire 20 reporters, we'll go out of business.

  a Firing reporters will help.   **b** Firing reporters won't help.

3 Unless we charge for online access, we won't increase revenue.

  a Charging will help.   **b** Charging won't help.

4 Even if we stop home deliveries, we'll lose money.

  a Stopping home deliveries will help.   **b** Stopping home deliveries won't help.

5 Even if we find new advertisers, we won't make more money.

  a Finding new advertisers will help.   **b** Finding new advertisers won't help.

6 Unless we put more articles online, we won't attract new readers.

  a Putting more articles online will help.   **b** Putting more articles online won't help.

Over to You **Complete the sentences about being informed. Write two or more results for the conditions. Don't repeat the *if* clauses for the second or third results. Write sentences that are true for you.**

1 If people stop reading newspapers, *newspapers will go out of business. Many reporters will be unemployed.*

2 If people get only one source of news, _____

_____

3 If you only listen to people you agree with, _____

_____

4 If you are not an informed voter, _____

_____

4 Real Conditionals with Modals, Modal-like Expressions, and Imperatives

Grammar Presentation

Modals, modal-like expressions, and imperatives can be used in the main clause of real conditionals.	*If I watch a lot of TV, I may become more aware of political issues.* *If you have finished reading the paper, put it in the recycling container.*

4.1 Forming Real Conditionals with Modals, Modal-like Expressions, and Imperatives

A In present and future real conditionals with modals and modal-like expressions, use a present form of the verb in the *if* clause. Use a present or future modal or modal-like expression in the main clause.	*If you haven't heard the news yet*, you should read the newspaper. *If you are planning to vote*, you have to register. She might learn more about politics *if she subscribes to that political magazine.*
B In present and future real conditionals, you can use the imperative in the main clause.	*If you are at home tonight at 7:00 p.m.*, watch the president's speech.

▸▸ Modals and Modal-like Expressions: See page A3.

Grammar Application

Complete the sentences about being an involved citizen. Use the words in parentheses.

1 If people don't vote, *they must not be interested in politics* .
(be interested in politics / not / must)

2 If you haven't registered to vote yet, _____ .
(do it today / should)

3 People _____ if they want to become involved in
(volunteer / ought to)
their community.

4 People _____ if they enjoy teaching.
(tutor children / can)

5 If you want to become informed, _____ .
(watch the news / have to)

6 If people participate in elections, _____ .
(influence the outcome / might)

7 If you aren't happy, _____ .
(change things / could)

8 People _____ if they have not already tried to
(complain / not / should)
find solutions to community problems.

Pair Work **Answer the questions about how you think people can be better citizens. Write real conditionals and share them with a partner. Use *you* in the *if* clause and an imperative in the main clause. Use the phrases in the box or your own ideas.**

be aware of bias in the media	study both sides of an issue
research alternative news sources	volunteer

■ What should people do if they want to become better informed?

■ What should people do if they want to become better citizens?

If you want to become better informed, research alternative news sources.

A Listen to an interview about how to be an informed voter. As you listen, complete the chart. Check (✓) *Do* if this is something an informed voter should do. Check (✓) *Don't* if this is something an informed voter should not do.

Action	Do	Don't
1 register early	✓	
2 visit campaign headquarters		
3 visit candidates' websites		
4 rely on campaign ads		
5 pay attention to what media sources say		
6 be influenced by other people's opinions		

B Listen to the interview again. As you listen, complete the sentences with the words you hear.

1 If you __*aren't registered*__ to vote, __*register*__ early so you don't miss the deadline.

2 If you _____ to be an informed voter, _____ the local campaign headquarters for the candidates of both parties.

3 If you _____ to make the right choice, you _____ also _____ the websites of all the candidates.

4 _____ campaign ads for information about the candidates or the issues if you _____ to be an informed voter.

5 _____ attention to what media sources say about a candidate, either, if you _____ the truth.

6 Finally, _____ other people's opinions influence your vote if you _____ to make good choices.

5 Avoid Common Mistakes ⚠

1 **In future real conditionals, use the simple present in the *if* clause.**

        has
If my son ~~will have~~ time, he will buy tickets for the show.

2 **Remember that *if* clauses are followed by a comma when they start a sentence.**

If I get the time off work and the weather looks good⌄ I will join you.

3 **Remember to use *if*, not *when*, to describe possible future conditions.**

                if
We will cancel the speech ~~when~~ it rains tomorrow.

4 **In questions with *if* clauses, remember to use question word order in the main clause.**

              should
If I don't have a signal, what I ~~should~~ do?

Editing Task

Find and correct the mistakes in the paragraphs about the advantages of a campus blog.

                                 should
      If incoming students want to learn what this college is like, where⌄they ~~should~~ look?
If they visit the college website they can learn about sports and campus events. However,
incoming freshmen might want a more personal perspective. They may not have the time to
attend lectures and other events, or they may want some anonymity. I have decided to start a
5 blog that provides an alternative source of information and help.

      When I want the blog to be successful at helping students, I will need to provide
practical suggestions. For example, one concern may be, "If I want to meet people with
similar interests, what I can do?" I will tell that person places where he or she can post
requests on the school website and how to write his or her requests. I will also include ways to
10 safely respond to queries.

      In addition, if a student will have a problem with a professor, I will write about it in my
blog and provide possible ways to solve it. If people want to add advice, how they can do so?
They can share advice by commenting. If professors want to comment, they can, too.

      I will not try to write like a journalist and give a lot of facts. If students will want facts,
15 they can go to the college website. In contrast, I will give them personal advice that will help
them with everyday problems. If students want real answers to their problems they should try
my blog.

6 Academic Writing

Argumentative Writing

Brainstorm > Organize > Write > Edit

In this writing cycle (Units 24-25), you are going to write an argumentative essay for the prompt below. In this unit (24), you will learn to build support for arguments and to develop unified paragraphs. You will then brainstorm and organize ideas, and write body paragraphs.

> *Research an aging but culturally or historically important building in your city or country. What do you think should be done with it and why?*

Exercise 6.1 Preparing to Write

Work with a partner. Discuss the questions.

1 What responsibility do we have to preserve historic buildings?
2 What are some ways that people express their disagreement with decisions to tear down important buildings?
3 How might the media influence people's opinions on this type of issue? Give an example.

Exercise 6.2 Focusing on Vocabulary

Read the sentences and choose the best definitions for the words in bold.

1 The beautiful old train station closed in 1990 and has been **vacant** since then.
   a   busy   b   ugly   c   empty

2 Historic buildings that are converted to apartments often have high rent and are not **affordable** for working or middle class families.
   a   not expensive   b   average   c   small but comfortable

3 The athletic **facility** at the university has a new ice-skating rink.
   a   a building for a special purpose   b   a field   c   a place where people can meet

4 Despite the extra tax money, the government **maintains** that it has no money for public housing.
   a   continues to claim   b   finally understands   c deeply regrets

5 If the ancient buildings are allowed to **deteriorate** any more, the government will not be able to restore them as a historical site for tourists.
   a   grow worse   b   stabilize   c   strengthen

6 The old school is now a museum and is **prospering** as part of a growing art community.
   a   building   b   doing well   c   being optimistic

Dear Members of the County Board:

Tusing County Hospital (TCH), which has been standing **vacant** for more than ten years, has become an eyesore in our neighborhood. In spite of the fact that the government has spent millions of dollars studying the best use for the site, 5 we are still waiting for action. Let's stop trying to figure out how to save this out-of-date pile of bricks. Our neighborhood is expanding and **prospering**. If the board shows some leadership by adopting a proposal that embraces the future, it will not be seen as clinging to the past but rather as moving forward.

It has been argued that it would be cheaper to reuse the old building than 10 to tear it down and build a new one. Almost ten years ago, experts estimated that if the TCH building were saved it would cost more than 150 million dollars. This figure may have been true then, but over the last decade, the building has **deteriorated** considerably, which would no doubt add to the cost of any renovation[1] carried out today. Our experts agree that if the county decides to update this one hundred-year-old building to meet modern safety standards, it will actually be more expensive than starting from scratch.

15 What this neighborhood really needs is an up-to-date, green structure that will provide much-needed housing and retail space. If it is accepted, our proposal will replace the decaying hospital building with a hotel, apartments (including 15% **affordable** housing), and space for stores, restaurants, and medical offices. Just as important, construction of these structures, and the businesses that will be located in them, will provide good jobs for people in the community. How much longer do we have to wait for our leaders 20 to make the right decision for the future of our neighborhood? Please tear down TCH!

Respectfully yours,
New Neighborhood Group

Dear Tusing County Board:

Tusing County Hospital (TCH), which has welcomed patients and their families for almost a century, is a community landmark. The building is beautiful, but more beautiful than the structure itself is the statement it made to the city and the world. When it opened its doors in 1916, TCH offered an attractive, 5 modern **facility**, not just to the city's elite, but also to the poor. It sent the message that the poor are just as deserving of quality healthcare as the wealthy. People in the neighborhood called the hospital our Statue of Liberty. Let's make sure this site continues to serve all of our citizens by renovating it now.

Some opponents to our proposal have argued that renovation is too expensive, but a recent similar project demonstrated that this may not be the case. In fact, if we renovate, the cost will be about $25 per 10 square foot, which is less than even the most basic new construction, while also preserving the beauty of the original building. And, although it is often claimed that old buildings have a more significant environmental footprint compared with new construction, architect and sustainability expert Carl Elefante **maintains** that the greenest building is the one that is already built. New construction almost always has a 15 more serious environmental impact because it requires the use of all new materials.

If our group's proposal for renovation of the hospital is accepted, the site will continue to serve the community by providing affordable housing, medical clinics, a school, and a community center—resources that we badly need. However, if instead we allow developers[2] to take over the project, the guiding principle will be profit, not neighborhood preservation. The people who will benefit most will be the investors in the project, 20 not the people of our community. Please save the Tusing County Hospital building and our community!

Respectfully,
Citizens Neighborhood Coalition

---

[1] **renovation** (n) the repair of a building to bring it into good condition
[2] **developer** (n) an entrepreneur or company that buys land and builds on it

Read the texts on page 359. Work with a partner. Discuss the questions.

1 Which letter makes the argument that the hospital should be torn down?
2 What reasons does the letter give for its argument?
3 In addition to cost, why does the opposing letter argue that the hospital should not be torn down?

Exercise 6.4 Noticing the Grammar and Structure

Work with a partner. Complete the tasks.

1 Highlight all conditional sentences in the first letter. Choose one conditional sentence. Explain how the writer uses the form to persuade his or her readers.
2 Underline an opposing argument in each letter. How does each writer refute the opposing argument?
3 What kind of support do the coalitions use to strengthen their arguments?

Building Support for an Argument

When writers make an argument, they need to decide which facts are relevant and will support it. It is also important to include relevant facts when presenting an opposing argument. However, those facts should weaken the opposing argument.

Argument: To be an informed citizen, people need to get their news from a variety of sources.

Relevant fact to support the argument: Based on recent research, only 20% our news organizations in the United States are considered neutral.

Opposing argument: Many people maintain that news organizations in the United States are unbiased, neutral reporters of the news.

Relevant fact that weakens the opposing argument: However, nearly 80% of news organizations endorse political candidates in elections. If you endorse a political candidate, you are essentially supporting a particular party, which is not neutral and unbiased.

Exercise 6.5 Applying the Skill

Read a thesis and some facts about the news media. Write *T* if the fact supports the thesis. Write *O* if the fact supports an opposing argument.

Thesis: News organizations should not publish paper newspapers.

1 People no longer get their news from newspapers. Sales fell 28% in three years. _____
2 Many people prefer the tactile experience of reading a paper newspaper. _____
3 Companies do not get the return on their advertisements in digital news articles as they do in paper newspapers. _____
4 Newspapers are not sustainable due to the natural resources involved in printing them. _____

Maintaining Paragraph Unity

Paragraph unity means that the entire paragraph focuses on the main idea. All the other sentences in the paragraph should provide relevant background information or support for the main idea.

Exercise 6.6 Applying the Skill

Read the paragraph. Cross out any irrelevant sentences to create paragraph unity.

Before you support a candidate, you need to research that person. What does that mean? First, it is important to look at different sources for different viewpoints of the candidate. Visit websites, read a variety of newspapers, and watch the his or her speeches and interviews. Search engines are useful tools. Next, it is extremely important not to believe everything you hear about the person, even if it comes from a friend. Fortunately, researching is not very difficult. Lastly, do not listen to his or her campaign ads, which are created to distract many voters.

My Writing

Exercise 6.7 Brainstorming and Organizing Ideas

Read the writing prompt on page 358. Choose a building to write about.

1 Use the questions to brainstorm ideas for your essay.

- What should be done with the building? Why?
- What relevant facts might support your argument?
- What is an opposing argument? What facts might weaken it?

2 Share and discuss your ideas with a partner. Use the feedback to edit your notes.

Exercise 6.8 Writing Body Paragraphs

1 Write a possible thesis statement for your argumentative essay.
2 Write the first draft of 2-3 body paragraphs. Include an opposing argument in the first body paragraph. Use the grammar in this unit correctly.

Unreal Conditionals: Present, Future, and Past

Natural Disasters

1 Grammar in the Real World

ACADEMIC WRITING

Argumentative writing

A Think of some natural disasters in recent history. Were there any positive effects or changes that resulted from the disasters? Read the article about Hurricane Katrina. What is one positive effect of Hurricane Katrina?

B Comprehension Check **Answer the questions.**

1 Why is Hurricane Katrina considered a catastrophe?

2 What did Paul Vallas do to improve New Orleans's schools?

3 What are charter schools?

C Notice **Read the sentences from the article. Underline the main clause in each sentence.**

1 If they found a strong school superintendent, they could hope for real change.

2 If you had been a public school student in New Orleans prior to 2005, you would have had little hope for the future of your education.

3 Vallas knew that if state exam scores improved, the charter schools would be considered a success.

4 If Katrina hadn't happened, the school might have been closed down.

Is the situation in each main clause real or imaginary?

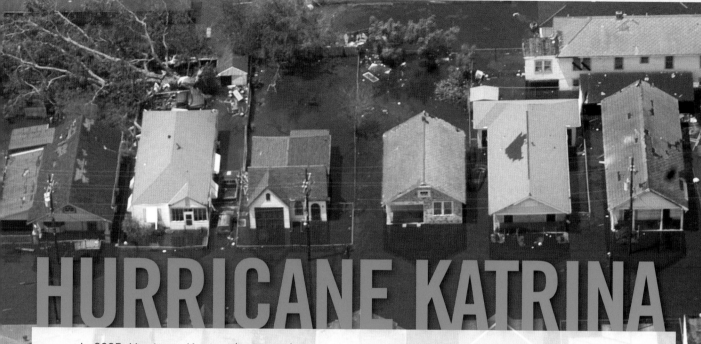

HURRICANE KATRINA

In 2005, Hurricane Katrina devastated New Orleans, Louisiana. The storm killed over 1,800 people and caused over $75 billion in damages. Certainly, Katrina was a catastrophe.[1] **People
5 wish it had never happened.** Nonetheless, some say Katrina saved the city's schools from failure. In fact, U.S. Education Secretary, Arne Duncan, said, "I think the best thing that happened to the education system in New Orleans was
10 Hurricane Katrina." Although some people thought Duncan's comment was inappropriate, is it possible that the storm did the city a favor and helped its school system?

**If you had been a public school student in
15 New Orleans prior to 2005,** you would have had little hope for the future of your education. With low test scores and high dropout rates, the New Orleans School District was already in trouble when the hurricane struck. The storm
20 destroyed almost every school in the city. State legislators realized the hurricane was tragic. They also knew it provided a fresh start to rebuild the city's schools. **If they found a strong school superintendent,** they could hope for real change.

---

[1]**catastrophe:** a sudden event that causes great suffering or destruction

25 In 2007, Paul Vallas was hired to rescue the poverty stricken and low-performing district. He knew that in order to succeed, he would have to make drastic changes. He hired top teachers and modernized classrooms. Vallas also started
30 several charter schools. Charter schools are independently run public schools. They control their own academics and policies but must show the state how their students have improved. Vallas knew that **if state exam scores improved,** the
35 charter schools would be considered a success.

Vallas received national praise for his experiment with charter schools. Student scores on state tests went up every year that he worked for the district. The Sophie B. Wright Charter
40 School is a good example. It was a failing traditional school before the hurricane. **If Katrina hadn't happened,** the school might have been closed down. Instead, it became a successful charter school.

45 As for Duncan's comment about Katrina, **some wish he had used a better choice of words.** A number of educational experts disagree. They say that in the end, New Orleans schools are only successful because of the work that Vallas
50 did to rebuild the school system.

2 Present and Future Unreal Conditionals

Grammar Presentation

Present and future unreal conditionals describe imagined situations (situations that are not true).	*If children got better grades on their exams, parents wouldn't be so worried.*

2.1 Forming Present and Future Unreal Conditionals

A Use the simple past or the past progressive in the *if* clause. Use the modals *could*, *might*, or *would* in the main clause.	*If I studied every day, I could pass all my tests.* (But I don't study every day, so I can't pass all my tests.) *Parents wouldn't worry so much about their children's future if their children's grades were improving.* (But the children's grades aren't improving, so their parents are worried.)
B In formal language, use *were* for the verb *be* for all subjects, including *I*. In informal language, native speakers often use *was* for the subject pronouns *I*, *he*, *she*, and *it*.	*If I were better at math, I would become an engineer.* (formal) *If I was better at math, I would become an engineer.* (informal)

▶▶ Conditionals: See page A14.

2.2 Using Present and Future Unreal Conditionals

A The *if* clause describes an imagined condition (something that is not true at the time of speaking or writing). The main clause describes the predicted result or possible outcome.	*If all public schools worked well, parents wouldn't choose private schools.* (But some public schools don't work well, so parents choose private schools.)
B Use *would* in the main clause to express the predicted result. Use *could* or *might* in the main clause to express something that is possible or doable.	*If teachers gave students study guides, more students would pass their exams.* (Passing is a predicted result.) *If students studied more for exams, more of them could/might pass.* (Passing exams is doable.)
C Use *could* or the past progressive in the *if* clause to describe an imagined possible situation.	*If the city could hire more teachers, we would have smaller classes.* (But they can't hire more teachers, so we have large classes.) *We wouldn't feel hopeful if schools weren't improving.* (But schools are improving, so we do feel hopeful.)

2.2 Using Present and Future Unreal Conditionals (*continued*)

D Use time words to show present or future time.	*We wouldn't have a place to learn if our school closed <u>next year</u>.* *If classes were smaller <u>today</u>, students might be more motivated.*
E Use unreal conditionals with *If I were you* to give advice. Use *I would* in the main clause.	<u>*If I were you*</u>, *I'd study harder.* (My advice is to study harder.) *<u>I wouldn't</u> drop out of school <u>if I were you</u>.* (My advice is to stay in school.)

⬈ Grammar Application

Exercise 2.1 Present and Future Unreal Conditionals

Complete the sentences about natural disasters. Use present and future unreal conditionals. If you are writing a main clause, use the modals in parentheses.

1 Their house is damaged, so they have to build a new one.

If their house weren't damaged, _**they wouldn't have to build a new one**_ (wouldn't).

2 We don't have flood insurance, so we have to pay for water damage.

**If we had flood insurance** , we wouldn't have to pay for water damage.

3 There aren't earthquakes here, so we don't need earthquake insurance.

If there were earthquakes here, _____ (might).

4 There's a tsunami[1] warning, so they have to leave the beach.

_____ , they wouldn't have to leave the beach.

5 We don't have a first-aid kit, so we aren't prepared for an earthquake.

If we had a first-aid kit, _____ (would).

6 There's a tornado warning, so José is going into the basement.

_____ , José wouldn't go into the basement.

7 The fire alarm is ringing, so we have to leave the building.

If the fire alarm weren't ringing, _____ (might not).

8 Everyone is worrying about the storm, so we are leaving.

_____ , we wouldn't be leaving.

[1]**tsunami:** an extremely high wave of water that is caused by an earthquake

Complete the statements made by earthquake experts. Use present and future unreal conditionals with *could (not)* in the *if* clause and *would (not)* in the main clause.

Dr. Sarah Green:

1 The government can't repair old bridges. Therefore, people don't feel safe.

If the government _*could repair*_ old bridges, people _*would feel*_ safe.

2 They can't build quake-proof bridges very quickly, so we aren't optimistic.

If the government _____

quake-proof bridges quickly, we

_____ optimistic.

Dr. Joe Wu:

3 Certain regions can build quake-proof buildings. Therefore, they don't suffer a lot of damage.

If certain regions _____ quake-proof buildings, they

_____ a lot of damage.

Dr. Rafael Rodriguez:

4 Some countries often can't avoid contaminated water after an earthquake. Therefore, people get sick.

If some countries _____ contaminated water after an

earthquake, people _____ sick.

5 Engineers aren't able to improve the water systems in all places, so people are not healthy.

If engineers _____ the water systems in all places, people

_____ healthy.

A Over to You Answer the questions with information that is true for you. Write your answers on a separate piece of paper. Use the ideas in the box or your own ideas. Write present and future unreal conditionals.

basement	escape	exit	higher ground
emergency services	evacuate	find shelter	take cover

What would you do if:

- you knew a hurricane were coming?
- an earthquake struck?
- you were driving and heard a tornado warning on the radio?
- you were within a half mile of a wildfire?
- you were at the beach and got a tsunami warning?
- you were in a heat wave?

If I knew a hurricane were coming, I would evacuate the area immediately.

B Group Work Brainstorm other answers to the questions in A. Share them with another group.

Exercise 2.4 *If I Were You . . .* for Advice

A Complete the conversations. Write sentences that give advice. Use *If I were you* and the ideas in the box. Sometimes more than one answer is possible.

~~build a new one~~	leave immediately	not go to work
get earthquake insurance	leave the building	stay indoors

1 **A** The house was damaged in the hurricane. What should we do?

   B *If I were you, I'd build a new one.*

2 **A** I live in an earthquake zone. What should I do?

   B _____

3 **A** There's a blizzard warning for tomorrow. What should I do?

   B _____

4 **A** Forecasters are predicting a terrible heat wave for tomorrow. What should we do?

   B _____

5 **A** There's a wildfire three blocks from our house. What should we do?

   B _____

6 **A** The fire alarm is ringing. What should we do?

   B _____

B Pair Work Take turns asking and answering the questions in A. Use your own ideas in your answers.

3 Past Unreal Conditionals

Grammar Presentation

Past unreal conditionals express situations that were not true in the past. They describe something that was possible but did not happen.	*If I had stayed home from school*, I would *have missed the exam*. (But I went to school, so I didn't miss the exam.)

3.1 Forming Past Unreal Conditionals

A Use the past perfect in the *if* clause. Use *could have*, *may have*, *might have*, or *would have* and the past participle of the verb in the main clause.	*If the city had hired more teachers, the schools might have improved.* (But the city didn't hire more teachers, and the schools didn't improve.)
B The *if* clause typically comes before the main clause, but it may also follow the main clause.	*The schools might have improved if the city had hired more teachers.*

3.2 Using Past Unreal Conditionals

A The *if* clause expresses the past unreal condition (a situation that was untrue in the past). The main clause describes an imagined result.	*If the hurricane had missed our city, the schools wouldn't have received money from the government.* (But it didn't miss our city, so the schools have received money.)
B Use *would have* in the main clause to express a predicted result.	*If you had applied, you would have gotten the job.* (Getting the job was a predicted result.)
C Use *could have* or *might have* in the main clause to express something possible or doable.	*I could have/might have passed the test if I had studied harder.* (Passing the test was doable.)
D You can use past unreal conditionals to express regrets or sadness.	*If I hadn't quit school, I would have become an engineer.* (But I quit school, and I regret it.)
E Use *If I had been you* to give advice indirectly. Use *I would (not)* in the main clause. *Had* is often contracted (*'d*).	*If I'd been you, I wouldn't have quit school.*

Grammar Application

Exercise 3.1 Past Unreal Conditionals

Complete the interview with a scientist who studied Mount Vesuvius, a volcano that erupted[1] in 79 CE near Pompeii, Italy. Use past unreal conditionals with the verbs in parentheses.

Reporter Today, I'm talking to Dr. Adam Gannon.

Dr. Gannon, we are all fascinated by Vesuvius, I think, because it practically erased an ancient city.

Dr. Gannon That's correct. If Vesuvius

hadn't erupted (not/erupt), Pompeii
(1)
would not have disappeared
(2)
(not/would/disappear).

Reporter So, Pompeii _____ (would/survived) if Vesuvius
(3)
_____ (not/explode)?
(4)

Dr. Gannon Yes, that's correct. On the other hand, if ash

_____ (not/cover) the city, it
(5)
_____ (not/would/be preserved).
(6)

Reporter The volcano caused other great changes, too, didn't it?

Dr. Gannon Yes. In fact, it completely changed the direction of a nearby river. The Sarno

_____ (would/stay) in the same place if
(7)
Vesuvius _____ (not/change) the course of the
(8)
river. It was a very powerful eruption.

Reporter How do we know so much about the eruption of Vesuvius?

Dr. Gannon We have the writer Pliny the Younger to thank for that. If he and his uncle

_____ (not/be) near Pompeii that day, we
(9)
_____ (not/would/know) much about the
(10)
eruption of Vesuvius. But we still don't know everything.

Reporter Fascinating. Thank you, Dr. Gannon.

[1]**erupt:** throw out smoke, fire, and melted rocks

A Group Work Look at the pictures and discuss these questions in groups: What does a volcanic eruption look like? What are some of the effects of a volcanic eruption?

Mount St. Helens,
Washington State

landslide

ash cloud

B Listen to a man talk about his experience surviving the 1980 Mount St. Helens volcano eruption. Circle *T* if the statement is true. Circle *F* if the statement is false.

1 The speaker and his family were hiking on the mountain the day the volcano erupted. T (F)

2 Falling trees hit the speaker and his friends. T F

3 The speaker thinks it's possible that many people on the mountain survived. T F

4 The speaker's wife wasn't affected by the eruption. T F

5 The sideways eruption of Mount St. Helens caused a lot of damage. T F

6 Ten years after the eruption, the speaker returned to his campsite. T F

7 Scientists didn't learn anything from the eruption. T F

C Listen again and check your answers.

D Complete the statements about the story. Use the words in parentheses to write past unreal conditionals with possible or predicted results.

1 If we hadn't gone camping that day, we *might have avoided the disaster*
   (**possible:** avoid / the disaster).

2 If we hadn't been in a hole, falling trees _____ (**possible:** hit) us.

3 If people hadn't been on the mountain, they _____ (**predicted:**
   survive).

4 If his wife had been with him, the eruption _____ (**possible:** affect) her.

5 If Mount St. Helens hadn't been a sideways explosion, it _____
   (**predicted:** not / do) so much damage.

6 If the speaker and his friends hadn't returned to the mountain, they
   _____ (**predicted:** not / see) the site of the destruction.

7 If the eruption hadn't happened, scientists _____
   (**predicted:** not / learn) how quickly plant and animal life can return.

4 Wishes About the Present, Future, and Past

Grammar Presentation

Sentences with *wish* express a desire for something to be different, or feelings of sadness or regret.	*I wish (that) every child could have a better education.* (Unfortunately, not every child can have a better education.)

4.1 Wish in the Present, Future, and Past

A *Wish* is followed by a *that* clause. Use a past form of the verb in the *that* clause, similar to conditional sentences. The word *that* is often omitted in informal speaking.	*There aren't enough teachers. We **wish that** we **could hire** more teachers.*
B Wishes about the present are followed by *that* clauses with verbs in the simple past or past progressive, or the modal *could*.	*I **wish (that)** we **had** more classrooms.* (We don't have a lot of classrooms.) *I **wish (that)** my son **were doing** well in school.* (My son is not doing well in school.) *Some people **wish (that)** they **could afford** to go to college.* (They can't afford to go to college.)
C Wishes about the future are followed by *that* clauses with *was / were going to* or the modals *could* or *would*.	*I **wish (that)** I **were going to have** time to meet you tonight.* (I'm not going to have time to meet you.) *She **wishes (that)** she **could go** to class tonight, but she has to work.* (She can't go to class tonight.) *We **wish (that)** the school **would build** a parking lot, but it's too costly.* (The school will not build a parking lot.)
D Wishes about the past are followed by *that* clauses with the verb in the past perfect.	*We **wish (that)** we **had had** more time to study for the test.* (We didn't have enough time to study.)

In academic writing, *wish* followed by a singular subject is more commonly followed by *were* than *was*.

Wish + singular subject + *were*					
Wish + singular subject + *was*					

The president wishes the solution to the problem were *simpler.* (more common in academic writing)

The president wishes the solution to the problem was *simpler.* (less common in academic writing)

 # Grammar Application

Exercise 4.1 Present and Future Wishes

Complete the sentences about a family's disaster. Write wishes in the present and future. Sometimes more than one answer is possible.

1 There isn't a lot of light. Ben _wishes (that) there was/were more light_ .

2 We don't have enough bottled water. We _____ .

3 The roof is leaking. Mom _____ .

4 We are running out of batteries. Paul _____ .

5 The electricity doesn't work. Dad _____ .

6 The Internet isn't working. Sue _____ .

7 The furniture is going to be ruined. Grandma and Grandpa _____

_____ .

8 We can't go to a hotel. We _____ .

Exercise 4.2 Past Wishes

Read the sentences about some past disasters. Then write sentences about the speakers' wishes. Use past wish forms. Sometimes more than one answer is possible.

1 An architect: The 1906 earthquake destroyed a historic building. There wasn't enough money to rebuild it.

I wish the earthquake hadn't destroyed the building./I wish
there had been enough money to rebuild it.

2 A surfer: They closed my favorite beach after the storm. They didn't let people in to clean it up.

_____

3 A historian: A flood destroyed the ancient city. There were no records of what life was like there.

_____

4 A student: A hurricane destroyed my high school. We weren't able to attend graduation.

_____

5 Avoid Common Mistakes ⚠

1 **When forming the present unreal conditional, use the past (not present) form of the verb after _if_.**

understood
If I ~~understand~~ my teacher, I would enjoy my class more.

2 **Remember to include a subject when forming an _if_ clause.**

she
She would feel safer if ∧ could stay with us during the storm.

3 **When forming the past unreal conditional, use the past perfect form in the _if_ clause.**

had not ruined
If the flood ~~did not ruin~~ his car, he would have arrived home safely.

4 **When making past unreal wishes, use the past perfect (not the simple past).**

had not moved
I wish I ~~did not move~~ to such a dangerous place.

Editing Task

Find and correct eight more mistakes in the story about Hurricane Ike.

 had
If Hurricane Ike ~~did~~ not come, we would have had an easier time. If the storm missed us, we would not have lived without electricity for two weeks. We would have been able to go to work and school. Our trees would look a lot better if had not been destroyed by the strong winds. For these reasons, some people wish that Hurricane
5 Ike never happened. However, I do not. If the storm did not come to Houston, we would not have learned many valuable lessons.

 First, we learned about our neighbors. We all came together to help each other before and after the storm. If I live in a different place, maybe I would not have gotten to know my neighbors in this way. Second, we learned good emergency survival skills.
10 If we had not learned to boardup our houses, might have been damaged. If another storm comes today, my house would be safe.

 Sometimes I wish that my family did not move to this city. However, I do not feel this way because of the hurricanes. The hurricanes have made our community stronger.

6 Academic Writing

Argumentative Writing

Brainstorm > Organize > Write > Edit

In Unit 24, you analyzed two letters and learned how to build support and unify paragraphs before brainstorming ideas and writing body paragraphs for the prompt below. In this unit (25), you will learn ways to integrate multiple sources to support your argument. You will then write, revise, and edit your essay.

> *Research an aging but culturally or historically important building in your city or country. What do you think should be done with it and why?*

Integrating Information from Multiple Sources

When you present an argument, you need to use facts to support your argument. Including facts from more than one credible source strengthens your argument and helps persuade your reader. When integrating multiple sources, it is necessary to show a connection between the sources in order to build coherence and improve the flow of your writing. Some common words and phrases you can use to connect multiple sources are: *in addition (to), another, like, likewise, similar (to), similarly, in the same way,* and *both.*

Natural disasters are caused by nature; however, human activity increases their frequency and intensity. **According to** *Agriculture Today*, when humans tear down trees, which leads to deforestation, our planet heats up, leading to global warming. **Similar to** *Agriculture Today*, Dr. Jonas Tomas notes that deforestation can have disastrous environmental consequences because it increases the risk of flooding.

Exercise 6.1 Applying the Skill

Work with a partner. Read the paragraphs and the source information. Then complete each paragraph by integrating the information from the two sources.

1 It is vital to reduce the number of deaths due to natural disasters have greatly increased over the last two decades. One effective strategy for saving lives in the future is to move people away from areas that are prone to natural disasters. _____

_____

_____

(*Source One*) Dr. Ross, a professor in Geophysics, has found that the largest fault line in California is moving.

(*Source Two*) The Center for Earthquake Studies has determined that an earthquake in this area could result in the death of hundreds of thousands of people.

2   Humans are directly responsible for the increasing number of number of hurricanes and the rising physical and economic costs. _____

_____

_____

Our planet is producing more energy, and 93% of this excess energy has been taken in by the oceans.

(Source One) According to the Meteorological Center, climate change, which has been a result of human behavior, is causing the increase. The waters of the Atlantic are warmer, and global warming has affected the circulation pattern.

(Source Two) Dr. Jonas holds global warming responsible for the increase.

Using Impersonal Statements

In most academic writing, when you state a position, there is no need to use phrases that mark it as your personal opinion such as *in my opinion, I think,* or *we should*. The reader understands that you are making a case based on your view of the subject.

Instead of writing a personal statement, express the same idea with an **impersonal statement**.

Personal statement: In my opinion, we need to take responsibility for the increase in natural disasters.

Impersonal statement: Humans need to take responsibility for the increase in natural disasters.

Exercise 6.2 Applying the Skill

Rewrite the sentences as impersonal statements. Compare your sentences with a partner's.

1 It is only my opinion, but I believe that city leaders did not act responsibly when they voted to allow construction on park land.

2 As far as I am concerned, it is always better to reuse and recycle the resources that we have instead of using up additional resources.

3 As I see it, a new convention center would be an incredible benefit for this city and its citizens, as it would provide both jobs and revenue.

4 It seems to me that by designating this neighborhood a historic area, we are telling all low-income homebuyers to stay away.

My Writing

Writers use **unreal conditionals** to explain and illustrate their ideas using hypothetical situations. Showing readers what is likely to happen if a particular change is made can help persuade them to support the thesis of an argument. Look at the following examples.

It is still very difficult to predict many earthquakes and volcanic eruptions. **If more money had been spent on research before the Northridge earthquake, scientists might have been able to warn people of the approaching disaster**.

Last year's fire moved very slowly. **If it had moved faster, firefighters would not have stopped it so quickly**.

Exercise 6.3 Applying the Skill

Review the body paragraphs you wrote in My Writing in Unit 24. Add two unreal conditional sentences to support your ideas.

Exercise 6.4 Writing Your First Draft

Write an argumentative essay that answers the prompt on page 374.
- Write an introductory paragraph with a hook, background information, and your thesis statement.
- Revise your body paragraphs. Use impersonal statements to present your ideas. Integrate multiple sources and use unreal conditionals to support and strengthen your argument.
- Write a concluding paragraph with a final thought, recommendation, or call to action.

Exercise 6.5 Revising Your Ideas

1 Work with a partner. Use the questions to give feedback on your partner's essay.

- Which of your partner's ideas seem strongest to you?
- Which of your partner's ideas need to be explained more clearly?
- What could your partner add or remove to make the essay stronger and easier to understand?

2 Use the feedback from your partner to revise the ideas and content of your essay.

Exercise 6.6 Editing Your Writing

Use the checklist to review and edit your essay.

Did you answer the prompt completely?	
Does the introductory paragraph provide a good description of the building?	
Is your position definitely and clearly stated in your introduction?	
Does each paragraph include a topic sentence?	
Did you use relevant evidence to build support for your argument?	
Is each paragraph unified?	
Did you include and refute an opposing argument?	
Did you use multiple sources of support and integrate them coherently?	
Did you use impersonal statements to make your writing more academic?	

Exercise 6.7 Editing Your Grammar

Use the checklist to review and edit the grammar in your essay.

Did you use present or future real conditionals correctly?	
Did you use unreal conditional sentences to support important ideas?	
Did you use the correct verb forms in the main and *if* clauses of conditional sentences?	
Did you avoid the common mistakes in the charts on pages 357 and 373?	

Exercise 6.8 Writing Your Final Draft

Apply the feedback and edits from Exercises 6.5 to 6.7 to write the final draft of your essay.

26 Conjunctions

Globalization of Food

1 Grammar in the Real World

ACADEMIC WRITING

Comparison and contrast

A Have you ever had fast food in a foreign country? Do you think the food looks and tastes the same everywhere that it is sold? Read the article about the globalization of fast-food chains. What do fast-food businesses do to their products to make customers happy?

B Comprehension Check **Answer the questions.**

1 What has Dunkin' Donuts done to succeed globally?
2 How has McDonald's changed its menu to attract vegetarians in India?
3 How is the United States affected by the globalization of fast food?

C Notice **Find the sentences in the article and complete them. What is the function of the missing words? Circle *a* or *b*.**

1 That is not surprising since sweet foods are popular with

Americans, _____ you might not be able to

find that donut in other countries.
a to add information
b to show a contrast

2 In Indonesia, they sell donuts filled _____ with

red bean paste _____ with lychee and orange.
a to emphasize additional negative information
b to emphasize surprising information

3 Adapting their products to local preferences is a way

to keep customers happy _____ to keep

business booming.
a to add information
b to show a contrast

The Globalization of FAST FOOD

Do you want a glazed[1] donut for breakfast? Go to your favorite Dunkin' Donuts in Arizona, New York, **or** almost anywhere in the United States **and** you will find
5 it. That is not surprising since sweet foods are popular with Americans, **but** you might not be able to find that donut in other countries. Instead, in parts of Asia you might find green tea or mango mochi ring donuts. In Korea, they offer kimchi[2] croquettes, donuts filled with
10 pickled[3] vegetables. In Singapore, you would find donuts filled with wasabi[4] cheese **and** seaweed cheese. The wasabi creates a very hot-tasting donut that appeals to people in Singapore. In Thailand, Dunkin' Donuts makes delicious Kai-yong donuts, a combination of
15 glazed donut and shredded chicken that is topped with a spicy Thai chili paste. In Indonesia, they sell donuts filled **not only** with red bean paste **but also** with lychee[5] **and** orange. Thinking globally **but** acting locally has been one of the reasons for Dunkin' Donuts' success in over 32
20 countries **and** over 10,000 restaurants worldwide.

American fast-food chains, like Dunkin' Donuts, seem to be everywhere, **but** these days they are serving **both** food from their U.S. menus **and** food adapted to the tastes **and** customs of other cultures in other countries.
25 McDonald's is another example. In India, there are many people who do not eat meat, **so** McDonald's in India serves only vegetarian burgers **and** prepares non-vegetarian (chicken and fish) meals in a separate area. McDonald's is one of the largest fast-food restaurants
30 worldwide. More than one third of its 33,000 restaurants are located outside the United States. Adapting to local cultures is very important.

The globalization of the fast-food industry is happening with restaurants from all over the world.
35 Pollo Campero, a fast-food restaurant that began in Guatemala in 1971, started adding stores in **both** Europe **and** the Middle East after expanding in Central America. In 2002, it opened its first restaurant in the United States **and** has been growing ever since. In order
40 to appeal to health-conscious consumers in the United States, Pollo Campero decided to offer customers a choice: **either** a healthier, grilled chicken **or** a lightly fried chicken. Grilled **or** fried, the uniquely seasoned chicken has become popular with **both** immigrants from
45 Latin American countries **and** Americans from other cultural backgrounds.

These days, more and more chain restaurants are selling their food in different countries. Adapting their products to local preferences is a way to keep customers
50 happy **and** to keep business booming.[6] It appears to be a strategy for success.

---

[1]**glazed:** covered with a sweet, shiny coating made of sugar

[2]**kimchi:** a Korean dish of pickled vegetables

[3]**pickled:** preserved in a liquid containing salt or vinegar

[4]**wasabi:** a strong-tasting condiment

[5]**lychee:** a sweet, juicy fruit often found in Southeast Asia and other parts of Asia

[6]**boom:** grow rapidly, especially economically

2 Connecting Words and Phrases with Conjunctions

Grammar Presentation

<table>
<tr>
<td>
Conjunctions connect words and phrases.
Coordinating conjunctions include and, but, and or.
Correlative conjunctions include both . . . and, neither . . . nor, either . . . or, and not only . . . but also.
</td>
<td>
I love pizza, hamburgers, and hot dogs.
I eat not only fast food but also healthy food.
</td>
</tr>
</table>

2.1 Coordinating Conjunctions

<table>
<tr>
<td>A Use coordinating conjunctions to link two or more nouns, gerunds, verbs, or adverbs.

Use the same part of speech in linked words or phrases to create parallel structure. This makes speech and writing clearer.</td>
<td>Have you ever eaten pizza with <u>shrimp</u> or <u>olives</u>? (nouns)
I've been to fast-food restaurants in <u>Asia</u>, <u>Europe</u>, <u>Africa</u>, and <u>North America</u>. (proper nouns)
I don't like <u>cooking</u> or <u>baking</u>. (gerunds)
The meal is <u>unhealthy</u> but <u>delicious</u>. (adjectives)</td>
</tr>
<tr>
<td>B Use and to add information.</td>
<td>There are many vegetarians in India and the U.K.</td>
</tr>
<tr>
<td>Use but to show a contrast.</td>
<td>This food is cheap but very good. (But contrasts the price of the food and the quality.)</td>
</tr>
<tr>
<td>Use or to connect related ideas or items in a negative statement or to show alternatives.</td>
<td>I <u>don't like</u> hamburgers or pizza.
Do you want to eat at a restaurant or at home?</td>
</tr>
<tr>
<td>C When you connect three or more words or phrases, use a comma between each one.

Put the conjunction before the last word or phrase.</td>
<td>I select my food based on taste, nutritional value, and price.
Would you like to have juice, milk, or water with your meal?</td>
</tr>
</table>

2.2 Correlative Conjunctions

<table>
<tr>
<td>A Correlative conjunctions have two parts. They often emphasize equality between the words or phrases they connect.</td>
<td>Both fried foods and grilled foods are served here.
Fast food is neither delicious nor healthy.</td>
</tr>
</table>

2.2 Correlative Conjunctions *(continued)*

B Use *both . . . and* to add information. When connecting two subjects, use a plural verb.	*Both* the food *and* the atmosphere <u>are</u> wonderful.
Use *either . . . or* to emphasize alternatives. The verb agrees in number with the noun that is closest to it.	*Either* potatoes *or* rice <u>is</u> fine with me. (Use a singular verb with *rice*.) *Either* rice *or* potatoes <u>are</u> fine with me. (Use a plural verb with *potatoes*.)
Use *not only . . . but also* to emphasize surprising information. The verb agrees in number with the noun that is closest to it.	*Not only* two drinks *but also* dessert <u>comes</u> with this entree. (Use a singular verb with *dessert*.) *Not only* dessert *but also* two drinks <u>come</u> with this entree. (Use a plural verb with *drinks*.)
Use *neither . . . nor* to emphasize additional information in negative statements. The verb agrees in number with the noun that is closest to it.	*Neither* my parents *nor* my brother <u>wants</u> to try eel. (Use a singular verb with *brother*.) *Neither* my brother *nor* my parents <u>want</u> to try eel. (Use a plural verb with *parents*.)

Grammar Application

Exercise 2.1 Coordinating Conjunctions

Combine the sentences about global food. Use the coordinating conjunctions in parentheses. Sometimes more than one answer is possible.

1 There's a Taco Bell in Iceland. There's a Taco Bell in India. (and)

   There's a Taco Bell in Iceland and in India.

2 Starbucks operates in Asia. It operates in Europe. It operates in Latin America. (and)

3 The U.S. branch doesn't have vegetarian burgers. It doesn't have lamb burgers. (or)

4 Would you prefer to try something unusual? Would you prefer to try something familiar? (or)

5 Vegans don't eat eggs. Vegans don't eat cheese. Vegans don't eat yogurt. (or)

6 The food is cheap. The food is very healthy. (but)

7 The coffee is expensive. The coffee is very popular. (but)

A Read the monthly sales report from Branch #345. Then complete the report to headquarters. Circle the correct correlative conjunctions.

Branch #345 – Shanghai, China – June

PRODUCTS

Frozen Yogurt and Smoothies	Drinks	Snacks
frozen yogurt: **55%**	coffee: **50%**	chips: **59%**
smoothies: **45%**	tea: **43%**	cookies: **41%**
	mineral water: **5%**	
	milkshakes: **2%**	

FLAVORS OF FROZEN YOGURT AND SMOOTHIES

Western Flavors	chocolate: **3%**
	vanilla: **2%**
Asian Flavors	dragon fruit: **55%**
	lychee: **40%**

Report to Headquarters on Branch #345

This branch offers (both)/ neither Western (and)/ or Asian flavors. Asian flavors seem to be
                        (1)   (1)
more popular. For example, dragon fruit and lychee are the most popular flavors this month.

Most customers tend to choose **neither/either** dragon fruit **nor/or** lychee yogurt. Therefore,
                                        (2)   (2)
please note that **both/neither** chocolate **and/nor** vanilla is selling well at this branch.
                        (3)   (3)

Neither/Not only frozen yogurt **nor/but also** smoothies are popular at this branch.
            (4)   (4)
Either/Neither mineral water **or/nor** milkshakes sold well this month. The reason is that
            (5)   (5)
most customers prefer **neither/either** coffee **nor/or** tea. **Both/Neither** coffee **and/nor**
                                (6)   (6)   (7)   (7)
tea are selling well. It is interesting to note that customers are buying snacks. Surprisingly,

neither/not only chips **nor/but also** cookies are selling well.
        (8)   (8)

I recommend that we create more locally flavored products to offer at this location.

B Group Work In groups, choose a country that you know well. Discuss possible frozen yogurt flavors and types of drinks and snacks that you think would or would not sell well in this country. Then write five sentences about your choices with correlative conjunctions.

Both chocolate and vanilla would sell well in Mexico.

Exercise 2.3 More Correlative Conjunctions

Combine the sentences about the availability of items in a Latin American coffee chain's global locations. Use the correlative conjunctions in parentheses.

1 Milk is available in the United States. Juice is available in the United States. (both . . . and)

Both milk and juice are available in the United States.

2 Tea is inexpensive in Egypt. Tea is very popular in Egypt. (both . . . and)

3 You can use your own mug at coffee shops in the U.K. You can use a store cup at coffee shops in the U.K. (either . . . or)

4 Donuts are available in the United States. Muffins are available in the United States. (not only . . . but also)

5 Recycling is encouraged in China. Reusing cups is encouraged in China. (not only . . . but also)

6 Generally, forks are not available in Chinese restaurants. Generally, knives are not available in Chinese restaurants. (neither . . . nor)

7 Hot dogs are not typically eaten for lunch in the Dominican Republic. Pizza is not typically eaten for lunch in the Dominican Republic. (neither . . . nor)

3 Connecting Sentences with Coordinating Conjunctions

Grammar Presentation

The coordinating conjunctions *and*, *but*, *or*, *so*, and *yet* can connect independent clauses.	Kevin doesn't eat meat, *but* he eats fish. Jennifer is a vegetarian, *so* we shouldn't put meat in the lasagna.

3.1 Connecting Sentences with *And*, *But*, and *Or*

A	Use a comma before the coordinating conjunction when you connect two complete sentences. The comma implies a pause.	*Starbucks opened in 1971,* **and** *it has become an international success.* *The café sold muffins,* **but** *it did not sell sandwiches.* *Consumers liked the food,* **so** *sales were good.*
B	When you connect sentences with the same subject with *and* or *or*, you do not need to repeat the subject. The result is a compound verb. Do not use a comma with compound verbs. If the modals or the auxiliary verbs are the same, you do not have to repeat the modals or auxiliaries.	CLAUSE, + AND + CLAUSE *We ate at that restaurant last week,* **and** *we really liked it.* VERB + AND + VERB *We ate at that restaurant last week* **and** *really liked it.* *Karen can ride with us,* **or** *she can meet us at the restaurant.* *Karen can ride with us* **or** *meet us at the restaurant.* *My brother has visited India,* **and** *he has eaten fast food there.* *My brother has visited India* **and** *eaten fast food there.*
C	In some writing, such as in newspapers and magazines, sentences begin with conjunctions like *and* and *but* to emphasize information. Do not do this in academic writing.	*The changes to the menu attracted many new customers.* **And** *the company's profits rose significantly.*

3.1 Connecting Sentences with *And*, *But*, and *Or* (continued)

D Use *and* to connect an independent clause that adds information. You can also use *and* to show a sequence of events.	*He is an excellent cook, and I love his recipes.* *This restaurant changed its chef, and now it is very popular.*
Use *but* to introduce contrasting or surprising information.	*This is supposed to be a good Mexican restaurant, but my Mexican friends don't like it.*
Use *or* to introduce a choice or alternative. It is often used in questions or statements with modals of possibility.	*We could have seafood, or we could make pasta.* *Could you prepare the meal, or should I ask Sam to prepare it?*

3.2 Connecting Sentences with *So* and *Yet*

A Use *so* to connect a cause and its result.	CAUSE RESULT *Henry doesn't like pizza, so we ordered pasta.* *That spice is rare in my country, so I substitute a different one.*
Use *yet* to connect contrasting ideas or surprising information. *Yet* sometimes expresses a stronger contrast than *but*.	*Cathy doesn't eat clams, yet she eats oysters.* *The restaurant serves wonderful food, yet it is known more for its music.*
B Use a comma to combine sentences with *so* and *yet*. Do not use a compound verb.	*Mary is a vegetarian, so she eats tofu.* NOT *Mary is a vegetarian so eats tofu.*

Grammar Application

Exercise 3.1 Connecting Sentences with *And*, *But*, *Or*

Complete the sentences about a European supermarket chain that opened stores in the United States. Circle the correct conjunctions. Add commas when necessary.

1 FoodCo opened 100 stores in the United States in 2008, **and** / but the managers expected to have great success in certain areas.

2 First, they studied the new market **but / and** they even sent anthropologists to study U.S. eating and shopping habits.

3 They opened stores in wealthy neighborhoods **or / and** they also opened some in low-income neighborhoods.

4 The trend in the United States is toward "big box" stores[1] **and / but** FoodCo decided to open small, convenience-type stores.

[1]"big box" store: a very large store that sells almost everything, including food

5 Convenience stores in the United States usually do not sell fresh produce **but / or** FoodCo has changed the definition of *convenience store* with its new stores.

6 FoodCo has positioned itself as a healthy convenience store **and / or** it provides high-quality groceries and produce at reasonable prices.

7 Customers can use FoodCo's shops to pick up last-minute items **but / or** they can do their weekly shopping there.

8 Now shoppers in low-income neighborhoods have a choice. They can buy junk food at a convenience store **but / or** they can buy healthy products at a FoodCo shop.

Exercise 3.2 Connecting Sentences with *So* and *Yet*

Complete the article about Chinese-American dishes. Use *so* or *yet*. Add commas when necessary.

Many Chinese restaurants serve dishes that are not authentic. Chinese restaurant owners wanted to be successful in foreign countries __, *so*__ they adapted
(1)
dishes to local tastes. Here are some examples: Fortune cookies are popular desserts in many Chinese restaurants _____ they were never popular in China. In
(2)
fact, the cookies were actually invented in Japan and then introduced to the United States by an immigrant in the early 1900s (although some people dispute this and say that a Chinese immigrant invented them first). General Tso's Chicken is another example. No one is absolutely certain of its origin _____ it appears on many
(3)
U.S. Chinese restaurant menus. It's fried chicken with a sweet sauce. Fried chicken is a traditional American dish _____ a clever Chinese restaurant owner probably
(4)
invented it to appeal to American tastes for sweet sauces. Chop suey is another Chinese-American invention. There are many legends about its creation _____
(5)
no one really knows for sure how it came about. In one story, a Chinese-American dishwasher created the dish from leftover bits of meat and vegetables. The man received part of his pay in food _____ he took what he could find at the end
(6)
of the day. Customers asked about the delicious-smelling creation _____ the restaurant manager put it on the
(7)
menu. Some of these dishes may seem inauthentic _____ they have been extremely popular in the
(8)
United States since the 1900s.

Exercise 3.3 Combining Sentences

Combine the sentences about the localization of food. Use the conjunctions in parentheses. Omit the subject and use a compound verb when possible. Add commas when necessary.

1 You can travel to many countries. You can still find dishes from home. (and)

You can travel to many countries and still find dishes from home.

2 I have eaten tacos in China. I have ordered kimchi in France. (and)

_____

3 You might get an authentic dish abroad. You might find a local version of it. (or)

_____

4 I often find international dishes abroad. They are usually adapted to local tastes. (but)

_____

5 Beef isn't eaten in some countries. A fast-food chain might sell lamb burgers. (so)

_____

6 I travel constantly. I never miss food from home. (yet)

_____

_____

Exercise 3.4 Using *So* and *Yet*

Over to You On a separate piece of paper, complete the answers about local food tastes. Write sentences that are true for you. Discuss your ideas with a partner.

1 How do supermarkets in your neighborhood address local tastes?

Supermarkets in my neighborhood want to address local tastes, so

they have an imported-food section .

2 How might an international food company adapt a product to local tastes?

People in _____ like _____ , so _____ .
       (name a country)   (food or taste)

3 What inauthentic ethnic dishes are sometimes very popular?

_____ is inauthentic, yet _____ .
(name of dish)

4 Reducing Sentences with Similar Clauses

Grammar Presentation

When you connect sentences that have similar clauses, you can often reduce the words in the second clause.	*Shrimp is one of my favorite foods. Chicken is one of my favorite foods.* *Shrimp is one of my favorite foods, and chicken is, too.*

4.1 Reducing Sentences

A In sentences with *be* as the main verb, use the *be* verb in the reduced clause.	*Their Chinese food isn't very good, but their Thai food is.*
B For other verb forms with auxiliaries, you can reduce the verb form in the reduced clause.	*My brother didn't eat fast food in college, and I didn't, either.*
For the present progressive or past progressive, keep the form of *be* and omit verb + *-ing*.	*The price of beef was rising last month, but the price of chicken wasn't.*
For simple verb forms, use *do/does* (*not*) or *did* (*not*).	*I don't like this restaurant, and Lisa doesn't, either.* *We went out to eat, and so did Victor.*
For the present progressive or past perfect, use *have/has* or *had* and omit the past participle.	*The cost of eating out has risen, and the cost of cooking at home has, too.*
For modals or future forms, use the modal or future form by itself.	*Jason can join us for lunch, and Liz can, too.* *I won't eat fried food, and Greg won't, either.*
C Use *and . . . too* or *and so* to combine two affirmative sentences. Use: • *and* + subject + auxiliary + *too* • *and so* + auxiliary + subject Note that the order of the auxiliary and subject are reversed in *and so* reduced clauses. We usually use a comma before *too*.	AFFIRM. SENT. + AFFIRM. SENT. *I ate there yesterday. She ate there yesterday.* AND + SUBJ. + AUX. + TOO *I ate there yesterday, and she did, too.* AND SO + AUX. + SUBJ. *I ate there yesterday, and so did she.*

4.1 Reducing Sentences (continued)

D Use *and . . . not*, *either* or *and neither* to combine two negative sentences. Use:

- *and* + subject + auxiliary + *not*, *either*

- *and neither* + auxiliary + subject.

NEG. SENT. + NEG. SENT.

I don't have any coffee. Kim doesn't have any coffee.

AND + SUBJ. + AUX. + NOT, EITHER

I don't have any coffee, and Kim doesn't, either.

AND NEITHER + AUX. + SUBJ.

I don't have any coffee, and neither does Kim.

E Use *but* to combine an affirmative and a negative sentence.

AFFIRM. SENT. + NEG. SENT.

The beef is dry. The chicken isn't dry.

AFFIRM. CLAUSE + BUT + NEG. CLAUSE

The beef is dry, but the chicken isn't.

NEG. CLAUSE + BUT + AFFIRM. CLAUSE

The chicken isn't dry, but the beef is.

F You can also use *too, so, either,* and *neither* in separate sentences in speaking and less formal writing.

Use *too* and *so* for two affirmative sentences. Use *either* and *neither* for two negative sentences.

Japanese food is delicious. Korean food is, too.

Japanese food is delicious. So is Korean food.

The coffee isn't warm. The tea isn't, either.

The coffee isn't warm. Neither is the tea.

Exercise 4.1 Reducing Sentences with Similar Clauses

Combine the sentences about food localization in India. Use coordinating conjunctions. If there are two lines, write the sentence in two different ways.

1 Americans like fast food. Indians like fast food.

   Americans like fast food, and Indians do, too.
   Americans like fast food, and so do Indians.

2 Some U.S. food companies are successful in India. Some U.S. food companies aren't successful in India.

3 Beef isn't popular in India. Pork isn't popular in India.

4 McDonald's adapts its menu to local tastes. Pizza Hut adapts its menu to local tastes.

5 Pizza Hut doesn't serve meat in some regions. McDonald's doesn't serve meat in some regions.

A Group Work Match the words with pictures of food. Tell the group which foods you have eaten raw.

_b_ **1** eel

_____ **2** jellyfish

_____ **3** sea urchin

_____ **4** seaweed

_____ **5** tuna

a

b

c

d

e

B Listen to the interview with the chef of a restaurant. Circle *T* if the statement is true. Circle *F* if the statement is false.

1 The chef is talking about Asian dishes that he serves at his restaurant.　Ⓣ　F

2 All the dishes he offers are popular with his customers.　T　F

3 The chef has adapted some dishes to local tastes.　T　F

4 The chef does not plan to make any changes to his menu.　T　F

C Listen again. Rewrite the statements to match what the chef says. Use reduced forms.

1 Raw fish is getting more popular. Seaweed salad is getting more popular.

Raw fish is getting more popular _**, and so is seaweed salad**_ .

2 Tuna has been selling well. Eel hasn't been selling well.

Tuna has been selling well, _____ .

3 Jellyfish didn't sell well last month. Sea urchin didn't sell well last month.

Jellyfish didn't sell well last month, _____ .

4 Spicy noodles have sold well. Cold noodles have sold well.

Spicy noodles have sold well, _____ .

5 This restaurant can't get customers interested in Thai dishes. Our other restaurants can't get customers interested.

This restaurant can't get customers interested in Thai dishes,

_____ .

6 We'll probably stop offering Thai dishes. The other branches will probably stop offering Thai dishes.

We'll probably stop offering Thai dishes, _____ .

7 We won't serve that. Most other Asian restaurants won't serve that.

We won't serve that, _____ .

8 The ice cream has been selling well. The cake has been selling well, too. The ice cream has been selling well, _____ .

5 Avoid Common Mistakes ⚠

1 **Use _or_ to connect ideas in a negative sentence.**

          _or_
There were no nuts in the vegetarian ~~and~~ the meat dishes.

2 **Use _both_, not _either_, when joining ideas with _and_.**

     both
They use ~~either~~ butter and oil for cooking.

3 **Use _either_, not _too_, after a negative verb.**

         either
They do not eat pork, and we don't, ~~too~~.

4 **Do not use a comma when a conjunction joins two phrases.**

Most local people love durian fruit~~,~~ but dislike the smell.

Editing Task

Find and correct eight more mistakes in the paragraphs about food.

Intercultural Dinners

          both
  My roommate and I come from different cultures, so ~~either~~ our eating habits and food preferences differ. Fortunately, we have some food preferences in common. I do not eat junk food, and he does not, too. There are no cookies and other desserts in our house. Instead, we have either fresh fruits and nuts for snacks.

5   However, we have some differences. I eat either rice and pasta every day. My roommate, however, thinks meals with rice, and dishes with pasta will make him gain weight, so he does not want to eat them often. Likewise, I do not like to eat a lot of meat and dairy products because I believe they are not healthy. Fortunately, I do not complain about his tastes, and he does not complain about mine, too. When we

10 cook, we try to make food that represents either his culture and mine.

6 Academic Writing

Comparison and Contrast

Brainstorm > Organize > Write > Edit

In this writing cycle (Units 26-28), you are going to write an essay that answers the prompt below. In this unit (26), you will analyze a text and brainstorm and organize ideas about the topic.

> *Not all products and services fit the same business model. Some might have a more successful introduction in a mobile setting. For others, a mobile setting would not be appropriate. Compare and contrast two products or services regarding their potential as mobile businesses.*

Exercise 6.1 Preparing to Write

Work with a partner. Discuss the questions.

1 What influences a person to start a business, their passion to do something or their desire to make money?
2 Describe two modern businesses that reflect the fast-paced nature of the 21st century.
3 How would you define *mobile retail*? Describe an example of a mobile retail business.
4 What other types of businesses might be successful in a mobile setting?

Exercise 6.2 Focusing on Vocabulary

Read the definitions. Complete the sentences with the correct form of the words in bold.

> **aspiring** (adj) wishing to become successful
>
> **component** (n) a part that combines with other parts to form something bigger
>
> **fluctuate** (v) to change frequently from one level to another
>
> **outweigh** (v) to be greater or more important than something else
>
> **proposition** (n) a proposal or suggestion, especially in business
>
> **revenue** (n) the money that a business receives regularly

1 The price of oil has _____ dramatically in recent years, falling from $102 a barrel to just over $26 in 2016, and back up to $75 in 2018!

2 The entrepreneur tried to persuade the bank officers to give him a loan, but they found his business _____ risky and poorly organized.

3 The _____ chef took a lower-level job at a famous New York restaurant to gain experience and connections in the business.

4 The agricultural company convinced the government regulators that the benefits of its new pesticide _____ the risks.

5 The spread of technology and the movement of labor are two _____ of globalization.

6 Amazon's _____ in 2018 was almost $233 billion.

Starting out Mobile

Perhaps you make the world's best peanut butter cookies, or maybe you have always helped your friends and neighbors by fixing their computers. Many businesses are started by people who have hobbies or special talents and want to turn these interests into a business. Yet, scaling up from a hobby to a real business, such as a bakery, restaurant, or store, requires both business know-how and a substantial investment. In reality, many entrepreneurs do not have enough of either the knowledge or the money, but it is often the high financial investment needed to start a brick-and-mortar[1] business that keeps them from taking the first step.

These days, an increasing number of **aspiring** business owners have found a way to make the transition[2] from hobby to business not only more gradual but also less expensive or risky than putting up the money for a building and its equipment right away. They are taking their dreams and talents on the road—in trucks. The first entrepreneurs to do this were in the food business. In recent years, a wave of food trucks have arrived on the scene, serving everything from gourmet muffins to Argentinian empanadas to Korean tacos. Food trucks became a way for aspiring chefs to try out recipes and test the waters before making a big investment in a traditional, brick-and-mortar business.

Beginning on a small scale has its advantages compared with starting a traditional business. The most important of these is the relatively modest size of initial start-up costs. These costs, which consist primarily of the truck, a license, and any required equipment, usually come to $20,000–$30,000, a fraction of what it would cost to start a store or restaurant. Similarly, overhead costs are generally lower. Mobile business owners must pay for gas, of course, but other utility payments are modest. With such tightly controlled costs, mobile businesses often break even[3] in a year or two. In contrast, success comes to brick-and-mortar businesses much more slowly, and they often fail within the first two years. In short, mobile businesses are relatively low-risk **propositions**.

The success of food trucks has inspired other entrepreneurs to consider starting out on wheels. Rich Harper once ran a chain of gyms, but his real interest was boxing. In 2005, he bought an old truck, equipped it with some gym equipment, and took to the streets—all for a total start-up cost of $6,000. His business quickly turned a profit and is still going strong. Instead of trying to convince customers to visit his facility in an already crowded market, he brings the boxing ring to customers all over his state.

Today, there are trucks that sell flowers, shoes, clothes, and all kinds of specialty food items. There are also trucks that provide services, such as hair styling, dog grooming, and repair of high-tech devices. While mobile retail has grown steadily in the past decade, it is not without problems. Weather, the fact that gas prices **fluctuate**, and the difficulty of finding a place to park are all challenges that mobile entrepreneurs have to deal with every day. These business owners, however, feel the advantages **outweigh** the disadvantages. In the United States, the mobile food business alone—the largest in the mobile retail sector— generates an average annual **revenue** of over $2 billion.

Once convinced that their business has achieved sufficient success, some successful mobile entrepreneurs move on to open brick-and-mortar locations. Others, like Rich Harper and his boxing gym, are satisfied to stay mobile. In an interesting twist, some brick-and-mortar business owners, like their mobile counterparts, have learned from their competition and have added a mobile **component** to their businesses. The truck sells their products or services and acts as a marketing tool to bring more business into the store. Either as stand-alone businesses, or as extensions of stores, mobile retail appears to be here to stay.

[1] **brick-and-mortar** (adj) existing as a physical building, especially a store
[2] **transition** (n) a change from one state or condition to another
[3] **break even** (idiom) to earn only enough to pay expenses

Read the text on page 393. Work with a partner. Discuss the questions.

1 How do many businesses get started?
2 What was the first type of business to take advantage of a mobile setting?
3 What are two advantages of starting on a small scale?

Exercise 6.4 Noticing the Grammar and Writing

Complete the tasks. Then compare your answers with a partner's.

1 Highlight the conjunctions in paragraphs 1 and 6. Why does the writer include a correlative conjunction in the last sentence of the article?
2 What two things is the writer comparing? Underline the sentences in paragraphs 1 and 2 that help you determine your answer.
3 What is the main idea of paragraph 3?
4 What does the writer conclude after comparing and contrasting these two types of businesses?

Using Signal Words and Phrases to Compare and Contrast

Comparing is showing how two or more things are the **same** or **similar**. **Contrasting** is showing how two or more things are **different**. When writing essays, writers often compare or contrast people, things, or ideas to make their presentations clearer and to focus on advantages and disadvantages. They often use signal words and phrases to alert the reader when they are comparing or contrasting.

In an interesting twist, some brick-and-mortar business owners, **like** their mobile counterparts, have learned from their competition…

These days, an increasing number of aspiring business owners have found a way to make the transition from hobby to business not only **more** gradual but also **less** expensive or risky **than**…

In the first example, the use of **like** signals a similarity between mobile and brick-and-mortar businesses. In the second example, the use of **more** and **less than** signals a difference.

Exercise 6.5 Understanding the Skill

Read each sentence. Indicate if the writer is stating a similarity (S) or a difference (D). Underline the signal words or phrases.

1 In spite of the popularity of eating out, cooking at home is much healthier. _____

2 Hamburgers from the same fast food restaurants in different countries taste the same. _____

3 Unlike the long lines at fast food restaurants in some Asian countries, they are usually shorter in Western Europe. _____

4 Similar to a food truck, a fast food restaurant needs to work quickly and efficiently. _____

My Writing

Using Venn Diagrams

A **Venn diagram** is a graphic organizer that can help you organize your ideas when comparing and contrasting two topics. It consists of two overlapping circles. The special characteristics (differences) of one topic are on the left side, while those of the second topic are on the right side. The shared characteristics (similarities) are in the middle.

Example: "Comparing Fast Food and International Food"

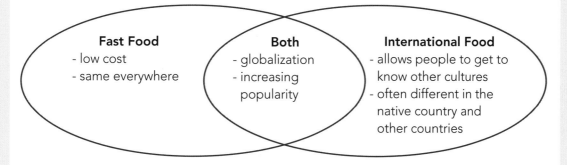

Fast Food
- low cost
- same everywhere

Both
- globalization
- increasing popularity

International Food
- allows people to get to know other cultures
- often different in the native country and other countries

Exercise 6.6 Applying the Skill

Work with a partner. Complete the tasks.

1 Brainstorm at least three products or services that could be set up as mobile businesses.
2 Discuss the advantages and disadvantages of each one.
3 On your own, choose two of the products or services for your essay. Use a Venn diagram to compare and contrast them.
4 Share your Venn diagram with your partner for feedback. Add any new ideas.

Exercise 6.7 Writing a Paragraph

Use your Venn diagram to write a paragraph about the two products or services. Include a topic sentence, at least two similarities or differences with supporting details, and a concluding sentence. Use coordinating or correlative conjunctions to show similarities or differences.

Adverb Clauses and Phrases

1 Grammar in the Real World

ACADEMIC
WRITING

Comparison and
contrast

A What are some normal behaviors that can become problems under certain circumstances? Read the web article about shopping addiction. When is shopping an addiction?

B Comprehension Check **Answer the questions.**

1 Why aren't shopping addictions considered a serious problem by most people?

2 What problems can a shopping addiction lead to?

3 What are two ways in which shopaholics can treat their problem?

C Notice **Find the sentences in the article and complete them. Then circle the meaning of the words.**

1 _____ these people do not need more clothes or electronics, they keep buying them.
   a The words introduce contrasting ideas.   b The words give a reason.

2 _____ shopping may be seen as an amusing addiction, society does not always consider it a serious problem.
   a The word introduces contrasting ideas.   b The word gives a reason.

3 _____ shopaholics enjoy the excitement, they often feel depressed or guilty after a shopping trip.
   a The words introduce contrasting ideas.   b The words give a reason.

SHOPPING ADDICTION:
When Spending Hurts

Some people have closets filled with new clothes that they do not wear. Others have desks covered with electronics that they 5 never use. **Even though these people do not need more clothes or electronics,** they keep buying them. They cannot help themselves. **Although many** 10 **people like to shop,** some people shop too much. If someone is unable to control spending, he or she may be a shopping addict, or "shopaholic." **Because** 15 **shopping may be seen as an amusing addiction,** society does not always consider it a serious problem. As a result, many people do not recognize they have a 20 problem that needs treatment. However, if this addiction is not treated, it can ruin a person's life.

Shopping can activate[1] chemicals in the brain associated 25 with pleasure, **so some people get a natural "high"[2] while**

shopping. Also, some people shop **because it makes them feel in control.** This often happens 30 **when they face difficulties in their personal or professional lives.** These feelings could be signs of shopping addiction. **While it may appear to some that** 35 **many more women than men are affected by this addiction,** current statistics show that this is not true. The percentage of men addicted to shopping is about the 40 same as the percentage of women (around 5 percent).

Like most addictions, a shopping addiction can cause serious problems. First of all, 45 it is difficult for addicts. **Even though shopaholics enjoy the excitement,** they often feel depressed or guilty after a shopping trip. **Spending** 50 **more money than they have,** many shopaholics have financial problems. **As they spend,** they

may lie to their families about their spending habits. These lies are 55 almost always hurtful and can even destroy the family.

Fortunately, shopping addiction can be treated. **In order to change their behavior,** 60 shopping addicts must admit that they have a problem and then seek help. In addition, shopping addicts should always take a friend along **when they need to** buy 65 something. Most shopping addicts only overspend when they shop alone.

While shopping is usually a harmless activity, an addiction 70 to shopping can cause financial and personal problems. Therefore, people should understand the signs of a shopping addiction **so that they can get help.** Shopping 75 should be a constructive activity, not a destructive one.

[1]**activate:** cause something to start

[2]**high:** a feeling of being excited or full of energy

2 Subordinators and Adverb Clauses

Grammar Presentation

Adverb clauses show a relationship between ideas in two clauses. They begin with subordinators, such as *although* and *because*.	*Although she enjoys wearing new clothes,* she doesn't enjoy shopping. Eric doesn't go shopping often *because he doesn't like to spend money.*

2.1 Forming Adverb Clauses

A An adverb clause has a subject and a verb, but it is a dependent clause. It is not a complete sentence.	MAIN CLAUSE DEPENDENT CLAUSE She shops *because it makes her feel good*
B In general, use a comma when an adverb clause begins the sentence.	*Although I sometimes buy things I don't need,* I'm not a shopping addict.

2.2 Using Adverb Clauses

A Use *because* and *since* to give reasons. *Because* is more common.	*Because shopping is necessary,* shopping addicts aren't easily recognized. Treatment is important for shopping addicts *since it is very difficult to overcome this problem on one's own.*
B Use *although*, *even though*, and *though* to show a contrasting idea or something unexpected. *Although* is a little more formal. Use a comma with adverb clauses that include these subordinators, whether they begin or end the sentence.	*Even though shopping addicts enjoy shopping,* they feel depressed afterward. She spends a lot on clothing, *though she doesn't make much money.*
C Use *while* to show contrasting ideas. Use a comma whether the adverb clause begins or ends the sentence.	Shopping addicts buy things they don't need, *while nonaddicts tend to buy mostly things they need.*
D You can use *as*, *since*, *when*, and *while* in adverb clauses to express time relationships.	It has been six weeks *since he went shopping.* *While she was at the mall,* she bought many useless things.

Grammar Application

Exercise 2.1 Adverb Clauses

Combine the sentences about shopping addiction. Use the subordinators in parentheses. Add commas when necessary. Sometimes more than one answer is possible.

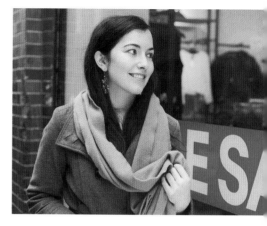

1 We are surrounded by advertising messages. It is often difficult to avoid shopping. (since)

   Since we are surrounded by advertising
   messages, it is often difficult to
   avoid shopping.

2 Many people feel that it is patriotic to shop. Some politicians say that it is good for the economy. (because)

3 We may not need items. We sometimes want what others have. (even though)

4 Shopping addiction seems to be a recent problem. It has almost certainly existed for centuries. (although)

5 Addicts may shop to escape negative feelings. Normal people shop to buy things they need. (while)

6 Normal shoppers use the items they buy. Compulsive shoppers often do not use them. (while)

A Complete the interview with a shopping addict. Rewrite each pair of sentences as one sentence. Use one of the subordinators in parentheses.

Jane   So, Claire, how did you know you were a shopping addict?

Claire I saw a show on TV. I realized I was an addict. (when / since)

1   *When I saw a show on TV, I realized I was an addict.*

Jane   I understand that you're getting help.

Claire Yes. My insurance pays for it. I was able to sign up for therapy. (because / although)

2   _____

Jane   Is your therapy helping?

Claire Definitely. I've only been in therapy a short time. I'm feeling better already. (although / when)

3   _____

Jane   How are things different now?

Claire I only buy what I really need. I'm spending much less money. (since / although)

4   _____

Jane   Describe a recent shopping trip.

Claire I was at the mall yesterday. I only went to one store. (even though / since)

5   _____

         I had a list. I only bought things I truly needed. (since / while)

6   _____

Jane   Good for you! Thank you for sharing your story with us.

B Listen to the interview and check your answers.

Group Work What are some ways to avoid bad shopping habits? Write five sentences using adverb clauses. Use the ideas in the unit and your own ideas.
Decide as a group which two ideas are the most effective and give reasons.

You should take a friend with you when you shop.

3 Reducing Adverb Clauses

Grammar Presentation

Sometimes you can reduce adverb clauses to *-ing* forms. The subject of the main clause must be the same as the subject of the adverb clause.	*While he was shopping*, he bought things he didn't need. *While shopping*, he bought things he didn't need.

3.1 Reducing Adverb Clauses

In many cases, you can reduce adverb clauses. Omit the subject, and use the verb + *-ing*.	*While he was shopping*, he bought a jacket. *While shopping*, he bought a jacket.

3.2 Reducing Clauses That Give Reasons

You can reduce clauses that give reasons when the verb is in the simple past, present perfect, or past perfect. For the simple past, omit the subordinator and the subject, and use the verb + *-ing*. For the present perfect and past perfect, change *have* to *having*. The *-ing* forms usually begin the sentences.	*Because he was cautious*, he didn't spend much money. *Being cautious*, he didn't spend much money. *Since she has gotten help*, she no longer shops so often. *Having gotten help*, she no longer shops so often.

3.3 Reducing Time Clauses

A You can reduce a time clause when the verb is in the present progressive or past progressive. Omit the subject and the form of *be*.	You can save money *while you <u>are going</u> to college*. You can save money *while going to college*. *While he <u>was shopping</u>*, he bought a jacket. *While shopping*, he bought a jacket.
B You can also reduce a time clause with a verb in the simple present or simple past. Omit the subject, and use the verb + *-ing*.	She started shopping at malls *before she <u>realized</u> that shopping was addictive*. She started shopping at malls *before realizing that shopping was addictive*.

Complete the sentences about Mike and Eric, two hoarders.[1] Rewrite the reason clauses in parentheses as reduced clauses.

1 _Buying new things all the time_ , Mike filled his apartment with useless items.
(because he bought new things all the time)

2 _____ , he took action.
(because he understood that he had a problem)

3 _____ , he had no savings.
(because he had spent so much money on clothes)

4 _____ , Eric is now able to keep his
(since he has received treatment)
apartment much cleaner.

5 _____ , he no longer feels anxious.
(because he has worked with a therapist)

6 _____ , he no longer hoards useless items.
(since he has gotten help)

[1]**hoarder:** a person who collects large supplies of things, usually more than he or she needs

Exercise 3.2 Reducing Time Clauses

Complete the sentences about a compulsive spender. Rewrite the time clauses in parentheses as reduced clauses.

1 _While shopping online_ , Amy was ecstatic.
 (while she was shopping online)

2 _____ , she was in an altered state.
 (while she was spending money)

3 Amy had spent over $30,000 _____ .
 (before she got treatment)

4 _____ , Amy decided to join Debtors
 (before she spent more money)
 Anonymous (DA).[1]

5 _____ , Amy learned how to budget.
 (after she joined DA)

6 She also got help with her credit _____ .
 (after she started DA)

7 Amy has changed her behavior _____ .
 (since she received treatment)

[1]**Debtors Anonymous (DA):** an organization that helps compulsive spenders

4 Subordinators to Express Purpose

Grammar Presentation

Some subordinators can express a purpose.	He got help for his shopping addiction *so that* he could feel better. (= He got help for the purpose of feeling better.)

4.1 Using Subordinators to Express Purpose

A Use *so* or *so that* to show a reason or purpose. Clauses with *so that* usually come after the main clause.	People go to psychologists *so that* they can talk about their problems. I keep track of my money *so* I don't spend too much.
B You can also show a reason or purpose with *in order to* or *to* when the subject of the main clause and the adverb clause are the same. Do not repeat the subject.	Shopping addicts buy things they don't need *to* feel good. (= Shopping addicts buy things they don't need so that they feel good.) Shopping addicts may get help *in order to* stop shopping. (= Shopping addicts may get help so that they stop shopping.)

Grammar Application

A Complete the sentences from the book *Consumer World*. Put the subordinators in parentheses in the right place in the sentences.

                                                             in order to

  1 Psychologists have shown that we actually need very little feel happy. (in order to)

  2 Some people buy things feel good about themselves. (to)

  3 Some people acquire things they have a sense of who they are. (so that)

  4 It's also possible that people acquire things feel secure. (in order to)

  5 They buy a lot feel that they are financially secure. (in order to)

  6 They buy a lot they are prepared for any emergency. (so that)

  7 Find out how little you really need, think about what you would do if you had to move. (to)

  8 I think that have true peace of mind, you should have as little as possible. (in order to)

B Group Work Discuss the questions with your group. Use *in order to, so, so that,* and *to* in your discussion.

  ■ Does owning things make people happy?

  ■ What are some of the problems that owning things can cause?

  ■ What do people have to do to be truly happy?

  ■ What are some ways to live with less?

  A *In order to be truly happy, you should focus on people, not things.*
  B *I agree, but to have a happy life, you need some possessions.*

C Write sentences about your five best ideas in B. Use subordinators to express purpose.

  In order to be truly happy, you should focus on people, not things.
  Pretend you are moving so you can decide what to get rid of.

5 Avoid Common Mistakes ⚠

1   **Remember that *even though* is two words, not one.**

                             even though
     I bought a computer bag ~~eventhough~~ I do not own a computer.

2   **Use *even though*, not *even*, to create an adverb clause.**

     Even though
     ~~Even~~ it was late, the store was open.

3   **Do not start a new sentence with *because*, *whereas*, or *although* when the clause refers to the previous sentence.**

                        store because
     I returned the camera to the ~~store. Because~~ I did not really need it.

4   **Remember to use the verb + *-ing* in reduced clauses after words like *after*, *before*, *while*, and *when*.**

        watching
     When ~~watch~~ ads on TV, some people feel a strong urge to buy the products.

Editing Task

Find and correct eight more mistakes in the paragraphs about addictions.

           looking
After ~~look~~ at research, we see clearly that alcohol and drug addictions are serious physical conditions. Psychologists are now considering adding shopping to the list. Eventhough these experts say that shopping is as addictive as drugs, I disagree that it should be considered a serious addiction.

5   People who argue that shopping is addictive have good reasons. While shop, many people get a good feeling. They like spending money even they may not need to buy anything. However, after go home, they feel regret. They have spent money on something they did not want or need. Because buying something makes them feel a sense of power.

10   However, after examine the situation of over-shopping closely, one can see that many people are victims of advertising. Even they may not plan to buy something, a powerful advertisement can change their mind. If people did not watch so much TV, they would not feel the urge to shop as strongly. In this way, shopping addiction differs from drug and alcohol addictions, which create a chemical change in the body

15   that is very difficult to resist.

     Eventhough shopping too much is a serious problem, it should not be considered an addiction. If advertisements disappeared, society would not have this problem called shopping addiction.

6 Academic Writing

Comparison and Contrast

Brainstorm > Organize > Write > Edit

In Unit 26, you analyzed a text and brainstormed and organized ideas for the writing prompt below. In this unit (27), you will focus on ways to organize comparisons and contrasts and to write concise body paragraphs.

> Not all products and services fit the same business model. Some might have a more successful introduction in a mobile setting. For others, a mobile setting would not be appropriate. Compare and contrast two products or services regarding their potential as mobile businesses.

Organizing Comparisons and Contrasts

In formal essays and reports, writers often compare or contrast people, things, or ideas in order to make an argument. There are two common ways to organize a text that compares and/or contrasts topics:

- **Block organization:** The writer discusses all the features (cost, appearance, size) of one topic in a body paragraph and the features of the second topic in a separate body paragraph.
- **Point-by-point organization:** The writer compares and contrasts one feature at a time, usually one feature per paragraph. Point-by-point organization works best when there are clear parallel points for comparison.

Exercise 6.1 Understanding the Skill

Work with a partner. Complete the tasks.

1 Write the correct organizational pattern in each box below.

2 Think about the characteristics of shopping at a brick-and-mortar store and those of shopping online. Choose three characteristics and fill in both outlines.

Organizational pattern: _____	**Organizational pattern:** _____
Shopping in stores _____	Feature 1 _____
Feature 1: _____	Shopping in stores: _____
Feature 2: _____	Shopping online _____
Feature 3: _____	Feature 2 _____
Shopping online _____	Shopping in stores: _____
Feature 1: _____	Shopping online _____
Feature 2: _____	Feature 3 _____
Feature 3: _____	Shopping in stores: _____
	Shopping online _____

Exercise 6.2 Applying the Skill

Read an early draft of a student's essay about the food truck industry. The body paragraphs and conclusion are incomplete. Work with a partner. Discuss the questions.

Roy Choi is considered the pioneer of the modern food truck movement. He was born in South Korea but grew up in Los Angeles, surrounded by incredible diversity--including diverse food. He has worked in fancy restaurants and in food trucks. He was successful in both settings, but it was the dramatic and instant triumph of his first food truck, Kogi BBQ, that really shook up the food world. Choi says that working in each of the two settings taught him important lessons, allowing him to master both cooking and marketing.

Choi went to Culinary school and then started working in hotel restaurants. What he learned in the theoretical world of culinary education did not prepare him for the real world of a busy hotel's kitchen.… [differences between what he was taught and the real world…]

After years of classical cooking, he decided to make the switch to a smaller, less formal setting--a food truck. He wanted… [advantages & disadvantages of the two settings & what he learned]

[Conclusion]

1 Which organizational pattern does the writer use?
2 How could you reorganize the information to follow the other organizational pattern?
3 What would you include in the conclusion?

My Writing

Exercise 6.3 Organizing Ideas

Read the writing prompt on page 406. Use the questions to organize your body paragraphs.

1 Review your work in My Writing in. Unit 26 Do you have three distinct comparisons or contrasts?
2 Create an outline for your body paragraphs.
3 Share your outline with a partner. Use the feedback to edit your outline.

Writing Concisely

Good academic writing is **concise**, which means the writers say what they want to say directly using the fewest number of words possible. One way to write concisely is to reduce clauses to phrases. This not only makes the writing more efficient, but it also demonstrates the ability to use complex sentence structure.

Exercise 6.4 Writing Body Paragraphs

Write your first draft of 2-3 body paragraphs.
- Use signal words and correlative conjunctions to compare and contrast.
- Reduce clauses to make your writing more concise.

Connecting Information with Prepositions and Transitions

Technology in Entertainment

1 Grammar in the Real World

A How are video games today different from the games of 5 or 10 years ago? Read the article about a kind of animation technology that is being used in games today. How has it changed the look of video games?

B Comprehension Check **Answer the questions.**

1 What is "mocap"?

2 In what areas is mocap used?

3 Why isn't mocap used more often in movies and video games?

C Notice **Match the words in bold with their meaning.**

1 **Because of** the realism that mocap gives its animated figures, a common use for mocap is in video games. _____

2 **Furthermore,** mocap can be used in training for jobs such as firefighting. _____

3 **Despite** the expense, mocap technology is becoming more popular in many different areas. _____

a introduces additional information

b introduces a reason

c introduces contrasting information

MOTION CAPTURE TECHNOLOGY

Computer animation was first introduced in the late 1970s; **however**, today's animation is much more realistic than it was then. While the first animated video game characters moved in only two directions, today's animated game heroes can jump, kick, and spin. The use of sensors[1] to record these movements is called motion capture, or "mocap."

Because of the realism that mocap gives its animated figures, a common use for mocap is in video games. Video game creators use real people to help create their characters. With sports video games, for example, famous athletes are used **instead of** actors. **Consequently,** the games can feature each athlete's unique moves. How does it work? **First**, the athlete puts on a tight suit that has special markers[2] all over it. **Next**, he or she performs a sequence of actions. Video cameras record these movements using the markers. **Finally**, digital information is collected from the markers and the video. This information is used to create the movements of the video character.

Another common use of mocap is in movies. The makers of *Titanic* needed characters that could move realistically in a situation that would have been much too dangerous for a real actor. **As a result**, they used mocap. **Besides being** completely safe, it was a lot cheaper and easier than filming people falling off a sinking ship!

In addition to these uses, motion capture technology is used in medicine. **For instance**, doctors have patients in mocap suits walk on treadmills. The mocap information helps doctors diagnose problems such as weak bones. **Furthermore**, mocap can be used in training for jobs such as firefighting. New firefighters can use mocap games to practice moving through virtual[3] house fires. **Instead of** taking risks in a real setting, they can practice in a virtual reality.

Despite the expense, mocap technology is becoming more popular in many different areas. **Due to** its success so far, who knows what it will be used for next?

---

[1]**sensor:** a device that discovers and reacts to changes in such things as movement, heat, and light

[2]**marker:** a small, reflective dot that is taped to a figure

[3]**virtual:** created by a computer

2 Connecting Information with Prepositions and Prepositional Phrases

Grammar Presentation

Some prepositions and prepositional phrases can connect information to an independent clause. Like subordinators, these prepositions can be used to add information, give reasons, show contrasts, present alternatives, or give exceptions.

Video games look realistic today because of improvements in computer animation.

Despite the popularity of animation, most people prefer to watch live-action movies.

2.1 Using Prepositions and Prepositional Phrases to Connect Ideas

A One-word prepositions, such as *besides* and *despite*, and multi-word prepositions, such as *as well as, because of, in addition to*, and *in spite of*, are followed by nouns, noun phrases, or gerunds.	*Besides being very expensive, animated movies can take a long time to produce.* *Some animated movies are also popular with adults in spite of their appeal to kids.*
B Prepositional phrases, like adverb clauses, can come before or after the main clause. Use a comma when the prepositional phrase comes first.	*Video games usually use athletes instead of actors.* *Instead of actors, video games usually use athletes.*

2.2 Meanings of Prepositions Used to Connect Ideas

A Use *as well as, besides*, and *in addition to* to emphasize another idea.	*I enjoy animated movies as well as live-action movies.* *This TV has 3D technology in addition to high definition.* *Besides being a talented director, he is an excellent actor.*
B Use *as a result of, because of*, and *due to* to give reasons.	*Because of the high cost of tickets, many people don't go to the movies.* *As a result of voters' opinions, the director was nominated for an Academy Award.* *The movie's appeal is due to its special effects.*

2.2 Meanings of Prepositions Used to Connect Ideas (continued)

C Use *instead of* to give alternatives.	*Let's see a drama instead of a comedy.* *Instead of going out, they watched TV at home.*
D Use *except* or *except for* to give exceptions. When the main clause is a negative statement, you can also use *besides* to mean "except for."	*This composer wrote the music for all the Alien Adventures movies except the first one.* *Except for their parents, the audience was mostly children.* *Besides the parents of the children, there weren't any adults in the audience.*
E Use *despite* and *in spite of* to show contrasting ideas.	*Despite being made for children, this movie is enjoyed by adults.* *In spite of its short length, the movie was very powerful.*

Grammar Application

Exercise 2.1 Prepositional Phrases to Connect Ideas

Complete the paragraphs about one use of motion capture technology. Use the words in the box. Sometimes more than one answer is possible.

as well as	because of	due to	in addition to	instead of	~~in spite of~~

    <u>*In spite of*</u> the high cost of mocap, its use is expanding. For example, Ford
   (1)
Motor Company, a car manufacturer, is using mocap technology to create digital

humans.[1] _____ their human-like behavior, digital humans are used to
            (2)
study people's behavior in cars. _____ studying driver behavior, engineers
                        (3)
are also studying ways to make passengers feel more comfortable. For example,

_____ using a real human, the company uses a short digital female to test
    (4)
a short driver's ability to reach the gas pedal.

    Motion capture technology helps the company improve worker safety

_____ driver safety. _____ the technology's ability to
   (5)   (6)
replicate workers' movements, the company has reduced the number of assembly

line accidents.

[1]**digital human:** an electronic representation of a person

Complete the sentences about using mocap technology to help athletes recover from injuries and improve their speed. Circle the correct prepositions.

1 (In addition to)/Because of filmmakers, physical therapists are using motion capture technology to help injured athletes.

2 **As a result of/Instead of** an injury, athletes could lose their careers.

3 An athlete's career could be destroyed **because of/instead of** injuries.

4 Analyzing an injury without motion capture technology is not always accurate, **due to/besides** being time-consuming.

5 With motion capture technology, therapists accurately see the problem **in spite of/instead of** guessing where the problem is.

6 The success of motion capture technology with Olympic athletes is **in spite of/due to** its ability to analyze the athletes' movements at high speeds.

7 **Except for/Despite** the success of motion capture technology with athletes, it cannot replace the hours of practice that athletes need to succeed.

A Combine the ideas about the use of technology in health care. Use the prepositions in parentheses and the underlined words to create prepositional phrases.

1 Many hospitals are no longer using <u>paper medical records</u>. They are using electronic medical records. (instead of)

   Instead of paper medical records, some hospitals are using electronic records.

2 Everyone has <u>quick access to your records</u>. Doctors can share information with each other more easily. (Due to)

   _____

3 There are <u>many advantages to electronic records</u>. Some doctors still have serious concerns. (in spite of)

   _____

4 There should be <u>accurate information in the records</u>. The information could contain data input errors. (instead of)

   _____

5 There will be <u>a lot of security</u>. Hackers could still steal information from hospitals. (despite)

   _____

B Group Work Choose an area that is changing because of technology. Use one of the ideas below or your own idea. As a group, write statements that explain the technology, its effects, and the possible advantages and disadvantages of using it. Use prepositional phrases.

- high speed trains
- online learning
- use of cell phones instead of money to purchase products

3 Connecting Information with Transition Words

Grammar Presentation

Transition words are words or phrases that connect ideas between sentences. They are frequently used in academic writing and formal situations.	*It's important not to judge a movie's quality by whether it is animated or not.* **Furthermore,** *you should not assume that a movie with human actors is superior to an animated movie.*

3.1 Using Transition Words

A Transition words join the ideas in two sentences.	*Movie stars often do the voices in animated movies.* **However,** *their fans don't always recognize them.*
Coordinating conjunctions (*but*, etc.), subordinators (*although*, etc.), and prepositions (*in spite of*, etc.) combine two different sentences into one new sentence.	*Music in movies is very important for setting the tone,* **but** *most people don't pay attention to it.* **Although** *animated movies sometimes win the best picture award, they also have their own category.* **In spite of** *having a lot of famous actors, the movie did not get very good reviews.*
B Most transition words occur at the beginning of the second sentence and are followed by a comma. You can also use a semicolon between the two sentences that you combine.	*The studio executives choose a script.* **After that,** *they select a director.* *She is a very talented artist;* **moreover,** *her use of color is exceptional.*
Many – but not all – transition words can go in the middle of the sentence or at the end. When the transition word comes at the end, it is preceded by a comma.	*Most people,* **however,** *associate animation with movies.* *Most people associate animation with movies,* **however.**

3.1 Using Transition Words (continued)

C The short transition words *so*, *then*, and *also* are often used without a comma. *So* is used at the beginning of a sentence only in informal writing.

Use more formal transition words with the same meanings in academic writing: *afterward*, *in addition*, *therefore*.

My daughter enjoys animated movies a lot. *So* we take her to them pretty often. *Then* she usually wants to stop for a snack on the way home. I am *also* usually hungry after a long movie.

Children often enjoy animated movies. *Therefore*, their parents often take them to the movies. *Afterward*, it is not unusual to stop for something to eat. *In addition*, parents often buy a book or souvenir connected to the movie for their children.

3.2 Meanings of Transition Words

A To show a sequence or the order of events or ideas, use *first*, *second*, *then*, *next*, *after that*, and *finally*.

How do animators capture an athlete's movement? *First*, the athlete puts on a special suit. *Then* the athlete performs the action. *Next*, the computer collects digital information.

B To summarize ideas, use *in conclusion*, *to conclude*, and *to summarize*.

In conclusion, technological innovations will change many fields, including animation.

C To give additional information, use *also*, *furthermore*, *in addition*, and *moreover*.

Animation is used in movies, video games, and other entertainment industries. *In addition*, it is used in sports medicine.

D To give alternatives, use *instead*.

I had expected the movie to be boring. *Instead*, I thought it was quite entertaining.

E To give contrasting ideas, use *on the other hand* and *in contrast*.

The story was not very original. *On the other hand*, the animation was impressive.

F To give a result, use *as a result*, *consequently*, *therefore*, and *thus*.

The game was designed with animation. *Therefore*, the characters were very lifelike.

G To give examples, use *for example* or *for instance*.

Many animated movies are very popular. *For example*, Kung Fu Panda and Despicable Me were huge box office hits.

🌐 DATA FROM THE REAL WORLD

The most common transition words in writing are:	however, so, then, therefore, thus
The most common transition words in conversation are:	anyway, so, then, though

Grammar Application

Exercise 3.1 Transition Words to Show Sequence

A Pair Work Look at the steps involved in computer game design. Can you put them in the correct order? Make guesses with your partner and try to number the steps in order from 1 to 6.

_____ **a** Make a prototype (a model or "first draft") of the game and test it.

_____ **b** Work with the marketing team to get the game ready to sell.

_1_ **c** Decide on the theme and environment of the game.

_____ **d** Do research on the theme.

_____ **e** Figure out the goal of the game and the rules.

_____ **f** Make any necessary changes to the game.

B Now listen to a game designer describing her job. Were your answers correct?

C Listen again and complete the sentences. Use the sequence words in the box. Add commas when necessary.

after that	finally	~~first~~	next	second	then

1 _____*First,*_____ I decide on an overall concept for a game.

2 _____ I figure out the goal of the game and the rules.

3 _____ I do research on the theme.

4 _____ I use software to make a prototype of the game.

5 _____ I go back to the computer and make any necessary changes.

6 _____ I work with the marketing people.

Exercise 3.2 Transition Words for Academic Writing

Complete the paragraph about the differences between computer animation and traditional animation. Circle the correct transition words.

Computer-generated animation (CGA) is very popular today. The spectacular effects of CGA in big-budget movies impress many people. **Therefore /(However)**, in my opinion, CGA is not as pleasant to
(1)
look at as traditional animation (TA). **First / Afterward**, CGA does not
(2)
require the same skill as TA. Traditional animators draw by hand, and the resulting images look complex and rich in style. **Instead / To summarize**,
(3)
computer animators use software to produce images. These images often

Computer-Generated Animation

have a cold, hard look to them. <u>To conclude/Furthermore</u>, (4) with CGA, objects are often overly bright. This adds to the unnaturalness of their appearance. <u>In contrast/Thus</u>, the (5) images from TA are often soft and appear more natural. <u>In conclusion/Moreover</u>, TA produces better-looking (6) images that have more style as well as a lifelike appearance; <u>on the other hand /therefore</u>, it is better than CGA. (7)

Traditional Animation

Exercise 3.3 Using Transition Words

A Look at the brainstorming notes a student made for a paragraph comparing two movies. Use the words to write sentences to summarize the ideas. Use the notes to help you.

War of the Aliens	The Magical Forest
excellent computer graphics dull plot[1] unappealing characters bad dialog	poor animation interesting story likeable characters good dialog

[1]**plot:** story

1 excellent computer graphics/in contrast/poor animation

War of the Aliens had excellent computer graphics. In contrast, The Magical Forest had poor animation.

2 excellent computer graphics/however/dull plot

_____

3 furthermore/unappealing characters

_____

4 on the other hand/interesting story

_____

5 in addition/likeable characters

_____

6 moreover/good dialog

_____

7 in contrast/bad dialog

_____

8 in conclusion/a better movie than

_____

B Over to You Think of two movies you have seen that have animation or special effects. Which one was better? Why? Write four to six sentences comparing the two movies. Use transitions to add ideas and show contrasts.

Cowboys in Space was very popular. On the other hand, Cowboys in Space II didn't do very well.

4 Avoid Common Mistakes ⚠

1 The prepositional expressions *as well as, in spite of, despite,* and *in addition to* are followed by a noun phrase or a gerund, not a subject + verb.

the high costs
Despite ~~the costs are high~~, 3D TVs are becoming very popular.

using
The filmmakers used mocap in addition to ~~they used~~ digital technology.

2 Use *on the other hand,* not *in the other hand,* when contrasting points of view.

on
The movie industry has many career opportunities; ~~in~~ the other hand, it is very competitive.

Editing Task

Find and correct four more mistakes in the paragraph about the filmmaking industry.

the slow economy
Filmmaking is a durable industry. Despite ~~the economy is slow~~, the movie industry is doing well. People always seem to find money for entertainment. As a result, movie production companies often hire people because it takes many professionals to create a movie. In addition to they hire actors and directors, they hire tens of thousands of other professionals that are

5 not well known – for example, grips (people who set up and tear down the sets), production assistants, and camera operators. The jobs can be exciting and challenging; in the other hand, some can be low paying. As with most other careers, it is necessary to work hard and be ambitious to succeed. The work can also be especially tough for production crews – for example, camera operators, production assistants, and makeup artists – who work up to 18

10 hours a day. Despite they have long hours, these jobs can be difficult to find because there is a lot of competition for them. In general, moviemaking is seen as a glamorous profession, and some people want to be a part of that glamor more than anything else. Movies often require celebrities and artists; in the other hand, they also rely on many people with other skills. It is a growing industry, too. The Bureau of Labor Statistics states that employment opportunities for

15 people in the filmmaking industry will increase 12 percent between now and 2016. In short, this industry is competitive, but young people should pursue it if they have an interest in movies.

5 Academic Writing

Comparison and Contrast

Brainstorm 〉 Organize 〉 Write 〉 Edit

In Unit 27, you focused on ways to organize your essay and wrote the first draft of your body paragraphs for the prompt below. In this unit (28), you will write your introduction and conclusion, and then revise and edit your essay.

> *Not all products and services fit the same business model. Some might have a more successful introduction in a mobile setting. For others, a mobile setting would not be appropriate. Compare and contrast two products or services regarding their potential as a mobile business.*

Connecting the Conclusion to the Introduction

Introductory and concluding paragraphs are connected in several ways, but concluding paragraphs are usually shorter. Conclusions summarize the thesis statement and key ideas in the essay, and they clearly state inferences drawn from the body paragraphs. They also include a final thought or conclusion such as a recommendation, call for action, or request to reconsider ways of thinking. Strong conclusions often return to the hook. For example, if the writer began with a question, the essay should end with a clear answer. If the writer began with an anecdote or story, it should be mentioned in the conclusion.

Exercise 5.1 Applying the Skill

Work with a partner. Read the introductory paragraph of an essay on motion capture movies. Discuss ideas for the concluding paragraph. What will it include?

Have you seen the latest *Avengers* movie? The action and characters are all extremely life-like, and you may feel like you are in the room with them. That is because significant parts were filmed by motion, or performance, capture. Motion capture is a type of film recording that captures the movement of an actor, while the rest of the scene is generated on a computer. It looks and feels very different than traditional filmmaking. While both techniques are popular in today's movies, motion capture has several advantages over traditional filmmaking.

My Writing

Exercise 5.2 Planning and Writing Your Essay

Review your body paragraphs from My Writing in Unit 27. Complete the tasks.

1 Plan your introduction and conclusion.

- What is your thesis? What hook can you use to get your reader's attention?
- What are the main ideas in your body paragraphs?
- What important inferences can you draw from your body paragraphs?
- How can you link your conclusion to your introduction?

2 Write an introduction and conclusion for the ideas and content of your essay.

Exercise 5.3 Revising Your Ideas

1 Work with a partner. Use the questions to give feedback on your partner's essay.

- Which of your partner's ideas seem strongest to you?
- Which of your partner's ideas needs to be explained more clearly?
- What could your partner add or remove to make the essay easier to understand?

2 Use the feedback from your partner to revise the ideas and content of your essay.

Exercise 5.4 Editing Your Writing

Use the checklist to review and edit your essay.

Did you answer the writing prompt completely?	
Did you give some background information on mobile retail in your introduction?	
Did you use an appropriate organizational structure for comparison and contrast?	
Did you use signal words and phrases, and coordinating and correlative conjunctions to compare and contrast?	
Does your concluding paragraph include a final thought for your readers?	

Exercise 5.5 Editing Your Grammar

Use the checklist to review and edit the grammar in your essay.

Did you use coordinating and correlative conjunctions correctly?	
Did you use subordinators and adverb clauses correctly?	
Did you reduce adverb clauses correctly?	
Did you accurately connect information with prepositional phrases and transitions?	
Did you avoid the common mistakes in the charts on page 391, 405, and 417?	

Exercise 5.6 Writing Your Final Draft

Apply the feedback and edits from Exercises 5.3 to 5.5 to write the final draft of your essay.

Appendices

1 Irregular Verbs

Base Form	Simple Past	Past Participle	Base Form	Simple Past	Past Participle
be	was / were	been	hide	hid	hidden
become	became	become	hit	hit	hit
begin	began	begun	hold	held	held
bite	bit	bitten	hurt	hurt	hurt
blow	blew	blown	keep	kept	kept
break	broke	broken	know	knew	known
bring	brought	brought	leave	left	left
build	built	built	lose	lost	lost
buy	bought	bought	make	made	made
catch	caught	caught	meet	met	met
choose	chose	chosen	pay	paid	paid
come	came	come	put	put	put
cost	cost	cost	read	read	read
cut	cut	cut	ride	rode	ridden
do	did	done	run	ran	run
draw	drew	drawn	say	said	said
drink	drank	drunk	see	saw	seen
drive	drove	driven	sell	sold	sold
eat	ate	eaten	send	sent	sent
fall	fell	fallen	set	set	set
feed	fed	fed	shake	shook	shaken
feel	felt	felt	show	showed	shown
fight	fought	fought	shut	shut	shut
find	found	found	sing	sang	sung
fly	flew	flown	sit	sat	sat
forget	forgot	forgotten	sleep	slept	slept
forgive	forgave	forgiven	speak	spoke	spoken
get	got	gotten	spend	spent	spent
give	gave	given	stand	stood	stood
go	went	gone	steal	stole	stolen
grow	grew	grown	swim	swam	swum
have	had	had	take	took	taken
hear	heard	heard	teach	taught	taught

Irregular Verbs (continued)

Base Form	Simple Past	Past Participle	Base Form	Simple Past	Past Participle
tell	told	told	wake	woke	woken
think	thought	thought	wear	wore	worn
throw	threw	thrown	win	won	won
understand	understood	understood	write	wrote	written

2 Stative (Non-Action) Verbs

Stative verbs do not describe actions. They describe states or situations. Stative verbs are not usually used in the progressive. Some are occasionally used in the present progressive, but often with a different meaning.

Research shows that the 25 most common stative verbs in spoken and written English are:

agree	dislike	hope	love	see
believe	expect	hurt	need	seem
care (about)	hate	know	notice	think
cost	have	like	own	understand
disagree	hear	look like	prefer	want

Other stative verbs:

appear	deserve	mean	smell
be	feel	owe	sound
belong	forgive	recognize	taste
concern	look	remember	weigh
contain	matter		

Stative verbs that also have action meanings:

be	have	look	taste
expect	hear	see	think
feel	hope	smell	weigh

Using the present progressive form of these verbs changes the meaning to an action.
*Can you **see** the red car?* (= use your eyes to be aware of something)
*I'**m seeing** an old friend tomorrow.* (= meeting someone)
*I **think** you're right.* (= believe)
*Dina **is thinking** of taking a vacation soon.* (= considering)
*I **have** two sisters.* (= be related to)
*We'**re having** eggs for breakfast.* (= eating)
*He **is** in his first year of college.* (= exist)
*She **is being** difficult.* (= act)

3 Modals and Modal-like Expressions

Modals are helper verbs. Most modals have multiple meanings.

Function	Modal or Modal-like Expression	Time	Example
Advice less strong	*could* *might (not)*	present, future	He **could** do some puzzles to improve his memory. You **might** try some tips on improving your memory.
stronger	*ought to* *should (not)*	present, future	We **ought to** take a memory class next month. Greg **should** improve his memory.
	had better (not)	present, future	You**'d better** pay attention now.
Past Advice, Regret, or Criticism	*ought to have* *should (not) have*	past	She **ought to have** tried harder to improve her memory. You **should have** made an effort to improve your memory. He **shouldn't have** taken that difficult class.
Permission	*can (not)* *may (not)*	present, future	You **can** register for the class next week. You **may not** register after the first class.
	could (not)	past	You **could** ask questions during the lecture yesterday, but you **could not** leave the room.
formal →	*be (not) allowed to* *be (not) permitted to*	past, present, future	He **was not allowed to** talk during the test, but he **was allowed** to use his books. Students **will not be permitted to** refer to notes during examinations.
Necessity / Obligation	*have to* *need to* *be required to* *be supposed to*	past, present, future	I **have to** study tonight. She **needs to** quit her stressful job. You **won't be required to** take a test. He **is supposed to** tell you his decision tomorrow.
	must (not)	present, future	You **must** have experience for this job.
Obligation not to / Prohibition	*must not* *be not supposed to*	present, future	You **must not** talk during the exam. Students **are not supposed to** take their books into the exam room.

Modals and Modal-like Expressions (*continued*)

Function	Modal or Modal-like Expression	Time	Example
Lack of Necessity/ Choices or Options	*not have to* *not need to* *be not required to*	past, present, future	You **didn't have to** bring your notes. You **don't need to** study tonight. You **are not required to** bring your books.
Ability	*can (not)*	present, future	We **can** meet the professor at noon tomorrow.
	could (not)	past	I **could** understand the lecture, but I **could not** remember it.
	be (not) able to	past, present, future	She **wasn't able to** see very well from her seat.
	could have	past	I **could have** done well on that memory test.
	could not have	past	I **couldn't have** taken the test yesterday. I was in another state!
Probability	*can't* *could (not)* *(not) have to* *must (not)*	present	Hackers **can't** be interested in my data. He **could** be online now. She **has to** be at work right now. He **must not** be worried about data security.
	may (not) *might (not)* *ought to* *should (not)*	present, future	Your computer **may** be at risk of hacking. That software **might not** be good enough. That password **ought to** be strong enough. It **shouldn't** be difficult to find good software.
	could *will (not)*	future	The company **could** start using cloud computing next month. My sister **will** probably get a new computer soon.
	can't have *could (not) have* *may (not) have* *might (not) have* *must (not) have*	past	I **can't have** entered the wrong password! The expert **could not have** given you good advice. The company **may have** been careless with security. I **might have** written the wrong password down. Someone **must have** stolen all the passwords.

4 Noncount Nouns and Measurement Words to Make Noncount Nouns Countable

Category of Noncount Noun	Noun Examples	Measurement Words and Expressions
Abstract concepts	courage, luck, space, time	a bit of, a kind of *You had **a bit of** luck, didn't you?*
Activities and sports	dancing, exercise, swimming, tennis, yoga	a game of, a session of *They played **two games of** tennis.*
Diseases and health conditions	arthritis, cancer, depression, diabetes, obesity	a kind of, a type of *She has **a type of** diabetes called Type 2.*
Elements and gases	gold, hydrogen, oxygen, silver	a bar of, a container of, a piece of, a tank of *We have **tanks of** oxygen in the storage room.*
Foods	beef, broccoli, cheese, rice	a bottle of, a box of, a bunch of, a can of, a grain of, a head of, a loaf of, a package of, a piece of, a pinch of, a serving of, a slice of, a wedge of *I'll take **a serving of** rice and beef.*
Liquids	coffee, gasoline, oil, tea	a bottle of, a cup of, a gallon of, a glass of, a quart of *I would like **a cup of** tea.*
Natural phenomena	electricity, rain, sun, thunder	a bolt of, a drop of, a ray of *There hasn't been **a drop of** rain for three months.*
Particles	pepper, salt, sand, sugar	a grain of, a pinch of *My food needs **a pinch of** salt.*
Subjects and areas of work	construction, economics, genetics, geology, medicine, nursing	an area of, a branch of, a field of, a type of *There are a lot of specialty areas in **the field of** medicine.*
Miscellaneous	clothing, equipment, furniture, news	an article of, a piece of *I need **a piece of** furniture to go in that empty corner.*

5 Order of Adjectives Before Nouns

When you use two (or more) adjectives before a noun, use the order in the chart below.

Opinion	Size	Quality	Age	Shape	Color	Origin	Material	Nouns as Adjectives
beautiful comfortable delicious expensive interesting nice pretty rare reasonable shocking special ugly unique	big fat huge large long short small tall thin wide	cold free heavy hot safe	ancient antique new old young	oval rectangular round square triangular	black blue gold green orange purple red silver yellow white	American Canadian Chinese European Japanese Mexican Peruvian Thai	cotton glass gold leather metal paper plastic silk silver stone wooden woolen	computer evening government rose safety software summer training

Examples:

*That was a **delicious green Canadian** apple!* (opinion before color before origin)

*I saw the **shocking government** report on nutrition.* (opinion before noun as adjective)

*Wei got a **small oval glass** table.* (size before shape before material)

6 Verbs That Can Be Used Reflexively

allow oneself	challenge oneself	hurt oneself	remind oneself
amuse oneself	congratulate oneself	imagine oneself	see oneself
ask oneself	cut oneself	introduce oneself	take care of
be hard on oneself	dry oneself	keep oneself (busy)	talk to oneself
be oneself	enjoy oneself	kill oneself	teach oneself
be pleased with oneself	feel sorry for oneself	look after oneself	tell oneself
be proud of oneself	forgive oneself	look at oneself	treat oneself
behave oneself	get oneself	prepare oneself	
believe in oneself	give oneself	pride oneself on	
blame oneself	help oneself	push oneself	

7 Verbs Followed by Gerunds Only

admit	keep (= continue)
avoid	mind (= object to)
consider	miss
delay	postpone
defend	practice
deny	propose
discuss	quit
enjoy	recall (= remember)
finish	risk
imagine	suggest
involve	understand

8 Verbs Followed by Infinitives Only

afford	help	pretend
agree	hesitate	promise
arrange	hope	refuse
ask	hurry	request
attempt	intend	seem
choose	learn	struggle
consent	manage	tend (= be likely)
decide	need	threaten
demand	neglect	volunteer
deserve	offer	wait
expect	pay	want
fail	plan	wish
forget	prepare	would like

9 Verbs Followed by Gerunds or Infinitives

begin	like	regret*
continue	love	start
forget*	prefer	stop*
get	remember*	try*
hate		

*These verbs can be followed by a gerund or an infinitive, with a difference in meaning.

10 Expressions with Gerunds

Use a gerund after certain fixed verb expressions.

Verb expressions	
spend time / spend money waste time / waste money have trouble / have difficulty / have a difficult time	I **spent time helping** in the library. Don't **waste time complaining**. She **had trouble finishing** her degree.

Use a gerund after certain fixed noun + preposition expressions.

Noun + preposition expressions	
an excuse for in favor of an interest in a reason for	I have **an excuse for not doing** my homework. Who is **in favor of not admitting** him? He has **an interest in getting** a scholarship. He has **a reason for choosing** this school.

11 Verbs + Objects + Infinitives

advise	force	remind	ask*
allow	get	request	choose*
cause	hire	require	expect*
challenge	invite	teach	help*
convince	order	tell	need*
enable	permit	urge	pay*
encourage	persuade	warn	promise*
forbid			want*
			wish*

* These verbs can be followed by an object + infinitive or an infinitive only, with a difference in meaning.

Examples:
My boss **advised me to go** back to school.
They **urged the advertisers not to surprise** people.
My department **chose* Sally to create** the new ads.
My department **chose* to create** the new ads.

12 *Be* + Adjectives + Infinitives

be afraid	be delighted	be encouraged	be lucky	be sad
be amazed	be depressed	be excited	be necessary	be shocked
be angry	be determined	be fortunate	be pleased	be sorry
be anxious	be difficult	be fun	be proud	be surprised
be ashamed	be easy	be happy	be ready	be upset
be curious	be embarrassed	be likely	be relieved	be willing

13 Verbs + Prepositions

Verb + *about*
- ask about
- care about
- complain about
- be excited about
- find out about
- forget about
- hear about
- know about
- learn about
- read about
- see about
- talk about
- think about
- worry about
- be worried about

Verb + *against*
- advise against
- decide against

Verb + *at*
- look at
- smile at
- be successful at

Verb + *by*
- be affected by
- be raised by

Verb + *for*
- apologize for
- apply for
- ask for
- care for
- look for
- pay for
- be responsible for
- wait for

Verb + *from*
- graduate from

Verb + *in*
- believe in
- find in
- include in
- be interested in
- involve in
- result in
- show in
- succeed in
- use in

Verb + *of*
- be afraid of
- approve of
- be aware of
- consist of
- dream of
- be guilty of
- hear of
- know of
- take care of
- think of
- be warned of

Verb + *on*
- concentrate on
- count on
- decide on
- depend on
- insist on
- keep on
- plan on
- rely on

Verb + *to*
- admit to
- belong to
- confess to
- listen to
- look forward to
- refer to
- talk to
- be used to

Verb + *with*
- agree with
- argue with
- bother with
- deal with
- start with
- work with

14 Adjectives + Prepositions

Adjective + **about**	Adjective + **by**	Adjective + **in**	Adjective + **to**
concerned about	amazed by	high in	accustomed to
excited about	bored by	interested in	due to
happy about	surprised by	low in	similar to
nervous about	Adjective + **for**	Adjective + **of**	Adjective + **with**
pleased about	bad for	accused of	bored with
sad about	good for	afraid of	content with
sorry about	ready for	ashamed of	familiar with
surprised about	responsible for	aware of	good with
upset about	Adjective + **from**	capable of	satisfied with
worried about	different from	careful of	wrong with
Adjective + **at**	safe from	full of	
amazed at	separate from	guilty of	
angry at		sick of	
bad at		tired of	
good at		warned of	
successful at			
surprised at			

15 Verbs and Fixed Expressions that Introduce Indirect Questions

Do you have any idea …?	I'd like to know …?	I don't know …?
Can you tell me …?	I wonder / I'm wondering …?	I'm not sure …?
Do you know …?	I want to understand …?	I can't imagine …?
Do you remember …?	Let's find out …?	We don't understand …?
Could you explain …?	Let's ask …?	It doesn't say …?
Would you show me …?	We need to know …?	I can't believe …?

16 Tense Shifting in Indirect Speech

Direct Speech	Indirect (Reported) Speech
simple present She said, "The boss is angry."	**simple past** She **said** (that) the boss **was** angry.
present progressive He said, "She **is enjoying** the work."	**past progressive** He **said** (that) she **was enjoying** the work.
simple past They said, "The store **closed** last year."	**past perfect** They **said** (that) the store **had closed** last year.
present perfect The manager said, "The group **has done** good work."	**past perfect** The manager **said** (that) the group **had done** good work.
will He said, "The department **will add** three new managers."	**would** He **said** (that) the department **would add** three new managers.
be going to She said, "They **are going to hire** more people soon."	**be going to** (past form) She **said** (that) they **were going to hire** more people soon.
can The teacher said, "The students **can work** harder."	**could** The teacher said (that) the students could work harder.
may Their manager said, "Money **may not be** very important to them."	**might** Their manager **said** (that) money **might not be** very important to them.

* Note: *should, might, ought to,* and *could* do not change forms.

17 Reporting Verbs

Questions	Statements				Commands and Requests	
ask	admit	convince	notify	show	advise	request
inquire	announce	exclaim	observe	state	ask	say
question	assert	explain	promise	suggest	command	tell
	assure	find	remark	swear	demand	urge
	claim	indicate	remind	yell	order	warn
	comment	inform	reply			
	complain	mention	report			
	confess	note	shout			

18 Passive Forms

	Active	Passive
present progressive	*People are speaking English at the meeting.*	*English is being spoken at the meeting.*
simple present	*People speak English at the meeting.*	*English is spoken at the meeting.*
simple past	*People spoke English at the meeting.*	*English was spoken at the meeting.*
past progressive	*People were speaking English at the meeting.*	*English was being spoken at the meeting.*
present perfect	*People have spoken English at the meeting.*	*English has been spoken at the meeting.*
past perfect	*People had been speaking English at the meeting.*	*English had been spoken at the meeting.*
simple future	*People will speak English at the meeting.*	*English will be spoken at the meeting.*
future perfect	*People will have spoken English at the meeting.*	*English will have been spoken at the meeting.*
***be going to* (future)**	*People are going to speak English at the meeting.*	*English is going to be spoken at the meeting.*
Questions	*Do people speak English at the meeting?* *Did people speak English at the meeting?* *Have people spoken English at the meeting?*	*Is English spoken at the meeting?* *Was English spoken at the meeting?* *Has English been spoken at the meeting?*

19 Relative Clauses

	Identifying	Nonidentifying
Subject Relative Clauses	Many people **who/that support the environment** recycle.	My sister, **who lives in Maine**, loves being outside.
	Electricity **that/which saves energy** is a good thing.	People power, **which is a way to create energy**, is popular.
	They are the scientists **whose research has won awards**.	Brad Pitt, **whose movies are well known**, gives a lot of money to environmental causes.
Object Relative Clauses	Detectives are people (**who/whom/that**) **I respect tremendously**.	The character Sherlock Holmes, who/**whom Arthur Conan Doyle created**, was a fictional detective.
	Evidence (**which/that**) **criminals leave at the crime scene** is called forensic evidence.	Evidence from criminals, **which we call forensic evidence**, can help police solve cases.
	The person **whose car the thieves stole** was a friend of mine.	Arthur Conan Doyle, **whose medical clinic not many patients attended**, had time to write his stories.
Object Relative Clauses as Objects of Prepositions	There's the police officer (**that/who/whom**) **I spoke to**. (informal) There's the police officer **to whom I spoke**. (formal)	There's Officer Smith, **who/whom I spoke to yesterday**. (informal) There's Officer Smith, **to whom I spoke yesterday**. (formal)
	Police found evidence from the crime scene under the chair (**that/which**) **I was sitting on**. (informal) Police found evidence from the crime scene under the chair **on which I was sitting**. (formal)	The door, **which I entered through**, had been broken during the robbery. (informal) The door, **through which I entered**, had been broken during the robbery. (formal)
Relative Clauses with *Where* and *in Which*	It's a city **where you can find Wi-Fi almost everywhere**. It's a city in **which you can find Wi-Fi almost everywhere**.	The city of Atlanta, **where my sister lives**, is very large. The city of Atlanta, **in which my sister lives**, is very large.
Relative Clauses with *When* and *During Which*	Night is a time **when many students study for exams**. Night is a time **during which many students study for exams**.	Joe prefers to study at night, **when his children are asleep**. Joe prefers to study at night, **during which his children are asleep**.

Relative Clauses (*continued*)

Participle Phrases	Students **concerned with the environment** should get involved in environmental groups on campus.	Millennials, **raised in the era of technology, cell phones, and the Internet**, understand technology very well.
	The expert **giving tomorrow's talk on Millennials** is very well known.	The movie Twilight, **starring Millennials**, is based on a book by Gen Xer Stephenie Meyer.
Prepositional Phrases	The computers **in our classroom** are fast. Young workers **low in self-esteem** are unusual.	
Appositives		Jan Smith, **the president of Myco**, will be speaking at noon today. Jan Smith (**the president of Myco**) will be speaking at noon today. (formal writing)

20 Conditionals

Situation	Tense	*If* clause	Main clause	Example
Real Conditionals	present	simple present	simple present	If a website **is** popular, people **talk** about it.
	future	simple present	future	If you only **listen** to one station, you **will hear** only one opinion.
Unreal Conditionals	present	simple past or past progressive	would, could, might + base form of verb	If I **studied** every day, I **would pass** all my tests. If I **weren't dreaming** all day, I **would pass** all my tests.
	future	simple past	would, could, might + base form of verb	If our school **closed** next year, we **wouldn't have** a place to learn.
	past	past perfect	would have, could have, might have + past participle	If the city **had hired** more teachers, the schools **might have improved**.
Wishes	**Tense**	*that* clause		**Example**
	present	simple past, past progressive, could		I wish (that) schools **were improving**.
	future	were going to, would, could		I wish (that) the teachers **were going to** give us a party.
	past	past perfect		I wish (that) I **had studied** more.

Glossary of Grammar Terms

action verb a verb that describes an action.

> I **eat** breakfast every day.
> They **ran** in the 5K race.

active sentence a sentence that focuses on the doer and the action.

> **Jorge played** basketball yesterday.

adjective a word that describes or modifies a noun.

> That's a **beautiful** hat.

adjective clause see **relative clause**

adverb a word that describes or modifies a verb, another adverb, or an adjective. Adverbs often end in -ly.

> Please walk **faster** but **carefully**.

adverb clause a clause that shows how ideas are connected. Adverb clauses begin with subordinators such as *because, since, although, and even though.*

> **Although it is not a holiday**, workers have the day off.

adverb of degree an adverb that makes other adverbs or adjectives stronger or weaker.

> The test was **extremely** difficult. They are **really** busy today.

adverb of frequency an adverb such as *always, often, sometimes, never,* and *usually* that describes how often something happens.

> She **always** arrives at work on time.

adverb of manner an adverb that describes how an action happens.

> He has **suddenly** left the room.

adverb of time an adverb that describes when something happens.

> She'll get up **later**.

agent the noun or pronoun performing the action of the verb in a sentence.

> **People** spoke English at the meeting.

appositive a reduced form of a nonidentifying relative clause. Appositives are formed by removing the relative pronoun and the verb *be*, leaving only a noun phrase.

> Jan Smith, **an expert on Millennials**, will be speaking at noon today.

article the words *a/an* and *the*. An article introduces or identifies a noun.

> I bought **a** new cell phone. **The** price was reasonable.

auxiliary verb (also called **helping verb**) a verb that is used before a main verb in a sentence. *Do, have, be,* and *will* can act as auxiliary verbs.

> **Does** he want to go to the library later? **Have** you received the package? **Will** he arrive soon?

base form of the verb the form of a verb without any endings (-s or -ed) or *to*.

come   go   take

clause a group of words that has a subject and a verb. There are two types of clauses: **main clauses** and **dependent clauses** (*see* **dependent clause**). A sentence can have more than one clause.

MAIN CLAUSE   DEPENDENT CLAUSE   MAIN CLAUSE
I woke up when I heard the noise. It was scary.

common noun a word for a person, place, or thing. A common noun is not capitalized.

mother   building   fruit

comparative the form of an adjective or adverb that shows how two people, places, or things are different.

*My daughter is **older than** my son.* (adjective)

*She does her work **more quickly** than he does.* (adverb)

conditional a sentence that describes a possible situation and the result of that situation. It can be a real or unreal condition / result about the present, past, or future.

If a website is popular, people talk about it. (present real conditional)

If I had studied harder, I would have passed that course. (past unreal conditional)

conjunction a word such as *and, but, so, or*, and *yet* that connects single words, phrases, or clauses.

*We finished all our work, **so** we left early.*

Some more conjunctions are after, as, because, if, and when.

consonant a sound represented in writing by these letters of the alphabet: *b, c, d, f, g, h, j, k, l, m, n, p, q, r, s, t, v, w, x, y,* and *z*.

count noun a person, place, or thing you can count. Count nouns have a plural form.

*There are three **banks** on Oak Street.*

definite article *the* is the definite article. Use *the* with a person, place, or thing that is familiar to you and your listener. Use *the* when the noun is unique – there is only one (*the sun, the moon, the Internet*). Also use *the* before a singular noun used to represent a whole class or category.

The *movie we saw last week was very good.*

The *Earth is round.*

The *male robin is more colorful than **the** female.*

dependent clause a clause that cannot stand alone. A dependent clause is not a complete sentence, but it still has a subject and verb. Some kinds of dependent clauses are adverb clauses, relative clauses, and time clauses.

After we return from the trip, *I'm going to need to relax.*

determiner a word that comes before a noun to limit its meaning in some way. Some common determiners are *some, a little, a lot, a few, this, that, these, those, his, a, an, the, much,* and *many*.

These *computers have **a lot** of parts.*

*Please give me **my** book.*

direct object the person or thing that receives the action of the verb.

*The teacher gave the students **a test**.*

direct question a type of direct speech (see **direct speech**) that repeats a person's question.

*The president asked, **"Who were your best employees last month?"***

direct speech (also called **quoted speech**) repeats people's exact words. A direct speech statement consists of a reporting clause and the exact words of a person inside quotation marks.

*The manager said, **"Workers need to use creativity."***

factual conditional *see* **present real conditional**

formal a style of writing or speech used when you don't know the other person very well or where it's not appropriate to show familiarity, such as in business, a job interview, speaking to a stranger, or speaking to an older person who you respect.

Good evening. I'd like to speak with Ms. Smith. Is she available?

future a verb form that describes a time that hasn't come yet. It is expressed in English by *will*, *be going to*, and present tense.

*I'**ll meet** you tomorrow.*

*I'**m going to visit** my uncle and aunt next weekend.*

*My bus **leaves** at 10:00 tomorrow.*

*I'**m meeting** Joe on Friday.*

future real conditional describes a possible situation in the future and the likely result. The *if* clause uses the simple present. The main clause uses a future form of the verb.

***If** you only **listen** to one station, you **will hear** only one opinion.*

future unreal conditional describes an imaginary situation in the future. The *if* clause uses the simple past. The main clause uses the modals *would*, *could*, or *might*.

***If** teachers **prepared** students better for exams, more students **would pass**.*

gerund the *-ing* form of a verb that is used as a noun. It can be the subject or object of a sentence or the object of a preposition.

*We suggested **waiting** and **going** another day.*

*Salsa **dancing** is a lot of fun.*

*I look forward to **meeting** you.*

habitual past a verb form that describes repeated past actions, habits, and conditions using *used to* or *would*.

*Before we had the Internet, we **used to** go to the library a lot.*

*Before there was refrigeration, people **would** use ice to keep food cool.*

helping verb *see* **auxiliary verb**

***if* clause** the condition clause in a conditional. It describes the possible situation, which can be either real or unreal.

***If it rains tomorrow**, I'll stay home.*

imperative a type of clause that tells people to do something. It gives instructions, directions to a place, and advice. The verb is in the base form.

***Listen** to the conversation.*

***Don't open** your books.*

***Turn** right at the bank and then **go** straight.*

indefinite article *a / an* are the indefinite articles. Use *a / an* with a singular person, place, or thing when you and your listener are not familiar with it, or when the specific name of it is not important. Use *a* with consonant sounds. Use *an* with vowel sounds.

*She's going to see **a** doctor today.*

*I had **an** egg for breakfast.*

indefinite pronoun a pronoun used when the noun is unknown or not important. There is an indefinite pronoun for people, for places, and for things. Some examples are *somebody, anyone, nobody, somewhere, anywhere, nothing, everything*, etc. Use singular verb forms when the indefinite pronoun is the subject of the sentence.

***Everybody** is going to be there. There is **nowhere** I'd rather work.*

indirect object the person or thing that receives the direct object.

*The teacher gave **the students** a test.*

indirect question (also called **reported question**) tells what other people have asked or asks a question using a statement. There are two kinds of indirect questions: *Yes / No* and information questions. Indirect questions follow the *subject-verb* word order of a statement.

*Mia **asked whether** we **would begin** Creative Problem Solving soon.*

*The president asked **who** my best employees **were** last month.*

indirect speech (also called **reported speech**) tells what someone says in another person's words. An indirect speech statement consists of a reporting verb (see **reporting verb**) such as *say* in the main clause, followed by a *that* clause. *That* is optional and is often omitted in speaking.

*He **said** (that) she **was enjoying** the work.*

infinitive *to* + the base form of a verb.

*I need **to get** home early tonight.*

infinitive of purpose *in order* + infinitive expresses a purpose. It answers the question *why*. If the meaning is clear, it is not necessary to use *in order*.

*People are fighting **(in order) to change** unfair laws.*

informal is a style of speaking to friends, family, and children.

Hey, there. Nice to see you again.

information question (also called ***Wh-* question**) begins with a *wh*-word (*who, what, when, where, which, why, how, how much*). To answer this type of question, you need to provide information rather than answer *yes* or *no*.

inseparable phrasal verb a phrasal verb that cannot be separated. The verb and its particle always stay together.

*My car **broke down** yesterday.*

intransitive verb a verb that does not need an object. It is often followed by an expression of time, place, or manner. It cannot be used in the passive.

*The flight **arrived** at 5.30 p.m.*

irregular adjective an adjective that does not change its form in the usual way. For example, you do not make the comparative form by adding *-er*.

good → better

irregular adverb an adverb that does not change its form in the usual way. For example, you do not make the comparative form by adding -ly.

badly ➞ *worse*

irregular verb a verb that does not change its form in the usual way. For example, it does not form the simple past with -d or -ed. It has its own special form.

go ➞ *went*   *ride* ➞ *rode*   *hit* ➞ *hit*

main clause (also called **independent clause**) a clause that can be used alone as a complete sentence. In a conditional, the main clause describes the result when the condition exists.

After I get back from my trip, **I'm going to relax***.*

If I hear about a good story, **I move quickly to get there and report it***.*

main verb a verb that functions alone in a clause and can have an auxiliary verb.

They **had** *a meeting last week.*

They have **had** *many meetings this month.*

measurement word a word or phrase that shows the amount of something. Measurement words can be singular or plural. They can be used to make noncount nouns countable.

I bought **a box** *of cereal, and Sonia bought* **five pounds** *of apples.*

modal a verb such as *can*, *could*, *have to*, *may*, *might*, *must*, *should*, *will*, and *would*. It modifies the main verb to show such things as ability, permission, possibility, advice, obligation, necessity, or lack of necessity.

It **might** *rain later today.*

You **should** *study harder if you want to pass this course.*

non-action verb *see* **stative verb**

noncount noun refers to ideas and things that you cannot count. Noncount nouns use a singular verb and do not have a plural form.

Do you download **music***?*

noun a word for a person, place, or thing. There are common nouns and proper nouns. (*see* **common nouns, proper nouns**)

COMMON NOUN   PROPER NOUN

I stayed in a **hotel** *on my trip to New York.*   *I stayed in the* **Ace Hotel***.*

object a noun or pronoun that usually follows the verb and receives the action.

I sent **the flowers***. I sent* **them** *to* **you***.*

object pronoun replaces a noun in the object position.

Sara loves exercise classes. She takes **them** *three times a week.*

participle phrase a reduced form of an identifying relative clause. Participle phrases are formed by removing the relative pronoun and the verb *be*. Participle phrases can be used when the verb in the relative clause is in the form verb + -ing (present participle) or the past participle form.

He is the person **using the Internet too much at work***.*

particle a small word like *down, in, off, on, out,* or *up*. These words (which can also be prepositions) are used with verbs to form **two-word verbs** or **phrasal verbs**. The meaning of a phrasal verb often has a different meaning from the meaning of the individual words in it.

passive sentence a sentence that focuses on the action or on the person or thing receiving the action. The object is in the subject position.

*English **was spoken** at the meeting.*

past participle a verb form that can be regular (base form + -*ed*) or irregular. It is used to form perfect tenses and the passive. It can also be an adjective.

*I've **studied** English for five years.*

*The **frightened** child cried.*

past progressive a verb form that describes events or situations in progress at a time in the past. The emphasis is on the action.

*They **were watching** TV when I arrived.*

past unreal conditional describes a situation that was not true in the past. Past unreal conditionals describe something that was possible but did not happen. The *if* clause uses the past perfect. The main clause uses the modals *would have, could have,* or *might have* and the past participle form of the verb.

*If we **hadn't had** a hurricane, the schools **wouldn't have closed**.*

phrasal verb (also called **two-word verb**) consists of a verb + a particle. There are two kinds of phrasal verbs: separable and inseparable. (*see* **particle, inseparable phrasal verbs, separable phrasal verbs**)

VERB + PARTICLE

*They **came back** from vacation today.* (inseparable)

*Please **put** your cell phone **away**.* (separable)

phrase a group of words about an idea that is not a complete sentence. It does not have a main verb.

across the street   ***in the morning***

plural noun a noun that refers to more than one person, place, or thing.

students   ***women***   ***roads***

possessive adjective *see* **possessive determiner.**

possessive determiner (also called **possessive adjective**) a determiner that shows possession (*my, your, his, her, its, our,* and *their*).

possessive pronoun replaces a possessive determiner + singular or plural noun. The possessive pronoun agrees with the noun that it replaces.

*My exercise class is at night. **Hers** is on the weekend.* (hers = her exercise class)

preposition a word such as *to, at, for, with, below, in, on, next to,* or *above* that goes before a noun or pronoun to show location, time, direction, or a close relationship between two people or things. A preposition may go before a gerund as well.

*I'm **in** the supermarket **next to** our favorite restaurant.*

*The idea **of** love has inspired many poets.*

*I'm interested **in** taking a psychology course.*

prepositional phrase a reduced form of an identifying relative clause. Prepositional phrases are formed by removing the relative pronoun and the verb *be,* leaving only a prepositional phrase.

*The computers **in our classroom** are fast.*

present perfect a verb form that describes past events or situations that are still important in the present and actions that happened once or repeatedly at an indefinite time before now.

*Lately scientists **have discovered** medicines in the Amazon.*

*I**'ve been** to the Amazon twice.*

present perfect progressive a verb form that describes something that started in the past, usually continues in the present, and may continue in the future.

*He **hasn't been working** since last May.*

present progressive a verb form that describes an action or situation that is in progress now or around the present time. It is also used to indicate a fixed arrangement in the future.

*What **are** you **doing** right now?*

*I**'m leaving** for Spain next week.*

present real conditional (also called **factual conditional**) describes a situation that is possible now and its result. Present real conditionals describe general truths, facts, and habits. The *if* clause and the main clause use the simple present.

***If** you **control** the media, you **control** public opinion.*

present unreal conditional describes an imaginary situation in the present. The *if* clause uses the simple past or past progressive. The main clause uses the modals *would, could,* or *might.*

***If** I **studied** every day, I **could pass** all my tests.*

pronoun a word that replaces a noun or noun phrase. Some examples are *I, we, him, hers, it.* (*see* **object pronoun, subject pronoun, relative pronoun, possessive pronoun, reciprocal pronoun, reflexive pronoun.**)

proper noun a noun that is the name of a particular person, place, or thing. It is capitalized.

Central Park** in **New York City

punctuation mark a symbol used in writing such as a period (.), a comma (,), a question mark (?), or an exclamation point (!).

quantifier a word or phrase that shows an amount of something. In addition to measurements words, some other quantifiers are *much, many, some, any, a lot, plenty, enough,* etc.

*We have **three bottles** of juice and **plenty of** snacks.*

quoted speech *see* **direct speech**

reciprocal pronoun a pronoun (*each other, one another*) that shows that two or more people give *and* receive the same action or have the same relationship.

*Mari and I have the same challenges. We help **each other**.* (I help Mari, and Mari helps me.)

reflexive pronoun a pronoun (*myself, yourself, himself, herself, ourselves, yourselves, themselves*) that shows that the object of the sentence is the same as the subject.

*I taught **myself** to speak Japanese.*

regular verb a verb that changes its form in the usual way.

live ➞ live**s**

wash ➞ wash**ed**

relative clause (also called **adjective clause**) defines, describes, identifies, or gives more information about a noun. It begins with a relative pronoun such as *who*, *that*, *which*, *whose*, or *whom*. Like all clauses, a relative clause has both a subject and a verb. It can describe the subject or the object of a sentence.

*People **who have sleep problems** can join the study.* (subject relative clause)

*There are many diseases **that viruses cause**.* (object relative clause)

relative pronoun a pronoun (*who, which, that, whose, whom*) that connects a noun phrase to a relative clause

*People **who** have sleep problems can join the study.*

*There are many diseases **that** viruses cause.*

reported question *see* **indirect question**

reported speech *see* **indirect speech**

reporting verb a verb used to introduce direct speech or indirect speech. *Say* is the most common reporting verb. Other such verbs include *admit, announce, complain, confess, exclaim, explain, mention, remark, reply, report, state,* and *swear,* and *tell.*

*The president **said**, "We will change our system of rewarding employees."*

*The president **stated** that they would change their system of rewarding employees.*

result clause *see* **main clause**

sentence a complete thought or idea that has a subject and a main verb. In writing, it begins with a capital letter and has a punctuation mark at the end (. ? !). In an imperative sentence, the subject (*you*) is not usually stated.

This sentence is a complete thought.

Open your books.

separable phrasal verb a phrasal verb that can be separated. This means that an object can go before or after the particle.

***Write down** your expenses.*

***Write** your expenses **down**.*

simple past a verb form that describes completed actions or events that happened at a definite time in the past.

*They **grew up** in Washington, D.C.*

*They **attended** Howard University and **graduated** in 2018.*

simple present a verb form that describes things that regularly happen such as habits and routines (usual and regular activities). It also describes facts and general truths.

*I **play** games online every night.* (routine)

*The average person **spends** 13 hours a week online.* (fact)

singular noun a noun that refers to only one person, place, or thing.

*He is my best **friend**.*

statement a sentence that gives information.

Today is Thursday.

stative verb (also called **non-action verb**) describes a state or situation, not an action. It is usually in the simple form.

*I **remember** your friend.*

subject the person, place, or thing that performs the action of a verb.

People use new words and expressions every day.

subject pronoun replaces a noun in the subject position.

Sara and I are friends. We work at the same company.

subordinator a conjunction that connects a dependent clause and an independent clause. Some common subordinators include *although*, *because*, *even though*, *in order to*, *since*, and *so that*.

Although many people like to shop, some people shop too much.

superlative the form of an adjective or adverb that compares one person, place, or thing to others in a group.

This storm was the most dangerous one of the season. (adjective)

That group worked most effectively after the disaster. (adverb)

syllable a group of letters that has one vowel sound and that you say as a single unit.

There is one syllable in the word lunch *and two syllables in the word* breakfast. (Break *is one syllable and* fast *is another syllable.*)

tag question consists of a verb and pronoun added to the end of a statement. Tag questions confirm information or ask for agreement. The tag changes the statement into a question.

They don't live in Chicago, do they?   Geography is interesting, isn't it?

tense the form of a verb that shows past or present time.

They worked yesterday. (simple past)

They work every day. (simple present)

third-person singular refers to *he*, *she*, and *it* or a singular noun. In the simple present, the third-person singular form ends in *-s* or *-es*.

It looks warm and sunny today. He washes the laundry on Saturdays.

time clause a phrase that shows the order of events and begins with a time word such as *before*, *after*, *when*, *while*, or *as soon as*.

Before there were freezers, people needed ice to make frozen desserts.

time expression a phrase that functions as an adverb of time. It tells when something happens, happened, or will happen.

I graduated in 2020. She's going to visit her aunt and uncle next summer.

transitive verb a verb that has an object. The object completes the meaning of the verb.

She wears perfume.

two-word verb *see* **phrasal verb**

verb a word that describes an action or a state.

Alex wears jeans and a T-shirt to school. Alex is a student.

vowel a sound represented in writing by these letters of the alphabet: *a, e, i, o,* and *u*.

Wh- question *see* **information question**

Yes / No question begins with a form of *be* or an auxiliary verb. You can answer such a question with *yes* or *no*.

"Are they going to the movies?" "No, they're not."

"Can you give me some help?" "Yes, I can."

Index

Credits

Acknowledgements

The authors and publishers acknowledge the following sources of copyright material and are grateful for the permissions granted. While every effort has been made, it has not always been possible to identify the sources of all the material used, or to trace all copyright holders. If any omissions are brought to our notice, we will be happy to include the appropriate acknowledgements on reprinting and in the next update to the digital edition, as applicable.

Key: U = Unit.

Text

U17: Figure 1 adapted from Organization for Economic Cooperation and Development (OECD), Online Education Database, retrieved September 13, 2019, from https://stats.oecd.org/Index.aspx. See Digest of Education Statistics 2018, table 603.20. Reproduced with kind permission; Figure 2 adapted from OECD (2019), 'Education and earnings: Level of earnings relative to median earnings' by Educational Attainment, OEC. Stat, https://stats.oecd.org/Index.aspx?DataSetCode=EAG_EARNINGS, accessed on August 1, 2019. Reproduced with kind permission.

Photography

The following photos are sourced from Getty Images.

U1: Jose Luis Pelaez Inc/DigitalVision; SDI Productions/E+; Jacqueline Veissid/DigitalVision; Ajr_images/iStock/Getty Images Plus; XiXinXing; **U2:** Wavebreakmedia/iStock/Getty Images Plus; Nikada/E+; Universal Images Group; Jose Luis Pelaez Inc./digital vision; **U3:** Corbis/VCG; Dinodia Photos/Hulton Archive; Michael Gottschalk/Photothek; Jetta Productions/digital vision; Benoist SEBIRE/Moment; Tim Robbers/The Image Bank; Jon Kopaloff/FilmMagic; View Pictures/Universal Images Group; Paul Morigi/WireImage; **U4:** encrier/iStock/Getty Images Plus; Strickke/E+; Aaron Mccoy/Photolibrary; Stephen Simpson/The Image Bank; Newton Daly/DigitalVision; Andrew Brookes/Cultura; Deborah Kolb/Image Source; Jose Luis Pelaez Inc/DigitalVision; Hero Images; **U5:** Ariel Skelley/DigitalVision; monkeybusinessimages/iStock/Getty Images Plus; Tim Robbers/The Image Bank; Cosinart/iStock/Getty Images Plus; guvendemir/iStock/Getty Images Plus Unreleased; Image Source/DigitalVision; **U6:** AndreaObzerova/iStock/Getty Images Plus; Westend61; Hinterhaus Productions/DigitalVision; **U7:** Nattakorn Maneerat/iStock/Getty Images Plus; Tonivaver/iStock/Getty Images Plus; Phil Boorman/Cultura; Westend61; Hero Images; **U8:** Wavebreakmedia/iStock/Getty Images Plus; Bill Hinton/Moment; Hero Images; Kali9/E+; **U9:** Ridofranz/iStock/Getty Images Plus; Alexander Spatari/Moment; Bluestocking/iStock/Getty Images Plus; Monticello/iStock/Getty Images Plus; Yevgen Romanenko/Moment; Paci77/iStock/Getty Images Plus; Enter89/iStock/Getty Images Plus; Kolesnikovserg/iStock/Getty Images Plus; Pearleye/E+; **U10:** FotografiaBasica/E+; Gchutka/iStock/Getty Images Plus; KatarzynaBialasiewicz/iStock/Getty Images Plus; jacoblund/iStock/Getty Images Plus; Vgajic/E+; **U12:** Fahrul Junianto/iStock/Getty Images Plus; Alejandrophotography/E+; Klaus Vedfelt/DigitalVision; **U13:** Stu Meech/Moment; Sam Mellish/In Pictures; **U14:** Viaframe/Corbis; George Rose News; Monkeybusinessimages/iStock/Getty Images Plus; PhotoAlto/Eric Audras/Brand X Pictures; **U15:** IP Galanternik D.U./E+; MPI/Archive Photos; Darren pearson (dariustwin)/Moment; Seb_ra/iStock/Getty Images Plus; **U16:** okeyphotos/iStock/Getty Images Plus; H. Armstrong Roberts/ClassicStock/Archive Photos; Hulton Archive;

U17: Comstock Images/Stockbyte; Jon Feingersh/DigitalVision; Monkeybusinessimages/iStock/Getty Images Plus; Jacoblund/iStock/Getty Images Plus; U18: Bloom Productions/DigitalVision; Hero Images; Vm/E+; Caiaimage/Agnieszka Olek; U19: SDI Productions/E+; Caiaimage/Caiaimage/Robert Daly/OJO+; U20: julief514/iStock/Getty Images Plus; Jose A. Bernat Bacete/Moment; Istanbulimage/E+; Kosamtu/E+; NoDerog/iStock/Getty Images Plus; U21: GIPhotoStock/Cultura; Echo/Juice Images; Photobalance/iStock/Getty Images Plus; Maciej Lulko/Moment; U22: gorodenkoff/iStock/Getty Images Plus; Steve Allen/Stockbyte; Monty Rakusen/Cultura; Stephen Chernin; Andersen Ross Photography Inc/DigitalVision; U23: NurPhoto; PeopleImages/E+; JGI/Tom Grill; Johnny Greig/E+; Juanmonino/E+; Simon Marcus Taplin/Corbis; U24: bruev/iStock/Getty Images Plus; Bloomberg Creative Photos; Skynesher/iStock/Getty Images Plus; Franckreporter/E+; U25: onfilm/E+; 1001nights/E+; Huntstock/Brand X Pictures; Kickstand/iStock/Getty Images Plus; Joshuaraineyphotography/iStock/Getty Images Plus; Stocktrek Images/Richard Roscoe; U26: martinedoucet/E+; Lew Robertson/Photolibrary; Will Heap/Dorling Kindersley; ilietus/iStock/Getty Images Plus; SolStock/E+; Cgissemann/iStock/Getty Images Plus; chengyuzheng/iStock/Getty Images Plus; MIXA Co. Ltd.; LUNAMARINA/iStock/Getty Images Plus; Troscha/iStock/Getty Images Plus; GlobalP/iStock/Getty Images Plus; U27: Csondy/E+; Michaelpuche/iStock/Getty Images Plus; Carlos Ciudad Photography/Moment; Gavin Jackson/ArcaidImages; U28: Handout; BSIP/Universal Images Group.

The following photos are sourced from other libraries. U3: Jackie ellis/Alamy Stock Photo; U9: Jose Luis Stephens/Alamy Stock Photo; Myronovych/Shutterstock; U15: ClassicStock/Alamy Stock Photo; U19: Keith Crowley/Alamy Stock Photo; U21: WENN Ltd/Alamy Stock Photo; U24: Artur Marciniec/Alamy Stock Photo; U25: FEMA/Alamy Stock Photo; U26: Catinsyrup/Shutterstock; U28: Everett Collection Inc/Alamy Stock Photo.

Illustrations

Maria Rabinky; Monika Roe; Rob Schuster; Shelton Leong.

Audio

Audio production by John Marshall Media.

Typeset

Q2A Media Services Pvt. Ltd.